Teaching as the Learning Profession

Teaching as the
Learning Profession

Handbook of Policy and Practice

Linda Darling-Hammond
Gary Sykes
Editors

Foreword by Lee S. Shulman

Jossey-Bass Publishers
San Francisco

Jossey-Bass books and products are available through most
bookstores. To contact Jossey-Bass directly, call (888) 378–2537,
fax to (800) 605–2665, or visit our website at www.josseybass.com.

Substantial discounts on bulk quantities of Jossey-Bass books are
available to corporations, professional associations, and other
organizations. For details and discount information,
contact the special sales department at Jossey-Bass.

 Manufactured in the United States of America on Lyons Falls Turin
Book. This paper is acid-free and 100 percent totally chlorine-free.

Library of Congress Cataloging-in-Publication Data

Teaching as the learning profession: handbook of policy and practice/
Linda Darling-Hammond, Gary Sykes, editors: foreword by Lee S.
Shulman.—1st ed.
p.   cm.—(The Jossey-Bass education series)
Includes bibliographical references and index.
ISBN 0-7879-4341-X (alk. paper)
1. Teachers—United States—Handbooks, manuals, etc. 2. Teachers—
Training of—United States—Handbooks, manuals, etc. 3. Teachers—
In-service training—United States—Handbooks, manuals, etc.
4. Teachers—Selection and appointment—United States—Handbooks,
manuals, etc. 5. Teachers' unions—United States—Handbooks,
manuals, etc. 6. Educational change—United States—Handbooks,
manuals, etc. I. Darling-Hammond, Linda, date. II. Sykes, Gary.
III. Series.
LB1775.2.T478   1999   99-19781
371.1'00973—dc21   CIP

FIRST EDITION
HB Printing 10 9 8 7 6 5 4 3 2 1

CONTENTS

FOREWORD

I was spending the 1980 academic year as a fellow at the Center for Advanced Study in the Behavioral Sciences on leave from my responsibilities as director of the Institute for Research on Teaching at Michigan State University. On a balmy May afternoon, I received a telephone call from Gary Sykes, a program officer at the National Institute of Education in Washington, D.C., who needed my help on a special project. The institute had funds to commission about eight papers that dealt with the intersection of educational policy and research on teaching. He wanted to hold a conference based on the papers, perhaps put them together into a book, and would I agree, he asked, to select (and hound) the authors, chair the conference, and edit the volume?

Thinking it was an awful idea but suffering from a lifelong inability to say no simply and directly, I proposed a set of impossible conditions. I proposed that the vast domain of research on teaching and its connections to educational policy could hardly be addressed in just eight chapters. He would need to find the resources to commission more than twenty contributions. Moreover, we would need to convene the authors before they began to write so they could develop a shared sense of the problems, then reconvene them after all had completed first drafts so they could critique one another's work and modify their own papers in the light of the others. Only then could we publish a respectable book. To my shock, Sykes came back a week later with the authorization to do everything I had proposed, and I was stuck with project. In 1983 *The Handbook of Teaching and Policy,* edited by Sykes and me, was published.

I had no idea how important the juxtaposition of *teaching* and *policy* would be to so many readers. One such reader was a young educational policy analyst at the RAND Corporation, Linda Darling-Hammond. When the handbook was published, she has since told me, its orientation and contents were an epiphany for her. Among others, I had written about the remote control of teaching as a serious problem for the field. Many of these ideas subsequently framed her work, and we in the world of education have profited extensively from her contributions. By the time the handbook was published in 1983, both Gary Sykes and I were at Stanford, where he completed his doctorate and worked with me on the initial studies that contributed to the Carnegie Forum on Education and the Economy's report on teaching, *A Nation Prepared: Teachers for the 21st Century* (1986), and then led to the current configurations of both the National Board for Professional Teaching Standards and of the Interstate New Teacher Assessment and Support Consortium. Sykes then moved to Michigan State University, where he serves as an outstanding scholar and teacher to this day. After distinguished service at both RAND and Teachers College, Columbia University, Linda Darling-Hammond has now come to Stanford, where she is the new Charles E. Ducommun Professor of Education, conducts research on teaching policy, and directs the teacher education program.

Nearly twenty years have passed since the papers for the original *Handbook of Teaching and Policy* were commissioned. How much has changed? How much remains the same? To what extent do the themes of the earlier work remain central to the intersections of policy and teaching practice today? In 1982 I concluded my final chapter for that book with the following observations:

> The teacher must remain the key. The literature on effective schools is meaningless, debates over educational policy are moot, if the primary agents of instruction are incapable of performing their functions well. No microcomputer will replace them, no television system will clone and distribute them, no scripted lessons will direct and control them, no voucher system will bypass them. It seems unlikely that increasing the financial rewards of teaching alone will suffice, though it is certainly necessary. The character of the work will have to change in order to attract and hold the more highly trained, talented, and committed teacher required for the 1980s and beyond [Shulman and Sykes, 1983, p. 504].

The argument that threads through this book is that although many kinds of policy are essential at all levels, there remains no better strategy than a significant and sustained investment in well-educated professional teachers. The more we learn from empirical studies of school reform—and this book demonstrates that we have learned quite a bit since 1983—the more irreplaceable classroom teachers turn out to be.

The answer as to why teachers are so hard to replace may lie in the distinction between *rules* and *standards*. We have come to understand that teachers are professionals precisely because they operate under conditions of inherent novelty, uncertainty, and chance. Although there may be curricula that strive to prescribe teachers' behavior with great precision, for most teachers a typical day is fraught with surprises. This is also the case for most other professionals— physicians, attorneys, journalists, social workers, and others. Therefore, their work cannot be controlled by rules, even though it must be governed by standards. Kathleen Sullivan, a distinguished constitutional scholar at Stanford, characterized that distinction in a recent review:

> Legal directives can take either of two forms: clear cut rules (drive no faster than 65 MPH) or flexible standards (drive safely for existing highway conditions). Rules constrain the discretion of decision-makers more than standards do, for they require the determination of fewer issues of fact. Those who favor rules stress their advantages of certainty, predictability, formal equality of treatment, and clear notice; those who favor standards counter that their approach is more substantively fair and accurate and more practical because capable of flexible adaptation [Lazarus, 1998, p. 16].

A consistent theme throughout this book is the importance of formulating guiding standards for teachers' work without straying into the error of stipulating rigid rules. Professionalism demands thoughtful, grounded actions under complex and uncertain conditions that are nevertheless guided by, rooted in, and framed by clear professional standards. A professional both acts wisely and can explain his or her actions.

Another consistent insight that the chapter authors in this book share is the recognition that professional teachers must be well educated, especially in the subject matter content they teach, and that their career-long professional education experiences must continue to be grounded in the centrality of that content. Here is a source of standards to which both conservatives and liberals alike can subscribe. We have come to understand the extent to which deep, flexible, and confident understanding of subject matter makes possible the kinds of professional autonomy and responsiveness that the teaching of all youngsters requires. We are also more clear than ever before that such knowledge is necessary but not remotely sufficient. The teacher must be a scholar, an intellectual, and a knowledge worker oriented toward the interpretation, communication, and construction of such knowledge in the interests of student learning. The accomplished teacher must understand both *Macbeth* and the complexities of learning and teaching literature to adolescents. Any good writer who has tried to teach another person to compose has felt the pain of knowing *how*, but not knowing how to teach.

This superb book also reminds its readers that the most critical part of the terrain in the landscape of teacher development is the quality of teacher educators and the effectiveness of the programs they conduct. Until teachers in colleges and universities come to recognize that they are all teacher educators, and thus take responsibility for the knowledge of their students, little progress on the subject matter front will be achieved. Until faculty members in schools and colleges of education take responsibility for the demonstrated competence in content, pedagogy, and performance in the classroom of the students whom they admit as well as those they graduate, little progress will be made. Formal assessments for teachers may well be important in moving us toward those goals, but a concerted commitment by educators will be the real key.

If there is an inherent conflict between policy and practice, it lies in the tension between simplification and generalization on the one hand and individuation and localization on the other. Policies are normally defined for general circumstances, typically devoid of nuance or conditionality. Practice, on the other hand, is terrifyingly local and specific. Policymakers are most comfortable with clear rules; professional practitioners become uneasy even with fairly flexible standards. This book comes to teach us that if the improved student learning we require for all students in a democracy is to be accomplished, both the policymakers and the professionals must come to appreciate their joint responsibility to craft a new alliance. Each must recognize, appreciate, and ultimately respect the constraints and civic obligations under which the other operates. Moreover, policymakers must understand that the most effective schools are institutions that are designed to be educative for their teachers. Readers of this book will discover that within its pages lies an impressive array of findings, analyses, interpretations, and proposals that can guide the needed efforts to design such settings.

Teaching as the Learning Profession is far more than a superb book title. It is a mandate for the stakeholders in whose hands lies the future of America's teachers, and through them, America's students.

Reference

Lazarus, E. "Closed Chambers." *New York Review of Books,* Oct. 8, 1998, p. 16.

Shulman, L. S., and Sykes, G. (eds.). *Handbook of Teaching and Policy.* White Plains, N.Y.: Longman, 1983.

April 1999

Lee S. Shulman
President,
The Carnegie Foundation
for the Advancement of Teaching
Menlo Park, California

INTRODUCTION: TEACHING AS THE LEARNING PROFESSION

Gary Sykes

This book is based on a deceptively simple premise coupled with a hypothesis. The premise is that the improvement of American education relies centrally on the development of a highly qualified teacher workforce imbued with the knowledge, skills, and dispositions to encourage exceptional learning in all the nation's students. The related hypothesis is that the key to producing well-qualified teachers is to greatly enhance their professional learning across the continuum of a career in the classroom. We underline this hypothesis in the book's title. Teaching par excellence must become the learning profession in order to stimulate greater learning among students.

As we advance these ideas, we also acknowledge their status as starting points for policy development, the ongoing creation of new practices, and the pursuit of inquiries to test their merit. The chapters combine arguments with analysis, proposals for new policies and practices with reviews, and reports of contemporary research. As a collection, the chapters are unified in their basic perspectives even as they range across a broad set of topics. In part their unity derives from their origin. The majority of chapters were solicited as background analyses for the National Commission on Teaching and America's Future (NCTAF). Formed in 1994 with support from the Rockefeller Foundation and the Carnegie Corporation of New York, NCTAF was a thirteen-person deliberative body made up of prominent educators and public officials. The commission was chaired by Governor James Hunt of North Carolina; its executive director, one of this book's coeditors, was Linda Darling-Hammond. The other coeditor, Gary Sykes, served as a consultant to the commission.

Over its two-year tenure, the commission held hearings and received testimony from many sources, initiated and synthesized research, and consulted widely with lay and professional organizations and individuals. These labors resulted in a report (NCTAF, 1996) to the nation issued in September 1996. Subsequent reports have tracked progress toward NCTAF's recommendations as well as amplifying basic assumptions (Darling-Hammond, 1998; NCTAF, 1997). The NCTAF report organized a call to action around five major recommendations that bear repeating:

- Get serious about standards for both students and teachers.
- Reinvent teacher preparation and professional development.
- Fix teacher recruitment, and put qualified teachers in every classroom.
- Encourage and reward teacher knowledge and skill.
- Create schools that are organized for student and teacher success.

Following the release of its report, the commission identified a number of states that agreed to serve as sites for implementation of report recommendations, and it engaged in a series of dissemination activities. At this writing, this work continues along with several related developments. In late 1997 the U.S. Education Department (USED) made two large awards for activities in support of the NCTAF agenda. The National Partnership for Excellence and Accountability in Teaching (NPEAT) brings together the major organizations with a stake in teacher quality, together with a consortium of universities within which is lodged a comprehensive R&D agenda. NPEAT is dedicated to bringing research to bear on the improvement of teaching and teachers in the United States through creation of a national partnership. At nearly the same time, the USED awarded the new Center for the Study of Teaching and Policy (CTP) to another group of researchers. This new research center will pursue a parallel set of inquiries that also reflects many of the themes set forth in the NCTAF report.

We mention these developments not only to indicate the evolving context in which this book has been produced, but also to underscore the centrality of these issues to American education. Cultivating and supporting a qualified teacher workforce increasingly is regarded by a wide spectrum of interests as vital to the nation's educational welfare. Yet educators and public officials recognize a host of problems that must be addressed, ranging from the quality of teacher education to state standard setting, district recruitment and selection routines, and the organization of schools for teacher learning. At the same time, recent developments offer promise that headway is possible in many of these areas. The National Board for Professional Teaching Standards (NBPTS) and its companion project, the Interstate New Teacher Assessment and Support Consortium (INTASC), have launched historically significant efforts to develop high and rigorous teaching standards that constitute one representation of knowledge and skill in teaching. The National Council for the Accreditation of Teacher Education (NCATE) is also redefining its standards for programs and institutions of teacher preparation, moving toward a performance-based orientation. Many states have begun to enact new policies that better support quality teaching. And the so-called new unionism, championed in various ways by the National Education Association (NEA) and the American Federation of Teachers (AFT), directs the efforts of both organizations to issues of school and teacher quality.

These are but a few developments we might mention that indicate receptivity to the multifaceted agenda for the improvement of teaching. This book makes a timely contribution to these issues, with an audience in mind of teachers, teacher educators, school administrators, and policymakers. The chapter authors were asked to draw out the implications of their arguments and analyses for the improvement of both educational practice and educational policy. Chapters are of various kinds. In some cases, including the contributions by Mary Kennedy and by Richard Elmore and Deanna Burney, the chapters present evidence from empirical studies. Other chapters, such as those by Ann Lieberman and Maureen Grolnick and by Charles Thompson and John Zeuli, weave research results into arguments and analyses. Still other chapters, including those by Gloria Ladson-Billings; Willis Hawley and Linda Valli; Barnett Berry, Linda Darling-Hammond, David Haselkorn, and Elizabeth Fideler; Judith Warren Little; and Darling-Hammond and Milbrey McLaughlin derive implications from reviews of literature. A final cluster of chapters, by Deborah Ball and David Cohen, Magdalene Lampert and Ball, Gary Sykes, and Julia Koppich and Charles Kerchner, draw on a range of literature to advance arguments and recommendations.

The term *handbook* typically has two denotations. It can refer to a practical compendium of information that practitioners may consult for guidance in their specialized field, or it can refer to a comprehensive review of the status of knowledge on a reasonably well-bounded academic subject. We employ the term in the volume's subtitle to conjure both meanings. Many of the chapters contain guidance in the form of principles, precepts, recommendations, and implications. Educational practitioners, we believe, will find this content useful. The chapters also review and synthesize the literature associated with the term *policy and practice,* which is increasingly common in educational discourse. Its use reflects the growing efforts by governmental and nongovernmental agencies at all levels of the educational system to influence what transpires in the classroom. Consequently the book also will be of use to researchers and educators who teach courses in this area within graduate and undergraduate programs.

A PREVIEW OF CHAPTER CONTENTS

The book presents chapters in four areas, beginning with reconsiderations of teacher education, proceeding to ongoing professional development, then to how schools serve as sites for teacher learning, and finally to policy-related issues in teacher learning. We note, however, that many of the chapters treat both policy and practice issues in their analyses and recommendations. Readers interested in policy issues will find relevant discussions in chapters throughout the book.

The opening chapter by Deborah Ball and David Cohen sets the stage. They propose what they term a "revolution" in professional education for teachers, but not in the usual sense involving politics, large structural change, or the creation of new organizations. Theirs is a quiet but profound revolution in ways of thinking and in the culture and norms that guide teacher learning at early and advanced career stages. As with other authors in this collection, they are skeptical of reform from "the outside in" that involves grand, governmental programs and large policy changes intended to drive subtle, complex alterations in teaching and learning. They frame their task as envisioning how deep changes in the content and pedagogy of professional education might transform teacher learning as one basis for long-term improvement in American education. Their proposals center on describing and providing examples of what it means for teachers to learn "in practice" and "from practice," taking care to distinguish their conception from the habit of unmediated "learning from experience." Central to their ideas are a curriculum situated in the critical activities of the profession, a rich collection of materials fabricated or modified to allow the close study of teaching, a stance of critical inquiry directed toward cases or instances of practice, and a discourse community whose norms support such study as a collective activity generated substantially by teachers themselves. Because the aim of such professional education is reformed rather than received teaching practice, Ball and Cohen along with several other authors in the book advocate the intentional creation of disequilibrium or dissonance as a basis for revisioning and rethinking the nature of teaching and learning. Thus may professional education serve the broad aims of educational reform at the instructional core.

Chapter Two by Magdalene Lampert and Deborah Ball amplifies and extends these ideas with particular attention to how new technologies may be employed to create rich learning materials and opportunities for teachers. Based on the authors' extensive experience in creating and using a multimedia archive of their own elementary mathematics teaching as a site for the study of instruction, they illustrate how such "electronic environments" provide both mechanical and conceptual tools for explorations into teaching. Their work draws on another powerful idea reflected across chapters, the situated nature of knowledge in teaching, which requires that teachers learn how to size up and respond to specific events in classrooms. Hypermedia access to videotape of classroom situations and artifacts of instruction such as teacher plans or student journals allows students to practice both interpreting classroom events and formulating responses and actions. Teaching as both knowing and doing may be supported by such applications of technology.

Mary Kennedy continues the analysis of teacher education in Chapter Three based on results from the Teacher Education and Learning to Teach (TELT) study, which she directed. Introducing the term *enactment* as shorthand for putting ideas into practice, she explores the challenge set forth in the first two chapters, which is to orient teacher education around appealing but operationally under-specified visions of reformed practice that may not yet be widely available for emulation and modeling. Drawing on evidence from the TELT study, which con-centrated on learning to teach writing, she illustrates complexities in translating reform talk about teaching into teaching practice that is indexed to, or situated in, the particularities of actual classrooms and students. Her results illustrate the kinds of influence that teacher education program orientations are likely to exert, as well as the limits of those influences. In concluding with implications for pol-icy, she emphasizes among other points the importance of the content of pro-grams rather than their structural characteristics.

The final chapter in Part One, by Gloria Ladson-Billings, complements the first three by focusing on the cultural and social characteristics of students as critical context and content for teacher education. Preparing teachers for diver-sity proceeds out of a history of dispute over the relative emphasis accorded to a single, unifying culture or an acknowledgment of diversity patterned along complex, intersecting lines of class, race, gender, and ethnicity. Of overriding significance in these debates over unity and diversity may be the uniformity of the teacher workforce (middle class, white) in relation to a student population that is increasingly diverse, racially and culturally. More than at any other time in our history, teachers must work with children who are culturally different from themselves. What kind of preparation equips teachers for this critical as-pect of their work? Ladson-Billings reviews the current status of multicultural education, profiles several innovative programs, and concludes with thoughts on an agenda for research in this area.

Part Two contains chapters that explore issues in the professional develop-ment of teachers. Chapter Five by Willis Hawley and Linda Valli establishes a set of consensus principles for effective professional development, culled from a wide variety of sources. In presenting a synthesis in the form of eight key prin-ciples, the authors argue that the literature on professional development converges powerfully. The issue is not one of disagreement among experts, but of how to translate widely accepted principles into organizational and instructional prac-tice. The chapter serves as a practical guide while posing a puzzle: if educators are in substantial agreement about characteristics of effective professional development, then why is such practice not widespread?

Several of the chapters in this book supply answers in the form of critiques and analyses of the status quo, but one answer also may be that each of Hawley and Valli's principles requires complex, well-coordinated responses from multiple educational actors that are difficult to initiate and sustain. In the next chapter, Gary Sykes explores the implementation of two of these principles in detail (numbers one and six), which together advocate anchoring teacher professional development in the assessment of student learning. Following an assessment of its current status, Sykes proposes a number of leads in policy and practice for strengthening the teacher-student learning connection in professional development.

Part Three of this book assembles chapters that explore the organizational context for teacher learning. Barnett Berry, Linda Darling-Hammond, David Haselkorn, and Elizabeth Fideler contribute a review that draws together evidence on teacher supply and demand, recruitment pathways into teaching, district selection and hiring practices, and induction programs for beginning teachers. Framed as a comprehensive, contemporary synthesis, the chapter makes an important point in treating these not as discrete topics but as interrelated aspects of a policy and organizational approach to attracting a highly qualified workforce. While pointing to exemplary programs and practices, the chapter also makes a strong case that recruitment, selection, and induction too often are mismanaged, neglected, or poorly implemented, tracing failures to both state policies and to district and school organizational routines. Recruiting new teachers along with their preparation and their support in the workplace are arguably what might be termed the infrastructure of teacher quality. This chapter provides an in-depth analysis of the recruitment functions, together with recommendations for future improvements.

Judith Warren Little next sets forth a wide-ranging set of school conditions that support teacher learning in the context of their daily work. While the professional development opportunities scheduled outside the regular workday are clearly one important resource for school improvement, the manner in which schools daily organize and manage teacher time and attention is equally critical. Little's chapter provides a systematic review of such organizational factors. The chapter's framework extends the existing literature on this topic by explicitly considering those factors that link teacher learning to student's academic achievement, and so continues this motif running through the volume's chapters.

Treated as an organizational function, professional development implicates the work of school administrators, but relatively few accounts describe how school superintendents and principals manage this function. Richard Elmore and Deanna Burney contribute one such account in Chapter Nine based on a case study of Community School District 2 in New York City. The central figure in this case is the district superintendent, Anthony Alvarado, whose leadership focuses squarely on instructional improvement through teacher development. The case details not only the strategies, structures, and processes that have evolved to support teacher learning but also the organizational ethos (a term Little also invokes) that permeates the district. Instructional improvement, the chapter reveals, cannot be one among a number of priorities if it is to result in better student learning. It must be the sole priority, the residing passion among all educators, and it must reach into all elements of administrative and teaching practice. Such single-minded (and tough-minded) management may be relatively rare in American education, but the case suggests what can be accomplished when leadership insists on learning as the priority.

Networks that join teachers within and across schools constitute another robust context for teacher learning. The term *network* enjoys a rich history in the social sciences, and its referents range from patterns of informal contacts (such as the infamous "old boys' network") to systematically devised organizations (such as the National Diffusion Network). In Chapter Ten Ann Lieberman and Maureen Grolnick report results of their study of sixteen networks in education. Networks are attractive because they link teachers to outside sources of knowledge and expertise (often other teachers) useful in the pursuit of such goals as school and instructional improvement and policy implementation. But not all networks are effective, and they all face common problems and tensions. Educators have interest in networks as a familiar form of reform as exemplified in such organizations as the Coalition of Essential Schools, and policymakers too have begun to use networks in policy enactment. The chapter describes network operations in terms of five organizational themes and then explores five tensions that all networks must manage. Their analysis serves as a useful guide to both the potential and the limitations of networks as a reform strategy.

The final part of this book, on policy for teacher learning, begins with a chapter by Julia Koppich and Charles Kerchner on the future of teacher unionism. Their title draws a distinction between what they call the first half of teaching—salaries and working conditions—and the second half—the actual work of teaching itself. A critical context for school reform is labor management relations, as it has been structured for some forty years through the process of collective bargaining. Although states vary in the labor laws regulating the employment of teaching, the negotiated contract has become a pervasive instrument of policy. Yet organized teachers today are uneasy about industrial-style unionism as their primary form of affiliation and advancement. While they seek to press claims for fair and equitable wages and working conditions, they also seek to be involved centrally in educational improvement. Might traditional unionism evolve toward new forms of negotiation and agreement with public bodies that provide teachers greater scope over issues of educational quality? This is the question Koppich and Kerchner set out to answer. Their chapter contains a number of bold yet practical proposals for transforming teacher organizations into partners in school reform, while recognizing that labor disputes and their resolution will continue to occur. They argue for a scaled-down contract coupled to a substantial compact that sets forth agreements about instruction. And they call for enactment of a new law of work that transforms the statutory framework regulating labor-management relations in education.

The penultimate chapter, by Charles Thompson and John Zeuli, returns to a set of issues that previous authors (Ball and Cohen, Sykes, Elmore and Burney) have treated. They pursue a complex argument and analysis about the necessary and sufficient conditions for building teacher learning into systemic reform, conceived as the coordination of multiple policy instruments that supply guidance to instruction. Fortified with examples drawn from their studies of mathematics and science instructional policy in Michigan, they take up what is arguably the greatest challenge to instructional policy: how to encourage transformative learning among teachers on a broad scale so that the new standards for teaching and learning may be enacted. Their argument begins by establishing the case for the centrality of teacher learning as a policy target; next describes the nature of student learning now sought by reformers, characterized as "thinking to learn"; then reviews what teachers need to know and why what currently passes for systemic reform is insufficient; provides some examples of teacher learning that appear promising; and finally reconceives the policy problem of "scaling up" reform as one of learning, not engineering.

The final chapter, by Linda Darling-Hammond and Milbrey McLaughlin, supplies an integrative summary of the book in the form of policy guidance for the improvement of teaching. Reforms, they argue, may be placed into three broad families: standards based, school based, and development based. Each family has its own logic and its own implications, but Darling-Hammond and McLaughlin argue that each ultimately relies on the others for long-term impact. In reviewing examples of effective policies in support of good teaching, they conclude with a call for patient development and testing of such policy as a critical investment in the improvement of teaching.

Although the chapter authors are in substantial agreement on many issues and converge in their basic support for systemic reform, greater attention to the relationship between teacher and student learning, and more ambitious conceptions of learning for teachers and students alike, the book offers differing opinions on the role of governmental and professional interests in sponsoring reforms. Darling-Hammond and McLaughlin, for example, conclude tentatively that a combination of government action with professional expertise will be necessary to stimulate transformational teacher learning on a broad scale. However, Thompson and Zeuli express skepticism that government will be able to play a constructive role; they place greater confidence in professional sources. Reform networks may be of the grassroots variety, extending lateral contacts among teachers around particular visions of improvement. But they may also be organized by government and include elements of hierarchy and formality associated with government interventions. Taken together, then, the book raises but does not resolve questions about roles and role relationships in the reform of teaching and learning. Reforming the system of education at the instructional core, we might conclude, is likely to require concerted actions by public and professional interests, whose terms must be worked out continuously, in ongoing fashion. Resolving these terms in local, state, and national contexts is a critical issue in that arena that we identify as policy and practice.

References

Darling-Hammond, L. "Teachers and Teaching: Testing Policy Hypotheses from a National Commission Report." *Educational Researcher,* 1998, *27,* 5–15.

National Commission on Teaching and America's Future. *What Matters Most: Teaching for America's Future.* New York: Author, 1996.

National Commission on Teaching and America's Future. *Doing What Matters Most: Investing in Quality Teaching.* New York: Author, 1997.

THE EDITORS

LINDA DARLING-HAMMOND is the Charles E. Ducommun Professor of Education at Stanford University, where her research, teaching, and policy work focus on issues of school restructuring, teacher education, and educational equity. She is also executive director of the National Commission on Teaching and America's Future, a blue ribbon panel whose 1996 report, *What Matters Most: Teaching for America's Future,* has been widely acclaimed as a blueprint for transforming educational policy so that all children are guaranteed access to high-quality teaching. The commission's work has led to ongoing reforms in the preparation of teachers and to policy changes affecting teaching and schooling at all levels of government. Darling-Hammond's most recent book, *The Right to Learn: A Blueprint for Creating Schools That Work* (Jossey-Bass, 1997), was awarded the Outstanding Book Award from the American Educational Research Association in 1998.

GARY SYKES is professor of educational administration and teacher education at Michigan State University, where his professional activities concentrate on policy related to teacher professionalization and school choice. He serves on the management committee of the National Partnership on Excellence and Accountability in Teaching, with responsibility for research on teacher professional development. He also is conducting several studies on educational choice policies in Michigan. His most recent publications include a chapter for the forthcoming *Handbook of Research on Educational Administration* and a chapter in *The Role of the University in the Preparation of Teachers* (1999).

THE CONTRIBUTORS

DEBORAH LOEWENBERG BALL, professor, School of Education, University of Michigan.

BARNETT T. BERRY, associate director, National Commission on Teaching and America's Future.

DEANNA BURNEY, assistant superintendent for curriculum, Camden, New Jersey.

DAVID K. COHEN, John Dewey Professor, School of Education, University of Michigan.

RICHARD F. ELMORE, professor, Graduate School of Education, Harvard University.

ELIZABETH FIDELER, vice president for research and policy, Recruiting New Teachers.

MAUREEN GROLNICK, education program officer, American Council of Learned Societies.

DAVID HASELKORN, president, Recruiting New Teachers.

WILLIS D. HAWLEY, professor of education and public affairs, University of Maryland.

MARY M. KENNEDY, professor, School of Education, Michigan State University.

CHARLES TAYLOR KERCHNER, professor, Graduate School of Education, Claremont College.

JULIA E. KOPPICH, president, Julia E. Koppich & Associates.

GLORIA LADSON-BILLINGS, professor, Department of Curriculum and Instruction, University of Wisconsin–Madison.

MAGDALENE LAMPERT, professor, School of Education, University of Michigan.

ANN LIEBERMAN, professor and co-director, National Center for Restructuring Education, Schools, and Teaching. Currently on leave at Stanford University.

JUDITH WARREN LITTLE, professor, Graduate School of Education, University of California, Berkeley.

MILBREY WALLIN MCLAUGHLIN, professor, Education and Public Policy, Stanford University.

CHARLES L. THOMPSON, associate professor of teacher education, College of Education, Michigan State University.

LINDA VALLI, associate professor, College of Education, University of Maryland.

JOHN S. ZEULI, academic instructor, Avon Park Youth Academy.

Teaching as the Learning Profession

PART ONE

RETHINKING
TEACHER EDUCATION

CHAPTER ONE

Developing Practice, Developing Practitioners

Toward a Practice-Based
Theory of Professional Education

Deborah Loewenberg Ball and David K. Cohen

The past decade has seen a tidal wave of proposals to reform education. Seeking to improve what students get from school, reformers advocate changes in standards and assessment, school organization and decision making, and curriculum. The vision of a better education is complex. Teachers are to help diverse learners become competent and skilled, understand what they are doing, and communicate effectively. Schools are to be connected with their communities, and all students are to succeed in ways they currently do not and never have before in the history of American public education. If such plans are to move in any significant way beyond rhetoric to permeate practice, significant professional development will be crucial, for such instruction is not commonplace. Nor could teachers change instruction in these ways simply by being told to do so. Teachers would need opportunities to reconsider their current practices and to examine others, as well as to learn more about the subjects and students they teach.

Reformers routinely invoke the need for professional development, and there is no shortage of in-service workshops for teachers. Although a good deal of money is spent on staff development in the United States, most is spent on sessions and workshops that are often intellectually superficial, disconnected from

We acknowledge our colleagues Magdalene Lampert, Linda Darling-Hammond, Gary Sykes, and Helen Featherstone for their help in thinking about these ideas. We also thank Virginia Richardson and Gary Sykes for their helpful comments on an earlier draft of this chapter.

deep issues of curriculum and learning, fragmented, and noncumulative (Cohen and Hill, 1997; Little, 1994). Rarely do these in-services seem based on a curricular view of teachers' learning. Teachers are thought to need updating rather than opportunities for serious and sustained learning of curriculum, students, and teaching. Instead they are offered one-shot workshops with advice and tips of things to try, catalogues filled with blackline-master activities for the latest educational ideas (cooperative learning, problem solving, literary analysis, or something else), six-step plans for a host of teaching challenges, and much more. These offerings get a steady stream of subscribers. Participation in modal staff development is the professional equivalent of yo-yo dieting for many teachers. Workshop handouts, ideas, and methods provide brief sparks of novelty and imagination, most squeakily practical. But most teachers have a shelf overflowing with dusty vinyl binders, the wilted cast-offs of staff development workshops. Since professional development is rarely seen as a continuing enterprise for teachers, it is only occasionally truly developmental. One reason is that many people see teaching as mostly common sense and perceive little need for professional learning. Another is that teaching has been seen and organized as a career in which sustained learning was not required for adequate performance. Still another is that there is no coherent infrastructure for professional development. It is not the responsibility of any easily identifiable group or agency, and so it happens everywhere—and hence lacks consistency, coherence, and curriculum.

Recent reforms challenge this perspective on teaching and its improvement. A great deal of learning would be required for most teachers to be able to do the kind of teaching and produce the kind of student learning that reformers envision, for none of it is simple. This kind of teaching and learning would require that teachers become serious learners in and around their practice, rather than amassing strategies and activities.

Despite considerable expenditures on professional development, resources are severely lacking to improve available opportunities for professional learning. Although money is important, the critical missing resources are not fiscal. Missing, for instance, is the common conviction that professional learning matters to instruction. Instead, a widely held belief is that teachers' practices change as a product of changes in curriculum, standards, and assessments. Missing as well are carefully constructed and empirically validated theories of teacher learning that could inform teacher education, in roughly the same way that cognitive psychology has begun to inform the education of schoolchildren. Teacher learning instead is usually seen as either something that just happens as a matter of course from experience or as the product of training in particular methods or curricula. Yet another missing resource is coordination among various elements of professional education. American education lacks anything remotely resembling a comprehensive perspective on professional learning, across time, or over topics or purposes. Such coordination would be impossible without a highly educated cadre of educators whose responsibilities prominently included the education of teachers and administrators. In the absence of these key resources, the system limps along, with teachers collecting material from a wide range of sources, their teaching experience the principal site for their individual and idiosyncratic development.

Those who want teaching and learning to become much more ambitious face a significant challenge: how to construct a substantial approach to professional learning—one that takes a comprehensive perspective on the relations between professional development and the improvement of teaching and learning, in a system in which professional development, like other education, has been superficial and fragmented, the commitment to and belief in serious professional development is quite limited, and theories of professional learning have been implicit and undeveloped.

It would be easier if schools were the problem—that is, if teacher education programs did a solid job of preparing teachers for good practice, which was then corroded by the schools. Then we could focus on practicing teachers. But the stage is set years before, in teachers' initial preparation. Although some teacher educators have aimed for more ambitious teaching and learning, many have not. And even when they aim high, preservice teacher education offers a weak antidote to the powerful socialization into teaching that occurs in teachers' own prior experience as students. What Dan Lortie (1975) called the "apprenticeship of observation" is typically more potent than formal teacher education, and the lessons of that apprenticeship ordinarily are reinforced by intending teachers' experience in most university courses, student teaching, and professional work. All of these things have reinforced the conservatism of practice, with its didactic approaches to teaching and facts-and-skills conceptions of knowledge. Teachers hone their skills within that frame of reference and have few opportunities for substantial professional discourse.

Thus we confront an educational system that seems poorly equipped to produce deeper and more complex learning in students as well as teachers. Weak teacher education, inherited conservative traditions, and little professional capacity for learning and change combine to inhibit reform.

Our response is to sketch a comprehensive approach to teachers' professional development. We situate this in a theoretical sketch of teacher learning, which we believe is essential to frame any sensible approach to teacher education. We then explore what it would take to reconstruct professional education in ways that could improve teachers' capacity to encourage deeper and more complex learning in their students. Such a reconstruction would require many changes in teacher education, but two are of leading importance.

First, professional education would have to acquire a fundamentally different content and character than it now has, in which all its elements coherently supported acquisition of the knowledge, skills, and dispositions that would enable teachers to encourage this sort of learning. Second, teacher education also would have to become sufficiently powerful to immunize teachers against the conservative lessons that most learn from practice. Until practice has changed, most intending teachers would arrive in their professional education having learned didactic conceptions of learning and teaching as students. And once finished with their professional education, those same teachers' experience in school would reveal the difficulty of sustaining thoughtful work when surrounded with more traditional colleagues, administrators, and parents. Teacher education would have to become an agent of professional countersocialization, no easy task.

Unless initial teacher education can prepare beginning teachers to learn to do much more thoughtful and challenging work, and unless ways can be found, through professional development, to help teachers to sustain such work, traditional instruction is likely to persist in frustrating educational reform, and reformers' visions are likely to continue not to permeate practice broadly or deeply.

Although many reformers have broken their lances on that problem since Horace Mann first attempted a solution, we think it could be solved. If teachers' professional learning could be situated in the sorts of practice that reformers wish to encourage, it could become a key element in a curriculum of professional development. A practice-based curriculum could be compelling for teachers and would help them to improve students' learning. If such teaching, and learning how to do it, became the object of continuing, thoughtful inquiry, much of teachers' everyday work could become a source for constructive professional development. Hence we propose new ways to understand and use practice as a site for professional learning, as well as ways to cultivate the sorts of inquiry into practice from which many teachers could learn.

Many advocates approach the problem of poor professional development with proposals to restructure teachers' roles, time, and relationships, but we do not. Although they may ultimately be needed, changes in the organization of professional practice or schools do not by themselves lead to better instruction or learning. To affect what teachers might learn, one must consider the curriculum and pedagogy of professional development: what teachers would have opportunities to learn and how they would be taught (Elmore, Peterson, and McCarthey, 1996). Any design for improved professional learning must be grounded in the cornerstones of education: what needs to be learned (content), the nature of that content and what that implies about how it might be learned (theories of learning), curriculum and pedagogy (with what material and in what ways the learners can be helped to learn that content, given who they are, the nature of what there is to be learned, and theories of how it is best learned). This chapter offers a set of ideas for such a design for professional development.

Our proposals are ambitious, but we want an approach that will work within American education as it stands. We propose to improve teachers' knowledge and classroom practice. As Milbrey McLaughlin wrote, "Implementation is a problem of the smallest unit," and we think it makes most sense to begin there, rather than trying to turn the system upside down from the outside, based on large increases in money or potent new instruments of coordination. Hence we offer ways to challenge and change common conceptions of practice at their roots, in ways that link the development of better practice to practitioners' development, and in doses that teachers might find usable and manageable. For reasons that we will explain near the end of this chapter, this seemingly more modest strategy seems more likely than more dramatic and grandiose strategies to thrive and grow. As the changes in practice and professional learning matured, they would generate the capabilities needed to change the system dramatically, but they would have done so at its base, where the capacity for change is most critical, and which external changes in structure and operations cannot produce. The ideas sketched here are intended to help to plot a new direction for teachers' professional education that could make a difference tomorrow as well as in the long haul.

We organize the chapter around three basic questions. First, what would teachers have to know, and know how to do, in order to offer instruction that would support much deeper and more complex learning for their students? Second, what sort of professional education would be most likely to help teachers to learn those things? Third, what do these ideas imply for the content, method, and structure of professional development?

WHAT WOULD TEACHERS NEED TO KNOW?

Researchers and educators have quite dramatically changed their views of learning and knowledge in the past several decades. Those changes have led them to dramatically different views of what students should do in classrooms and how teachers should teach. We begin from these developing conceptions of knowledge, teaching, and learning, and ask: What would teachers need to know in order to teach in the ways that researchers and educators imagine they should?[1]

First, teachers would need to understand the subject matter they teach, in ways quite different from those they learned as students. For example, they need to know meanings and connections, not just procedures and information. It is not enough to know that when you multiply:

$$\begin{array}{r} .75 \\ \times .25 \\ \hline \end{array}$$

you count the number of places in the two multipliers (.75 and .25 together have "four places") and then "count over" that number of places from the right in the calculated answer (1875), resulting in .1875. Students are likely to come up with the answer 18.75. Speculating about why they may do this requires teachers to be able to see the procedure through students' eyes in the light of other things students know—for example, that when adding two decimals, one lines up the numbers and preserves the location of the decimal point:

$$\begin{array}{r} .75 \\ +.25 \\ \hline 1.00 \end{array}$$

And explaining why the multiplication algorithm works is very different from being able to execute it correctly. Why does the answer for the product of .75 and .25 have four decimal places? What representation or models could function to endow the multiplication, or the conventional procedure, with meaning? What does .75 × .25 mean? What is a real-life situation for which .75 × .25 is a sensible calculation? Answers to such questions are essential to teaching with understanding and are founded on a deeper, more conceptual kind of knowledge than most of us have acquired from our own experiences in math classes.

Understanding the ideas is not all that teachers need. They also need to understand what reasoning in particular fields entails—such as what counts as "proving" something in mathematics as compared with proving something in history or biology, and, more broadly, what habits of mind are associated with scientific thinking versus literary interpretation or art criticism. They also need to see ways that ideas connect across fields, and to everyday life, so that they can appropriately select and use contexts, problems, and applications. In such matters it helps to know something about how particular ideas evolved in the history of a field, for students' thinking sometimes parallels historical developments. Understanding current controversies in certain fields can also help in knowing where knowledge is changing or contested rather than agreed on.

Second, in addition to knowing the material they are teaching, teachers would need to know about children—what children are like, what they are likely to find interesting and to have trouble with, in particular domains. They would need to become insightful in listening to and interpreting children's ideas about academic subjects. They would need ways to expand the interpretive frames they likely bring to their observations of students so that they could see more possibilities in what students could do. And they would need to come to see children as more capable of thinking and reasoning, and less as blank slates who lack knowledge. Some of this knowledge is general—about children of certain ages, for instance. Some of it is particular—what this child believes, how she works, what she means by what she has drawn or written or said. Learning to attend to one's students with insight requires expertise beyond what one gathers from one's own experience. What one enjoyed, thought, or felt as a child may afford helpful speculation about one's students, but is insufficient as a professional resource for knowing learners.

Third, teachers would need to learn that knowing students is not simply a matter of knowing individual children. Because teachers often teach children who come from backgrounds different from their own, they would need to become acquainted with cultural differences, including differences in language, class, family, and community. Gender, taken for granted in everyday experience, is another critical matter for teachers to understand. Through a complex interplay of regard for individuals and groups, teachers have to understand their learners. Honoring differences in teaching is a complicated matter, for teachers need to suspend habitual notions that presume sameness and to appreciate distinction, which requires the capacity to bridge social and ethnic gulfs and sensitivity to the adjustment and adaptation needed to reach each student. Yet teachers also need to connect with their students, and for this it is important not to see students as the "other." That requires seeking common ground, expecting all students to learn, and not differentiating expectations of students. Teachers bring their own experiences based on race, class, gender, and culture, and these are both resource and liability in relating to students.

Moreover, teachers would need to develop and expand their ideas about learning, including what it means to learn, what helps children (or anyone else) learn, and how to "read" children to know more about what they are thinking and learning. Longstanding beliefs and assumptions about learning would need to be examined. For example, is it true that children learn best in bite-sized pieces, each one "learned" before another could be? Do we know that all learning proceeds from the concrete to the abstract, and what is meant by either? Is it true that learning needs to be "fun," and what does that mean anyway? What do we know about when students can best grasp certain ideas, and about the relationship between developing skills and developing understanding? How do differences among learners affect how they learn?

Teachers also would need to know pedagogy. In order to connect students with content in effective ways, teachers need a repertoire of ways to engage learners effectively and the capacity to adapt and shift modes in response to students. What is entailed in using discussion as a medium for instruction? How can student exploratory projects be appropriately framed and guided? When might a clear expository presentation or explanation be called for, and what distinguishes a skillful presentation from a less skillful one? Examining how the curriculum is constructed as teachers and students interact over the material is vital to an increasingly developed practice. Teachers also need to learn to discern the constituents of the culture of a classroom, to have ideas about the kind of classroom culture that supports learning goals and about how to construct such a culture.

One conclusion we draw from this sketch is that little of the knowledge we have discussed is found in most teachers' experience as public school students or teachers, let alone in their social worlds. These sorts of knowledge and learning would require that teachers move far beyond their own personal and educational experience. However that might be done, it would be the antithesis of the "apprenticeship of observation" that now is such a powerful influence on most teaching.

LEARNING IN AND FROM PRACTICE

Even if teachers knew all these things, they would not know nearly enough to teach in the ways that researchers and educators think they should, for the knowledge we have sketched could be used only in complex interactions in the unpredictable situations that we call classrooms. In addition, the sorts of teaching we have discussed would render the interactions more complex, unpredictable, and difficult to monitor and manage. Teachers could not do such work unless they knew how to learn in the contexts of their work. That would require the capability to attend to and learn about individual students' knowledge, ideas, and intentions. It also would require the capability to stand back from and analyze their own teaching, to ask and answer such questions as: What is working? What is not working? For whom are certain things working or not working? To teach well, given reformers' ambitions and the situational and uncertain nature of teaching and learning, teachers would need to use what they learn to correct, refine, and improve instruction.

This implies that practice cannot be wholly equipped by some well-considered body of knowledge. Teaching occurs in particulars—particular students interacting with particular teachers over particular ideas in particular circumstances. Despite the significance of the knowledge that we discussed above, no amount of such knowledge can fully prescribe appropriate or wise practice. Hence an additional answer to the first question at the outset of this chapter—"What would teachers need to learn?"—is that much of what they would have to learn must be learned in and from practice rather than in preparing to practice. Or, perhaps better, they would have to learn, before they taught and while teaching, how to learn in and from practice. Teaching requires improvisation, conjecturing, experimenting, and assessing. Teachers must be able to adapt and develop practice.

It has become popular to talk about teachers as lifelong learners and about teaching as something that one learns over time, but the content of such phrases typically is less than clear. What distinguishes learning from and improving one's practice, from simply "becoming experienced"?[2] We think it wiser to ask more specifically: What might it take to learn in practice, and to learn from practice?

First, teachers would have to learn to size up a situation from moment to moment. For example, in addition to learning formal knowledge about children's thinking, teachers would need to learn how to elicit children's ideas and how to interpret them in the context of classroom work. This is inquiry into teaching in teaching. The knowledge of subject matter, learning, learners, and pedagogy is essential territory of teachers' work if they are to work as reformers imagine, but such knowledge does not offer clear guidance, for teaching of the sort that reformers advocate requires that teachers respond to students' efforts to make sense of material.[3] To do so, teachers additionally need to learn how to investigate what students are doing and thinking, and how instruction has been understood, as classes unfold. Conducting such investigations of student learning is essential to the new pedagogies that reformers urge, as well as to effective traditional instruction.

Second, teachers would have to learn to use such knowledge to improve their practice. All teachers accumulate experience, and some inquire into children's ideas. But neither experience nor inquiry improves teaching. Teachers would need to learn how to use what they learn about students' work and ideas to inform and improve teaching. That could include using their learning about first graders' thinking about stories to broaden understanding of what helps first graders learn to write. To develop this kind of knowledge, teachers would need intellectual tools that could help them to examine their own work with care and some detachment, to challenge their own thinking, and to draw reasonable conclusions from their inquiries, including generalizations that could help them to navigate future situations.[4]

Third, in order to do these things, teachers would need to learn how to operate experimentally in response to students and situations. Some of this is evident from what we already have said. Teachers would need to know how to frame, guide, and revise tasks and to pose and reformulate questions, so as to learn more about students' ideas and understandings. Such learning is not only produced in response to what arises, but also includes a kind of predictive, imaginative anticipation. What might students say or do? How might this particular student hear or see this? What might happen if I end this discussion and try to explain it myself? Much of what teachers need to know must be known and learned in context and in the moment. Knowledgeable teachers may not know the particulars in advance, but they can anticipate many likely elements of students' response to assignments and classroom situations.

Our argument is not that teachers should become researchers or teacher researchers. Rather, it is that a stance of inquiry should be central to the role of teacher. In order to teach in the ways we have sketched, teachers must be actively learning as they teach. The best way to improve both teaching and teacher learning would be to create the capacity for much better learning about teaching as a part of teaching. Teachers can certainly learn subject matter, as well as knowledge of children, learning, and pedagogy, in a variety of courses and workshops. But the use of such knowledge to teach depends on knowledge that cannot be learned entirely in advance or outside practice.

Since such knowledge is situated in practice, it must be learned in practice (Feiman-Nemser and Remillard, 1995). To propose otherwise would be like expecting someone to learn to swim on a sidewalk. Reading situations, the moves, the decisions—each of these is contextualized and shaded with subtleties of time, tone, person, topic—and it is in the unique combinations of these that the professional knowledge that we have been discussing can be created. Professional development could be substantially improved if we could develop ways to learn and teach about practice in practice. But what we mean by "in practice" is not obvious.

PROFESSIONAL EDUCATION FOR PROFESSIONAL LEARNING

To understand what we mean by learning in practice, we must first consider the basic requirements of professional education. First, professional education must be education for professional practice if it is to be either professionally responsible or usable. Thus a conception of the practice itself, and what it takes to practice well, should lie at the foundation of professional education. Second, any defensible education requires a sense of its purposes, a map of the relevant terrains in which to work, and a conception of what is involved in learning to operate in that terrain—that is, ideas about appropriate curriculum and pedagogy, the materials and experiences best suited to help people learn, and how to engage them. Third, since such schemes do not apply themselves, ideas are needed about the kinds of knowledge, skill, and other qualities crucial to teaching teachers in these ways. To satisfy these three basic requirements would be to realize the key elements of professional education for the practice of teaching.

We expand on these requirements to develop our conception of learning in practice. On our first point—what is distinctive in the professional education of teachers—we believe that at the core, it is about learning professional performance. To learn anything relevant to performance, professionals need experience with the tasks and ways of thinking that are fundamental to the practice. Those experiences must be immediate enough to be compelling and vivid. To learn more than mere imitation or survival, such experiences also must be sufficiently distanced to be open to careful scrutiny, unpacking, reconstruction, and the like.

On our second requirement, the primary purpose of teacher education is to cultivate the knowledge, skills, and values that will enable teachers to be highly effective in helping students to learn. It is also to develop the personal resources necessary to foster such learning. One element of such professional learning, then, is that it would be centered in the critical activities of the profession—that is, in and about the practices of teaching and learning. This does not necessarily mean that teachers should be educated in public schools, for we do not hold a narrow view of practice. As in medicine and law, to be "in" practice is not necessarily to be in an operating room or a courtroom. One is "in" a realm of legal practice when one drafts or comments on appellate briefs in a legal library, by considering a variety of briefs and other sources that bear on the matters in question. Centering professional education in practice is not a statement about either a physical locale or some stereotypical professional work. Rather it is a statement about a terrain of action and analysis that is defined first by identifying the central activities of teaching practice and, second, by selecting or creating materials that usefully depict that work and could be selected, represented, or otherwise modified to create opportunities for novice and experienced practitioners to learn.

The investigation of practice would be another key element in any professional approach to learning. In order to prepare people who were truly able to use knowledge to learn in and from practice, professional education would emphasize questions, investigations, analysis, and criticism. Crucial questions about teaching and learning would be one part of the frame of such work, and evidence of professional work—teaching and learning—would be another part. Investigating such questions and bringing salient evidence to bear would be central activities in the acquisition and improvement of professional knowledge. Thus, the pedagogy of professional education would in considerable part be a "pedagogy of investigation" (see Lampert and Ball, 1998). Such work could not be carried on without the development of suitable tools of professional analysis, and the development of such analytic tools would be another key requirement for creating a more deeply professional education.

Finally, the activities we have sketched could not be adequately cultivated without the development of more substantial professional discourse and engagement in communities of practice. Continuing thoughtful discussion among learners and teachers is an essential element of any serious education, because it is the chief vehicle for analysis, criticism, and communication of ideas, practices, and values. In the education of professionals, discourse serves additional purposes, which are related to building and sustaining a community of practitioners who collectively seek human and social improvement. The discourse of teacher education should also help to build collegiality within the profession and create a set of relations rooted in shared intentions and challenges. Such discourse should focus on deliberation about and development of standards for practice and on the improvement of teaching and learning.

This analysis leaves open many questions about what sort of study and analysis, and what the other elements would be. It remains to be shown how teacher education and professional development could be designed to make room for the inquiry-oriented teacher education that we propose. In fact, to say that teacher education should be centered in practice seems both reasonable and perplexing. Many tasks of teaching can be exploited as fruitful sites for inquiry and learning: selecting and developing curriculum materials, planning instruction, and assessing student work, for example. In the course of these tasks, teachers may puzzle, weigh alternatives, draw on what they know or can access as resources for judgments and decisions. But teachers also know that these things often are done on the run in the midst of busy days, and that there can be little time for puzzling or alternative weighing. How could professional education be centered in practice and still be thoughtful?

The key to our answer is that being "centered in practice" does not necessarily imply situations in school classrooms in real time. Although the bustle of immediacy lends authenticity, it also interferes with opportunities to learn. Being situated in a classroom restricts attention to the sort of teaching underway in that particular class. Further, being so situated confines learning to the rush of minute-to-minute practice. Better opportunities can be created by using strategic documentation of practice. Copies of students' work, videotapes of classroom lessons, curriculum materials, and teachers' notes all would be candidates. Using such things could locate the curriculum of teacher education "in practice," for they could focus professional learning in materials taken from real classrooms that present salient problems of practice. For instance, samples of students' work on two-digit multiplication, combined with the relevant curriculum materials and videotapes of the class in which the topic was taught, could be used to inquire into what students learned, and whether it was what the teacher intended. (See Lampert and Ball, 1998, and Cohen in Lampert and Ball, 1998.) Teachers and intending teachers could investigate what students seemed to have learned, and in the course of such analysis could probe other fundamental issues, among them these: What might it mean to know two-digit multiplication? To what big mathematical ideas is two-digit multiplication connected? Could there be more than one reasonable answer to the problem? For any answer, what sort of evidence for learning can reasonably be adduced from what is available? And if such documentation of practice included several different approaches to teaching the same topic, teachers and intending teachers would have the material with which to explore such issues in a comparative perspective, which would sharpen and deepen their examination of the issues.

Some disequilibrium is required for such learning. It would not be sufficient simply to see what one already assumes about students, learning, and content; one would also need to see others' assumptions, differences in their content and effects, or unexpected effects of one's own ideas or practices. Examples include the writing of a six-year-old boy who cannot yet read, or serious conceptual fissures in the thinking of an accomplished seventh-grade math student.[5] Such challenges to extant assumptions can be enormously productive exactly because seeing problems in their own, other teachers', or their students' work can spur reconsideration, more systematic inquiry, and learning about practice. For example, when teachers see the correct test of a student whose interview or open-ended writing reveals a profound misunderstanding of the material, they may begin to realize that the evidence that they have taken for learning is not necessarily adequate. Similarly, it is useful for teachers to notice that a student who says little in class and seems inattentive and unconnected can produce thoughtful written work.

These points are underscored in classrooms in which the tasks are less controlled and the discourse more open. One reason is that the possibilities for students' performance expand, and another is that the sensible but wrong ways students can think will also be more visible. More access to students' work can also unsettlingly reveal the complexity of the subject matter that ordinarily escapes adult notice. For example, in Ball's third-grade class, it turned out that her students did not necessarily think that 4/4 was equivalent to 5/5, even though they did think that 4/4 and 5/5 were each themselves equivalent to one whole—that is, that $4/4 = 1$ and that $5/5 = 1$. Some argued that 4/4 is less than 5/5 because "there are fewer pieces." Some argued that 4/4 is more than 5/5 because "the pieces are bigger" (Ball and Wilson, 1996). This episode was captured on videotape, and teachers who have viewed it have been disturbed by the children's misconceptions, enchanted by their imagination, worried about the students' potential confusions, and concerned over the teacher's role.

Such videotape provides an example of what we mean by the term *in practice,* and they have provoked many useful discussions about mathematics, about learning and teaching, and about third graders. Situating professional development in such materials, examples, and incidents—each of which may stimulate some productive disequilibrium—would create a new terrain for learning. The sorts of materials that can be used to constitute the terrain include written cases of teaching, multimedia cases or the raw materials of such cases, observations of teaching, teachers' journals, and examples of student work that are embedded in evidence about teaching.

We are not arguing that all examples of such material would qualify; in fact, much would not. One particularly crucial entry criterion for records that might be included is that they not merely reinforce extant practices, beliefs, or ideas, for practice-centered professional learning of the kind we are describing would be contrary to teachers' conventional socialization in two respects. It would intervene in the isolation of practice, in which the only material for learning is one's own practice. By enabling encounters with very different practices, such work would broaden and diversify teachers' knowledge and create opportunities to see new versions of teaching and learning, and to understand things differently. Moreover, the use of such materials could do so in a more considered way than is possible in lived practice, under conditions in which teaching and learning can be held still, studied, analyzed, and contrasted. Teachers could "have" and scrutinize a variety of experiences, learning to operate as thoughtful professionals (Cohen, in Lampert and Ball, 1998).

A second crucial entry criterion for candidate records of practice is that they be used to focus teacher education on the investigation of practice—that is, to make systematic study and analysis of learning and teaching the core of professional education. To do so, teacher educators and teachers would have to cultivate the capacities to investigate teaching and learning, develop new claims on the basis of such investigation, and defend them with evidence and argument. Simply looking at students' work would not ensure that improved ways of looking at and interpreting such work will ensue. It would be crucial to develop and debate ideas about what to look at, ways to describe what is observed, and conceptions of what is sufficient evidence for any given claim. If we want to say that a given student understands even and odd numbers, what would we use to support that conclusion? If he says that 1, 3, 5, and 7 are all odd numbers, is that adequate evidence that he understands what an odd number is? What can we say with confidence about his understanding? Working with various specks of evidence—something he said in class, a homework paper, an explanation he gave to the child sitting next to him—teachers engage in real inquiries of practice. Examining student thinking is a core activity of practice, and fundamentally also a matter for investigation. The fragility of understanding—their own as well as the children's—is a phenomenon that teachers encounter uneasily. After all, they are responsible for helping children learn and for reporting on what they have learned. Teachers have to learn how to frame and explore conjectures, how to bring evidence to bear on them, how to weigh the often-conflicting information they get, to make well-supported judgments.

Careful focus on developing ways to study and analyze teaching and learning is one of the key elements of the professionalism we envision. It also could intervene in the taken-for-granted ways of seeing and interpreting teaching and learning that are developed through the apprenticeship of observation. The more teachers developed methods of professional inquiry, articulated ways of knowing, and determined standards for knowledge in practice, the more teachers would have interpretive power, which could contribute to improving both their own teaching and their own and others' learning. They should be less likely simply to see in terms of what they bring, but might be able to see new things and consider more alternatives, analyze students' learning more finely, and consider their practice more deeply and in more complex ways.

That sort of work would cut against the conventional socialization to teaching by changing what teachers talk and think about, which we term the *discourses of practice* (Lampert, forthcoming). Rather than centering as it does currently on a "rhetoric of conclusions," the discourse would emphasize more the "narrative of inquiry." Instead of a definitiveness of answers and fixes, the focus would be on possibilities, methods of reasoning, alternative conjectures, and supporting evidence and arguments. It could legitimate and invest authority in a stance of deliberative uncertainty in and about practice. With such conversations, conducted from such a stance, teachers' practice could be improved by acknowledging the limits of knowledge in practice, expanding teachers' capacity to grasp the nature of these uncertainties, and improving their capacity to manage and learn from them with thoughtful analytic—that is, not purely idiosyncratic—consideration of alternatives. Working in the company of other professionals enables them to compare their interpretations and decisions with others', to confront the inherent inconclusiveness and incompleteness of knowledge, and still to strive for reasoned and reasonable professional judgment.

Creating and sustaining an inquiry-oriented stance such as this is a social enterprise. It can be done alone in some rare cases, but such cases require either special working conditions or almost heroic efforts on the part of the inquiring teachers, or both. Therefore a third element in our conception of professional education is to make professional learning more of a collective endeavor. The purpose here would be to create new capacity for professionals to learn from one another, capitalize on existing capability, and thus break down the traditional isolation of teachers' work and broaden their opportunities to learn.

To do such work would require the development of communities of practice designed to enable practitioners to cultivate more substantial professional discourse. That would entail the construction of more extensive common analytic and descriptive vocabularies and terms of reference, which would expand opportunities for more concrete and precise professional communication about practice (Stein, Silver, and Smith, 1994). The opportunity to engage in such conversation can provide a means for teachers to represent and clarify their understandings, using their own and others' experiences to develop ideas, learn about practices, and gain a more solid sense of themselves as contributing members of a profession, as participants in the improvement of teaching and learning and their profession, and as intellectuals (Stein, Silver, and Smith, 1994; Pfeiffer, 1998).

We emphasize the importance of situating professional discussion in concrete tasks or artifacts of practice, because they ground the conversation in ways that are virtually impossible when the referents are remote or merely rhetorical. Lacking such grounding, a common analytic vocabulary, and strong norms of analysis, professional conversation tends to become an exchange of buzzwords and slogans more than specific descriptions and analyses with concrete referents. Imagine physicians discussing the treatment of tetanus by discussing only how patients described their illness, how the physicians felt about that disorder, what patients said, how often they saw cases of tetanus, what patients looked like, and the like. Few patients would get well, and many would die, because physicians' discourse did not deal with any of the medically relevant issues. In fact physicians discuss specific medications and related treatments, their effects in particular sorts of cases, patients' physical symptoms and responses to treatment, and prevention. An analogous example in education would be teachers' discussion of a videotape in which a class is working with base ten blocks to learn decimals. Such an example offers a specificity that cannot be paralleled by a general conversation about the use of manipulatives in the absence of solid records of practice. Similarly, talking about "performance assessment" or standards is substantially deepened if it is centered on a set of student papers. Recall the earlier example of teachers watching a third-grade discussion about equivalent fractions. Groups of teachers who have watched this same video have disagreed, debated, raised questions, and pursued more information together. Rather than relying on vague terms and language, the communication can be grounded in real phenomena of practice. And in the context of discussing complex and not completely clear concrete elements of teaching and learning, a more useful and discriminating language of practice could develop. Such concreteness can be the beginning of serious intellectual work rather than a low-grade alternative, focused more on personal opinion and preference without recourse to evidence and relevant analysis.

One reason that records of practice are so important to changing the discourse of practice, and hence improving teaching, is that in conversations about them, teachers could hardly avoid grappling with standards: What is good teaching? What is a good enough paper? Which response to this question shows that students understand? Where do we agree? Where do we disagree, and why? Such discussions could make much more public the bases of knowing in and about teaching and learning. That, in turn, could help to create a shared enterprise of constructing knowledge in and from practice. Developing standards in practice that reflect shared vocabularies and values could develop practice beyond the currently private enterprise that it often is. Shared standards can still produce differences of interpretation and action, but within a common framework of consideration and value. Teachers might argue over whether a given student's explanation reflected appropriate grasp of a text, but would agree on seeking to ascertain that, with common ideas about evidence. They would come into contact with the reality that different people can look at the same phenomenon and see different things and interpret them in different ways. Such encounters can expand the perspectives with which teachers can examine their own practice, as well as to stimulate discussion of the "obvious," the taken-for-granted.

By highlighting the importance of teachers' access to and participation in communities of practice, we signal the need for teachers to be linked with a wider discourse beyond their local circle of colleagues, whether through subject matter organizations, study groups, university-school partnerships, or other groups or networks. An important goal should be to expand the community of educators and education resources to which teachers turn to inform and support their work, a shift from the pattern in which teachers focus exclusively on their own work or the work of those close by, with little external contribution, challenge, or support (Lord, 1994).

Our argument is based on the conviction that developing communities of practice with shared approaches to the study and analysis of teaching could help to build norms for knowledge and discourse within the profession. The current norms, captured concisely in the popular American maxim that "every teacher has to find his or her own style," actually work *against* teachers' learning. They also work against the development of collective capability as a profession, for it preserves the individualistic, polite, and standardless culture of teaching. Lacking concreteness and common ground, teachers (when they even have opportunities to talk or work collectively) often talk past and around one another. They rarely grapple with core elements of their work, seeking to discover and use their differences in assumptions, experience, and reasoning. Instead, they politely reaffirm teachers' needs to do what fits them personally. The construction of knowledge in practice is paradoxically confined to the private world of each practitioner, its status as knowledge thus peculiar (Little, 1990).

Orienting professional learning toward the joint professional study and analysis of teaching and learning would knit professional development inextricably into the practice of teaching. It would convert professional development from its traditional role of training or remediation external to the work of teaching into a core dimension of professional practice. It would simultaneously work to convert practice from a process of private trial and error and implementation to a more publicly deliberative process of inquiry and experiment. This is no small change on either front. Our proposal merges two agendas— the improvement of practice and the improvement of professional development—into a single reform aimed at both the development of practice and the development of practitioners.

TOWARD A CURRICULUM AND PEDAGOGY FOR PROFESSIONAL EDUCATION

Our proposal aims at fundamental change in teaching and teacher education, but it would not require massive or revolutionary change, with huge shifts in resource allocation or government. It would require deliberate development of the profession. We sketch some examples of what would be entailed in creating such opportunities for professional learning, to offer a sense of what the opportunities might look like and how they would draw on the elements of a theory of professional education outlined in the previous section.

Such professional education would depend partly on finding ways to use practice as a site for inquiry, in order to center professional learning in practice.

One way to do this lies within the course of teachers' everyday work—in the regular tasks of planning, selection, enactment, reflection, and assessment. There is no shortage of material; the key lack is of ways to turn the work of teaching into material for inquiry and learning. Another way to make inquiry into practice more available to teachers is to document and collect artifacts of practice and make them available for teachers' examination and inquiry. For such opportunities for inquiry to be educative would depend on the development of a pedagogy for teacher education that would focus on new capacities for the study of practice; once begun, the work could spur the development of such a pedagogy. Questions, ways of observing, methods of annotation and comparison, access to others' perspectives—all of these would expand the opportunities for learning from practice.

The development of such a pedagogy would require significant change in the culture of professional learning, which goes beyond finding ways to use practice as a site for inquiry. Because teaching has long lacked ways for teachers to work on the improvement of practice as a group, creating such a new pedagogy and opportunities to learn thus would require creating venues, norms, and conditions for teachers to inquire collectively into problems of teaching and learning and to participate in communities of practice. Leadership would be required for such arrangements, which opens up questions about who would provide it, what such roles would entail, and what leaders would need to know. In this section, we explore further each of these elements of professional learning.

A Curriculum for Professional Learning

A central element of our argument is that professional development could be improved by seeking ways to ground its "curriculum" in the tasks, questions, and problems of practice.[6] One way to do this is to use the actual contexts of teachers' ongoing work: their efforts to design particular units of instruction, try different classroom organizations, assess students' learning. Another would be to collect concrete records and artifacts of teaching and learning that teachers could use as the curriculum for professional inquiries—for example, students' work, curriculum materials, videotapes of classroom teaching, teacher notes, and student assessments. These could be drawn from teachers' own ongoing work or be specially collected from others' practice, and catalogued and made available to be shared and accessed. These sites of practice would then be used to develop usable knowledge of content, students' learning, and teaching.

Consider an example of what it might mean to do this within teachers' own ongoing work. In two local middle schools, the mathematics teachers have been worrying a lot about the implementation of a new state-mandated performance assessment. The test was to be given at the beginning of eighth grade. Last year, when the draft assessment was piloted at their school, test scores plummeted. Since the state assessment test has always been a worry—eighth graders have always done less well than fourth graders, raising concerns about the middle school program—these teachers are anxious to understand better what students need to know to do well on the new assessment. Two teachers volunteer to organize material from the pilot administration, such as students' test portfolios and the scoring sheets. Because these were their own students, the teachers also have the student records. Each teacher gets a packet of portfolios, scoring sheets, and a few other records for ten students drawn from all classes.

In preparation for the first meeting, they pore over the assessment but feel that they do not adequately understand either what the tasks are asking or the ways in which students' work was scored. They decide to begin by doing one of the tasks themselves. In three separate sessions they complete the task and analyze closely what it "covers" mathematically, and what one needs to know and be able to do to perform the task successfully. They then consider their students' performances on the same task and begin to see more about the different ways in which the students interpreted and approached the task. Over the course of several meetings, they repeated this cycle of doing one of the assessment tasks themselves, discussing and analyzing the mathematics entailed and then examining the middle schoolers' work on the same task. Doing the tasks is actually enjoyable, and they find that they are much better able to "see" the students' work and thinking after they have dug mathematically inside the tasks themselves. Later in the year the teachers develop a short list of the understandings that the assessment seems to tap and the problems they saw in students' work. This raises a host of questions about how to help students do better, and where to seek resources for their own learning. One of the teachers proposes attending the state National Council of Teachers of Mathematics affiliate conference, coming up soon in a nearby city, for she notices that a number of sessions target the new state assessment and at least a couple of them seem to address the teachers' questions about ways that might help them improve their teaching of these mathematical ideas, and hence, their students' learning.

Several elements of professional education we have already discussed are evident in this extended example. The teachers are bent on improving students' performance on the new state assessment, and they construct a way to investigate mathematics, assessment, learning, and teaching using their need to look more closely at the test to understand it. The material for their investigation is their own students' last year's tests. The immediacy and anxiety of the situation is a pressing incentive to participate—using a real task of practice as the context for their work. Their investigation of what was causing students to do so poorly on the test took them to an opportunity to deepen their own understanding of mathematics, students' thinking and interpretation, and the structure and worth of tasks. Although any one of them could have done this investigation alone, working together greatly enhanced what was possible to consider and to learn, for their ideas differed about the mathematics, the tasks, and particular students, and the discussions broadened what any one person could do. Finally, the teachers created for themselves an opportunity to learn mathematics: in order to understand the nature of the tasks and their students' performance, the teachers had to focus on the mathematics. Too often the "study of teaching" overlooks the central role subject matter plays in the practice of teaching. In this example, the teachers used their understanding of the mathematics and their own mathematical explorations to learn more about the assessment, students' work, and mathematics.

In this instance, teachers drew on data from their own teaching, and it seemed to work. This can be awkward if someone is particularly unreflective or defensive, and it can be hard to get enough distance on an example when it is from one's own practice. Moreover, some data are difficult to locate in one's work—videotape of very young children discussing mathematics or an entire year's worth of documentation of a single child. Another way to make practice more available to teachers is to document and collect artifacts of practice and to archive such material in ways that make them available for teachers' examination and inquiry. This would be a new kind of material, drawn directly from practice: records of teaching and learning that could be examined, discussed, and experimented with. The quality of these materials would be adequate for close examination but would not be polished or glossy. In fact, if the quality is too slick, some evidence suggests that their credibility suffers, and teachers suspect that the examples are contrived. Although such material would be outside the regular activities of teaching, its distance from teachers' own classrooms offers opportunities not proffered within the dailiness of their own work. For example, looking collectively at a videotape of a lesson from some teacher's classroom whom they do not know makes possible a kind of critical scrutiny and interpretation not likely to be possible in talking about their own or their colleagues' practice. They can explore alternative appraisals, they can disagree, and they can raise critical concerns in ways that would be much harder, at least at first, in discussing the practice of people with whom they work. Such analytic conversation about teaching and learning has not been part of either the norms of teaching or professional development. Moreover, archival records allow a special kind of access to practice not as easily done in the course of ongoing work. Teachers can look closely at multiple points back and forth across time, can look at multiple sources of evidence around a single event, can look together at the same phenomena with others. Commentaries produced by others can broaden the richness of the archive, expanding the multiplicity of perspective that teachers can learn to bring to the material and to issues of practice. The concreteness of the material can expand teachers' experience by making the experiences of a particular teacher intimately available to others (Lord, 1994).

Take now a second example in which a group of teachers works on a set of issues grounded in others' practice. A group of seven teachers from three different elementary schools in the same district decides to study two fourth graders' and two fifth graders' writing across an entire school year—not students from their school. They examine copies of stories, journal entries, notes, and the writing the children did in math class. They have several goals in mind. One is to develop their capacities to see things in children's writing—to increase and deepen what they can notice and describe. Another is to get better at helping children with their writing. Toward that end, two of the teachers focus particularly on the comments that the teachers have written to these students in response to these different kinds of writing, and they talk about the kinds of issues that they might raise in a writing conference with each of the students. A third goal is to develop a more shared sense of standards for evaluating students' writing. As they move increasingly in the direction of encouraging their own students to write, they feel quite uncertain about what should count as a satisfactory piece of writing. Suspecting that their standards might vary depending on the student as well as on the particular context of the writing (for example, explaining a solution to a mathematics problem versus writing a story) only makes the puzzle thornier.

As they talk together about a few pieces of children's writing, they find themselves disagreeing about the quality and key features of some of the work. At first they defer to one another, treating the conversations more as an opportunity to share their ideas. But after a few times, their meetings evolve into more of a forum for working on hard issues together, hence going away thinking a little differently or understanding something a little more. They argue, sometimes vehemently and with conviction, but they also find themselves stimulated and learning. After a year, one of the teachers who is an avid e-mail user convinces the others to get e-mail accounts too, and some of their conversations begin to take place in writing (although they also continue to meet regularly). One interesting by-product of their expansion onto the Internet is that they are writing to one another, and sometimes voluminously. They comment on this, noting that they had been doing little writing of their own for years, and that this is refreshing and even useful since they themselves are working on writing.

How are the elements of improved professional education, which we sketched earlier, evident in this example? First, the group had purposes, some shared and some individual: to learn to look more skillfully at students' writing, to get better at what they do to help children's writing improve, to develop a more shared sense of standards for what counts as good writing—for whom, in what contexts, under what conditions. Their work was grounded in a central activity of practice—examining and appraising children's writing—but the children were not their own students. The stance of the teachers was one of puzzlement and inquiry: How can we get better at looking at children's work? What makes sense to do to help any particular student with some particular text? What are the standards we hold for children's writing? What is good enough? The teachers are working as a collective, and finding that there are things they can learn to do and say with one another that improve what they could learn alone. The disagreements, uncomfortable at first, emerge as particularly challenging and useful for extending their capacity. Although their meeting takes time, they find it so valuable and so useful to their own learning and practice that they tend to have little difficulty finding meeting times. As in the first instance, teachers' own versatility and fluency with the content becomes a strand of their professional learning.

Each of these approaches offers possibilities. Using artifacts and records of practice, teachers have opportunities to pursue questions and puzzles that are deeply rooted in practice, but are not of their own classrooms. In the context of their own students, concerns, and responsibilities, teachers have depth, care, and interest that creates an immediacy for work and could mobilize incentives for learning. Studying both other teachers' practice and one's own offers opportunities to exploit the regular professional tasks of teaching. Yet the pull of the personal and the immediate in the case of one's own classroom can mitigate against reflection, analysis, and investigation of alternative perspectives and courses of action. Moreover, the current norms of teacher interaction and discourse do not readily support the kinds of joint consideration of one another's practice that would be useful. Creating common ground on which individual teachers and groups might work, compare thinking, explore alternatives, and play imaginatively would offer a meeting place for a new kind of professional work, although one still familiarly connected to practice. Paradoxically distant from the intensely personal and private world of the individual teacher's classroom, this new work would be designed to be no less deeply rooted in the intellectual, emotional, and moral realities of practice.

Three features stand out about such a curriculum for professional education. One is that it centers professional inquiry in practice. Using real artifacts, records, moments, events, and tasks permits a kind of study and analysis that is impossible in the abstract. Second, it opens up comparative perspectives on practice. In the traditionally individualistic structure of teaching, teachers rarely see teaching other than their own. Looking closely at student work produced in a different classroom offers teachers a chance to learn from others' practice. Third, it contributes to collective professional inquiry. Typically when U.S. teachers talk, they do not share commonly accessible referents. They mention students, topics, assignments, and lessons, but rarely are they able to examine such examples jointly. When they do, one teacher shares an anecdote from his or her own classroom. The example often is not in a concrete form to which others can have equal access, examining it unrestricted by the sharing teacher's interpretation. The approach that we propose would enable teachers to approach concrete phenomena of practice on equal footing, with room for each person's reactions, interpretations, conjectures, and analyses.

Doing such work would not require turning teaching inside out, changing its structure, or massive funding. Work of the sort that we describe could be woven into and around work in schools, professional development, and schools of education. To make this happen would still be no simple matter. One large reason is that selecting, collecting, and organizing the records of practice that would provide the material for such professional development would be a major undertaking. Merely collecting, organizing, and reproducing (with adequate technical fidelity) examples of instruction on videotape would be difficult. Constructing a rich and various multimedia database from those materials would be time-consuming. Creating such databases in ways that are both easily accessible to novices and deeply educative is no mean feat. Users would need access to both the multimedia environments and to guidance knowledgeable enough to help them use the materials.

Even if such materials could be collected, catalogued, and made accessible, another challenge would be to design ways of working with such materials. Just as providing innovative materials, media, and tools does not in itself reform and reformulate children's learning, neither will even the most clever construction and infusion of new materials change the focus and means of teachers' learning.

A Pedagogy of Professional Development

Although using the regular tasks of teaching, or materials such as those we have described, could help to create a new class of opportunities for teachers' learning, even such compelling occasions and materials themselves would not be enough. Used alone, they would most often be used in the conventional teachers' discourse in which personal style and individualism are primary and in which there is little analysis. The subtle and complex challenges of teaching and learning thus would remain invisible, much as conventional mathematics instruction leaves third graders' naive view of fractions unseen and untouched, even when new materials are used. Many schools have added colorful concrete models of fractions, but that does not ensure different engagement of the content, for students and teachers can continue to use conventional rules about fractions and fraction operations and use the models to substantiate those rules.

The same is true for the study of teaching. The kind of professional curriculum that we have sketched would be unlikely to support professional inquiry unless it was embedded in particular ways to engage and pursue issues. We refer to this as *pedagogy of professional development*. The key components of such a pedagogy are the sorts of tasks in which teachers would engage around materials of practice, the nature of the discourse that would be needed to support learning with and from these tasks and materials, and the roles and capabilities of teacher educators and leaders who would provide guidance for this work.

In order for materials of practice to serve as a medium for productive professional learning, teachers would need to engage in tasks grounded in the activities of practice. Using records of practice affords opportunities to investigate and construct knowledge central to teaching, so fruitful tasks for teachers' learning are those on which teaching itself depends. For example, one task central to teachers' work is figuring out whether and what students are learning. Teachers select materials and design lessons with the goal of affecting what students know and can do, but to figure out whether these designs are working depends on examining their effect for students, and assessing students' performance is no easy matter. Using suitable records of practice, teachers could study and discuss students' work, comparing what they notice, how they interpret it, and how they evaluate the quality of the work. Discussing such questions with other professionals would create opportunities to encounter differences in attention, interpretation, and judgment—crucial matters that are most often engaged alone and with little or no external referent. Teachers would learn from one another's views and interpretations, thus extending and enhancing their own capabilities. And teachers could develop shared standards for good work, progress, and learning.

Another potentially generative task would be analysis of students' assignments. Teachers could take a mathematics problem, a writing assignment, or a science experiment, and analyze the territory it makes possible. They could analytically probe what domains of the subject work on the assignment would entail. Teachers could explore the thinking that the assignment called for by doing it themselves and then comparing their work. Both would create opportunities for teachers to discern the content entailments of assignments and to learn some of the content. They could learn how unpacking a student task can help teachers delve into the associated or underlying ideas. Discussing the assignment with one another would enable them to see others' paths and connections and others' ways of working and solutions. Such discussion would both expand teachers' own understanding and extend their view of the terrain.

Many other sorts of tasks would similarly follow the contours of practice: planning lessons, selecting materials, listening to students, asking questions, figuring out what to do next. For example, teachers could design next steps for a class after watching and discussing a videotape of a lesson; they could frame and word specific questions to navigate student thinking as observed in videotape or children's work; they could weigh and compare alternative representations or tasks, courses of action, and materials.

We have added to the ideas we sketched earlier, about using records and materials of practice to build a curriculum of professional development, by proposing ways to set professional learning tasks that would use such records and materials. As with curriculum designed for students, even the best materials are not self-enacting. Learners will be more likely to thrive if materials are framed by appropriate and artfully designed tasks, and such task design and use is a central element in any plausible pedagogy.

Further, a pedagogy of professional development depends not only on the tasks created for profitable work, but the ways in which those tasks are engaged and discussed. Because few tasks are self-enacting, much learning requires teaching that helps learners to perform tasks in which they learn the vocabulary and syntax of the domain in question, and learn how to use them. One example is developing tools for the study and analysis of teaching and learning. Some such tools are skills of observation—ways of seeing, hearing, and noticing the many details of classrooms. Others concern the methods of interpretation, analysis, weighing competing views, and framing fruitful conjectures in particular subjects.

A second large element in learning how to engage a set of professional learning tasks would be the development of a disposition of inquiry. One way to put the aim here is to help teachers learn the intellectual and professional stance of inquiry—the situation of oneself that would support their generation of multiple conjectures about an issue in practice, their production of alternative explanations, and their efforts to weigh them rationally. In order to inquire, especially into one's own practice, professionals must cultivate dispositions as well as technical and intellectual knowledge and skills. These would include learning to avoid leaping to definitive conclusions, cultivating the disposition to frame interpretations as conjectures, and thus how to identify and use appropriate evidence. Learning the technical and intellectual skills and knowledge would be impossible without learning the disposition, and vice versa.

Thus the pedagogy of teacher education would be one in which critique would be valued and in which the learning teachers would be expected to argue with others and with themselves and to explore arguments among plausible explanations or approaches. Learning such dispositions would depend also on learning new norms of interaction. This would create disequilibrium at times, for teachers would encounter ideas and perspectives, evidence and possibilities, quite different from what they assumed. They would have to unlearn the politeness norm that dominates most current teacher discourse. They would have to learn to be tenacious, to probe their own and others' ideas and interpretations, to doubt and be skeptical. And they would have to learn to combine intellectual aggressiveness and a willingness to take risks with a humility about the incompleteness and uncertainty of their own ideas.

All this would require a substantial revision in the norms of professional relations and discourse. It would require learning to have respect for others and their views, but also being able to hold ideas and interpretations out for scrutiny, discussion, and debate in ways that were not seen as personal challenges to individuals. The sort of learning we propose would require that teachers see disagreement as productive, not as something to cover up.

The pedagogy of professional development we have been sketching would require something of a revolution—not in political or social structures but in professional knowledge and culture. It could not arise through spontaneous generation, but would require the participation of teacher educators. Everything we have been discussing in this section would depend for its existence on professionals who planned, developed, and led opportunities for teachers' learning—teacher educators, staff developers, and teacher leaders, as well as principals and other leaders. Like other teachers in any context, these teacher developers would need to understand the content terrain itself—in this case, the practice of teaching, including the subjects taught and the learners of those subjects. For teacher educators to use records of practice in fruitful ways, they would need well-cultivated knowledge, skills, sensibilities, and insight about key issues of teaching and learning. They would need to be themselves skilled observers of teaching, to be curious about practice, and to have multiple ways of thinking about student work, classroom discussions, and content representations.

In addition to being insightful students of practice themselves, these teacher developers would need to understand teachers as learners and have a repertoire of ways to engage different teachers in fruitful professional learning. They would need to be good listeners, so they could hear and respond to the wide range of reactions and stances that teachers might bring to a professional development setting. They would need to be able to establish rapport and trust with a variety of learning professionals, and be able to help them form relationships, even a sense of community, with one another. All of this would depend on extensive knowledge of teaching and learning—of both school students and professionals—and considerable interpersonal skill.

Ironically, while the role of the teacher educator is critical to any effort to change the landscape of professional development, it is a role for which few people have any preparation and in which there are few opportunities for continued learning: there is little professional development for professional developers. Yet the changes we sketch are so extensive that, like the teachers with whom they work, teacher developers would need to seek and create opportunities for learning grounded in the practice of professional development. Hence the scheme we have been sketching would require the creation of more formal opportunities for people who do this work to talk with one another, and to do many of the same things we have proposed for teachers: to watch videotapes of professional development sessions, examine materials created for teachers' learning, analyze teachers' projects, listen to teachers' discussions and interpret what they are thinking and learning. Doing such work would be a major change in how teacher developers learn and do their work, but it would be crucial to the improvement of professional development.

CAN THESE PROPOSALS WORK IN THE UNITED STATES?

Our ideas envision a kind of professional education that is rooted in both study of teaching practice and knowledge of teacher learning. Such professional education would be unlike most of the current opportunities teachers have, which usually are brief workshops or in-service programs. Although our emphasis on learning in and from practice superficially resembles the surface features of teachers' professional education, of which the overwhelming proportion is "from experience," uncharted experience alone is an unreliable and often unhelpful guide. We have proposed a set of ways to turn teachers' experience to educative rather than reproductive ends.

Any sensible reader would now ask how such approaches might be arranged so they could spread widely and deeply within the profession. Then they would ask whether, if the ideas did spread, how they might avoid simply reproducing the kind of fragmented, unfocused, and superficial work that already characterizes professional development. Without ways to seek and create much greater coherence in teachers' professional learning, this strategy could be just another name for the existing haphazard collage of experience and workshops, pasted together with little connection. The payoffs for practice and students' learning could be just as fragmented and ephemeral.

We do not have a six-point program and can only begin to answer the questions. Figuring out how to maintain quality in any enterprise as far-flung as American education is a terrific challenge, and working out a detailed plan would take time and extensive consultation. But we can identify three components that seem essential.

First, more people in professional development and the improvement of teaching would need to address systematically what it might mean to center teachers' opportunities for learning in practice and contrast that with conventional wisdom about teachers' learning on their own, from their own experience. The ideas we have sketched in this chapter themselves need development. Discussing them and engaging in some preliminary experiences of this kind could help to begin to develop the capabilities needed to redesign teachers' opportunities to learn.

Second, a small number of such learning opportunities should be designed and used as examples of practice-based professional development. Records of their use should be created—in effect, written and video cases of how such things work and do not work. Having such instances would make it possible to engage the ideas in ways that are grounded in practice of professional development, concretizing the discussion. Those cases should be studied and distributed widely. Companion materials should also be designed that describe ways to organize and carry on such activities. The materials should be vivid enough to be compelling, concrete enough to provide resources for others' efforts, and open enough to avoid being converted into lists of abstract principles and "shoulds."

Third, alternative curricula for grounding professional development in practice should be explored. For example, it would be fruitful to develop alternatives for embedding teachers' opportunities to learn subject matter in materials of practice—in student work, curriculum materials, or classroom videotapes.

Similarly, how might opportunities to learn about students—their development, language, and culture, learning—be designed around opportunities to look closely at students in action? What sorts of materials would support such opportunities? What considerations might there be in designing opportunities to learn? What might be some of the most productive tasks that engage teachers and support serious and sustained learning?

One idea that underlies these proposals is that the problem is not a lack of investment in teacher development, or that "professional development" is not on anyone's mind. The problem lies more subtly in common thinking about what teachers need to learn and how they can best do it. As the analysis thus far suggests, we think that the ordinary culture, knowledge, and professional norms of teaching and teacher education are at the core of the problem. If reform does not address those, nothing will work. But if steps were taken to begin to develop the sort of attack on those problems we have proposed—through discussion, the construction of some examples, and focused curricular thinking— capacity for a different sort of professional development would grow.

Put a little differently, we have proposed to turn professional development into a professional activity centered on the development of practice and practitioners. That would be critical if the knowledge that teachers acquire were to fit with the nature of the work—its challenges, uncertainties, and complexity. Like complex learning anywhere else, learning to teach merits greater and more serious attention than it has too long had. If reformers want learning to improve, then continued careful development of professional development itself will be essential. Joining the development of practice to the development of practitioners is an avenue for that agenda.

Notes

1. We are not arguing that these developing conceptions are either complete or correct, but they seem both more adequate and more promising than many earlier ideas.

2. To highlight the complexity of "learning from experience," Philip Jackson points to the difference between two twenty-year teaching veterans, commenting that one had twenty years of experience while the other had one year of experience twenty times.

3. This is related to, but not the same as Schön's (1983) "reflection-in-action."

4. See Dewey's (1933) distinction between empirical and scientific thinking.

5. See Erlwanger's famous case of Benny, a student whose teacher thought he was advanced, but who had privately constructed idiosyncratic understandings of fractions and of mathematics. But the curricular approach in Benny's classroom made it possible for him to continue to progress officially, his personal constructions unrecognized.

6. See Beasley, Corbin, Feiman-Nemser, and Shank (1997) for an extended example of what is possible and what it takes to establish a curriculum and culture of profession.

References

Ball, D. L. "Teacher Learning and the Mathematics Reforms: What Do We Think We Know and What Do We Need to Learn?" *Phi Delta Kappan,* 1996, *77*(7), 500–508.

Ball, D. L., and Wilson, S. W. "Integrity in Teaching: Recognizing the Fusion of the Moral and the Intellectual." *American Educational Research Journal,* 1996, *33,* 155–192.

Beasley, K., Corbin, D., Feiman-Nemser, S., and Shank, C. "Making It Happen: Creating a Subculture of Mentoring in a Professional Development School." In M. Levine and R. Trachtman (eds.), *Making Professional Development Schools Work: Politics, Practice and Policy.* New York: Teachers College Press, 1997.

Cohen, D. K., and Hill, H. "Instructional Policy and Classroom Performance: The Mathematics Reform in California." Unpublished manuscript, University of Michigan, 1997.

Dewey, J. *How We Think.* Buffalo, New York: Prometheus Books, 1991. (Originally published 1933.)

Elmore, R. F., Peterson, P. L., and McCarthey, S. J. *Teaching, Learning, and Organization.* San Francisco: Jossey-Bass, 1996.

Feiman-Nemser, S., and Remillard, J. "Perspectives on Learning to Teach." In F. Murray (ed.), *The Teacher Educator's Handbook.* San Francisco: Jossey-Bass, 1995.

Lampert, M. "Studying Teaching as a Thinking Practice." In J. Greeno and S. Goldman (eds.), *Thinking Practices.* Hillsdale, N.J.: Erlbaum, forthcoming.

Lampert, M., and Ball, D. L. *Mathematics, Teaching, and Multimedia: Investigations of Real Practice.* New York: Teachers College Press, 1998.

Little, J. W. "Norms of Collegiality and Experimentation: Workplace Conditions of School Success." *American Education Research Journal,* 1982, 325–340.

Little, J. W. "The Persistence of Privacy: Autonomy and Initiative in Teachers' Professional Relations." *Teachers College Record,* 1990, 509–536.

Little, J. W. "Teachers' Professional Development in a Climate of Educational Reform." *Educational Evaluation and Policy Analysis,* 1994, *15,* 129–151.

Lord, B. "Teachers' Professional Development: Critical Colleagueship and the Role of Professional Communities." In N. Cobb (ed.), *The Future of Education: Perspectives on National Standards in Education.* New York: College Entrance Examination Board, 1994.

Lortie, D. C. *Schoolteacher: A Sociological Study of Teaching.* Chicago: University of Chicago Press, 1975.

Pfeiffer, L. "Becoming a Reform-Oriented Teacher." Unpublished doctoral dissertation, Michigan State University, 1998.

Schön, D. *The Reflective Practitioner: How Professionals Think in Action.* New York: Basic Books, 1983.

Stein, M. K., Silver, E., and Smith, M. S. "Mathematics Reform and Teacher Development: a Community of Practice." Unpublished manuscript, Learning Research and Development Center, University of Pittsburgh, 1994.

CHAPTER TWO

Aligning Teacher Education with Contemporary K–12 Reform Visions

Magdalene Lampert and Deborah Loewenberg Ball

The current reform movement in education takes aim at the common assumptions about knowing and worthwhile knowledge that have dominated public schools for decades. If K–12 teaching is to adopt a different stance toward what it means to know and what is worth knowing, then teacher education will need to change in these ways as well. In this chapter we look at the knowledge demands of the reform vision—for students and for teachers. We explore how teacher education might be designed to help teachers prepare to teach and the potential of innovative uses of technology to support the preparation of teachers. We use the subject of mathematics to illustrate our argument because it is a subject we are deeply familiar with, as both teachers and teacher educators. Nevertheless, the arguments we make are intended to apply to all K–12 subjects.

KNOWING IN SCHOOL: AN EXAMPLE FROM MATHEMATICS

Consider the problem of adding three-fourths to two-fourths. Should a teacher settle for the answer "five-fourths," or its mixed number equivalent, "one-and-one-fourth"? Or should we take a more ambitious view that would have students

This work was supported by grants from the National Science Foundation, the Spencer Foundation, Michigan State University, and the University of Michigan. We gratefully acknowledge our colleagues and students who have contributed to our thinking and ideas in this chapter: David Cohen, Angie Eshelman, Ruth Heaton, Mark Rosenberg, and Kara Suzuka. Each of us contributed equally to the work on these ideas and the writing of this chapter.

33

asking questions like: "Three-fourths of what?" "Two-fourths of what?" and "Why do you want to add them?" "What do you mean by three-fourths? or two-fourths? and what do you mean by adding them?" This latter way of thinking about the problem may seem esoteric and quibbling. Nevertheless, asking these kinds of questions in school mathematics lessons is fundamental to the current reform movement in education, which identifies knowing a school subject with the practices associated with intellectual and practical work. Why might we want K–12 learners and teachers to worry about the kind of quantity to which these numbers refer?

Someone doing mathematical work might argue that adding three-fourths to two-fourths results in five-eighths or simply note that the total is less than two but greater than one. Traditionally in school, teachers and textbooks would label these assertions incorrect or not accurate enough. But what if we were to look more deeply into the reasoning behind these assertions, as educators are now exhorted to do? We might find out that in the first instance, the student was referring to an experience with athletic competitions: "two-fourths" refers to winning two out of four games in the first half of the soccer season, and "three-fourths" refers to winning three out of four games in the second half of the season. We would then agree that the team had won a total of five out of eight, or five-eighths of its total games.

Another person, basing his reasoning on experience with a different kind of mathematical work, might be trying to find out how much butter is needed altogether if a cake calls for three-fourths of a cup of butter and the frosting for two-fourths. Since the store sells butter by the pound, the baker would need to buy two pounds of butter altogether. Still a third person, responsible for the neighborhood swimming pool, notices that in one case of chlorine (containing four one-gallon jugs), three are full, and in another case, two are full, and concludes that she has the necessary five gallons for balancing the pool's chemicals. Her friend might say it is one and a quarter cases, and they would agree on how much there is left.

In our ideal classroom, students with experiences like these (figuring out soccer team records, buying butter, and figuring out how much chlorine is left for the swimming pool) would engage in a discussion with their teacher and reflect on the conditions under which each of the different ways of thinking about adding two-fourths and three-fourths makes sense. They would invent and learn about how to represent the additions in mathematical symbols, and they would talk about other scenarios that fit each model of "fractions" and "addition." In the process of such talking, the teacher might suggest that they could more easily relate all of these different phenomena in mathematical ways if they agree to call the number that comes first (or "on top") in the fraction the *numerator* (because it tells the number of parts to the whole), and the number that comes second ("or on the bottom") in the fraction the *denominator* (because it tells the name of the kinds of parts you are working with). The teacher would suggest that students with their different examples consider the benefits and disadvantages of a rule like this one: "When the denominators are the same, add by adding the numerators and keep the same denominator." After doing this sort of work, the students might be asked to use what they had learned from their investigation of "three-fourths plus two-fourths" to consider a problem like how to measure the sum of one-eighth of a teaspoon of sugar and three-fourths of a cup of sugar when combining two recipes. They would come to know that there is a rule for adding fractions with unlike denominators, but they would also understand when and when not to apply it. Fundamentally they would begin to appreciate the importance of the unit in talking about quantities.

These students could be said to know how to do both the practical and the intellectual work of mathematics, as well as how to communicate about why the solutions to various kinds of problems make sense. Would we agree that they know how to add fractions? Would we agree that the student who insists that three-fourths plus two-fourths must always be five-fourths knows how to add fractions? The examples force us, and the students and teachers who are trying to effect the reforms we have in mind, to ask: What does it mean to know how to add fractions? To know anything in mathematics? More than a vast set of algorithms and rules, mathematical knowing entails considering the specifics of the context and using resources of abstraction and pattern to gain control and perspective. Specific problems cannot be fully anticipated. Enmeshed in a mathematical or real-world context, knowers choose, apply, and invent ways of making sense.

To specify the implications of these aspects of knowing for teaching, learning, and assessment in K–12 education, David Perkins and Howard Gardner have developed something they call the "performance perspective" on understanding (Boix Mansilla and Gardner, 1998). In Perkins's terms,

> In brief, this performance perspective says that understanding a topic of study is a matter of being able to perform in a variety of thoughtful ways with the topic, for instance, to: explain, muster evidence, find examples, generalize, apply concepts, analogize, represent in a new way, and so on. . . . Understanding something is a matter of being able to carry out a variety of "performances" concerning the topic . . . that show one's understanding, and at the same time, advance it by encompassing new situations. We call such performances "understanding performances" or "performances of understanding" [Perkins, 1993, p. 7].

A classroom in which performance understanding is the norm reflects an ambitious vision of K–12 education. Helping students develop such understanding goes considerably beyond what has been expected heretofore of students and teachers in public schools. Whether this vision should be the one we embrace as a society is not an issue that we take up here. We consider instead what the vision implies for the practice of teaching and, consequently, for the education of teachers.

KNOWING IN TEACHING:
AN EXAMPLE FROM A DIVERSE CLASSROOM

Consider the problem of the teacher faced with a class of thirty students, five of whom have their hands raised and presumably want to speak. Of those five, two are girls, three are African American, one has not yet volunteered to speak since the beginning of the school year, and one raises his hand at every opportunity and almost always has something interesting to say. Who is to have the floor? This is both a practical problem, since the teacher does need to call on somebody, and an intellectual problem, because the act of giving students the floor needs to be understood in relation to a host of other problems and their solutions. Should we accept the idea that a teacher who has had the appropriate kind of preparation can know which of these students to call on first? This way of thinking about knowledge is as common in traditional teacher education as the notion that the correct answer to three-fourths plus two-fourths is five-fourths is in traditional mathematics education.

In this example, a teacher faces a class in which five diverse students want to speak at the same time. What does the teacher need to know in this situation in order to manage it? A host of general considerations about the particular students comes to mind: race, gender, class, achievement levels of particular students, past mathematical experience in school. There are theories that can inform the teacher's decision—theories about engaging minority students, about girls, power, and discourse. There are also aspects of the subject matter that may be useful to the teacher in making a decision about whom to call on. What all these kinds of understanding have in common is that they are constituted out of something already known before the problem arises in the situation at hand. It assumes that in the situation, the teacher can, in split-second fashion, draw on her repertoire of understanding and ideas and attempt to apply them.

Researchers have learned a great deal about what sort of knowledge teachers need to bring to teaching. For example, the work initiated by Lee Shulman and his colleagues (Shulman, 1986, 1987) has moved knowledge of subject matter to center stage. Shulman advanced a conception of content knowledge combined with understandings of learning and learners, and lobbied it as the kind of knowledge of content that teachers needed. "Pedagogical content knowledge," or knowledge of the best and most useful representations, of what topics students are likely to be interested in, and of the kinds of difficulties students are likely to have with specific academic concepts and procedures, drew attention to the special ways in which teachers needed to understand content. It also made more visible the ways in which the knowledge teachers need is both varied and interactive. The framework of pedagogical content knowledge made plain that teaching children to add fractions sensibly, as in our example, would depend on the teacher's own understanding of key ideas about number as well as her understanding of what helps children develop their knowledge of fractions. This perspective shaped our ideas about what teachers need to know in order to teach well. It also raised a set of complicated questions about how teachers could develop such ways of knowing content. In addition to this work on subject matter, researchers have recently explored other domains of knowledge essential to teaching, such as knowledge of students and knowledge of students' cultures and contexts.[1]

Still, knowing teaching is more than applying prior understandings. It also depends fundamentally on being able to know things in the situation: to know things that one cannot know in advance of any particular encounter. Let us return to the teacher who faces a class of thirty students, five of whom have their hands raised to speak. In the situation, this teacher needs to know things she could not know when the school year began, the day before, or even minutes before. Looking for various cues, she must know who is vying to speak. She must know who has not spoken recently, and it helps to know what different students have been working on, so that she has a sense of who might say what if called on. She might know which children are engaged at the moment and who is drifting off. She might seek to have a sense of the dynamics among the students this morning. But students are not all she needs to know. She needs to have a sense of where the class is in their exploration of the problem. How is the mathematics developing? Are there key ideas that might be highlighted here? Are any misunderstandings developing? Would a rediversion of the question help? We could keep elaborating this list of things that the teacher needs to know in the situation. From moment to moment, the teacher must observe, infer, interpret, conjecture. Her conclusions, although tentative, are knowledge claims to herself. The assertions she makes to herself function as knowledge. She knows them the best she can in the moment, and must act, treating what she knows as both reasonably reliable and also provisional.

What are some recurrent themes in this kind of knowing in teaching? Making no attempt to be comprehensive, we offer some illustrations. Our claim is that teaching is more than the application of knowledge, and it is more than a site for thoughtful reasoning and reflection. In practice, we argue, teachers know things; they make claims to themselves based on what they can see, hear, sense. An unexplored and underappreciated area of teacher knowledge, knowing in teaching is critical to both teaching and teacher learning. One theme in this kind of knowing is knowing who is engaged. Teachers work with groups of students and are responsible for keeping them involved in experiences and activities aimed at helping them learn. Teachers must continually appraise who is paying attention and who is disengaged. Visual clues are not always reliable. Students can paste attentive looks on quiet faces, and lively, fidgety, chatterers may be following the flow. Teachers must do their best to keep track of who is in and who is tuning out. Another example of this knowing in teaching is knowing what particular students understand. Basic to their work, knowing who is "getting it" is critical. Are students getting a sense of the importance of the "unit" in fractions? What do they think it means for two fractions to be equivalent? How do they think fractions, with like denominators and with unlike denominators, are added? Just as with figuring out who is paying attention, determining what students understand is far from straightforward. Students produce correct answers with incomplete or incorrect reasons; incorrect answers can also mask sound understandings and reasoning. Across two or three dozen students and with these endemic uncertainties, teachers must make ongoing, usable assertions about what students know.

Teachers must know if something they are doing is working. They must know when to move on and when to spend more time on an idea. They must know what a student's comment means, and they must know what a student's silence means. Each of these themes could be elaborated and linked to a set of questions the teacher needs to know the answers to as she works.

Calling these judgments "knowledge" highlights the sense in which teachers observe, interpret, reach conclusions, and act based on what they know in the situation. The knowledge is uncertain, provisional, evolving. Yet in the moment, teachers' assertions have the epistemological status of knowledge and must function as such (Scheffler, 1965). Teachers make decisions and design moves based on what they know. What they must know is much more than what they can know in advance; they must know in the context of practice.

PREPARING TEACHERS TO KNOW

Traditional beginning teacher education courses and in-service workshops for practicing teachers have been organized to help educators acquire the knowledge and skill thought to be crucial to teaching. In courses and workshops, educators learn theories and methods of teaching, and in classroom settings, they practice using what they have been taught. The assumption, held by instructors and learners at the university as well as by teachers, field supervisors, and learners in classrooms, is that knowledge is acquired in course work and applied in practice (Feiman-Nemser and Buchman, 1986).

This divide between theory and practice, however, has left a critical gap unattended (Dewey, 1964). Student teachers are often in the end most influenced by what they see their cooperating teachers do or by their own memories from school. The effect of teacher education is often small. Although they collect ideas, learn theories, and develop some strategies, beginning teachers often report that their professional preparation was of little use or practicality (Feiman-Nemser, 1983; Lortie, 1975; Tabachnik, Popkewitz, and Zeichner, 1979–1980). The first years of teaching are often characterized as a period of sink or swim, during which novices cope with the many demands of the job, borrowing and inventing ideas as they go. It is during those years that teachers think they "learn to teach," by themselves, from experience, or by picking up tips from fellow practitioners. In-service workshops are usually required by school districts and not highly valued as sources of knowledge about improving instruction.

A second gap in teacher education lies between reform visions of teaching and the traditional pedagogy of teacher education. Prospective and practicing teachers learn about constructivist theories of learning, communities of learners, and authentic tasks, but often the courses and workshops in which they hear about these ideas are taught in ways that do not make use of the very same ideas. With little or no firsthand experience with learning of the kind that reformers advocate, neither beginning nor experienced teachers have adequate images of what these ideas mean, what it might mean to draw on them in practice, and the complications they raise for teaching and learning.

If teacher education is going to prepare teachers for the kind of ambitious teaching that reformers envision, then reformers of teacher education will need to look carefully at what it means to know something in teaching, just as the architects of the K–12 reform have looked at what it means to know something in school subjects. Teacher education will have to be designed to help prospective teachers develop flexible understandings and ways of knowing in and about teaching. This means being prepared to teach. It also means being prepared to know in teaching. Teachers need to be prepared for the more predictable parts of practice: teaching a song, helping children learn addition facts, discussing the weather. And they will also have to be prepared for the unpredictable: what to do or say when a child gives a solution that the teacher does not understand, how to assess the momentum of a discussion, talking with parents.

Because what there is to be known in teaching cannot be known entirely in advance, an essential part of the practitioner's role is to figure out what is right practice in the situation, as opposed to looking only to experts to identify which strategies to apply. Still, although the answer to what is right practice is not standardized, neither is it entirely an idiosyncratic matter of personal style, where anything goes. Making decisions about right practice is not relativistic, but responsible within a community of practice.

So what might it mean to orient teacher education courses and workshops in such a way that teachers would be better prepared to meet the challenges of knowing that they will face as teachers? These goals for the reform of teacher education parallel the goals of the school reform vision. The National Council of Teachers of Mathematics, for example, argues for all K–12 students to be engaged—not only in acquiring, but also in building and communicating about—mathematical knowledge:

> Goals such as learning to make conjectures, to argue about mathematics using mathematical evidence, to formulate and solve problems and to make sense of mathematical ideas are not just for some group thought to be "bright" or "mathematically able." Every student can—and should—learn to reason and solve problems, to make connections across a rich web of topics and experiences, and to communicate mathematical ideas [National Council of Teachers of Mathematics, 1991].

We might imagine that every teacher, not only professional leaders or teacher-researchers, would engage in learning to reason and solve pedagogical problems, to make connections across a rich web of topics and experiences, and to communicate pedagogical ideas. If assertions about who to call on in the scenario presented earlier were considered as conjectures—that is, as tentative judgments, open to revision in the course of thinking the problem through with other members of one's professional community—then teachers could take on a more direct responsibility for creating practical and intellectual knowledge that could be used in classrooms. If teachers and prospective teachers were encouraged to examine assumptions about what makes something good teaching or about how one event in the classroom is related to another, they would be more adequately prepared for the multifaceted problems they will face in their own classrooms from one minute to the next.

WHAT KIND OF TEACHER EDUCATION AIMS TOWARD THESE GOALS?

One possibility that we have been exploring in our work is to orient teacher education around the investigation of the practices of teaching and learning, rather than to center it solely on the provision of knowledge and skills to be applied in practice. Investigation is an appealing idea. In any field, conducting an investigation entails using the extant knowledge of the field and simultaneously constructing new frameworks. Investigation has also been part of the current reform in school subject matter instruction. Whether they are studying temperature or democracy, poetry or probability, students are to learn from investigating ideas, that is, from working on problems, talking with others about potential solutions, building on their own ways of thinking about concepts, and engaging with big disciplinary ideas. In mathematics lessons, for example, students would be expected to investigate situations in which probabilistic events occur, construct ways of representing mathematical patterns, and debate the applicability of classic strategies for finding needed information. Working in parallel, we have been exploring what this kind of pedagogy might offer to the way we teach beginning teachers about teaching (Lampert and Ball, 1998).

Although *investigation* could describe a teacher's private inquiry into his or her own practice, we focus our discussion here on investigations conducted in common using some set of materials representing practice: videotapes, children's work, teacher notes and reflections, curriculum materials, and guidelines. The focus here is on the idea of a group of teachers using a common set of materials drawn directly from practice—the same classroom and the same set of students—to pursue different questions important to learning about teaching and learning. Since such investigations are unusual, at least in the United States, the participants in this kind of teacher education would also need to be developing terms and rules of discourse for talking about practice.[2]

Imagine a teacher education class in which students are intently watching a short video segment from a whole class discussion in a third-grade class. On the video, the children are disagreeing about whether 4/4 is equivalent to 5/5. A number of children are arguing vigorously that 5/5 is "more" because there are more pieces. Several others argue that 4/4 and 5/5 are the "same amount." The teacher on the video asks clarifying questions, and guides the turns taken by children in the discussion, but she does not step in and explain equivalent fractions. A number of the children on the video do not say anything in the discussion, some seeming to write or draw in their notebooks.[3]

The teacher education students are quiet, riveted on the screen. Occasionally they chuckle at a child's comment or point at and whisper about something in the video. At the conclusion of the segment, the instructor flips on the lights and asks the students to write for a few moments in their notebooks, jotting down what stood out to them, what puzzled them, what confused them, what they wondered. A few pore over a paper transcript as they write. After a few minutes, the instructor asks for comments and questions. The comments pour out.

"She should have told them that 5/5 is the same! I was so frustrated with the discussion going on and on!"

"I was impressed with that little girl's—is her name Mei?—ability to explain her thinking."

"I was amazed at how comfortable the children seemed. I never would have gone to the board like that when I was that age. In fact, I wouldn't do it now!"

"Yeah, how did the teacher get the kids to talk like that, and to talk to one another so much? In my math classes, the teacher could never get anyone to talk."

"I wondered what the kids had done before about fractions. Had they used manipulatives to see how two fractions can be equivalent?"

"A lot of children seemed to be bored."

"I didn't think they were bored. Did you see how that one boy who never talked was leaning toward whoever was speaking, and how he reacted to different things the other kids said?"

"What did the teacher do next?"

"What should kids know about equivalent fractions at this age?"

"Why were so few boys talking? Is that always the case in this classroom?"

The instructor does not comment and records the students' questions on the board. After about ten minutes of this, she flips an overhead with this list of other information:

children's writing from their notebooks

fraction quizzes

third-grade math textbook and goals and objectives for third grade in this state

teacher's journal

videotapes from previous and subsequent class sessions

She begins, "Here is a list of other materials I am making available for you today. I want you to spend a few minutes thinking about the questions, inferences, and assertions we have up here on the board and select something you'd like to pursue using something on this list." A low hum of talk can be heard in the class as the teacher education students bend over their notebooks, glance up at the board, and comment to others nearby. The instructor then invites students to share what they are thinking of doing. This time she offers suggestions or connects each idea to something that someone else has already volunteered. After about twenty more minutes, the students are set off to pursue their issue using the materials.

Like the elementary mathematics students in the vignette at the beginning of this chapter who investigated the sum of three-fourths and two-fourths by drawing on their experiences with mathematical work, these teacher education students draw on their own experiences with learning and teaching to try to make sense of the phenomenon they are investigating. They also draw on research they have read in various academic fields like philosophy, sociology, psychology, and anthropology. And they draw on their knowledge of the mathematical content: fractions. By participating with others, they will be exposed to a variety of interpretations of what is going on and what is important. By using other representations of the practices of teaching and learning gathered from the same classroom, they will develop a richer, more complete sense of the teacher and students in the lesson on the tape and develop the capacity to understand their actions and ways of thinking.

The teacher educator in this situation would prompt the students to examine the assumptions behind their assertions and look for evidence in the materials representing practice to elaborate their understanding. She would encourage them to examine and articulate the relationships among multiple aspects of the teaching and learning they have observed. She might introduce the term *registers* for talking about talk to help her students distinguish between formal mathematical talk and ordinary talk about quantitative relationships. She might have them consider the wisdom of pedagogical truisms like, "Only those students who verbally participate are engaged." Together the teacher educator and her students would search for ways to represent and communicate about what they know and try to interpret the representations and communications of others. They would revise and refine their questions. They would be producing what Perkins and Gardner call "performances of understanding" (Boix Mansilla and Gardner, 1998).

Using the idea of investigation to orient work in teacher education centers the focus on inquiring into concrete phenomena of practice. What are these children understanding about fractions? How can one decipher the children's writing and drawings, and how can one learn to listen well enough to figure out what they think and what they know, across boundaries of age, culture, and understanding? What are the elements of fraction knowledge to listen and look for in their talk, drawing, and writing? Investigations begin with something that is unknown and puzzling. The teacher education student might have a general pedagogical question with which she or he is absorbed, such as, "What do manipulatives contribute to learning?" or "How does the teacher decide when to follow the children and when to make insertions or sharply focus or turn the children's work?" Investigations can also be rooted in the specifics of the setting, such as, "Is Michael getting it?" or "What are the qualities of this classroom's culture, and how have they developed?" or "Who seems to be participating?" Investigation is a stance as well as an approach. Rooted in a tradition of inquiry-based teacher education, investigations approach teaching as complex, intriguing, and uncertain. Although they are focused, they must take account of the complexities of the context.

In an investigation, teacher education students pursue questions. These may be their own puzzlements and curiosities, or they may be questions that an instructor frames. The focal questions of investigation are rooted in practice and are at once specific and general. A question about a particular child is a question about both that child and children more broadly, about children's understandings of this particular content, and about the general challenge of what it means to know children. A question about a particular teacher's decision is a means both to understanding a single lesson and to learning the workings of a specific classroom. But it is also more broadly about teacher role and teacher thinking. A question about what children learned about a particular problem is also a question about that kind of problem and the attendant possibilities and pitfalls. Figure 2.1 illustrates the interrelationships of the concrete and the general in pursuing investigations of teaching.

Investigations draw on but are not restricted to current theories and formal knowledge about teaching and learning in general or a particular kind of teaching and learning. Instructors help teacher education students access and use ideas of the field, and they also encourage students to make novel conjectures and advance possible novel interpretations. Engaging with situated questions of practice can support a context for the intertwining of knowledge use and knowledge construction.

Investigations rarely reach definitive conclusions; rarely are they complete. As one group of teachers with whom we worked exclaimed, "We just keep discovering more questions!" Instead of questions leading to answers, questions tend to multiply. In trying to understand what a particular child meant in a specific context, other questions arise about that child, other children, the problem

Figure 2.1. Interconnections Between the Particular and the General in Investigating Particular Phenomena of Practice.

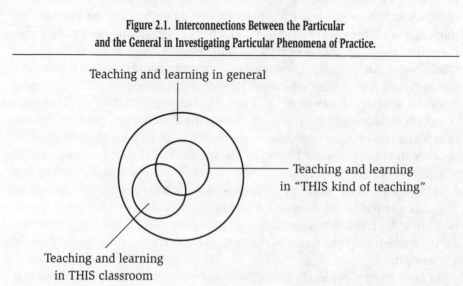

at hand, and the classroom environment. The subject matter itself often becomes more complex and worthy of a more careful examination. Just as knowledge in teaching is virtually always incomplete, tentative, and connected, so is the knowledge developed in investigating teaching. The big questions—"How do manipulatives contribute to students' understandings of fractions?" or "When does the teacher tell, and when does she hold back and press the students?" or "What is being covered in a curriculum where children do fewer problems but do them more thoroughly?"—are never concluded once and for all. Investigations help to uncover both the connectedness and the uncertainties of knowing in teaching.

By doing investigations like the one described, intending and practicing teachers have the opportunity to learn about the relationship between knowing and doing in teaching. They gather information from representations of practice that enable them to appreciate the teacher's construction of knowledge in the situation. They come up against evidence that knowledge is incomplete, uncertain, and context bound, and yet the teacher must act. As they develop an appreciation for a teacher and her students as people in a relationship over time, they have the opportunity to recognize that knowledge of facts and principles is used in connection with another kind of knowing, more moral or empathetic than cognitive. Yet they remain outsiders to that relationship, making them better able to look at it from multiple perspectives.

Investigations offer sites for exploring multiple interpretations. Looking at a set of student papers, prospective teachers will find that they do not always see the same things in the students' work. What looks to one person like a serious lack in a child's understanding can be seen as imaginative and clever by another. While one person sees a child as inattentive or frustrated, another person may see evidence that the child is listening intently. The inferences we make in teaching and learning are rooted in the evidence we apprehend and use, and the ways in which we interpret it. Discussing specific interpretations together with others reveals the multiplicity of perspectives that can be convincing around a single event or issue. Through such discussion, possibilities exist for teacher education students to develop multiple voices in their own heads. They can learn to generate for themselves alternative ways of hearing, seeing, and interpreting, and come to appreciate their initial interpretations as possible and not necessary.

How might a pedagogy of teacher education oriented around investigation restructure the relations of knowledge and practice? Table 2.1 offers one preliminary view of this restructuring, showing ways in which investigations might support the development of ways of knowing more consonant with the views of knowledge and learning that are fundamental to K–12 education, and the necessary teacher education. We see from the table that as new ways of knowing are acquired (italics), they must be integrated with more familiar approaches.

Table 2.1. Restructuring Ways of Knowing in Teaching.

	Common Understandings About Knowing and Learning Encountered in Traditional K–12 and Teacher Education	Understandings of Knowledge Acquisition and Use That Are Consonant with Reformers' Visions of K–12 Education
Sources of knowledge	Textbooks Researchers/experts People with more experience	Textbooks Researchers/experts People with more experience *Self: not opinions but reasoned judgment* *Arguments with oneself and with others*
Nature of knowledge	Rules Definitions Facts Theories	Rules Definitions Facts Theories *Conjectures to be tested, discussed, and revised in the context of work on problems*
Connections between what you know and what you do	Remember Practice Apply	Remember Practice Apply *Manage dilemmas* *Empathize* *Consider multiple perspectives and possible interpretations*

HOW CAN NEW TECHNOLOGIES HELP?

In every field of endeavor, the capacity to collect and use information has been dramatically increased by new technologies. The introduction of investigations of practice as a method for studying teaching depends on having access to large collections of information about practice in the form of raw representations of the activities of teaching and learning. New hardware for putting representations into a computer and taking them out for viewing, new software for cataloguing these representations and annotating them, and new programming language for creating customized records of what users do with the information can be combined into an "investigator's working environment" for use by teacher educators and beginning and practicing teachers to learn the kind of knowing in teaching we have described above. We conclude this chapter by identifying three ways in which new technologies can support the access and use of such representations in teacher education settings:

- Increased capacity to document practice
- Improved potential to study practice outside of the time, space, and relational constraints of ongoing work in classrooms
- Added support for professional discourse

The hardware, software, and multimedia information together constitute an electronic environment in which teachers and teacher educators can investigate practice.[4] This environment does not replace the classroom, in which the teacher or student teacher learns by being a practitioner. Nor does it replace academic course work or focused workshops in which conceptual frameworks or specific pedagogical techniques are taught and learned. The kind of work that can be supported in this environment is unique, offering opportunities for learning not easily had through field experience or in classes or workshops.

In order to create an electronic environment in which teachers and teacher educators can investigate practice, the first task is to collect, file, and catalogue representations of practice that document the activities of teaching and learning and participants' perspectives on those activities. Improvements in tools for collecting information in multiple media, including miniaturization and easy translation between digital and analogue forms of storage, make it possible to capture high-quality representations of many different aspects of teaching and learning practices without significantly disrupting the ecology of the environment in which those practices occur. For example, scanning, together with database software, could save and catalogue children's daily work using a process no more complex than photocopying. Slides of the work on the chalkboard, taken automatically every five minutes by a digital camera, would provide an animated record of the graphic representations that accompanied talk in a lesson and could be electronically linked to an audiotape using time code.

The technology makes it increasingly possible to capture and make available aspects of what there is to see, hear, and know in practice. Examining raw materials from practice—videotape, for example—provides access to the less verbal and less analyzed texts of teaching: body movements and facial expressions, tone and timing, pattern and style, the unedited and uninterpreted expressions of children. Such opportunities are crucial in learning to teach, because so much of teaching entails hearing and seeing, as well as interpreting such information.

New programming languages for building complex and relational databases mean that access to multiple representations is fast and easy. Search strategies can be used that make it practical to keep a collection of representations in a relatively undigested form, meaning that teacher educators and teacher education students can go directly to instances of classroom teaching and learning and build their own links among them without having their view of those instances filtered through the conceptual frameworks of others. This is similar to the overwhelming volume of unprocessed "data" surrounding teachers in the moment-to-moment reality of teaching. At the same time, representations can be organized in multiple ways, drawing on conceptual frameworks of not only academic disciplines like psychology, sociology, and philosophy but also on perspectives of parents, children, subject matter specialists, and the like. Being able to link the raw data to such multiple perspectives can enhance teachers' capabilities to make sense of the flood of information in which they swim.

If a database of this sort has been collected and electronically filed and catalogued, new technologies make it possible to get access to it in ways that substantially enrich the study of teaching and learning. Multimedia workstations link computers with sources of textual, graphic, audio, and video information and make it possible for users to create and store information in all of those media as well. Even without computer control, video and audio can be used to stop in the middle of an activity to think, write, or talk about it; replay the activity over; and chunk activities together in different ways for different analytic purposes. Given a lesson video, for example, one can try to figure out where the important transitions between activities are from the teacher's point of view and then use the same tape to consider that question from the points of view of different students. With computer-controlled video and audio and the capacity to annotate these media electronically, one can make comments at various points and keep records of multiple streams of commentary on the same instance of practice. With software for capturing audio, video, and graphics, investigators can make scrapbooks of their journeys through the year as a case by pasting movies of lessons or excerpts from children's and teachers' work into a text processing, spreadsheet, or database application. All of these and other such capacities can support teachers in developing multiple perspectives and frames of reference with which to interpret information and make conjectures in practice. In these ways, the technology supports the possibilities of preparing beginning and practicing teachers to know in teaching.

The power of current computing technologies to process large amounts of information in multiple media—video, audio, graphics, and conventional text—means that representations of teaching and learning practices need not be limited to verbal, linear information. We can store what gets written on the chalkboard during a discussion, for example, and look at it alongside what students write in their notebooks and what participants say. Being able to replay and rearrange events of practice make possible a kind of analytic thinking crucial to skilled, constructive, and reflective practice.

In addition, the technology can facilitate communication about teaching. Nonverbal representations of the multiple ways in which those practices can be thought about can be produced. Color and graphics can be used to show maps of relationships among social and academic considerations in the teacher's choice of a problem for the class to work on, for example. This opens up many more channels for communication about practice, and makes those channels available for collaborative study outside the time and space constraints of the classroom. It also may support the development of teachers' communication skills and capacities. In talking with others, using novel and conventional modes of representing aspects of teaching and learning, teachers can develop language and shared referents for communicating about teaching.

Because computers have the capacity to store large amounts of information and relations between pieces of information, it is possible to consider an entire year of classroom lessons, together with teachers' and students' reflections on those lessons and relevant background information, as a "case" of teaching and learning. Given the nature of the K–12 reform vision, this capacity is central to improving the study of teaching, for unlike traditional instances of teaching and learning, which could be understood as discrete bits of communication between teacher and learner about discrete bits of subject matter, the reforms we envision focus on problems that touch on many interrelated subjects and extend over many days of work. Within this work organization, teachers are expected to assess students' performances of understanding that do not come in simple packages like standardized tests. The difference between what a teacher plans and what actually happens in lessons is much greater when teaching is expected to take account of how learners think about the topic at hand. And if we are to be responsive to the increasing diversity in our classrooms, simple mechanisms for describing what is taught and learned are inadequate. If we are to teach and learn in K–12 classrooms in the ways that reformers envision, we cannot adequately keep track of or try to understand what is happening by looking at a few lessons or a few curriculum units or a few pieces of children's work. A corpus of all of these pieces of information and more is needed to represent accurately the kind of practice we want beginning and experienced teachers to study.

The technologies we have described have the potential to support a rich analytic discourse about practice among professionals in the field of education. By representing teaching and learning in terms of the year in one classroom as a case, they would make it possible for teacher educators and intending and practicing teachers to get to know another teacher and the students in the class without intruding on the fragile relationship that underlies the work they do together. Looked at from the other side, this means that their understanding of what is happening in that setting is less intruded on by the need to create and maintain an identity and a set of relationships with the people in that setting. For example, beginning teachers need not worry about whether the children they are observing should call them by the first names. This may seem like a trivial matter, but from the perspective of a young teacher education student, trying on what it means to be a "grown-up," such a consideration can interfere with giving full attention to the myriad issues in the classroom around her.[5] In order to develop new capacities for the sort of knowing in teaching we are examining here, it is important to cut down on these kinds of interferences, especially at the beginning of learning teaching.

Using new technologies means that this personal yet detached way of knowing a teacher and a class can be shared among a group of investigators, giving them a common multimedia "text" on which to focus their conversation. Other ways of giving intending and practicing teachers access to classroom activities for analysis (like field placement or mentoring) have each participant in a class or workshop looking at different teachers and classes, or the same teachers and classes on different days, making it impossible to use common referents to build shared meaning for the terms of discourse. Having a common text to study promotes the possibility of education professionals developing as a community of inquirers in ways that are parallel to the communities of inquirers that reformers would like to see them create in K–12 schools.

As educators, we currently lack practical or theoretical language for communicating about classroom activity. Having opportunities to examine practice in the concreteness of its unedited and unanalyzed flow, and to talk about what one sees and hears, and how one interprets that, can support the development of language for communicating about practice. Developing language that is useful in the context of careful examination of practice can contribute to the professional discourse of teaching, to teachers' exchanges with one another. It can also contribute to the internal conversations teachers have with themselves as they watch, listen, and try to make sense.

With the increasing availability of telecommunications, the sort of multimedia environment for studying teaching that we have described can be expanded across time and geographical distance. With relational database programming, it is possible to imagine the expansion of discourse about practice beyond face-to-face, local professional groups to more public discourse in the profession as a whole, using the same raw representations of teaching and learning to develop a shared understanding of the reforms. If commentaries on the representations and ways of organizing the representations could become part of the database as well, discourse could be incorporated into the electronic environment. This would make it possible for groups meeting in different places at the same time or in the same place at different times, or even in different places at different times, to be part of the same professional conversation about teaching and learning. For example, the environment could include the information that groups in several teacher education settings were interested in the question, "How can teachers cover the curriculum if we are supposed to spend a day or even a week on one problem?" In different locations, investigators could use materials representing teaching and learning in one particular classroom across the year. They could take various paths into that material, annotating various pieces of information from the classroom and arranging collections of information for reflection. With powerful relational databases, it would be possible to communicate across time and distance, examining the history of use and annotation for particular instances of teaching and learning and their representations, thus expanding the shared referents for a language of practice beyond local conversations.

ON THE HORIZONS FOR TEACHER LEARNING: USING TECHNOLOGY TO ALIGN TEACHER EDUCATION WITH THE CONTEMPORARY REFORM VISIONS

Technology has the potential to create workspaces for teachers' and teacher educators' learning that differ in important ways from the kinds of opportunities that exist in current settings and relationships. We conclude by discussing three distinctive features of these new workspaces.

First is the content of practice and tools for working with that content. Technology makes it possible to access close, concrete, inside information about teaching and learning, teachers and students, subject matter and classrooms. Although this is the central material of practice, and thus of learning practice, such information is never available to prospective teachers and teacher educators. And in the classroom, information whizzes by even the practicing teacher. Developing skills to see more, hear more, interpret multiply does not automatically come with the opportunity. The having of teaching experience does not necessarily make it possible to learn in and from teaching. It is a paradox of learning to teach that the very material of practice is so rarely available to those who seek to learn it. Technology makes it possible to collect and explore concrete materials of practice and use such information to investigate and develop understandings of teaching and learning.

Second, technology makes it possible to manipulate such materials of practice in constructively imaginative ways. Videotape can be stopped, replayed, and played in slow motion; a child's presence in September can be arrayed for comparison next to her stance in May; patterns of teacher talk can be examined across time. Playing with the data not only allows purposive exploration; it also can allow space and tools for the pedagogical imagination to fly in ways that cannot be done in real time by either observers or teachers. Ideas, interpretations, questions, and ways of looking can be developed through such playful work.

Third is the possibility for supporting a kind of professional discourse and joint work and exchange that is often hampered for a host of complicated practical and cultural reasons. Although the work we are describing can certainly be done by individual teachers, groups of teachers can expand their opportunities for learning by the possibilities of coming together with others to talk about teaching and learning. That it need not be the practice of any of the participants can free the norms of niceness that often hinder critical discussion. That the objects of inquiry are stored for access rather than occurring in real time can free the geographic boundaries that divide and isolate teachers. That the material can be collectively accessed and investigated can increase interpretations, considerations, and conjectures, substantially expanding the opportunities for educators' learning, in this environment as well as in classrooms to which they can later take others' eyes, ears, and voices.

Technology offers both mechanical and conceptual tools for use in teacher education. It can improve our mechanical capacities because of the kinds of processes and interactions that it makes possible in the study of teaching. It can improve our conceptual capacities because it can support new ways to conduct inquiry teaching, new ways to think about sharing the results of that inquiry, and new ways to make use of knowledge constructed through that inquiry.

Notes

1. Books such as Reynolds (1989) enumerated and analyzed the understandings needed in order to teach.

2. This approach to teacher education is common in Japan and China, but can be found only in rare and special circumstances in the United States. See, for example, Lewis (1998) and Paine and Ma (1993) for descriptions of teacher investigations in Japan and China and Stein, Silver, and Smith (1998) for a U.S. example.

3. This episode is taken from a videotape from Deborah Ball's class. Both of us have used this particular videotape with prospective and practicing teachers as well as teacher educators; the vignette we use here is a composite from our experiences in using such tape.

4. We describe our work in building and using such an environment in teacher education in Lampert and Ball (1998).

5. Dewey ([1904] 1964) wrote about ways in which the concerns of beginning teachers interfered with the attention they could give to deeper issues of teaching and learning.

References

Boix Mansilla, V., and Gardner, H. "What Are the Qualities of Understanding?" In M. S. Wiske (ed.), *Teaching for Understanding: Linking Research with Practice.* San Francisco: Jossey-Bass, 1998.

Dewey, J. "The Relation of Theory to Practice in Education." In R. Archambault (ed.), *John Dewey on Education.* Chicago: University of Chicago Press, 1964. (Original work published 1904.)

Feiman-Nemser, S. "Learning to Teach." In L. Shulman and G. Sykes (eds.), *Handbook of Teaching and Policy.* New York: Longman, 1983.

Feiman-Nemser, S., and Buchman, M. "The First Year of Teacher Preparation: Transition to Pedagogical Thinking." *Journal of Curriculum Studies,* 1986, *18,* 239–256.

Lampert, M., and Ball, D. *Teaching, Multimedia, and Mathematics: Investigations of Real Practice.* New York: Teachers College Press, 1998.

Lewis, C. "A Lesson Is Like a Swiftly Flowing River: How Research Lessons Improve Japanese Education." *American Educator,* Winter 1998, 12–17, 50–52.

Lortie, D. *Schoolteacher: A Sociological Study.* Chicago: University of Chicago Press, 1975.

National Council of Teachers of Mathematics. *Professional Standards for Teaching Mathematics.* Reston, Va.: Author, 1991.

Paine, L., and Ma, L. "Teachers Working Together: A Dialogue on the Organizational and Cultural Perspectives of Chinese Teachers." *International Journal of Educational Research,* 1993, *19,* 675–697.

Perkins, D. "An Apple for Education: Teaching and Learning for Understanding." Paper presented at the Ed Press Conference, Jun. 10, 1993.

Reynolds, M. *The Knowledge Base for Beginning Teachers.* New York: Pergamon and the American Association of Colleges of Teacher Education, 1989.

Scheffler, I. *Conditions of Knowledge: An Introduction to Epistemology and Education.* Chicago: University of Chicago Press, 1965.

Shulman, L. "Those Who Understand: Knowledge Growth in Teaching." *Educational Researcher,* 1986, *15*(2), 4–14.

Shulman, L. "Knowledge and Teaching: Foundations of the New Reform." *Harvard Educational Review,* 1987, *57,* 1–22.

Stein, M. K., Silver, E., and Smith, M. S. "Mathematics Reform and Teacher Development: A Community of Practice Perspective." In J. G. Greeno and S. Goldman (eds.), *Thinking Practices in Mathematics and Science Learning.* Hillsdale, N.J.: Erlbaum, 1998.

Tabachnik, R., Popkewitz, T., and Zeichner, K. "Teacher Education and the Professional Perspectives of Student Teachers." *Interchange,* 1979–1980, *10*(4), 12–29.

CHAPTER THREE

The Role of Preservice
Teacher Education

Mary M. Kennedy

Ideas about teacher education are strongly influenced by a received wisdom about learning to teach. Most citizens in the United States who have thought much about teaching subscribe to the received wisdom, and most teachers subscribe to it as well. The most vocal and visible group not subscribing to the received wisdom is teacher educators. Here is why.

According to received wisdom, teaching is fundamentally a self-evident practice. What to teach should be obvious if you know your subject, and what to do at any given moment should be obvious from the situation. Therefore learning to teach consists of two main parts: you learn the subject you intend to teach through college-level liberal arts courses, and you refine your technique and personal style through experience in your own classroom. Most versions of the received wisdom end here. Some versions add a small role for teacher education, acknowledging that there might be some benefit from studying child psychology or perhaps research on teaching. But the role of teacher education is still considered to be relatively modest.

Even reform movements, which usually acknowledge that there might be more to teacher learning than meets the eye, often subscribe to the received wisdom and concentrate more attention on continuing professional development than on preservice teacher education. Consistent with received wisdom, reformers tend to believe that a great deal of teacher learning occurs in the context of practice, that teachers can continue to refine their techniques throughout their careers, and that this is where reform efforts should be concentrated.

This chapter is adapted from Kennedy, M. M. *Learning to Teach Writing: Does Teacher Education Make a Difference?* New York: Teachers College Press, 1998. Reprinted by permission of Teachers College Press.

54

There is much to be said for received wisdom. Many teachers will attest th,
it describes their experience of learning to teach, and many studies of teacher
education programs indicate that teacher education is indeed a weak intervention. Comparisons of teachers who have received different amounts or kinds of
teacher education often indicate only slight differences between groups, thus
suggesting that teachers are learning the things that matter most from either
their liberal arts courses or their own experiences teaching.

There is, though, an invisible element in learning to teach that the received
wisdom does not mention. The sociologist Dan Lortie pointed out over twenty
years ago that teachers go through a lengthy apprenticeship of observation in
that they spend their entire childhoods observing teachers teach. Lortie suggested that the endurance of traditional teaching practice derives in part from
the fact that teachers are highly likely to teach in the way they themselves were
taught.[1] Their experiences in primary and secondary schools give them ideas
about what school subject matter is like, how students are supposed to act in
school, and how teachers are supposed to act in school. Thus, when they begin
to teach, they adopt the practices of their former teachers. If their elementary
teachers represented the school subject of writing as a set of grammar rules, for
instance, rather than as a way to organize thoughts and communicate ideas,
they will tend to teach writing this way themselves.

The apprenticeship of observation is an important omission from the received
wisdom model of teacher learning, yet it is likely that the model itself would
not work if the apprenticeship were not there. This apprenticeship gives teachers a frame of reference that allows them to interpret their experiences and gives
them some ideas of how to respond to them. That is, one reason teachers are
able to learn to teach almost exclusively through their own teaching experiences
is that they know what is supposed to happen. Their frame of reference enables
them to judge their daily successes against a standard of expectations. Consequently the received wisdom model of teacher learning seems to work because
teachers have already learned so much about what the practice of teaching consists of. Absent an a priori frame of reference, it is not clear that the received
wisdom model could account for teacher learning.

We could revise the received wisdom model of teacher learning, of course,
so that it provided a more complete picture of teacher learning. We could say
that teacher learning consists of three parts(First, teachers learn what the task
of teaching is through their apprenticeship of observation, then they learn their
subject matter through their liberal arts courses in college, and then they develop their own technique and style through their own teaching experiences.
And, of course, they can still learn some incidental things about learning theory, child development, or classroom management through their preservice
teacher education courses.

The received wisdom model of teacher learning, then, is a reasonably accurate rendition of how most teachers learn to teach, if we add the proviso that teachers engage in an apprenticeship of observation that provides them with a frame of reference for deciding what is appropriate and inappropriate classroom behavior. But the received wisdom model is less useful when teachers are expected to learn a version of practice that they have not already examined for thirteen years, for it does not include a place for teachers to learn alternatives to traditional teaching.

In fact, if teachers must draw on their apprenticeship of observation in order to learn to teach, then most reform proposals are doomed. Reformers will not improve teachers' practices by changing the caliber of people who enter the profession, for teachers of all kinds bring the same apprenticeship to their work. Nor can they improve teaching practice by changing the number of course credits teachers are required to take in one subject or another, or by changing the rewards and sanctions that govern teachers. Reformers can change teaching practices only by changing the way teachers interpret particular situations and decide how to respond to them.

That teachers already have a clear frame of reference for interpreting and evaluating classroom situations introduces problems for education reformers. Reformers by definition want to change the frame of reference. They want teachers to teach differently. They want teachers to see differently. For reformers, the received wisdom model of teacher learning will not work for two reasons. First, it does not include a time and place for teachers to learn a different conception of the task of teaching, and second, it does not acknowledge that teachers already have a frame of reference that might actually hinder the learning of a different conception of teaching.

In fact, the kind of teaching that reformers envision requires teachers to shift their thinking so that they have different ideas about what they should be trying to accomplish, interpret classroom situations differently, and generate different ideas about how they might respond to these situations. Such a shift in thinking might be analogous to Kuhn's (1970) famous description of paradigm shifts in scientific communities, although teachers' ideas are not nearly as elaborated as those of scientists. Still, teachers function within frames of reference, and they use these frameworks to formulate their plans, interpret their experiences, and respond to classroom events. So when reformers ask for an entirely different type of teaching, they are asking teachers to shift to an entirely different frame of reference. This is no simple task.

Reform might be easier if reformers could describe—indeed, prescribe—the practices they wanted, but they cannot. The kind of teaching that reformers want requires teachers to encourage students to develop their own ideas, and then to respond intelligently to those ideas. This kind of teaching requires a lot of spontaneous judgments. It is often difficult to know how to interpret a particular student's remark or to discern the sources of confusion that are frustrating a student. Evidence of student learning is obscure at best, and it is hard for teachers to judge their own success. Sometimes a carefully wrought lesson misfires, and sometimes a lesson hastily thrown together is wildly successful.

This ambiguity makes teachers' frames of reference especially important, for teachers draw on these frames of reference to interpret the situations they face, make sense of what happens in their classrooms, and make decisions about what to do next. These frames in turn are likely to derive from their own childhood experiences in classrooms.

An important role for preservice teacher education (PTE) is to change these initial frames of reference. Preservice teacher education is ideally situated to foster such a shift in thinking. It is located squarely between teachers' past experiences as students in classrooms and their future experiences as teachers in classrooms. From their experiences, teachers develop the ideas that will guide their future practices. If these ideas are not altered during preservice teacher education, teachers' own continuing experiences will reinforce them, cementing them even more strongly into their understandings of teaching, and reducing the likelihood that these ideas might ever change.

Whether preservice teacher education can do this is not known. To address this question, I turn to findings from a study of the influences of teacher education, the Teacher Education and Learning to Teach (TELT) study. This study was designed to examine teachers' interpretations of and responses to a set of prespecified situations. In the TELT study, instead of testing teachers for their knowledge about ideas such as "authentic tasks" or "engagement in learning," we presented them with hypothetical classroom situations and asked them what they thought about these situations and how they thought they would respond to them.

TEACHER EDUCATION AND LEARNING TO TEACH STUDY

The TELT study was designed to see what teachers learned from teacher education programs—not what they could recite about important educational ideas, but how they interpreted particular situations and proposed to respond to them. Researchers followed teachers from the time they entered their programs through their completion of those programs. Over one hundred teachers were followed as they participated in nine programs. Teachers were asked at several times during this process how they would respond to a set of specific classroom situations. The situations were such that teachers' interpretations and responses could, and did, differ from one situation to another. Moreover, the ideas and ideals they claimed to care about could be, and often were, incompatible with the ideas that occurred to them in the face of these specific situations.

The TELT study concentrated most of its examples of teaching within the context of two specific subjects, mathematics and writing. In this chapter I focus on teachers' thinking about writing situations. The teaching of writing is a good example of the problem of frames of reference because there are many laudable ideas within the reform rhetoric for writing, and they differ substantially from traditional practices in teaching writing. The reform argument in writing runs something like this:

1. In the past, the subject of writing has consisted of a set of prescriptions: rules for when to capitalize, how to punctuate, which verb tenses to use in different sentence constructions. These have been taught to students with little regard for why they matter. The assumption in the past has been that once students are adults and have some reason to write, all of the rules will be there, waiting to be applied.

2. What we have failed to do in writing is help students learn to generate ideas and translate those into texts: to formulate their thinking, wrestle with ideas and with the meaning of words, go through the difficult processes of thinking, drafting, revising, rethinking, envisioning audience response, and so forth that are part of writing when it is done in the real world for authentic purposes.

3. Moreover, we suspect that all of this attention to prescriptions in writing may divert students' attention to their original purposes and inhibit their ability to engage in serious thought about their purposes and how to achieve them.

4. Therefore, the teaching of writing should change so that (1) students engage in authentic writing tasks for real audiences; (2) teachers serve as coaches, mentors, or facilitators rather than as judges and arbiters of what should be done and how and when; (3) prescriptions are taught in the context of these projects, when students are ready to publish their papers, rather than earlier in the process, when students are still formulating their ideas and trying to express them.

None of the reformers claim that prescriptions should not be taught. Rather, they suggest that the orientation toward prescriptions should change so that prescriptions have a purpose within an authentic writing context. However, teachers may not be able to see prescriptions through this frame of reference if they have acquired a different frame of reference from their apprenticeship of observation. They may not be clear about exactly how much attention should be given to prescriptions, relative to the concepts and processes of writing. Yet when they are alone in their classrooms, trying to teach in this new way, they must interpret each situation by themselves and must decide by themselves whether it calls for attention to prescriptions or to some other aspect of writing. Writing, then, is similar to many of the other subjects that have been involved in reform rhetoric in that it requires teachers to make a great many ad hoc decisions, and consequently is very dependent on the frame of reference that teachers use to make those decisions.

Writing is also representative of other subjects in the sense that many of its ideas appear in the rhetoric of other subjects: the idea of student engagement is there, as is the idea of authentic tasks, the idea of teachers' working as facilitators rather than as purveyors of absolute truths, and the idea of students' constructing their own understanding of important ideas in writing through their experiences working with these ideas. But all of these ideas are only vaguely defined, and teachers are necessarily left to their own devices to envision what they might do in any particular teaching situation. Consider, for instance, the concept of ownership. *Ownership* sometimes means that the student chooses the topic or format or genre for texts, sometimes that the student, rather than the teacher, makes the major decisions about the progression of the piece, and sometimes that the project is an authentic project rather than an assignment. Not only are there many meanings to this idea, but any of these definitions of ownership can conflict with the idea of ensuring that students learn to comply with prescriptions, because eventually, the teacher must inform the student of relevant language conventions. At some point, the teacher must impose some rules on the student's text and insist that it conform with these conventions. Without a clear and detailed understanding of ideas such as ownership, teachers may have difficulty envisioning a practice that gives students ownership of their own products while at the same time ensuring that they learn language conventions.

Initial Frames of Reference

To see how teachers' frames of reference influence their teaching decisions, consider one particular classroom situation that we asked teachers to interpret and respond to: a story written by a student named Jesse. Jesse's story appears in Figure 3.1. Like the texts of most other novice writers, Jesse's story contains many errors in punctuation and grammar. But it also contains evidence, to a teacher who is disposed to look for it, that Jesse is thinking about his writing and is developing strategies for achieving his own purposes. We received this story from a second-grade teacher who told us of the original "Jesse's" intentions. In this story, Jesse wanted to include quoted material. He had never used quoted material before, and had received no formal instruction in how to indicate quoted material. But he had noticed that when his teacher read stories to the class, the teacher always paused prior to reading a quotation. Jesse therefore decided to insert pauses before his quoted material, and chose to insert periods to indicate those pauses.

Figure 3.1. Jesse's Story.

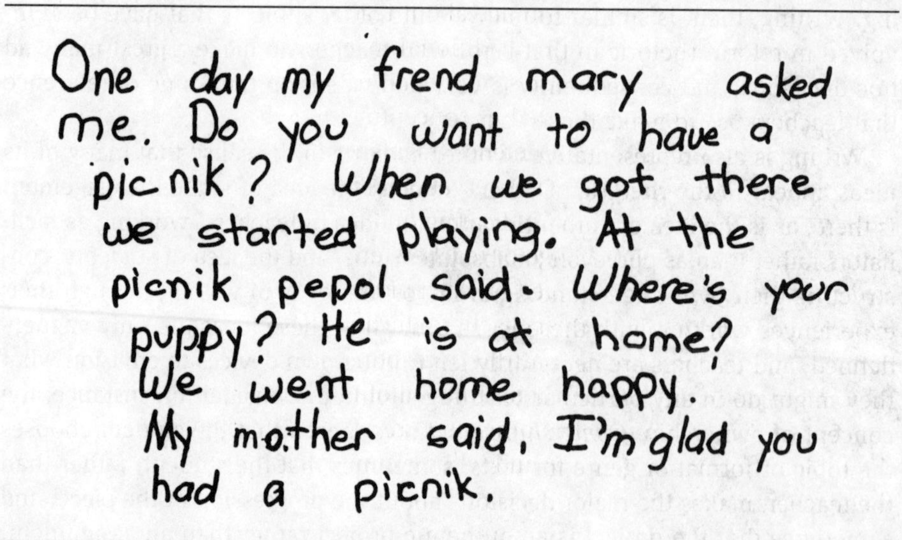

One day my frend mary asked me. Do you want to have a picnik? When we got there we started playing. At the picnik pepol said. Where's your puppy? He is at home? We went home happy. My mother said, I'm glad you had a picnik.

In the TELT study, we asked teachers attending each of our sample programs to examine Jesse's story and talk about how they would respond to Jesse if he were a student in their own classrooms. As I examined teachers' interpretations of and proposed responses to Jesse's story, I found that I could group teachers' comments into three main categories of ideas.

- Comments reflecting the traditional prescriptive frame of reference. Teachers whose interpretations and responses fell into this category wanted to help students learn the rules of grammar, punctuation, and so forth. When examining Jesse's story, for instance, they were likely to discuss its errors, and when proposing a response, they were likely to enumerate all of the errors.

- Comments drawing on a conceptual frame of reference. Teachers using this frame tended to think that concepts were important in writing—concepts such as chronology and flashback, for instance. When examining Jesse's story, these teachers were likely to say that Jesse understood the main parts of a story—beginning, middle, and end—or that Jesse understood chronology.

- Comments reflecting an interest in students' strategies and purposes. When examining Jesse's story, for instance, teachers using this frame of reference were likely to comment on the meaning of Jesse's story—to say that they were confused about the significance of the puppy, for instance.

Teachers were free to comment in any way they wanted, and their comments reflected their own frames of reference about teaching and learning. A teacher whose ideas derived mainly from traditional teaching practices, for instance, would be likely to notice that Jesse's story had numerous incomplete sentences, while a teacher who was interested in conceptual understanding might notice that there was a pattern to these sentence fragments—that they always appeared prior to quoted material. Such an observation could lead to the deduction that Jesse had invented a method for indicating quoted material.

Table 3.1 shows the percentage of teachers entering each program category in the TELT study who commented on each of these features of Jesse's story at the time they were entering their teacher education programs. Two important points can be made about the pattern of responses shown in the table. First, across most program groups, a larger fraction of teachers noticed Jesse's errors in prescription than noticed any other feature of Jesse's story. This pattern is very similar to the patterns we found when examining teachers' interpretations

Table 3.1. Categories Teachers Noticed in Jesse's Story, Before Participating in Teacher Education.

What Was Noticed in the Story	Traditional Management Orientation		Reform Orientation		Total Number of Interviewees Noticing This Aspect
	University Based	Field Based	University Based	Integrated	
	Urban U (n = 13)	State AR (n = 8)	Elite C and Normal U (n = 11)	Collaborative U and Independent U (n = 21)	
Jessie's compliance with prescriptions					
Mechanics, other rules	*77 percent*	50 percent	45 percent	*19 percent*	30
Jesse's understanding of concepts					
Concepts, ideas	31	25	18	29	14
Jesse's strategies or purpose					
Content of the story	*31*	50	64	52	27
Apparent purpose	23	13	9	24	10

Note: Each figure indicates the percentage of people who raised a particular concern, but the total exceeds 100 percent because teachers could raise as many issues as they wanted.

Italicized figures indicate that a group's response rate in this row differs by at least 20 percentage points from the average response rate for the row.

U = University; C = College; AR = Alternate Route Program

and responses to other teaching situations as well. That is, across all the situations we presented and across all interview occasions, the most frequent comments reflected a concern about how well students complied with prescriptions. In this case, when examining Jesse's story, teachers noticed the many grammatical and punctuation errors Jesse made, and when asked how they would respond to Jesse, they proposed to correct these various grammar and punctuation errors. This should not be surprising, in that ensuring compliance with prescriptions has been the main idea guiding the teaching of writing in the past.

The second important point that needs to be made about Table 3.1, however, has to do with the group in the right-most column. The programs represented in these columns subscribed to many of the reformers' ideals. They represented the school subject of writing as a purposive activity that required a unique pedagogy. Moreover, neither of them is a preservice teacher education program; both work with practicing teachers who can profit from their own experiences teaching as they participate in the programs. One is an in-service program, the other an induction program. The idea of working with practicing teachers rather than preservice teachers is consistent with the received wisdom model of teacher learning, which asserts that the most important phase of teacher learning is that which occurs in the context of practical experience. These programs capitalize on this important phase of learning by working with teachers while they are maintaining full-time teaching practices.

One important corollary to the fact that these programs are working with practicing teachers is that the teachers themselves already had their bachelor's degree and their teaching certificate. They did not need these programs in order to teach. This fact turns out to be important when we look at their interpretations of Jesse's story. Notice that teachers entering these programs interpreted Jesse's story remarkably differently from teachers entering all the other programs. Far fewer of them noticed Jesse's compliance with prescriptions, for instance. Thus, even before they participated in these programs, they were already guided by different frames of reference than other teachers were guided by. These teachers, then, were probably not like most practicing teachers. Instead, they represent a subgroup of the population—a group that happens to be interested in the same ideas reformers are interested in. So these reform-oriented programs have somehow managed to recruit teachers who were already sympathetic with the reform agenda and already interpreted classroom situations differently than other teachers did.

With the important exception of these teachers, though, most teachers, across a wide range of programs, interpreted Jesse's story as revealing how well the student was complying with language prescriptions. Only a small fraction of teachers saw evidence of concepts that Jesse understood or did not understand, and in fact, none looked closely enough to notice that there was a systematic pattern in Jesse's sentence fragments so that they could infer that Jesse had an idea in mind when he created these fragments. These teachers were using the frames of reference that they had developed during their thirteen-year apprenticeship of observation to interpret Jesse's story.

Interestingly, these frames of reference are closely tied to concrete situations. That is, teachers often espoused different ideas when they talked about teaching in general, and yet they turned to their traditional frames of references when they face particular situations. This tendency was especially apparent in a set of interview questions that had to do with teaching students to organize their writing. In one question, we asked teachers what they thought students needed to know in order to organize their writing. Teachers' responses to this question revealed their espoused ideas about teaching organization. In another question, we asked teachers to examine and comment on a student paper that was disorganized (the student's text is shown in Figure 3.2). Responses to this question revealed the frame of reference that teachers used to interpret this particular

Figure 3.2. The Dolphin Essay.

Dolphins are really not fish. Other fish have gill to breath in air and blow out again.
Dolphins are like other big, big water animals they eat other small water animal
The ocen is the only place that Dolphins can live.
The reason that the Dolphins can only live in the ocen is because the Dolphins have to   live in salt water. Dolphins are somewhat reladed to sharks and whales.
There are only one kind of Dolphins. There are very few places that have Dolphins.
Matter of fact there are only two places that have dolphins.
The two places that have Dolphins are the coast of Maine and Alaska are the only two places that have Dolphins. The Dolphins can weigh up to three tons. In 1963 a man was killed by a Dolphin.
The Dolphins name was Julie. The way they tell is the markins on the Dolphins tale.

situation. In a third question, we asked them how they would actually respond to this student author if he or she were in their classroom.

By examining the relationship between teachers' responses to these various questions, we can see the extent to which teachers used the same or similar frames of reference when considering these different questions. The relationship between responses to the first two questions is shown in Table 3.2. The rows in the table represent the kinds of knowledge or understanding that teachers espoused when considering what students needed in order to organize their writing. The distribution of responses across the rows suggests that teachers mentioned these different ideas in roughly equal proportions. That is, there was no apparent domination of prescriptions or concepts or strategies in teachers' thinking about what organization entailed.

The columns in Table 3.2 represent the aspects of this particular student's text that teachers noticed as they examined it. What they attended to reflects the frame of reference they used to interpret this particular situation. The distribution of ideas across the columns shows that even though teachers were almost evenly concerned about each kind of knowledge when they discussed organization more generally, they were more likely, when interpreting this particular student paper, to focus on how well the student complied with prescriptions.

If teachers interpreted this situation using the same ideas they espoused about organization, we would see large numbers in each of the diagonal cells.

Table 3.2. Relationship Between Espoused Ideas and What Teachers Noticed in Examining the Dolphin Report (Number of Teachers Mentioning Each Combination of Ideas).

Ideals Espoused in Response to Question About What Students Should Know	Ideals Enacted in Response to a Student Paper			
	Author's Compliance with Prescriptions	Author's Understanding of Concepts	Author's Purpose, Content of Paper	Author's Effort
Know facts and prescriptions	23	15	18	3
Understand concepts	15	13	24	2
Have a purpose, ideas	18	15	21	3
Have general capability	8	5	8	3

Note: Teachers may volunteer more than one idea as important to learning to organize a text, and they may also notice more than one thing when examining the dolphin report.

That is, a teacher who thought students should know all the relevant facts and prescriptions would respond to the paper by enumerating all the prescriptions that needed to be fixed. One who thought students should understand important concepts would respond to the paper by introducing important concepts the student appeared to understand or not to understand. Table 3.2 suggests that there is very little relationship between the ideas teachers mentioned as generally important in learning to organize a text and the ideas they saw as relevant when they examined this particular disorganized text. For instance, among teachers who claimed that knowledge of prescriptions was important to organization, twenty-three commented on the author's compliance with prescriptions, fifteen interpreted the paper in terms of some important concepts that the student appeared to understand or not to understand, and another eighteen interpreted the paper in terms of the student's apparent purpose. Regardless of which ideas they thought were generally important to learn in order to organize one's writing, they drew on all of the different ideas to interpret this particular situation. Table 3.2 shows that every possible combination of espoused and enacted ideas occurred.

Table 3.2 shows only the relationship between espoused ideas about learning organization and ideas used to interpret this student's paper. Yet to be considered are teachers' proposed responses to this student. Just as teachers may draw on different ideas when they discuss a topic in general and interpret a particular situation, they may also draw on different ideas when they devise a response to a situation. Table 3.3 displays the relationship between teachers' interpretations of the dolphin report and their proposed responses to its author.

Table 3.3. Relationship Between What Was Noticed
in the Dolphin Report and Proposed Responses to Its Author.

What Was Noticed in the Report	Number Mentioning This Idea	Teacher's Proposed Response			
		Correct Errors	Impart Knowledge	Facilitate Purpose	Encourage Only
Author's compliance with prescriptions	52	50 percent	38 percent	4 percent	6 percent
Author's understanding of concepts	14	29 percent	36 percent	77 percent	
Author's strategies or purposes					
Content	45	36 percent	49 percent	9 percent	
Purpose	19	32 percent	47 percent	16 percent	

Table 3.3 shows that there was very little relationship between the ideas that guided teachers' interpretations of this dolphin report and the ideas that guided their response to the student. Almost every combination of ideas appeared, so that teachers who noticed prescriptions when they first examined the paper proposed sometimes to correct those errors, sometimes to impart knowledge, sometimes to facilitate the student's purpose, and sometimes simply to encourage the student without providing any instructional guidance at all. Similar distributions appear on the other rows.

But Table 3.3 also shows us that regardless of which ideas teachers attended to when they examined the dolphin report, they were still highly likely to propose to correct the errors in the text or impart some knowledge to the student. Just as more teachers appeared in the first column of Table 3.2, so more teachers appear here in the first column of Table 3.3.

We have, then, a situation in which teachers tend to be more and more influenced by prescriptive ideas as they move closer and closer to the action of teaching. When teachers discuss organization in general, they give roughly equal attention to each of these three ideas about writing. When they interpret the dolphin report, they focus more on prescriptions than they had in their general discussion, and when they propose responses to the author, they focus even more on prescriptions than they had when they first examined the text. As teachers move closer and closer to the action of teaching, their frame of reference turns more toward the traditional view of writing as requiring compliance with prescriptions.

Frames of reference are important guides for teachers. They enable teachers to interpret the situations that arise in their classrooms and provide them ideas for how to respond to those situations. The evidence from the TELT study also suggests that although teachers may espouse ideas about teaching that deviate from the narrow prescriptive tradition, they are less likely to act on those espoused ideals. The tremendous advantage of asking teachers to respond to particular classroom situations, from a research point of view, is that these situations enable us to get past the ideals that teachers claim to subscribe to and into those they are likely to enact.

To see how teachers move from their espoused ideals to their interpretations of particular situations, consider Ginger, a teacher candidate who was sympathetic with reform rhetoric in part because her experiences as a student had reinforced it. Ginger had written for her school newspaper when she was young, and through that experience she discovered the satisfaction of writing for her own purposes rather than to please the teacher. As a teacher candidate, she wanted her students to like school and to like writing, and she thought that one way to accomplish that goal was to give them meaningful projects rather than assignments that served no purpose other than fulfilling the teacher's requirements. Yet when we presented Ginger with Jesse's story, Ginger felt compelled to enumerate all of its errors:

> What I'd try to do is sit down with him and say, "So let's look at this and, you know, let's try and correct some of the little things you have wrong, like the punctuation, the spelling, and the capitalization and things like that." And also some of his sentence structure would—using question marks when it's really a statement and should have a period.

After having said all of this, Ginger does discuss the meaning she sees in the student's text:

> I think once you did that you could look at the story and say, "Well, you kind of jumped here, you know? See, you're talking about this and all of a sudden we went to this. Can you kind of explain? Tell me what happened in between," type of thing.

This last segment of her response is closer to what reformers generally mean when they suggest that teachers be facilitators rather than dispensers of pre-scriptions. But although Ginger proposes this response, she puts the prescriptions first, and only after those are corrected does she mention that the story is a bit hard to follow. If this had been a real student, presumably Ginger would have made the student correct all of the spelling and punctuation errors, only then to be told that the story needed more revision. Ginger's interpretation of this situation apparently was that the errors were so numerous that they needed attention.

These discrepancies appeared in response to other questions as well. One particularly frequent discrepancy appeared when teachers talked about their ideal of caring for students. Leslie is a good example of a teacher who cares about caring. When she entered her teacher education program in an open en-rollment university, she had already married and raised her children. She wanted to teach because she felt she had been successful as a parent. However, Leslie's own childhood experiences in education had not all been positive, and these experiences were the source of her conception of teaching. Her parents were not well educated and had essentially told Leslie as a child that they could not help her with her schoolwork. Leslie also had had some bad experiences in school, once being chastised so severely by a teacher that she stayed home for a week in embarrassment. She wanted to be different from that teacher. She wanted to be caring, wanted her students to like her, to like school, and to like learning.

This ideal of caring was a strong theme in Leslie's discussion of teaching; it was a value that had sustained her throughout her preparations for teaching.

She said, "I want to build children's confidence. I don't want to crush them. And I hope I can be sensitive to different children and their needs." What we do not know from these conversations is how Leslie would translate that ideal into particular classroom situations. To be sensitive to different children and their needs would require Leslie to be able to perceive those needs in particular situations and be able to generate responses that appropriately reflect her ideal of caring.

One of the particular situations we asked Leslie to respond to was this:

> **Imagine that you are teaching in your third-grade classroom, and one of your students says, "This is boring. Why do we have to learn this?" How would you respond?**

Like most of the other situations we presented, this one is brief but contains much within it. The first sentence announces the student's boredom. It is a plea for sympathy, for sensitivity, for some sort of response that will alleviate the boredom. The second sentence asks for a justification for the task. It could be interpreted as asking for an explanation of the value of the content being learned, but it could also be interpreted as challenging the teacher's authority to make curriculum decisions. Given Leslie's espoused ideal of caring, we might expect her to interpret the situation as presenting a plea for relief, and we might expect her to devise a response that would either alleviate the boredom or at least offer a sympathetic ear to the student. For instance, she might propose to try to learn more about why the student felt bored, or to ask how other students felt about the lesson. Or she could propose to utter some sympathetic words to the student, encouraging the student to stick with the work a little longer.

But Leslie did not interpret this situation as calling for sympathy. Instead she interpreted the student's comment as a challenge to her authority and said:

> I think I would really be tough, because he's bored and he doesn't want to work on organizing. Ah, I'd ask him, "Well, how would you do it if you were the teacher and you knew your students needed to organize their papers? Because you're going to need to write papers throughout school and even after school. And, ah, we want to hear your ideas but we can't understand them if they're not organized."

Leslie was not alone in her interpretation of this situation or in her proposed response. Many teachers who espoused an ideal of caring interpreted this situation as calling for something other than caring. An interesting comparison to Leslie is Dena, who entered teaching from a very different direction. Dena had not originally intended to teach. When she finished college, she went to work as a stockbroker. But in her free time, she volunteered to help various charities, and through these activities she decided she preferred helping people more than managing money. She eventually found her way into an alternative route program. When we asked Dena what her goal would be for her students, she talked at length about her own experiences in school:

> I desperately reach down in myself and remember how I was when I was in sixth, seventh, and eighth grade and even high school. I felt so lost sometimes and I felt that I had no direction. What am I going to do with myself, where am I going to go? I remember these thoughts so vividly all the time. I felt so dumb sometimes. Maybe they're going through the same things I went through.

Dena took a job in a Catholic school and translated her concern into lessons on the golden rule. She wanted her students to think about themselves and their lives, and to think about how they would apply ideas such as "doing good to others." Yet when we asked Dena about the bored student, she responded,

> No matter what they say to me, they're not going to embarrass me because I usually have something to say back to them or the kids have something to say back to them. Because if they start looking like they're making a monkey out of themselves, not me, the kids will say, "Why don't you shut up?" or something, to the kid, not to me.

Responses to Jesse and to the author of the dolphin report indicate that teachers' thinking is dominated by a concern for how well students are complying with prescriptions; they show us too that teachers' ideas become more and more dominated by prescriptions as they move closer and closer to the action of teaching. Responses to the bored student suggest that this tendency to espouse ideas different from those one enacts is not limited to subject matter issues.

There are several plausible hypotheses for why these patterns appear in our interviews. One hypothesis is that these teachers subscribed to multiple, and sometimes conflicting, ideals. That is, Ginger may indeed want writing to be meaningful, but she also wants to ensure that students learn to comply with prescriptions. And Leslie and Dena may indeed want to be caring and compassionate teachers, but they may also want to ensure that their students treat them respectfully. Another hypothesis is that their ideals were not strong enough to overcome the frames of reference they had developed during childhood, so when they faced particular situations, their childhood frames of reference dominated their interpretations and their proposed responses in spite of their intentions to think and do otherwise. Yet a third hypothesis is that these teachers thought they were enacting their ideals. Since terms like *caring* and *ownership* can mean different behaviors to different people, perhaps Ginger, Leslie, and Dena were in fact enacting their ideals, but they meant something different with these terms than reformers are seeking.

There is probably some truth in all three of these hypotheses. Most teachers necessarily hold multiple and conflicting ideals. All of us do. We want teachers who are strict and do not tolerate inappropriate behavior, yet we also want teachers who are sympathetic and sensitive to students' needs. We want teachers who give students autonomy and encourage independent learning, and yet we want teachers who will ensure that students learn particular academic content. This is why teachers' interpretations of each situation are so important, for it is in their interpretation that they decide which ideals should be pursued in this circumstance. It is also likely that these teachers had not had as much experience with their ideals as they had had with the traditional approach to teaching. In fact, their ideals were often framed as alternatives to the specific experiences teachers had had themselves. Leslie and Dena held caring as an ideal precisely because they felt their own teachers had not been sufficiently caring. And Ginger held ownership as an ideal because she had not experienced ownership in her classes. Therefore, none of these teachers had many specific examples to fill out the details of their espoused ideals. Finally, given their extensive experience with the traditional approach to teaching, it is likely that these teachers may have meant different things with the terms *ownership* and *caring* than others might infer. The meanings they ascribe to these terms may be embedded within a traditional frame of reference. That is, perhaps Ginger took prescriptions for granted to such an extent that it seemed appropriate to ask Jesse to correct all his errors before she responded to the content of his story. Perhaps too Leslie and Dena assumed their own authority to such an extent that when they said they wanted to be caring, they did not mean *empathetic* but instead meant that they wanted to be at least benevolent in their exercise of authority.

If all of these hypotheses have merit, then the ideas that Ginger, Leslie, and Dena enact at any given moment cannot be predicted from knowledge of their espoused ideals. Without a clear sense of how teachers' ideals translate into classroom behaviors, with multiple ideals influencing their interpretation of classroom situations, and with the vagaries of the language of classroom ideals, these teachers' interpretations of classroom situations, and their responses to them, will depend heavily on a frame of reference we may never see and they may never be aware of.

This is the problem of enactment. There are at least three parts to this problem. First, the language we use to talk about our ideas can be used in the context of many different frames of reference. Thus, one teacher who claims to want students to have a sense of ownership over their writing may say this from a frame of reference that attends mainly to how well students comply with prescriptions. Another teacher may say the same sentence, but her sentence may emanate from a frame of reference that attends mainly to creating a classroom atmosphere in which students work separately and independently on projects of their own choosing. The second part of the problem is that even within a particular frame of reference, most ideas, especially those that stand behind our ideals, are associated with a wide range of specific behaviors. This second part of the problem is not unique to teaching, but is fundamental to virtually all discussions of human behavior. If I were to tell you that a mutual acquaintance seemed angry, you might envision any number of behaviors I might have seen. If you were to describe yourself as generous, I might envision any number of behaviors you might engage in. We could both be wrong in our behavioral translation of one another's descriptions. So, too, with teaching, in which terms like *ownership* and *caring* can have numerous legitimate behavioral translations. And this leads to the third problem of enactment. Novice teachers and their university faculty are highly likely to draw on different frames of reference when they talk about teaching. Novice teachers often approach the formal study of teaching with a frame of reference they developed during their childhood, while their university faculty are likely to approach the formal study of teaching from the perspective of reformers. When teacher educators discuss attitudes such as curiosity or teaching approaches such as cooperative grouping, novices may envision a wide range of behaviors that might be meant by these terms. Moreover, it is likely that all the sentences spoken by faculty will be interpreted in the light of novices' initial frames of reference, rather than in the light of a reform frame of reference.

There is also a strong likelihood that even if novices are persuaded by their faculty's ideas and are persuaded to adopt a different frame of reference to thinking about teaching, they will not know what actually to do to enact these new ideas. To pursue any particular teaching idea or ideal, teachers need to be able to recognize particular situations as calling for that particular idea. Teachers may acquire numerous important ideas about teaching when they are studying in college, and they may even have some visions of what to do to enact these ideas yet be unable to recognize situations that call for these ideas.

The problem facing preservice teacher education is not merely one of giving teachers a new frame of reference, but in addition of giving them the behavioral enactments that accompany these ideas. Psychologists refer to this kind of knowledge as *situated knowledge,* meaning knowledge that is understood through specific situations rather than, or in addition to, knowledge that is understood abstractly. It is through specific situations that we learn most of the concepts we use every day. Situated learning enables us to recognize everything from a beanbag to a bar stool as a "chair." Formal definitions of chairs do not prepare us for these varied examples.

In ordinary conversations, when I tell you someone was angry, I can depend on our shared cultural experience and shared situated understanding of this term to help you understand what I mean. Even if you envision different behaviors than I actually witnessed, you are likely to envision behaviors that I would also count as examples of angry behavior. Situated knowledge of these terms is central to our ability to communicate using language. Our shared experiences in a common culture and a common language enable us to narrow the range of possible behavioral meanings such a term might have.

But the terms we use to describe teaching practices, especially reformed practices, do not have the benefit of shared behavioral meanings. We cannot draw on our shared experiences to understand the meaning of a kind of teaching that none of us has experienced. Teachers, teacher educators, and policymakers use a common language to describe their ideas about teaching, but each interprets these terms in the light of his or her own frame of reference.

One might reasonably ask whether teacher education programs that adopt a reform orientation toward teaching can actually influence teachers' interpretations and proposed responses to particular teaching situations. One can imagine several possibilities. Teacher educators may use reform rhetoric, and novices may interpret that rhetoric in terms of their extant frames of reference, so that no fundamental changes in thought occur. Or students might be persuaded to change their frame of reference and yet be unable to enact these new ideas because they do not have enough behavioral understanding of the terms to enact them. Or, finally, students might learn both a new frame of reference and a set of enactments for these new ideas. The question is, Can reform-oriented preservice teacher education programs influence enactments?

INFLUENCES OF PRESERVICE
TEACHER EDUCATION PROGRAMS

One problem in posing the question as I have is that not all programs of teacher education subscribe to the reform agenda. In fact, the programs participating in the TELT study can be roughly classified according to whether they were traditional or reform oriented. Reform-oriented programs tried to persuade teachers to attend less to how well students complied with prescriptions and more to how well students formulated and expressed their ideas. They wanted students to learn concepts such as voice, main idea, and chronology that are important when translating ideas into text, they wanted them to be familiar with the iterative processes that are involved in translating ideas in texts, and they wanted students to write things that were important and meaningful to them. In contrast, the traditional teacher education programs concentrated on classroom management issues such as how to organize classroom activities, keep students busy, and discipline students who were disruptive. They tended not to address the content that would be taught. I was interested in comparing teachers who attended these different types of teacher education programs to see whether the programs influenced teachers in different ways. To illustrate these possibilities,

I describe two examples of teacher education classes that were observed as part of the TELT study.

As an example of a traditional teacher education class, consider a class we observed in an alternative route program. In this class novice teachers were learning to examine lessons they had already taught by reteaching them in front of their peers. After each novice teacher taught her lesson, Professor Dickenson led discussions in which the novice teachers analyzed the focal lessons. Dickenson's focus, however, was not on the substance of the lesson but on how it was packaged—on how the focal teacher had organized and presented the lesson. On the day we observed, a focal teacher gave a writing lesson intended for third-grade pupils. She wrote the three parts of a paragraph on the board as "(1) beginning sentence, (2) middle sentences, and (3) ending sentence." She then asked her mock pupils what each set of sentences should do. Other novice teachers, playing the role of pupils, volunteered that the beginning sentence should tell us the main idea, that the middle sentences should tell us more about the main idea, and that the ending sentence should restate the main idea. Then the focal teacher said she wanted students to write their own paragraphs. These paragraphs would be about the wind. In preparation for their writing, she wrote on the board, "(1) kinds of wind, (2) sounds made by the wind, (3) other words for wind." After some brainstorming about what one might say about each of these topics, she had the students write their paragraphs.

With the mock lesson finished, Dickenson led the novices through an assessment of this lesson. She guided the students' analysis of the lesson with a handout that listed the features of a good lesson. Here is a partial transcript of that list:

- Anticipatory set: Were the students told what they were to learn and how it related to prior lessons?
- Were students given a chance to practice what they were taught?
- Did the teacher close by having students identify what the session's learning was?
- Did the teacher assign homework based on the day's learning?

In the group analysis that followed, novice teachers tried to translate the ideas on this handout into the specific activities this focal teacher had done. With respect to anticipatory set, for instance, they noted that the focal teacher had opened the lesson by saying, "Today we are going to use what we know about paragraph writing." They commented on the fact that the focal teacher had used the board, the teacher had given students an opportunity to practice what they had learned at the close of the lesson, and so forth. Only a very brief exchange had to do with the content of the lesson, and this consisted of an argument between two teachers over whether this was a science lesson or a writing lesson. Dickenson quickly ended the dispute by saying it was both.

Had she been so inclined, Dickenson could have directed novices' attention to at least three substantive points about this lesson. First, the focal teacher never said what paragraphs are for, why anyone would want to learn about them, or how they can be used to communicate with others. Second, she provided definitions for the three parts of the paragraph that were virtually indistinguishable. All three parts were used to tell the main idea. Third, when the focal teacher had pupils write their own paragraphs, she defied her own definition by developing a paragraph outline that had three ideas (kinds of wind, sounds of wind, other words for wind) rather than one. Thus, although Dickenson did encourage novices to examine specific instances of practice and to assess these instances against some broad criteria, her criteria did not address the content of what was taught, but instead addressed only how it was organized and presented.

A university class taught by Professor Smith illustrates the converse of this lesson in two ways. First, Professor Smith focused exclusively on substantive ideas rather than ideas about how to package or present lessons. Professor Smith strongly promoted reform ideas about teaching writing and eschewed what he called the "formalist ideal"—the notion that you could teach students proper structures and forms. He listed many reasons why he rejected the formalist ideal, cited research on how professional writers write, and referred the students to some interviews with writers. The second way in which Smith's class differed from Dickenson's was that Smith provided no enacted meanings for the ideas he presented. He gave no examples of what any of these ideas might look like in real classrooms. He did eventually ask his students, most of whom were already teaching, how these new ideas might influence their own teaching of writing, and he encouraged them to discuss their teaching experiences. But even during this discussion, Smith offered nothing to help his students connect their experiences to the ideas he had presented. For instance, one student described her frustration in getting students to write an opinion essay. She said it was as if the students had no opinions about anything, even when she put a quotation on the board for them to respond to. Professor Smith could have helped this student translate his ideals into enactments by asking several questions about what the assignment was, how she had gone about preparing students for it, what students actually said or did that made her think they could not do the work, and so on. But he did not. Or he could have offered some hypotheses for why the lesson failed to motivate students. He could have pointed out, for instance, that this teacher had assigned both the content and the format of the writing project rather than encouraging students to write their own pieces. As other teachers offered speculations about the lesson, Smith neither affirmed nor questioned anyone's speculations. His only remark was a mock surprise that teenagers would not have any opinions. Although many students agreed that this was a frustrating event, and some offered their own frustrating experiences, Smith asked no questions, encouraged no analysis of the lesson, offered no suggestions about what else could have been done, and offered no critique of the student's lesson. His lack of ability, or of willingness, to translate his ideas about teaching writing into action meant that his students had to figure out for themselves what these ideas really meant. Rhetoric about such things as engaging students in intellectual activities and making school subject matter more meaningful and more authentic says little about how teachers decide what to do at any particular moment.

The distinctions I make between these two broad program orientations are based in part on program rhetoric and in part on interviews with and observations of faculty. Ideally we would want to distinguish programs by the extent to which they provide students with situated ideas rather than, or in addition to, abstractions, but this is a difficult classification to make. Programs could promote situated meanings through case discussions, video clips, school-based observation assignments, or even vivid descriptions couched in lectures. Moreover, even knowing that any of these types of situated descriptions had been provided to students would not automatically assure us that students were acquiring situated understandings of important ideas. It could mean only that teachers are witnessing examples of teaching, something they have already done throughout their lives. What is more important is whether the situations teachers see or hear about are interpreted in terms of important reform ideas. If they are not, teachers will surely interpret these situations with the frames of reference they already have.

A popular proxy for situated knowledge is the location of the program: programs located in schools rather than universities are often presumed to provide more situated knowledge. The problem with location, however, is that we cannot know the extent to which programs attach important ideas about teaching and learning to the many behaviors that novices observe. Some programs in schools might give teachers a great deal of situated understanding, all of which is consistent with the frame of reference they already had. Others might give teachers a new frame of reference for interpreting the classroom situations they see. The great confidence that reformers and others place on classroom experiences reflects their attachment to the received wisdom model of teacher learning, and fails to acknowledge the importance of frames of reference in learning to teach. Still, because location is presumed to be so important, I did distinguish between TELT study programs that were located primarily in colleges and universities and those that were located primarily in schools so that I could compare their relative influences on teachers and teaching. Thus, I was able to distinguish programs that were oriented toward traditional teaching or toward reform teaching and programs that were located primarily in universities or primarily in schools.

Since teachers participating in the TELT study were asked to respond to the same situations before and after they participated in their programs, it is possible to see the extent to which their interpretations of these situations, and their proposed responses to them, changed during this period of time. It is also possible to compare the changes (or lack of changes) that occurred among teachers attending reform-oriented programs with those of teachers attending traditional programs, and to compare changes among teachers whose programs were provided mainly in schools with those of teachers whose programs were provided mainly in university settings.

Finally, it is possible to distinguish two different kinds of program influences. Most people, when asked how programs might influence teaching, would say they expect to see learning. That is, they would expect to see changes in teachers' interpretations of or responses to these particular situations. An equally important influence could be called an *enrollment influence*—that is, teacher education programs can recruit teachers into the profession who are already inclined to use one frame of reference rather than another. I found both kinds of influences when examining these programs. Enrollment influences were apparent when teachers entering a particular program already interpreted situations and responded to these situations differently than other teachers did, even before they had learned anything from the programs themselves. I showed an enrollment influence in Table 3.1 when examining teachers' interpretations of Jesse's story. It was clear that teachers entering two of the programs already differed from other teachers, even before they began the programs. Learning influences, on the other hand, were apparent when teachers drew on different ideas at the end of their programs than they had drawn on at the outset.

Just as it would be a mistake to assume that all programs are oriented toward reform, so too it would be a mistake to assume that all enrollment influences or all learning influences were in the direction of the reform. There were some teachers participating in the TELT study who already embraced reform ideas from the start, and then changed toward traditional thinking. One such example is Chad. Chad was a black man who believed writing was essential to black people and was committed to making writing meaningful for his students. His ideals for teaching writing were consistent with much of the reform rhetoric in that he wanted students to take ownership of their own writing and to learn to use it for their own purposes. At one point in the interview, he said,

> If we can read, if we can write, we have a greater understanding of ourselves and we have greater definition of who we are and what we present to the world. They are powerful skills. They put us in control of our lives. I want students to see how writing can become a powerful tool to them so that they do not have to be resigned to whatever the limits were of the previous generation in their families, you see, but that they can go light years beyond if they can write.

We asked Chad, both before and after his teacher education program, to respond to the dolphin report. The first time Chad read the paper, he overlooked the technical problems and focused on the content, saying,

> I would ask the student some searching questions that he would be able to answer and then suggest that, with his own answers, he further develop a conclusion.

Chad's proposed response was consistent with his espoused ideas about teaching writing and consistent with reform rhetoric about teaching writing. Chad had wanted writing to be meaningful for his students, wanted them to write for authentic purposes and to learn to use writing to formulate and express their own ideas. His method of encouraging such expression was to ask the student searching questions—questions that would stimulate the student to refine his thinking and his text.

Despite Chad's apparent interest in reform ideas, he had much to learn. For instance, Chad did not say what a searching question might be for this student or what he would do if the student could not answer his searching question. If Chad had entered a reform-oriented program, he might have received some help in clarifying his situated understanding of these ideas. Because Chad's program had a traditional orientation, though, it did not provide that assistance.

Chad's program was an alternative route, suited for someone who was changing professions in midcareer. It was largely a school-based program and oriented toward traditional ideas about teaching. Chad's mentors provided no help in figuring out what a searching question might be and in fact encouraged him to be more prescriptive. By the time Chad had completed his alternative route program, he had adopted a more prescriptive response to this student. When asked to respond to this author at the completion of his program, Chad said:

> I would tell her that unless she is going to introduce lots of new information, we don't need a new paragraph [at one location in the text]. A couple of sentences don't make a new paragraph.

Chad began his program hoping to make writing more meaningful for his students and envisioned himself asking searching questions to help students improve their writing. But Chad's program pursued a different set of ideas and encouraged him to attend more to prescriptions. By the time he completed the program, Chad's proposed response to this student was more prescriptive, and this change is an example of a program influence on Chad's learning.

In Tables 3.4 and 3.5, I summarize the number of times I found evidence of each kind of influence. Table 3.4 lists the number of enrollment influences each program group had when teachers responded to each particular teaching situation I analyzed, and Table 3.5 lists the number of learning influences each

Table 3.4. Summary of Program Enrollment Influences
on Ideas Elicited Across All Interview Questions.

	Traditional Management Orientation		Reform Orientation	
	University Based (Urban U)	Field Based (State AR and District AR)	University Based (Elite C., Normal State U, Research State)	Integrated (Independent U, Collaborative U)
Immediate concerns				
What was seen in Jesse's story	2			1
Proposed responses to Jesse		1		1
Criteria for grading Jesse's story		1		1
What was seen in the dolphin report	2			2
Proposed responses to the dolphin author	1			1
Proposed response to the question about verb choice			1	1
Ideals Aspects of subject matter relevant to learning organization				
Situation-relevant subject matter knowledge Number of principles shared about *none* with is or are			-1^a	
Total	5	2	1,−1	7

Note: Number of times when entrants in one program group mentioned an idea noticeably more often than other program entrants.

[a]These teachers offered more misinformative principles than any other group of program entrants. Although no program rhetoric addressed the question of informative versus misinformative content, I am assuming they would take misinformation as a negative.

Table 3.5. Evidence of Program Influences on Teacher Learning Across All Interview Questions.

	Traditional Management Orientation		Reform Orientation	
	University Based (Urban U)	Field Based (State AR and District AR)	University Based (Elite C., Normal State U, Research State)	Integrated (Independent U, Collaborative U)
Immediate concerns				
What was seen in Jesse's story		2	1	
Proposed responses to Jesse	2[a]		1	1
Criteria for grading Jesse's story	N.A.		2	2
What was seen in the dolphin report			1	
Proposed responses to the dolphin author		1		
Proposed response to the question about verb choice	N.A.			
Ideals				
Aspects of subject matter relevant to learning organization				
Situation-relevant subject matter knowledge				
Number of principles shared	N.A.	−1[b]	1,−1[b]	−1[b]
Total	2	3,−1	6,−1	3,−1

Note: Number of noticeable changes in teachers' ideas from the beginning to the end of the program within each program group.

[a]One of these changes was a decrease in the proportion of teachers who proposed to give encouragement only, with no substantive comments on the story. I do not have information on program views toward encouragement without specific feedback, but am assuming they would all prefer teachers to provide some sort of substantive comment. Consequently I considered this a positive, rather than a negative, change.

[b]These teachers noticeably decreased the number of principles they provided to the student with the verb choice question. I do not have data indicating whether programs would prefer for teachers to say more or less on an issue like this but am assuming that since the student asked for information, and since the reductions resulted in fewer than one principle offered per person, all programs would view this change negatively.

program group appeared to have on the same set of teaching situations. The four columns in each table represent the four major program groups. There is just one program in the first column, representing a university-based program with a traditional orientation. The two programs in the second column are field-based programs, emphasizing similar content but presumably more able to provide enacted meanings for their ideas. Professor Dickenson's class, described above, was observed in this program group. The third column includes three reform-oriented programs housed in universities, and the two programs in the fourth column are reform-oriented, field-based programs.

Across all programs, beginning teachers demonstrated a strong tendency to draw on prescriptive ideas when they interpreted and responded to the situations we presented. Therefore, in this analysis, I was especially interested in seeing whether, and to what extent, reform-oriented programs helped teachers learn to draw on other ideas—either to teach their students important concepts about writing or to help students learn the processes of generating texts.[2] Either of these ideas would be closer to what reformers seem to want.

Tables 3.4 and 3.5 show the number of occasions when programs influenced teachers' responses to each of several particular situations. I defined an "influence" as any occasion when one group of teachers' responses to a given situation differed by at least 20 percent from the responses of the other groups. Recall from Table 3.1, for instance, that over half of the teachers entering most programs offered prescriptive interpretations of Jesse's story, while only 19 percent of teachers entering the two reform-oriented, field-based programs offered prescriptive interpretations of this particular situation. The difference constitutes evidence of an enrollment influence, and so I placed a 1 in that column. In a couple of places in each table, I used a negative number to indicate an instance in which a group of teachers differed from others but in the opposite direction from the program's orientation.

Five statements can be made from these tables. First, both tables have far more positive than negative numbers, suggesting that programs did in fact influence the ideas that teachers drew on to interpret and respond to these particular situations. With respect to enrollment influences, programs with traditional classroom management orientations enrolled teachers who were more likely to enact prescriptive ideas, whereas reform-oriented programs enrolled teachers who were more likely to draw on reform ideas. With respect to learning influences, traditional programs tended to reinforce teachers' prescriptive ideas, while reform-oriented programs tended to decrease references to those responses and increase references to ideas about concepts and processes. In other words, the differences I found were virtually always in the direction of program orientations. That these patterns of enrollment and learning are consistent with program orientations suggests that teacher education programs do indeed make a difference. The patterns were not random.

The second point about these patterns, however, is that program influences are slight. No program produced radical changes in the ideas teachers drew on, even though many produced some changes. Thus, although teacher education programs can and do make a difference in the ideas teachers used to interpret particular situations and to respond to them, none was able to alter radically their teachers' interpretations of or responses to these situations.

Third, there were more enrollment influences than there were learning influences. Across all situations and all program types, there were fifteen enrollment influences and fourteen influences on learning. The difference itself is slight, but the important point here is that influences through the process of enrollment were noticeable and just as likely to occur as learning influences were.

Fourth, with respect to program location, Table 3.5 shows that university-based programs demonstrated more influence on teacher learning than field-based programs did. This finding underscores the fact that locating a program in the field does not necessarily ensure that teachers will learn to translate important ideas into particular situations. One reason this difference occurred, of course, is that the field-based reform programs were enrolling teachers whose frames of reference were already oriented toward reform ideas, so there was less room for change. Still, I tallied more influences on learning in the third column of Table 3.5 than in any other column. This finding is particularly important in terms of the received wisdom of teacher learning, which gives a relatively minor role to university-based teacher education programs and a more potent role to liberal arts courses and learning from experience.

Finally, these influences, whether influences on enrollment or on learning, were associated with differences in program orientations, not differences in program structures. The university-based program group included four-year and five-year programs, with relatively more and less field experience, and with different specific courses listed in their curricula, but these differences were unrelated to the substantive orientations of the programs. Even the difference between field-based and university-based programs was not as great as the difference between programs with different orientations. In fact, just as some university-based programs had a traditional orientation and some had a reform orientation, so some field-based programs were traditional and some were oriented toward reform. This point is important to policymakers, for it suggests that the kinds of program features that they often try to influence—curriculum, duration, number of credit hours, or amount of field experience—are relatively less important than is the actual content that teacher educators teach within their individual classrooms.

The TELT study shows us that it is possible, though difficult, to help teachers develop new frames of reference so that they interpret classroom situations differently and envision different responses to particular situations. Before participating in these programs, many teachers espoused ideas that were consistent with reform rhetoric, but when faced with the situations we presented, they were unable to enact those ideas and turned instead to more traditional—usually prescriptive—responses. Those who attended programs with a reform orientation often learned alternative frames of reference for interpreting and responding to these situations.

IMPLICATIONS FOR POLICY

Findings from the TELT study throw some doubt on the received wisdom model of teacher learning. They show, for instance, that the content of teacher education programs is more important than their structure. Policymakers often regulate program structures to conform to the received wisdom model of teacher learning, a model that gives relatively little weight to the formal study of teaching and considerable weight to liberal arts courses and practical experience. By regulating program structure, policymakers hope to ensure that teachers receive an appropriate exposure to these various components of the curriculum. The TELT study included programs with a variety of structures: four-year and five-year programs, graduate and undergraduate programs, programs with extensive or less extensive field experiences. These program structures were less important than program content in influencing teacher enrollment or teacher learning. In fact, Professor Smith's program is often cited as an ideal approach to teacher education, in that it is a fifth-year program and consequently ensures that students receive a complete liberal arts program before beginning their formal study of teaching. Moreover, the students in his course were teaching concurrently with their university courses, a structural feature that should have enabled students to see connections between the ideas their professors espoused and their teaching experiences. But merely seeing such connections does not enable teachers to become better teachers. Smith's students were able to see that their students were not engaged in writing, and they expressed their frustrations at their inability to engage students in writing. But Smith was either unable or unwilling to help his students translate his ideas into interpretations of, and responses to, the classroom situations they described to him. Consequently, even though the students agreed on the ideals they wanted to enact and sympathized with one another's frustrations when trying to enact these ideas, they made no progress toward a better understanding of what they could actually do in their classrooms to enact these ideas. As long as professors like Smith are unable or unwilling to make that translation, the structural arrangement of this program offers no particular advantage to students.

The TELT study also raises doubts about the wisdom of alternative routes into teaching. Alternative route programs are also premised on received wisdom. In fact, they are based on a relatively strong version of it that gives almost no role to university-based teacher education. These programs try to recruit teachers who have not formally studied teaching but have received a bachelor's degree and have received high test scores on academic achievement tests. They then place these teachers in schools with mentor teachers to help them learn the practical aspects of teaching. Yet the two alternative route programs participating in the TELT study yielded few enrollment influences relative to other field-based programs and yielded few influences on learning relative to university-based programs.

Third, the TELT findings raise some doubts about the likelihood of in-service programs as a broad-based approach to reform. Since the two reform-oriented, field-based programs participating in the TELT study demonstrated more influence on enrollment than on learning, it is possible that such programs may never reach those teachers whose frames of reference depart most dramatically from reformers' ideas. To the extent that programs such as these enroll volunteers, their influence is likely to be limited to those who are already disposed toward reform ideas.

Finally, the TELT study indicates that university-based programs may have more influence on learning than the received wisdom model has assumed. Among the programs participating in the TELT study, university-based preservice programs had more influence on teacher learning than school-based programs did. Moreover, they had more influence over teachers' interpretations of particular situations than they had over teachers' espoused ideals. These findings fly directly in the face of the received wisdom model of teacher learning, which expects most practical learning to occur in school settings and assumes that the formal study of teaching has less influence because it is abstract and theoretical. In fact, policymakers who subscribe to the received wisdom model of teacher learning sometimes try to restrict teacher education curricula to a small number of courses and sometimes try to restrict the content of these courses to generic topics such as classroom management, thinking that all subject matter–related courses should be taught by the disciplines. These policies may, ironically, hinder teacher learning rather than enabling it.

Notes

1. While Lortie was the first to make this observation (Lortie, 1975), many others have since elaborated on this idea. See, for instance, Nemser (1983). See Haberman (1985).

2. Since teachers could propose virtually anything they wanted, including multiple responses, it was possible for teachers to increase their attention to other substantive ideas without necessarily reducing their attention to prescriptions. Or, conversely, they could reduce their attention to prescription without necessarily increasing their attention to other ideas. I therefore tallied references to each idea separately and counted changes in each of them as independent evidence

of program impact. A given situation could therefore produce multiple changes in teachers' responses to one situation: increases or reductions in enactments of combination of ideas.

References

Doyle, W. "Academic Work." *Review of Educational Research,* 1983, *53*(2), 159–199.

Duckworth, E. "Teaching As Research." *Harvard Educational Review,* 1986, *56,* 481–495.

Floden, R. E., and Clark, C. M. "Preparing Teachers for Uncertainty." *Teachers College Record,* 1988, *89,* 505–524.

Getzels, J. W., and Jackson, P. W. "The Teacher's Personality and Characteristics." In N. L. Gage (ed.), *Handbook of Research on Teaching.* Chicago: Rand McNally, 1963.

Haberman, M. "Does Teacher Education Make a Difference? A Review of Comparisons Between Liberal Arts and Teacher Education Majors." *Journal of Thought,* 1985, *20*(2), 25–34.

Jackson, P. W. *Life in Classrooms.* New York: Holt, 1968.

Kennedy, M. M. "Inexact Sciences: Professional Education and the Development of Expertise." In E. Z. Rothkopf (ed.), *Review of Research in Education.* Washington, D.C.: American Educational Research Association, 1987.

Kennedy, M. M. (ed.) *Teaching Academic Subjects to Diverse Learners.* New York: Teachers College Press, 1991.

Kuhn, T. S. *The Structure of Scientific Revolutions.* Chicago: University of Chicago Press, 1970.

Liston, D. P. (1986). "Teachers' Work and Teacher Education." *Review of Education,* 1986, *12*(2), 93–98.

Lortie, D. C. *Schoolteacher: A Sociological Study.* Chicago: University of Chicago Press, 1975.

Lytle, S. L., and Cochran-Smith, M. "Teacher Research as a Way of Knowing." *Harvard Education Review,* 1992, *62*(4), 447–474.

McNeil, L. M. *Contradictions of Control.* New York: Routledge, 1985.

Nemser, S. F. "Learning to Teach." In L. S. Shulman and G. Sykes (eds.), *Handbook of Teaching and Policy.* New York: Longman, 1983.

Reynolds, M. C. (ed.). *Knowledge Base for the Beginning Teacher.* New York: Pergamon Press, 1989.

Richardson, V. "Significant and Worthwhile Change in Teaching Practice." *Educational Researcher,* 1990, *19*(7), 10–18.

Schön, D. A. *The Reflective Practitioner: How Professionals Think in Action.* New York: Basic Books, 1983.

Schön, D. A. (ed.). *The Reflective Turn: Case Studies in and on Educational Practice.* New York: Teachers College Press, 1991.

Sykes, G. "Teacher Education and the Predicaments of Reform." In C. E. Finn, Jr., D. Ravitch, and R. T. Fancher (eds.), *Against Mediocrity: The Humanities in America's High Schools.* New York: Holmes and Meier, 1984.

Zeichner, K. M., and Liston, D. P. "Teaching Student Teachers to Reflect." *Harvard Educational Review,* 1987, *57*(1), 23–48.

CHAPTER FOUR

Preparing Teachers for Diversity

Historical Perspectives, Current Trends, and Future Directions

Gloria Ladson-Billings

Diversity has become a buzzword of U.S. society in the 1990s. Its supporters use it to reflect the potential benefits of multiple perspectives and encouraging full civic, economic, and social participation of all segments of the society (Banks, 1995; Grant, 1992). Its detractors use *diversity* to signify the rending of a united social fabric or common culture that makes individuals in the society not members of their ethnic, racial, or cultural groups but merely Americans (D'Souza, 1991; Schlesinger, 1991). Supporters of diversity point to the loss of human capital when society continues to exclude and exploit particular groups because of status characteristics such as race, class, and gender. But the press for inclusion is one that allows for and encourages acculturation, not assimilation. On the other hand, diversity's detractors have argued that too much emphasis on notions of pluribus take away from the possibility of a united and seamless unum.

This chapter explores the current demographic realities, how they affect schooling, and how colleges, schools, and departments of education prepare teachers for this reality. I situate my argument in a brief chronology or historical context of social change and school reform efforts that date back to before the turn of the century. I want to argue that the social conditions that precipitate certain changes rarely, if ever, are incorporated into the standards and practices of teacher education. Thus, the changing demographics of the nation's schoolchildren have caught schools, colleges, and departments of teacher education by surprise. Students are still being prepared to teach in idealized schools that serve white, monolingual, middle-class children from homes with two parents. Nevertheless, a variety of institutions of higher education (IHE) are working to rethink and remake their teacher education programs so that they more accurately reflect the issues and concerns of beginning teachers in urban and diverse school settings. Some of their promising practices may serve as a template for other institutions still struggling to prepare new teachers for a changing classroom reality.

AMERICANIZING THE IMMIGRANT

Truant boys in Boston, pursued by officer Oliver Spurr—most of them Irish children, probably wonder[ed] why they had to go to school where there weren't enough seats in classrooms and where signs were appearing all over town, "No Irish Need Apply."

German parents in Cincinnati, refus[ed] to send their children to a school that taught them to scorn their language and culture.[1]

There are probably striking comparisons to be made between the growth of nineteenth-century immigrants in America's urban centers of Boston, New York, Chicago, and Philadelphia with that of current immigrants into California, Oregon, Washington, Florida, Texas, and other areas of the country. Over time, immigrants have come to the shores of the United States seeking freedom and economic prosperity, fleeing persecution or famine. However, there is a tendency for a kind of historical amnesia to rewrite the immigrant experiences of the past and to valorize and naturalize their experiences as the way every group must "make it" in the United States.

Fortunately, the historical record is replete with examples of the ways that nineteenth-century immigrants were treated (Zinn, 1980; Takaki, 1993). When we consider their schooling experiences, we learn that while there is consensus about the notion of schools' serving an Americanizing function, there are divergent views as to interpretation and motivation of this effort (Olneck, 1995). Brumberg (1986) argues that New York City educators made connections between immigrant children's outward behavior and their inner identity. Thus, the schooling these immigrant children received explicitly transmitted middle-class values concerning health and grooming, manners, diet, food preparation, dress, recreation, accentless English, rights and duties of citizenship, as well as aesthetic and literary standards and myths and legends of U.S. history (Olneck, 1995). Brumberg interprets this process of Americanization as one of genuine sharing on the part of teachers who hoped to welcome the immigrant children into the American mainstream.

Another vision of the process of Americanization for immigrant children is put forth by Cohen and Mohl (1979). In a study of Gary, Indiana, they suggested that Americanizing the immigrant was tied to the "nativist impulse to regulate and reorder the behavior of immigrants coercively so as to ensure adherence to dominant social norms, and to ensure social stability" (Olneck, 1995, p. 311). Regardless of the intents and motives of nineteenth-century teachers toward immigrant students, there is no evidence that teachers of that era received any formal preparation for teaching immigrant children.

Tyack (1974) argues that like most of the workforce of the nineteenth century, teachers had little or no formal schooling for the work they were asked to do. The typical nineteenth-century teacher had a grammar school education, with approximately 25 percent of those teachers in urban areas (with graded schools) possessing a normal school diploma (Tyack, 1974). Since normal school training took place at the secondary level, urban teachers at best had a high school diploma. Thus, teachers' notions of how to teach immigrant children came from their own values and perspectives, as well as those espoused in the school community.

This quest to Americanize European immigrant children, with attempts to assimilate them into the American mainstream, did not extend to African American or American Indian children in the nation's public schools. Rather, African American and American Indian children were to be "Americanized" in separate and unequal schools (Tyack, 1974), often with untrained teachers. The main purpose of their schooling was to create a servant class capable of doing manual and repetitive work in a growing industrial society.

Today Americanization continues as Latin American and Asian Pacific families immigrate to the United States. In schools where there are adequate human and capital resources, students may receive bilingual services and English as Second Language (ESL) instruction. More often, students receive only ESL services, and in poor districts, both rural and urban, second-language learners receive little or no formal ESL service. Although school personnel may not be as overtly nativist and xenophobic toward recent immigrants as they were toward their turn-of-the-century counterparts, the message that these newcomers should conform to white, middle-class cultural forms and identity representations persists.

EDUCATION IN THE POSTWAR ERA

By the end of World War II public education in the United States had taken on a decidedly different appearance. Buoyed by a strong economy and burgeoning enrollment as the first of the baby boomers started school, public schools mirrored the "happy days" of the Eisenhower era. Not all groups enjoyed the fruits of this prosperity. In the South, African American students continued to be relegated to unequal, inferior schooling; the same was true for many Mexican American students in the American West and Southwest (Cruse, 1987).

When the widely discussed decision in *Brown v. Board of Education* (1954) declared segregated schools separate and unequal, the actual implementation of school desegregation had a negligible impact on teacher preparation. Those few African American students who attended previously all-white schools were expected to behave and learn in exactly the same way as white children. In fact, the nine African American children who were chosen to integrate Central High School in Little Rock, Arkansas, were selected because of their outstanding academic achievement and ability to "fit in" (Carson, Garrow, Harding, and Hine, 1987).

By the end of the 1950s both the cold war and the space race aggravated tensions between the United States and the Soviet Union. The public blamed the nation's failure to compete with the Soviet Union's space technology on inferior science and mathematics education. Teacher education became directed toward helping prospective teachers learn to understand and use the emerging curricula in mathematics and science. Issues of student diversity were not included in the preparation of teachers. In addition, as Spring (1989) points out, during the 1950s, public education came under attack because of the perception that professional educators had lost contact with traditional academic disciplines. It was during this era that the master of arts in teaching (M.A.T.) program and other fifth-year programs developed. These programs were designed to ensure that professional preparation courses did not limit prospective teachers' mastery of academic subjects. Once again, preparing teachers for culturally diverse classrooms was not a primary concern of teacher educators.

EDUCATION IN THE TURBULENT 1960S

During the social and political turmoil of the 1960s, students and teachers advocated for a more "relevant" curriculum (Cruse, 1987). School desegregation efforts occurred throughout the South, while educators in the urban North reconsidered the kind of schooling offered to African American students (Tyack, 1974). It was during this time that the language of cultural deprivation (Ornstein, 1971; Ornstein and Vairo, 1968; Bloom, Davis, and Hess, 1965; Bettelheim, 1965) began to shape school policy. The perception of African American and low-income students as "culturally deprived" and "culturally disadvantaged" precipitated the development of compensatory education programs funded initially by foundations and later by Title I of the Elementary and Secondary Education Act of 1965.

Compensatory education programs such as Head Start and Follow Through were designed to work against the supposed detrimental effects of low-income African American children's homes and families. Teacher education programs focused on helping prospective teachers identify "culturally deprived" students so they could be placed in the appropriate compensatory programs. Preservice teachers were not expected to make curricular or instructional changes to accommodate culturally diverse learners. Some special programs designed to prepare teachers for "urban" teaching were modeled after Peace Corps or VISTA programs in that prospective teachers were to spend a few years working with the "disadvantaged" before moving on to more prestigious and rewarding careers.

By the 1970s the black power and ethnic revitalization movements helped change the rhetoric from "cultural disadvantage and deficit" to "cultural difference." These movements created changes in curriculum offerings. African American, American Indian, Latino, and Asian American histories and studies proliferated at the high schools. However, instructional practices changed very little (Cuban, 1973). Little or nothing in teacher preparation addressed the idea that a changed curriculum might require a changed pedagogy.

EDUCATION REFORM IN THE 1980S

Soon after the 1983 Commission on Excellence in Education Report, *A Nation at Risk,* the Holmes Group (1986) and the Carnegie Task Force (1986) raised important questions about teacher preparation. Both of their reports called for greater professionalization of teachers. The Carnegie Task Force called for the establishment of a national certification board, raising standards in teacher education, and improving the status of teaching in order to attract more capable students to the profession. The impetus for the Carnegie Task Force was a growing concern about the ability of U.S. students to compete in a highly technological and global economy.

The Holmes Group was more tied to notions of "new knowledge about teaching practices [requiring changes in] teacher education and the organization of schools" (Spring, 1989, p. 69). Like Carnegie, the Holmes Group called for the abolition of undergraduate teacher education and raising the status of teaching. Although the Holmes Group called for increasing minority teachers, neither report addressed the need for the current and future teaching force to be prepared to teach an increasingly diverse public school population more effectively. Despite these commission calls for change in teaching and teacher education, Cuban (1984) argues that relatively no significant change has occurred in teaching in U.S. public schools throughout the twentieth century. Most classrooms are teacher centered rather than student centered. Teacher talk dominates the classroom, and instruction occurs primarily in whole class rather than small group settings. The reason for this lack of change is that "schools exist to serve larger social purposes and to instill behaviors required by the prevailing economic system. This produces teaching practices that emphasize uniformity, authority, and other traits required by bureaucratic organizations" (Spring, 1989, pp. 83–84).

Another reason for a lack of instructional change in teaching, according to Cuban (1984), is the organizational structure of our schools. Because schools still work on an efficiency model, class size, prescribed curricula, and maintaining order are the highest priority. Third, Cuban argues that teachers are socialized to conservative values and are resistant to change. New teachers' teaching is based on the kind of teaching they had in school and on that of cooperating teachers who supervised their preparation. These are the conditions under which teacher educators must attempt to effect changes that address the needs of a culturally diverse student population.

THE DEMOGRAPHIC IMPERATIVE

The reality of who attends the nation's public schools has not made much of a difference to those who would argue that "multicultural education" is another educational fad that distracts educators from the pressing need to improve basic literacy and numeracy skills. According to the College Board and the Western Commission for Higher Education (cited by Garcia, 1995) the U.S. nonwhite and Latino student population was projected to increase from 10.4 million in 1985–1986 to 13.7 million in 1994–1995. These students now constitute 34 percent of public elementary and secondary school enrollment, up from 29 percent a decade ago. During this same period white enrollment would rise by just 5 percent, from 25.8 million to 27 million, and the white percentage of the student population would drop from 71 percent to 66 percent. According to this study, by 2026 "we will have the exact inverse of student representation as we knew it in 1990: Hispanic and non-white students will make up 70 percent of our enrolled K–12 student body" (Garcia, 1995, p. 373). Garcia further suggests that "in the decades to come it will be virtually impossible for a professional educator to serve in a public school setting, and probably any private school context, in which his or her students are not consequentially diverse—racially, culturally, and/or linguistically" (p. 373).

At the same time the student population is undergoing dramatic demographic shifts, the teaching population remains primarily white and female. According to Banks (1991):

Even if we are successful in increasing the percentage of teachers of color from the projected 5 percent in [the year] 2000 to 15 percent, 85 percent of the nation's teachers will still be white, mainstream and largely female working with students who differ from them racially, culturally, and in social class status. Thus an effective teacher education policy for the 21st century must include as a major focus the education of all teachers, including teachers of color, in ways that will help them receive knowledge, skills, and attitudes needed to work effectively with students from diverse racial, ethnic, and social class groups [pp. 135–136].

The demographic imperative is not just about numbers of culturally diverse students. The social and economic conditions of these students also are a major concern. An abundance of data details the poor economic and social conditions under which many students of color exist. Thirty-three percent of all African American families live below the poverty level of $14,999 per year for a family of four (Daniels, 1998). Students of color are more likely to be poor, live with one parent, and drop out of school than their white counterparts (Darling-Hammond, 1998). Although nationwide the high school dropout rate is about 28 percent, cities with high concentrations of African Americans and Latinos, such as New York and Chicago, have dropout rates of over 40 percent (Wilson, 1998). African American students, compared to whites, are two to five times more likely to be suspended from school (Irvine, 1990). Although African American students make up 17 percent of the public school population, they comprise 41 percent of the special education population (Kunjufu, 1984). Strikingly, a black male child who was born in California in 1988 is three times more likely to be murdered as he is to be admitted to the University of California (*Fortune Magazine*, 1990, p. 18).

As the nation's student population is becoming more diverse, its teaching force is becoming increasingly monocultural. Both Haberman (1989) and Grant (1989) believe that our overwhelmingly white and mostly female teaching force will persist for the foreseeable future. And many of these new white teachers would prefer not to teach in urban settings in schools that primarily serve students of color (Grant, 1989). This inverse relationship between the race, culture, and background of the students and their teachers has played a major role in the development of multicultural teacher education.

For many years communities had come to depend on neighboring colleges and universities to supply teachers, a relationship that seemed satisfactory to the school districts. But as urban areas began to serve more culturally diverse and poor families, fewer teacher education programs were able to say with assurance that their graduates were prepared to educate effectively students from poor families and communities of color. Gradually schools, colleges, and departments of education began to redesign aspects of their teacher preparation programs to include courses and field experiences that addressed the needs of diverse students.

THE STATE OF MULTICULTURAL TEACHER EDUCATION

Several scholars have done comprehensive reviews of institutional attempts to prepare teachers for diverse classroom settings (see, for example, Gollnick, 1991; Grant and Secada, 1990; Ladson-Billings, 1995; Zeichner, 1992). The Commission on Multicultural Education (1978), working under the auspices of the American Association of Colleges of Teacher Education (AACTE), surveyed 786 member institutions in 1977. Four hundred and forty institutions responded to the survey, which attempted to determine whether some aspect of multicultural or bilingual education was included in foundations or methods courses. According to the directory the commission put together, forty-eight of the fifty states and the District of Columbia had at least one institution that offered a multicultural education course, major, or minor or a multicultural component within the foundations or methods courses.

The commission's survey was useful in describing the breadth of multicultural teacher education efforts, but it failed to provide any indication of the quality of these programs. This early work helped to influence the National Council for Accreditation of Teacher Education's (NCATE) attempt at developing standards to examine more systematically how teacher preparation programs addressed the multicultural education of its prospective teachers (Gollnick, 1991). In 1979 NCATE began requiring those institutions applying for accreditation to "show evidence of planning for multicultural education" (Gollnick, 1991, p. 226). By 1981 NCATE expected these institutions to provided this planned-for multicultural education. The first NCATE multicultural education standard stated in part:

> Provisions should be made for instruction in multicultural education in teacher education programs. Multicultural education should receive attention in courses, seminars, directed readings, laboratory and clinical experiences, practicum, and other types of field experiences [NCATE, 1982, p. 14].

In its 1990 revision of the accreditation standards, NCATE dropped the separate multicultural standard and integrated multicultural components into four different standards: the standard on professional studies, the standard on field-based and clinical experiences, the standards on student admission into professional education, and the standard on faculty qualifications and assignments.

Gollnick (1991) reported that "in its review of the first 59 institutions seeking accreditation under the current NCATE standards, NCATE found only 8 [13.6 percent] of the institutions in full compliance with [the] multicultural education requirements" (p. 234). Two of the most intractable areas of weakness seem to be institutions' inability to attract and retain a culturally diverse student body and the absence of culturally diverse faculty.

I have searched the ERIC database using the descriptors *diversity, multicultural education,* and *teacher education* for the period 1981 through 1993.[2] The search generated 209 entries, 68 of which seemed directly relevant to this investigation. Among the reasons some entries were deemed inappropriate for this discussion were the generic use of the term *diversity* (as meaning "variety" rather than "ethnic or cultural difference"), their emphasis on preparing college teachers or teaching assistants, or their focus primarily on special education or a particular subject matter discipline (not on preparing teachers for teaching culturally diverse students). Closer examination revealed that twenty-five (approximately 38 percent) of the relevant documents were data driven based on actual groups of prospective students, programs, courses, or short-term interventions. The remainder of the documents were opinion papers in which authors discussed needs, perceptions, and theoretical considerations surrounding multicultural teacher education.

Course Descriptions

Three of the "data-based" documents were course descriptions. Martin and Koppelman (1991) described a required human relations course for teacher education candidates designed to heighten prospective teachers' sensitivities to issues of diversity. The authors asserted that the course did have a positive impact on teachers' reported attitudes. Piscitelli (1990) described a ten-session inservice teacher education course designed to address the problems of content-area teachers in teaching limited-English-proficient (LEP) students. The author suggested that teachers who participated in the course were more successful than other colleagues in mainstreaming LEP students into regular course work. Cornelius (1990) described a course at New Mexico State University designed to provide prospective teachers with on-site visits to early childhood classrooms in Juarez, Mexico. The purpose of these visits was to compare and contrast classroom settings and share ideas with Mexican teachers.

Program Descriptions

Nine of the data-based entries were program descriptions. Here authors attempted to describe how foundations courses, methods courses, and field experiences were organized to reflect a general philosophical orientation toward preparing teachers for diverse classrooms (Baez and Clarke, 1990; Biddle and Lasley, 1991; Book, 1983; Clemson, 1990; Eppenauer and Smith, 1990; Ladson-Billings, 1991a, 1991b; Nava, 1990; Wheeler, 1990). Some of this work looked at programs that provided prospective teachers with international experiences so that they could understand difference and diversity as "normal" occurrences (Nava, 1990; Wheeler, 1990). Others looked at how courses that developed within a program structure oriented toward equity and social justice might elevate the intellectual rigor and discourse in "multicultural methods" courses (Ladson-Billings, 1991a, 1991b). Clemson (1990) described program change at the state level that involved colleges and universities, local schools, and state agencies. This collaboration featured more attention to issues of preparing teachers for culturally diverse schools and classrooms. Biddle and Lasley (1991), Book (1983), and Eppenauer and Smith (1990) all described university-based restructuring efforts to reorient prospective teachers toward the challenges of preparing to teach in culturally diverse, urban settings. Finally, Baez and Clarke (1990) reported on a community college program designed to help urban students begin the first steps toward teacher certification.

Surveys, Interviews, Questionnaires, and Tests

Ten of the data-based entries fell into this category. Although there were differences in methodological approaches and perspectives, this category in general contained studies that assessed prospective teachers regarding their multicultural knowledge, skills, abilities, and attitudes on entry into teacher education or completion of the teacher certification program, or both.

Larke (1990) assessed the cultural sensitivity of fifty-one female white and Mexican American elementary preservice teachers after they had completed a multicultural education course. The study's results indicated that one course was insufficient to change student attitudes toward diverse students. Most of the students preferred to work with students from white, middle-income communities. Hadaway and Florez (1988) discovered similar results among 125 preservice teacher education students.

Cooper (1990) used self-assessment questionnaires to compare student teachers working in Minnesota and Texas in an effort to identify connections between cross-cultural experiences and attitudes toward multicultural teaching. The study found that Texas students were more willing to demonstrate multicultural competence while Minnesota students were less willing. Heger and Engelhart (1991) described an effort to prepare candidates of color for two state tests that regularly screen such candidates out of teacher preparation programs. Both tests are aimed at sharpening students' college mathematics skills. According to Fields (1988) this kind of preparatory effort is necessary since test results of prospective teachers in nineteen states documented the failure of nearly thirty-eight thousand minority candidates.

Zimpher (1989) conducted one of the few longitudinal studies uncovered in this search. This study examined the perceptions of between 729 and 1,141 preservice teachers to develop an overall profile of the nation's teaching force. The last three years of the study indicated that students entering the teaching profession are relatively homogeneous in race, ethnicity, socioeconomic status, cultural experiences, and perceptions about cultural diversity. Sleeter (1989) surveyed 416 novice teachers in Wisconsin who had previously taken multi-cultural education training to determine how much of it they implemented in their classrooms. She found that the teachers' implementation of multicultural education varied by grade level and subject area. Elementary teachers more often reported having used multicultural materials and information in their classrooms than secondary teachers did. Teachers of literature and art used multicultural education materials more frequently than teachers of mathematics and science did. Indeed, mathematics teachers were more likely to regard multicultural education as irrelevant to their subject areas. Teachers were more likely to report that they included materials and information on women than on racial and ethnic groups. Physical educators almost exclusively focused on gender. Almost no materials and information were presented on social class.

Paine (1990) drew on the baseline data from the National Center for Research on Teacher Education to examine the approaches to learner diversity held by prospective teachers participating in five U.S. teacher education programs. The teachers appeared to value ideals of equality and fairness but had difficulty envisioning concrete pedagogical means toward supporting these values.

AACTE (1990) received 685 usable surveys from schools, colleges, and departments of education to identify the numbers of students in the teacher education pipeline by race and ethnicity. This response of approximately 57 percent indicates that the proportion of students of color entering teacher education program continues to be much lower than that of whites.

Olsen and Mullen (1990) conducted in-depth interviews of thirty-six California teachers to determine their perceptions of the challenges of teaching in diverse classrooms. The teachers suggested the need for the following conditions for creating effective teaching and learning in diverse classrooms: supportive leadership, collegiality among teachers, opportunities for interaction and coordination, new curriculum development and materials development, strong support services for students and families, small class sizes, school structures that promote integration, and policies that set a tone of support for diversity.

Experiments and Interventions

Only three of the usable entries from this search reflected attempts at educational experiments or interventions. Similar to Nava (1990), Mahan and Stachowski (1990) examined the effects of international experiences on prospective teachers. However, Mahan and Stachowski compared the experiences of the student teachers who participated in teacher preparation overseas with their colleagues who remained in U.S.–based programs. Students who were prepared overseas acquired more cross-cultural learnings than their counterparts did, exhibited broader perspectives in the content of their learnings, and acknowledged a greater variety of learning sources.

Grottkau and Nickolai-Mays (1989) conducted an empirical analysis of fifty-one education majors to determine the extent to which exposure to ongoing multicultural education experiences can change or reduce bias toward diverse groups. As contrasted with a control group of seventy-one college students who had not taken any multicultural education courses, the education majors demonstrated that prolonged exposure to cultural diversity can produce attitude changes in teacher education students.

McDiarmid and Price (1990) used data from pre- and postprogram questionnaires and interviews to describe the views of seventeen student teachers from five Michigan universities toward culturally diverse learners. The intervention was a three-day workshop intended to influence their views. The study found that the multicultural presentations had little effect on students' beliefs about the capabilities of learners, the use of stereotypes in making teaching decisions, or providing genuinely equal opportunities to learn challenging and empowering subject matter.

CONSENSUS FINDINGS ABOUT MULTICULTURAL TEACHER EDUCATION

Although much of the literature on multicultural teacher education remains fragmented, conceptually weak (Ladson-Billings, 1995), and methodologically flawed (Grant and Secada, 1990), there are some general consensus issues to be considered from those studies that have been carefully crafted. In general, those issues fall into the categories of student characteristics and program admissions procedures, homogeneity among teacher educators, student resistance to issues of diversity, cooperating teachers, and institutional commitment.

Student Characteristics and Program Admissions Procedures

Although separate issues, student characteristics and program admissions procedures are closely related. Hodge (1990), Grant (1989), Haberman (1989), and others document that "culturally encapsulated" (Zeichner, 1992, p. 4) groups of white students continue to be prepared by teacher education programs as if they will be teaching in homogeneous, white, middle-income schools. The data also indicate that most of these prospective teachers would rather not teach in diverse school settings. Although we know that prospective teachers would prefer not to teach the students who need to be taught in the nation's public schools, admission procedures continue to admit the same type of prospective teachers and screen out others (Fields, 1988).

Calls for attracting the best and brightest to teaching (Holmes Group, 1986; Carnegie, 1986) have focused on student grade point averages and standardized test scores. Rarely have they addressed student attitudes toward working with culturally and linguistically diverse students. However, Haberman (1991a, 1991b, 1995a) has written convincingly about the need to prepare "adults" who are "decent" for teaching in urban settings. According to Haberman (1995b), what constitutes the best and the brightest urban school teachers may look very different from what admissions policies and procedures demand. For example, the best and brightest urban schoolteachers are likely to have experienced living conditions similar to those of their students and are likely to have chosen to teach in urban settings. They may or may not have the highest grade point averages.

Currently teacher education programs throughout the nation are faced with demands to improve and ensure the quality of teacher education candidates. These demands are typically met by requiring more admissions tests with more stringent passing scores. Students who have best been served by the current education system continue to produce the best scores on these measures. Tests such as the Pre-Professional Skills Test (PPST), which is used throughout the nation, and the California Basic Education Skills Test (CBEST), which is used in California and Oregon, continue to screen out potential teachers of color. In addition states that test in-service teachers for recertification and relicensing find the greatest failure rate among teachers of color (Fields, 1988).

Homogeneity and Teacher Educators

Teacher educators are reluctant to address their own culpability in reproducing teachers who cannot (and will not) effectively teach diverse learners. Teacher educators overwhelmingly are white and male (Grant and Gillette, 1987). Ducharme and Agne (1989) found the education professoriat to be predominantly male: 65 percent to 35 percent female. But more severe than the gender distribution is the racial and cultural one:

> Minorities are much less represented in the education professoriat than are women. In the RATE study, 2.9 percent of the full professors are minority; 6.4 percent at the associate level; and 9.9 percent at the assistant professor level. The representation of minorities appears to be growing, but the growth may be short lived inasmuch as these institutions showed a total of only 8 percent minorities in doctoral programs [Zimpher, 1989, p. 75].

This dominance of white males on the faculties of departments, schools, and colleges of education is commensurate with their representation across college and university schools and departments (Howey and Zimpher, 1990). Teacher educators' own experiences with diverse others is limited. How can they teach what they themselves do not know? Teacher educators of color who have written about their experiences (King and Ladson-Billings, 1990; Hollins, 1990) describe students' initial shock and discomfort at having their first nonwhite teacher. Students' lack of experience in day-to-day interactions with people of color and in settings where people of color are in positions of authority over them can produce an interesting dynamic.

First, students' stereotypical beliefs about students of color may be mapped on to teachers of color. Their beliefs about the intellectual and character inferiorities of students of color may manifest themselves in their beliefs about and attitudes toward professors of color.[3] Second, students may perceive teachers of color as the very exceptions who prove that the system works, and if the masses of people would just work hard too, all could advance. Third, and a seeming contradiction to the second point, students may perceive teachers of color as exceptions in that they are not at all like the masses of people of color, thus bestowing on them the status of "honorary white person."[4] These scholars' ability to "separate" themselves from the masses of people of color is perceived to be instrumental in allowing them to succeed.

The challenge that teacher educators face is preparing students to do what they themselves do not have to do or may not be able to do. Most teacher educators teach in the rarefied environment of a white academy. Most of their students are white, with middle-class orientations. They teach people who have demonstrated their ability to learn in fairly conventional ways. If teacher educators believe their responsibilities lie solely with subject areas (mathematics education and social studies education, for example), they may feel that student teaching supervisors, cooperating teachers, or specially designed courses bear the major responsibility for helping students address issues of diversity.

Student Resistance to Issues of Diversity

Even when teacher educators assume responsibilities for helping to prepare prospective teachers to teach diverse learners effectively, these efforts may be met with resistance. Ahlquist (1991) notes that "teaching from an antiracist perspective often generates resistance" (p. 166), and King (1991) argues that prospective teachers are "dysconscious" in their racism. She refers to dysconsciousness as "an uncritical habit of mind (including perceptions, attitudes, assumptions, and beliefs) that justifies inequity and exploitation by accepting the existing order of things as given" (p. 135). King further asserts that "dysconscious racism is a form of racism that tacitly accepts dominant white norms and privileges" (p. 135).

Thus, teacher educators who want to teach students about inequity teach against the grain. Their work runs counter to the beliefs, attitudes, perceptions, and perspectives of most of their students. Students finds ways to minimize the impact of teacher educators who teach against the grain by challenging the legitimacy of their subject matter, their authority, and their credentials. Rothenberg (1988) pointed out that when she attempted to integrate issues of race, class, and gender into her courses, students both resisted and discounted the information. Ultimately, she concluded, one course has little or no impact on students' views of race, class, or gender because they often stand out as outliers or anomalies, which can easily be refuted with the volumes of counter-knowledge offered in other courses.

Cooperating Teachers

Hollins (1995) states that prospective teachers consistently cite the student teaching or practicum experience as the most significant part of the teacher preparation program. They often regard both their foundations and methods courses as meaningless and irrelevant to the task of teaching. The most significant person in the field experience appears to be the cooperating teacher (Hollins, 1995). Of course, cooperating teachers reflect some of the same problems of inadequate preparation for teaching diverse students as do student teachers and teacher educators. Hollins's (1995) work indicated that although prospective teachers hold their cooperating teachers and their field experiences in high regard, they rarely are prepared to analyze and critique either. To assist with the abilities of prospective teachers to understand and critique the field experience, Hollins (1990) argues that

> part of the teacher education curriculum should be aimed at re-socializing preservice teachers in ways that help them view themselves within a culturally diverse society. This could entail restructuring self-perceptions and world views. Part of designing appropriate experiences for preservice teachers is making meaningful connections between the students' personal/family histories and the social context of life as experienced by different groups within a culturally diverse society [pp. 202–203].

The need to help students and teachers recognize and interrogate their own culture is echoed by Banks (1991):

> Helping students understand their own cultural experience and to develop more clarified cultural and ethnic identifications is only the first step in helping them to better understand and relate to other ethnic and racial groups. They also need experiences that will enable them to learn about the values and attitudes they hold toward other ethnic and cultural groups, to clarify and analyze those values, to reflect upon the consequences of their values and attitudes, to consider alternative attitudes and values, and to personally confront some of their latent values and attitudes toward other races [p. 141].

Both Sleeter (1992) and Winfield (1986) have documented that in-service teachers may hold very negative attitudes toward the intellectual potential and abilities of students of color. Sleeter suggests that teachers have particular worldviews about how the society works that dictate the performance and possibilities of their students. If, for example, teachers believe that the society is a meritocracy where rewards are a direct result of the effort and hard work of individuals, students they perceive to be "lazy" or "unmotivated" are unlikely to do well in their classrooms.

Winfield (1986) has argued that in the case of students designated as at risk, teachers believe that students are either capable of improvement or merely maintained at a low level of achievement, and either the teachers are seen as responsible for that improvement or maintenance or they shift that responsibility. Only teachers who believe both that the students can improve and that improvement is their responsibility appear capable of effectively teaching diverse learners.

Unfortunately, most teacher education programs do not make fine distinctions between and among potential cooperating teachers. The need for cooperating teachers can be so great that any "warm body" will do. Some states require that prospective cooperating teachers take a course to prepare them for basic supervisory responsibilities. This course may or may not consider issues of teaching in cultural diverse settings. In addition, in schools with high numbers of African American, Latino, and American Indian students, there are likely to be more underqualified teachers (Oakes and Keating, 1988). Teacher shortages are greater and higher numbers of underqualified entrants to teaching are found in the inner city schools that most poor and racially and ethnically diverse students attend (Watson and Traylor, 1988). Thus, teacher education programs that include inner city, urban field experiences are more likely to place student teachers in classrooms with underqualified teachers where there is high degree of turnover.

So acute is the need for teachers in urban centers that many prospective teachers participate in nontraditional certification programs that provide no day-to-day exposure to cooperating teachers. These students serve as "interns," yet they have full classroom responsibilities throughout their training years (Gallegos, 1995). The positive aspect of this alternate certification route is that interns are not subjected to the negative beliefs and practices of poor cooperating teachers. The negative aspect is that they do not benefit from the knowledge, skills, and abilities of excellent cooperating teachers.

Alternate certification remains an untested way to reduce urban teacher shortages. States such as New Jersey and California have approved alternate teaching certification routes to attract college graduates, particularly those with training and expertise in mathematics, science, and second languages such as Spanish. Darling-Hammond (1994) has critiqued the widely publicized Teach for America (TFA) program for its failure to prepare prospective teachers adequately for urban classrooms:

It is clear from the evidence that TFA is bad policy and bad education. It is bad for the recruits because they are ill-prepared. They are denied the knowledge and skills they need, and many who might have become good teachers are instead discouraged from staying in the profession. It is bad for the schools in which they teach, because the recruits often create staffing disruptions and drains on school resources. The schools don't get the help they need, and more lasting solutions are not pursued. It is bad for the children because they are often poorly taught. With their teachers foundering, they are denied opportunities to fully develop the skills they need. They often lack continuity in instruction and are frequently exposed to counterproductive teaching techniques that can destroy their inherent desire to learn [p. 33].

Institutional Commitment

Whether prospective teachers, teacher educators, and cooperating teachers have knowledge, skills, abilities, and dispositions that support effective teaching and learning in diverse school settings, a key ingredient in ensuring success in this endeavor is the institutional commitment of the university, as well as that of the school, college, or department of education. Current efforts toward downsizing and restructuring (Womack, 1995) often mean that issues of cultural diversity are given lower priority, if they are considered at all. More devastating than this institutional downsizing have been the current setbacks in affirmative action (Hilton, 1995) and scholarship (Bennett, 1995) support for students of color.

Working with students on issues of cultural diversity may require differential allocations of professors' course loads. If institutions are unprepared to make these adjustments, teacher educators are unlikely to take on more work, particularly more challenging work. In addition, institutional reward structures may work against teacher educators' attempts at providing culturally diverse experiences for prospective teachers. For example, teacher educators with expertise in dealing with issues of effective teaching in culturally diverse settings are in high demand. School districts, professional associations, community organizations, and other college campuses (as well as their own campuses) request their help in staff development and in-service programs (Zeichner, 1991). However, this kind of service typically is not as highly regarded as research and scholarship that is published in high-status professional journals. The competing demands of providing service and publishing are particularly salient for untenured faculty. And scholars of color are more represented among the ranks of junior faculty.

How institutions respond to issues such as increasing the diversity of their faculties, administrators, and student population, as well as the need to reexamine their curricula and course requirements, campus climate, and reward structures, all signal the level of commitment and value placed on cultural diversity. Teacher education cannot be the sole campus entity for dealing with diversity. Rather, teacher education efforts toward preparing prospective teachers for cultural diversity will be enhanced by clear and unwavering institutional commitment to these principles.

EXAMPLES OF MULTICULTURAL TEACHER EDUCATION

Shulman (1987), a leader in teacher education reform, argued persuasively for the use of case knowledge in teacher education. Drawing parallels between teaching and other professions such as medicine, law, and business, Shulman pointed to the need to accumulate much more detailed qualitative information about what transpires in classrooms in order to build a more reliable knowledge base. When we have better understandings about the nature of classrooms—what teachers do, how and why they do what they do—we are more likely to prepare prospective teachers effectively for the realities of the classroom. A similar need for knowledge and understandings about teacher education programs exists, particularly teacher education programs that successfully prepare prospective teachers for diverse classrooms.

Here we look at five teacher education programs that attempt to prepare prospective teachers for diversity. Two of these cases reflect my firsthand knowledge and experiences as a teacher educator and consequently are more fully elaborated. Two of the other cases have been documented in the teacher education literature.[5] The fifth case is an innovative alternative program designed by a consortium of colleges and universities to serve one urban district.[6]

Santa Clara University

Santa Clara University is a Jesuit school located in the midst of northern California's Silicon Valley. Although the area has large Latino and Asian-American communities, the university's approximately eight thousand students are overwhelmingly white and upper middle class. Tuition exceeds $12,000 a year, and most students pursue degrees in the university's highly regarded engineering and business schools.

Teacher education in California occurs at the postbaccalaureate level. The fifth-year program at Santa Clara, housed in the Division of Counseling Psychology and Education, is a small program, never serving more than thirty to thirty-five students a year. In the mid-1980s two African American women scholars who directed and coordinated the program took advantage of the institution's expressed social justice mission in order to restructure the program. Typically regarded as a curricular extra, social justice generally resided in community service activities loosely connected to course work or to ministries in Latin America directed by some of the Jesuits. The director and the coordinator of teacher education made changes in the program to make issues of cultural diversity and social justice the centerpieces of the program (King and Ladson-Billings, 1990).

Because of the relatively small size of the program, all applicants are interviewed by a team of university faculty and public school personnel. Students are asked to talk about their background and why they are choosing a career in teaching. Students also are asked to discuss their experiences with culturally diverse others. Although the interview is not used to exclude students, it does serve as a piece of confirmatory information to accompany the applicants' files. Program faculty are aware that given the youth and level of maturity of most applicants, their responses necessarily reflect naiveté and inexperience. However, the interview is designed to identify and screen out students with openly racist and dogmatic perspectives against difference.[7]

The hallmark of Santa Clara's program is the cultivation of "informed empathy." Rather than a sense of "sympathy," where well-meaning students "feel sorry for" or pity others, the program's goal is to help prospective teachers "feel with" people different from themselves from a position of knowledge and information about how both they and others come to occupy the social positions they do. Students admitted to the program must participate in a one-week immersion experience prior to the start of classes. The purpose of this experience is to place students in social settings different from any they have already encountered. By serving in soup kitchens, homeless shelters, and other facilities designed to serve poor and dispossessed individuals and families, students are challenged to see a fuller range of the human condition and begin a year-long questioning of social inequity. The immersion experience is systematically debriefed, and the students are helped to make connections to classroom situations.

Santa Clara uses a cohort approach to teacher education. Students begin the program together in the fall quarter with courses and complete the program at the end of spring quarter. Five of their courses are directly related to issues of diversity and social justice: social foundations of education, cross-cultural and interpersonal communication, curriculum foundations, reading in the content areas (which requires students to work one-on-one with a youth who is a nonreader and is awaiting adjudication of his or her case in the juvenile justice system), and a course in second-language acquisition.

Throughout the program students are engaged in a practical experience. During the fall and winter quarters students are assigned to a half-day practicum in local public schools. During the spring quarter students participate in full-day student teaching. California State Department of Education guidelines specify that at least one of these placements must occur in a community whose population is different from that of the prospective teacher. Santa Clara strives to ensure that two of those placements are in culturally, linguistically, and economically different settings. Because the Division of Counseling Psychology and Education does not offer doctoral degrees, there are no graduate students to serve as supervisors. Instead, faculty members and public school practitioners fulfill this role.

Subject matter pedagogy is taught in at least two different ways depending on whether students are seeking certification at the elementary (multiple subjects) or secondary (single subjects) levels. Elementary students are presumed to be knowledgeable about basic elementary subject areas by virtue of their undergraduate training. The appropriate undergraduate major for elementary teacher candidates is liberal studies—preteaching. This major is divided into four broad areas: English language and communication, natural sciences (including mathematics), social sciences, and fine arts. These areas are compatible with the general knowledge section of the National Teachers Examination (NTE), which students who do not have the appropriate major must pass in order to complete the certification program. The curriculum foundations course serves as an integrated methods course where students are required to develop lesson and unit plans. Students also attend a directed teaching seminar where additional aspects of pedagogy are demonstrated and discussed.

Secondary students must have an approved undergraduate major before they are admitted to the program. The state's Commission on Teacher Credentialing (CTC) determines what courses are appropriate for each major. Thus, for example, an English major without requisite courses in writing, literature, and grammar may need to take additional course work before being admitted. However, as with elementary-level students, secondary students may take the designated NTE, such as English, mathematics, or life sciences, in lieu of an approved undergraduate major.[8]

Single-subject or secondary-level students also take a curriculum foundations course. However, because of the size of the program (typically between ten and twelve secondary students), each secondary student is assigned a faculty mentor in the College of Arts and Sciences. Thus, a student preparing to teach secondary mathematics is assigned to a math professor with whom to explore issues of secondary school mathematics pedagogy. Each secondary mentor is approved by the CTC. The secondary subject area mentor works in combination with the curriculum foundations teacher to develop subject-matter-appropriate experiences and assignments for the student. The secondary mentor also serves as a supervisor during student teaching. This allows for some continuity between curriculum and instruction. An aspect of the secondary curriculum course and directed teaching seminar is the use of a modified microteaching[9] experience. Here, students develop short lessons, ten to fifteen minutes long, that demonstrate their ability to teach a concept or skill. Students are required to teach both teacher-centered lessons (for example, minilecture, demonstration, experiment, explanation) and student-centered lessons (such as cooperative learning, discovery learning, inquiry-based learning). In each microteaching session, students are required to demonstrate how what they are teaching addresses the needs of diverse students. Some students may explain how the lesson may be adapted for students whose native language is not English. Others demonstrate adaptations for special needs students. Still others suggest ways that students' home culture can be used as a resource for learning. During the analyses of the microteaching, students are encouraged to think about different ways that teaching might take place in diverse settings.

The Santa Clara University teacher education program fully recognizes that a good portion of its students have never attended public schools and may have narrow conceptions of what it means to be a teacher now. By emphasizing equity and diversity issues, Santa Clara attempts to prepare students for teaching in the diverse classrooms of the San Francisco Bay Area and the Santa Clara Valley, in particular, and throughout the state of California, in general. Graduate follow-up surveys indicate that school administrators regard Santa Clara graduates highly.[10] Recent personnel changes may bring a shift in the focus in the Santa Clara program. However, most of the attention it has received in the teacher education literature has been as a result of its commitment to equity, diversity, and social justice.[11]

University of Alaska–Fairbanks

The challenge for teacher preparation programs in Alaska is an issue of both diversity and location. Although urban issues in Alaska mirror those throughout the rest of the country, most of Alaska comprises small, rural villages of between one hundred and three hundred American Indian or Alaskan Native peoples. Most of these villages maintain their own languages and cultural traditions. Because the population often is sparse in many regions, one teacher may be required to teach all of the children, K–12, in a village. The severe weather and poor road conditions mean that schools must be creative in the delivery of educational services. Correspondence programs are used extensively.

Because of these conditions, rural Alaska faces a high teacher turnover rate. Most teachers stay in the small community schools two years or less (Nelson-Barber and Mitchell, 1992). Most of the teachers who do not stay in the rural schools are non-Alaskan transplants from urban areas in the lower forty-eight states who come to Alaska with little preparation for the vast differences in language, culture, and lifestyle they will encounter.

The University of Alaska–Fairbanks has taken a two-pronged approach to meeting the needs of a diverse, diffuse rural state. One response is the Cross-Cultural Educational Development Program, which trains native teachers on-site in their communities (Barnhardt, 1982). As might be expected, only a small percentage of the Alaskan teaching force is composed of native teachers. Thus, the program seeks to help native teachers become fully credentialed and also to become educational leaders in their communities and serve as "culture brokers" between the school and the community.

The Teachers for Rural Alaska Program is designed to prepare nonnative and non-Alaskan teachers for culturally diverse rural classrooms. According to Kleinfeld and Noordhoff (1988, p. 3), "These schools demand highly competent faculty—teachers who can teach a wide range of academic subjects to high school students of enormously varied achievement levels and teachers who can create trust between the public school and a minority community wary of the western cultural domination that the school symbolizes."

A central aspect of the Teachers for Rural Alaska Program is the development of reflective and self-critical teachers. Philosophically the program believes that for teachers to be effective in diverse classrooms, they must have clear understandings of classroom decisions and actions. To assist in the implementation of this philosophy, the program has a strong community immersion component and a systematic use of teaching portfolios to assess prospective teachers.

University of Texas–Pan American

The University of Texas–Pan American (UTPA) is located close to the U.S.–Mexican border and boasts the country's largest bilingual, Latino student body. Unlike Santa Clara, which serves an affluent student body, UTPA is located in an economically depressed area, and its students generally represent the first generation of students to attend a college or university. UTPA's students, economically disadvantaged and linguistically diverse, often come to campus educationally underprepared for the challenges of university study.

UTPA has an open admissions policy, allowing any student with a high school diploma to enroll. The teacher education program requires that students have at least a 2.0 grade point average and the state-required minimum scores on the Pre-Professional Skills Test (PPST). Although UTPA has had one of the largest bilingual-bicultural teacher education programs in the United States, current legislative actions by the Texas state government have drastically curtailed the enrollment and graduation of prospective Latino teachers. To ensure that the state's mandates are not the only measures by which teaching competence is determined, UTPA is working to develop documentation strategies that include knowledge about community context and about cultural and linguistic diversity in its standards for teacher education.

Like the University of Alaska–Fairbanks, UTPA is working to employ an instructor-designed system for prospective teachers. Because of its participation in the Stanford Teacher Assessment Project (Nelson-Barber and Mitchell, 1992), it is likely that this system will use some form of portfolio assessment as a mechanism to provide documentation of teacher competence and illustrate for prospective employers the range of skills and competence UTPA graduates demonstrate.

University of Wisconsin–Madison

A large land grant university serving forty thousand students, the University of Wisconsin–Madison (UW) is perennially rated among the nation's top research institutions. Its school of education is rated among the top five for scholarly productivity and the quality of its graduates. Teacher education is one of the university's most popular majors. Because of the high demand of the major, the Department of Curriculum and Instruction, which administers the teacher education program, is highly selective in its admissions process. Although the entire elementary education program is grounded in a philosophy of social reconstruction (Zeichner, 1991), both the size and complexity of the elementary program caused a group of faculty to reconsider how to ensure that students are well prepared to teach diverse students.[12]

Beginning in the summer of 1994 UW initiated its Teach for Diversity (TFD) master's degree with elementary certification program. Unlike the other programs already examined here, this program was designed purposely to attract people committed to principles of equity and diversity who do not have a background in education. Students admitted to TFD must possess a bachelor's degree in a "teachable major or minor" (English, mathematics, history, life sciences, physical sciences), have a 3.0 grade point average on the last sixty undergraduate credits (or take the Graduate Record Examination), and submit a statement of purpose and three letters of recommendation from former college or university professors and/or employers. The applicants' statements of purpose and letters of recommendation are reviewed by an admissions committee of approximately twenty UW faculty and teachers from local public schools. The admissions committee recommendations help determine the cohort participants.[13]

TFD is a fifteen-month elementary certification program where prospective teachers begin to understand what it means to teach diverse learners by starting in the community. The experience consists of an initial summer session, fall semester, spring semester, and a final summer session. The first summer experience requires a six-week assignment in a community-based agency or neighborhood center, Salvation Army Day Camp, city-sponsored day camps, or enrichment programs. In addition to spending ten to twelve hours per week in a community placement, the students take two courses, (1) Teaching and Diversity and (2) Culture, Curriculum, and Learning. Students also take an eight-week seminar to process and debrief their community placement experiences.

During fall semester students are placed in one of three elementary school placements, where they spend the entire school year.[14] During this first semester of practicum, students are in their school sites for three days each school week, and they attend three integrated methods courses the other two days. A seminar also supports the practicum.[15] Students are required to develop a community service project during this semester also. In the spring semester students begin student teaching. Although they remain in the same school the entire year, the student teaching may occur in a classroom other than that of the practicum. Course work includes a state-required course in inclusive schooling and the on-going field experiences seminar. In the final summer of the program students enroll in courses entitled School and Society, and Child Development. These courses are taught by faculty in the School of Education's Educational Policy Studies and Educational Psychology departments, respectively. During this final summer students complete and defend their master's papers.

The truncated nature of the TFD program means that a few themes are emphasized and repeated throughout the preparation year. One such theme is that schools are community entities and teachers must understand the communities in which they teach. Another theme is that learning teaching methods is less important perhaps than learning to develop a "humanizing pedagogy" (Bartolome, 1994). A third theme is that teaching is an "unfinished" profession. Truly excellent teachers of diverse learners constantly work on their practice, looking for new and better ways to enhance learning. A fourth theme is that self-reflection is an important skill for teacher development. A theme of the entire TFD program is that we are all learners. The program faculty, administrators, cooperating teachers, faculty associates, and students are all part of an exciting experiment.

Pedagogical competence is accomplished in a variety of ways in TFD. The cohort nature of the program means that students' experiences vary depending on their placements. At least two kinds of placement experiences currently exist. In two of the school sites, student teachers are supervised by university faculty and graduate students who are experienced teachers. The university-based supervision includes two days per week when supervisors are in the school to observe students, confer with them and their cooperating teachers, and conduct the weekly seminar. At one of the schools, the university has entered into an agreement with the school district to pay a portion of the salary of one of the teachers who is released from classroom teaching to serve as an in-school supervisor. The in-school supervisor and a university faculty member conduct the weekly seminar.

The weekly seminar in both types of supervisory arrangements in the program is designed to develop the pedagogical skills of the cohort members. No cohort is larger than eight students, and each cohort has two supervisors. One feature of the seminar is the opportunity to have participants "tell teaching stories" (Gomez and Tabachnick, 1992). Here students talk about what worked for them in their attempts to teach and what did not. The cohort members support their members by acting as critical friends to each other. Students are encouraged to rethink and reteach unsuccessful lessons, skills, and concepts. The cooperating teacher plays a critical role in developing the prospective teachers' pedagogical competence. Lesson ideas, plans, and units must first be approved by the cooperating teacher, who also serves as a member of the students' supervisory team. The other team members are the university supervisors, the cooperating teacher, and a student teaching peer. This arrangement allows for students' teaching performance to be witnessed by multiple sets of eyes.

In the two cohorts that do not have in-school supervision, students are required to create a videotape of their teaching, which they share in the seminar. During the seminar students view and analyze each others' practice, asking questions about what, how, and why students teach. This opportunity to see oneself in pedagogical action has proved valuable for experienced as well as novice teachers. To be able to see oneself in the presence of others who are engaged in the same practice seems to be useful in eliciting meaningful discussion about how decision making and action work together in teaching (Ladson-Billings, 1994).

Another place where students develop their pedagogical competence is in the integrated methods courses. Here students must learn how to make connections and linkages between and among a variety of subject areas. This notion of integration is prevalent in current thinking about best practices in elementary education. Thus, students must learn how to use a piece of literature in a variety of ways. Instead of merely reading a story about pigs, students may learn about pig farming and the biology that explains a pig's anatomy and life systems, and calculate the profit being made in pork bellies on the commodities market. This use of knowledge in varied and increasingly sophisticated ways means that teachers will need to understand the deep structures of the content they teach.

TFD is expensive; it requires full faculty members as well as graduate students to teach and supervise. The program has been granted a three-year waiver to suspend many of the Department of Public Instruction's (DPI) rules. Whether the university continues the financial resources and institutional support and the DPI allows the continued alternate preparation will determine the viability of TFD for subsequent years.

Because TFD is in its infancy, little evaluation data have been collected to date. What information the program does have is anecdotal and impressionistic. The attrition rate is high. In the first cohort of twenty-one students, four failed to complete the teacher certification program. Five of the students did not complete the master's paper by the end of the second summer. In the second cohort one student withdrew after the first four-week summer course. A second student withdrew at the end of the second four-week summer course. Three students were not permitted to student teach. The program does not assume that the high attrition rate is a "bad" thing. Rather, program faculty understand the need to evaluate student performance carefully and discourage students who are not developing requisite teaching competencies.

By the end of the program TFD students are expected to have designed, planned, and implemented lessons in a variety of subject areas. They are to have assumed responsibilities for two weeks of lead or solo teaching. This means a gradual assumption of responsibility by teaching individual half-days and full days. TFD students are expected to demonstrate the ability to manage a classroom (at least as well as other beginning teachers), assess student performance, and communicate well with other adults—cooperating teachers, other teachers, administrators, and parents.

Despite the high rate of attrition, TFD students appear to be in demand, at least in the local school district. Graduates from the first cohort who wanted to stay in the area have been able to find either full-time, part-time, and temporary (substitute) teaching in and around Madison. How well they perform is yet to be determined.

Teachers for Chicago

The Teachers for Chicago (TFC) program was created to develop talented cohorts of culturally diverse teachers for the Chicago public schools in shortage areas such as mathematics, science, and bilingual and special education. The collaborative group involved in TFC includes the Chicago public schools, the Chicago Teachers Union, the Council of Chicago Area Deans of Education (from nine public and private colleges and universities in the Chicago metropolitan area),[16] and the Golden Apple Foundation for Excellence in Teaching.

TFC is a graduate-level teacher education program that requires participants to apply for admission to both TFC and one of the participating colleges or universities. The participants must successfully complete the Urban Teacher Interview Selection Process developed by Haberman (1995a). Prospective teachers complete a preservice orientation session and begin university course work prior to assuming responsibility in the classroom. Next, they commit to completing all course work required for Illinois teacher certification and all course work necessary to obtain a master's degree.

The TFC participants are required to complete three consecutive summers of course work and two years of an internship. This internship provides the participants with a salary and health benefits for their teaching and a stipend to cover university tuition. Completion of the program comes with a guarantee of full-time employment as teachers in the Chicago public schools for at least two years.

School principals and the chair of the local school council[17] must apply to secure interns from TFC. Teams of four interns are assigned to schools where they work under the supervision of a mentor teacher. Mentor teachers must be fully certified and have a master's degree. The mentor's record of commitment to professional development must be evident, for example, through course work, workshops, and conference participation. Mentors have the opportunity to become adjunct faculty of the participating college or university and receive compensation or university tuition credits.

The schools that participate in TFC must have three full-time vacant teaching positions. In urban schools this is not an unusual situation. The schools also must be open to innovative teaching and learning strategies. The principal's role in participating schools includes demonstrating enthusiastic support, agreeing to host the program for at least two years, selecting mentor teachers, supporting program participants with training experiences, and conducting twice-yearly performance appraisals.

The colleges and universities involved in TFC must offer both master's degrees and teacher certification. Unlike the previously described programs, TFC is not located in one institution, and its participants do not constitute a cohesive cohort. Rather, the program participants are characterized by principals as mature, professional, enthusiastic, dedicated, and creative. Over three years TFC has shown steady growth from 80 interns in the first group (1992–1994) to 315 interns in the third group (1994–1996). TFC looks carefully at the recruitment and selection of talented, mature people as a way to increase the teaching force for one urban school district. It may serve as a model for other urban districts throughout the nation.

Matching the Case Data with the "Wisdom of Practice"

Once again we look to Shulman's (1987) notion of a reconsidered teacher education that calls on researchers to pull on the "wisdom of practice" found in exemplary teachers and detailed in skillfully crafted cases. He defined this wisdom of practice as "the maxims that guide (or provide reflective rationalization for) the practices of able teachers" (p. 11). In the cases we examined, faculty and program administrators pay close attention to admissions, not merely to increase full-time equivalency (FTE) but to ensure that prospective teachers are committed to teaching in diverse classrooms. These programs also highlight diversity as an integral part of the preparation—in course work, field experience, and seminars. These programs all have some teacher educators of color whose perspectives are important aspects of the preparation. These programs are different from some of the state alternative certification programs because they understand that teaching is a learned profession that requires coaching and support over time.

In Zeichner's (1992) comprehensive review of preparing teachers for diversity, he succinctly delineated the elements that are hallmarks or wisdom of practice of effective multicultural teacher education. Although these key elements (singularly and in various combinations) are mentioned in many studies, there is very little empirical evidence to support their validity. However, most of these elements are found in the cases described:[18]

- Admission procedures that screen students on the basis of cultural sensitivity and a commitment to the education of all students
- Development of a clearer sense of prospective teachers' sense of their ethnic and cultural identities

- Examination of prospective teachers' attitudes toward other ethnocultural groups
- Teaching about the dynamics of prejudice and racism and how to deal with them in the classroom
- Curriculum that addresses the histories and contributions of various ethnocultural groups
- Teaching that includes information about the characteristics and learning styles of various groups and individuals (and the limitations of such information)
- Curriculum that gives much attention to sociocultural research knowledge about the relationship among language, culture, and learning
- Teaching about various procedures by which prospective teachers can gain information about the communities represented in the classroom
- Teaching about how to assess the relationship between the methods teachers use in the classroom and the preferred learning and interaction styles in their students' homes and communities
- Teaching about how to use various instructional strategies and assessment procedures sensitive to cultural and linguistic variations and how to adapt classroom instruction and assessment to accommodate the cultural resources that students bring to school
- Exposure to examples of successful teaching of ethnic- and language-minority students
- Opportunities for complete community field experiences with adults and children of other ethnocultural groups with guided reflections
- Opportunities for practicum and/or student teaching experiences in schools serving ethnic- and language-minority students
- Opportunities to live and teach in a minority community (immersion)
- Instruction that is embedded in a group setting that provides both intellectual challenge and social support

IMPLICATIONS FOR RESEARCH AND CHANGE

How do we know that multicultural (teacher) education is even possible? Critics from the left (McCarthy, 1990; Olneck, 1990) raise serious doubts about the ability of multicultural education to address the structural inequality of the society. They argue that multicultural education is an accommodationist strategy that fails to effect any real change. Critics from the right (D'Souza, 1991; Schlesinger, 1991) believe that multicultural education is divisive and threatens

American core values. Between these two opposite positions, multicultural education treads an increasingly tenuous line toward social change. For example, Sleeter (1995) relates an anecdote in which an invitation to write cautioned her and her coauthor against an essay that did "not serve as a forum for attacking society" (p. 92) and urged that it be written in a "positive, nonjudgmental tone" (p. 92). Thus, it appears that some educators and policymakers want a form of multicultural education that does not challenge existing social arrangements.

Despite the changing demographics that make our public schools more culturally and linguistically diverse and the growing body of knowledge on issues of diversity and difference, multicultural teacher education continues to suffer from a thin, poorly developed, fragmented literature that provides an inaccurate picture of the kind of preparation teachers receive to teach in culturally diverse classrooms. The research needs are multiple; I identify just a few here:

- We need more accurate information about the number of multicultural teacher education programs in the nation's schools, colleges, and departments of education.

- We need accurate data about the nature of multicultural teacher education programs—for example, on how the programs are structured.

- We need information about admissions practices into multicultural teacher education programs.

- We need information about the cost of multicultural teacher education programs.

- We need information about the qualifications and experiences of teacher educators charged with the responsibility of preparing teachers for diverse classrooms.

- We need information about the specifics of courses, readings, assignments, and pedagogical strategies that work to prepare teachers for diverse classrooms.

- We need information about how to assess the effectiveness of multicultural teacher education programs.

In addition to increasing our knowledge base about multicultural teacher education, we need to recognize the cautionary flags that work against our ability to effect real change in teacher education. The message of the Holmes Group has not been lost on policymakers. Campuses across the nation are questioning the need for continuing teacher education at both the undergraduate and graduate levels. The cry for increased subject matter knowledge has the potential to override the plea for more and better professional knowledge about teaching diverse student populations effectively.

Low-income communities of color are justified in their outrage about the conditions and quality of education their children receive. However, a wholesale abandonment of public schooling through "choice" programs primarily serves the interests of white, middle- and upper-income families who almost always have "better" choices. The only way to enlist the support of communities of color is to guarantee them access to teachers who are well prepared to teach their children. Unless schools, colleges, and departments of education commit themselves to the finest education for all students, ultimately they serve no children. Unless we prepare teachers for diversity, we prepare them for (a career of) disaster.

Notes

1. Both of these examples were cited in Tyack (1974).

2. Although I used the ERIC database as the basis for this chapter, I also reviewed other well-known publications, such as Sleeter (1992) and Dilworth (1992).

3. Distinguished legal scholar Derrick Bell was once a visiting scholar at Stanford University Law School. The law school's white students were suspect of Professor Bell's abilities and approached the dean to "quietly" set up a series of lectures by white professors to ensure that they would not be "disadvantaged" by being in Bell's class (Bell, 1994).

4. Middle-class African American writers such as Ellis Cose (1993), Jill Nelson (1993), and Sara Lawrence-Lightfoot (1994) discuss the ways African American professionals are "granted" temporary whiteness but still suffer the pain of racism and discrimination.

5. I was a teacher educator at Santa Clara University, Santa Clara, California, and am currently a teacher educator at the University of Wisconsin–Madison. Teachers for Rural Alaska has been documented by Barnhardt (1982), Kleinfeld and Noordhoff (1988), and Nelson-Barber and Mitchell (1992). University of Texas–Pan American has been documented by Nelson-Barber and Mitchell (1992), and Pan American University–Valley Schools (1988).

6. See Gallegos (1995).

7. In one instance, a student consistently expressed what she saw as her "religious mission" in the public schools. She believed it was her responsibility to "Christianize the unsaved" who attended public schools. When interviewers explained that state and federal law prohibited such proselytizing, she stated that they were persecuting her because of her religious beliefs. She was not accepted into the program because of a lack of flexibility in her thinking. Another student was denied admission because he indicated throughout the interview that he was applying only because his parents wanted him to attend the university. He had failed at several other career endeavors and was in danger of being cut off financially by his parents.

8. It is important to note that passing the NTE is in conjunction with students' having had some course work in an area. California also allows prospective (and in-service) teachers to add credentials by passing an NTE in an area in which they have minored or believe they have sufficient knowledge to teach. This "secondary authorization" often is restrictive. For example, secondary authorization in mathematics typically means a teacher can teach lower-level mathematics courses, such as general math or a first course in algebra. It does not authorize the teacher to teach geometry, trigonometry, or calculus.

9. This modified microteaching differs from the work pioneered at Stanford University in the late 1960s. The Stanford work required students to teach to peers short content lessons, fifteen to twenty minutes in length, that were videotaped. At the end of the microteaching session, students viewed their videotaped lessons and analyzed their own and others' practice. At Santa Clara peer teaching was not always videotaped. However, there was self and peer analysis of the teaching.

10. The California State Department of Education requires that all approved credential programs conduct a follow-up of its graduates. Santa Clara sends questionnaires to the graduates, their administrators, and two of their colleagues. The follow-up includes a rating scale of each program component, as well as some open-ended questions. Informal follow-up by telephone calls and face-to-face meetings indicates that some of the students most resistant to the program's emphasis on equity and diversity issues feel that it has been most beneficial to them in their teaching.

11. The program's director, Joyce King, has become an associate vice provost at the University of New Orleans. I served as program coordinator and am currently on the faculty at the University of Wisconsin–Madison. However, the current program director, Sara Garcia, was hired initially as the coordinator because of her commitment to the program goals. There is no reason to believe she will not maintain and enhance the program goals.

12. Several UW faculty members—Carl Grant and Ken Zeichner, B. Robert Tabachnick and Mary Gomez, Marianne Bloch and Bob Tabachnick and Bob Tabachnick and Ken Zeichner—all have conducted small (twenty-five students or fewer) cohort programs whose primary focus has been preparing teachers for diverse classrooms. Each of these programs was developed within the existing teacher education structure.

13. The admissions committee does not have ultimate authority for selection because students also must be admitted to the graduate school. It is possible for a student to be rated highly by the faculty admissions committee and fail to meet graduate school criteria. Unfortunately, this has meant that several promising prospective teachers of color have not been able to be admitted to the program.

14. Schools have been preselected for participation in TFD because of their cultural and economic diversity and the willingness of at least one-third of their faculties to work with UW in a new collaboration that allows experienced teachers to support new professionals and rethink their own practice.

15. The ongoing teacher education program at UW also has practicum and student teaching seminars. However, these seminars are led by graduate students who serve as their supervisors. Teach for Diversity seminars are conducted by faculty members who also supervise the students and serve as faculty associates for the elementary schools. In their role as faculty associates, faculty members may serve as resource persons and professional development leaders for the school.

16. The participating colleges and universities are Chicago State University, Columbia College, Concordia University, DePaul University, Loyola University-Chicago, Northeastern Illinois University, Roosevelt University, Rosary College, and Saint Xavier University.

17. As a result of Chicago school reform, each school is governed by a local school council with a majority parent membership. These local school councils have the power to hire and fire principals and make decisions concerning the appropriation of discretionary funds.

18. I previously delineated these elements in another work on this topic (Ladson-Billings, 1995).

References

Ahlquist, R. "Position and Imposition: Power Relations in a Multicultural Foundations Class." *Journal of Negro Education*, 1991, *60*(2), 158–169.

American Association of Colleges of Teacher Education. *Teacher Education Pipeline II: Schools, Colleges, and Departments of Education Enrollments by Race and Ethnicity.* Washington, D.C.: Author, 1990.

Baez, T., and Clarke, E. "Reading, Writing, and Role Models." *Community, Technical, and Junior College Journal*, 1990, *60*(3), 31–34.

Banks, J. A. "Teaching Multicultural Literacy to Teachers." *Teaching Education*, 1991, *4*, 135–144.

Banks, J. A. "Multicultural Education: Historical Development, Dimensions and Practice." In J. A. Banks and C. M. Banks (eds.), *Handbook of Research on Multicultural Education.* New York: Macmillan, 1995.

Barnhardt, R. (ed.). *Cross-Cultural Issues in Alaskan Education.* Vol. 2. Fairbanks: Center for Cross-Cultural Studies, University of Alaska, 1982.

Bartolome, L. "Beyond the Methods Fetish: Toward a Humanizing Pedagogy." *Harvard Educational Review*, 1994, *64*(2), 173–193.

Bell, D. A. *Confronting Authority: Reflections of an Ardent Protestor.* Boston: Beacon Press, 1994.

Bennett, C. "Research on Racial Issues in American Higher Education." In J. A. Banks and C. M. Banks (eds.), *The Handbook of Research on Multicultural Education.* New York: Macmillan, 1995.

Bettelheim, B. "Teaching the Disadvantaged." *National Educational Association Journal,* 1965, *54,* 8–12.

Biddle, J., and Lasley, T. "Portfolios and the Process of Teacher Education." Paper presented at the annual meeting of the American Educational Research Association, Chicago, 1991.

Bloom, B., Davis, A., and Hess, R. *Compensatory Education for Cultural Deprivation.* New York: Holt, Rinehart and Winston, 1965.

Book, C. "Alternative Programs for Prospective Teachers: An Emphasis on Quality and Diversity." *Action in Teacher Education,* 1983, *5*(1–2), 57–62.

Brumberg, S. E. *Going to America, Going to School: The Jewish Immigrant Public School Encounter in Turn-of-the-Century New York City.* New York: Praeger, 1986.

Carnegie Task Force on Teaching as a Profession. *A Nation Prepared: Teachers for the 21st Century.* New York: Author, 1986.

Carson, C., Garrow, D., Harding, V., and Hine, D. C. (eds.). *Eyes on the Prize: America's Civil Rights Years.* New York: Penguin Books, 1987.

Clemson, S. "Four Models of Collaborative Teacher Education: A Comparison of Success Factors and Maturation." *Action in Teacher Education,* 1990, *12,* 31–37.

Cohen, R., and Mohl, R. *The Paradox of Progressive Education: The Gary Plan and Urban Schooling.* Port Washington, N.Y.: Kennikat, 1979.

Commission on Excellence in Education. *A Nation at Risk.* Washington, D.C.: Author, 1983.

Commission on Multicultural Education. *Directing Multicultural Education Programs in Teacher Education Institutions in the United States.* Washington, D.C.: American Association of Colleges of Teacher Education, 1978.

Cooper, A. "Preparing Teachers for Diversity: A Comparison of Student Teaching Experiences in Minnesota and South Texas." *Action in Teacher Education,* 1990, *12*(3), 1–4.

Cornelius, G. "A Border Issue in Teacher Training: Respecting the Diversity of Children." *Journal of Educational Issues of Language Minority Students,* 1990, *7,* 111–118.

Cose, E. *The Rage of a Privileged Class.* New York: HarperCollins, 1993.

Cuban, L. "Ethnic Content and 'White' Instruction." In J. A. Banks (ed.), *Teaching Ethnic Studies, 43rd Yearbook.* Washington, D.C.: National Council for the Social Studies, 1973.

Cuban, L. *How Teachers Taught: Constancy and Change in American Classrooms 1890–1980.* White Plains, N.Y.: Longman, 1984.

Cruse, H. *Plural But Equal.* New York: Morrow, 1987.

Daniels, L. A. (ed.). *The State of Black America: 1998.* Washington, D.C.: The National Urban League, 1998.

Darling-Hammond, L. "Who Will Speak for the Children? How 'Teach for America' Hurts Urban Schools and Students." *Phi Delta Kappan,* 1994, *76*(1), 21–34.

Darling-Hammond, L. "New Standards, Old Inequalities: The Current Challenge for African American Education." In L. A. Daniels (ed.), *The State of Black America: 1998.* Washington, D.C.: The National Urban League, 1998.

Dilworth, M. E. (ed.). *Diversity in Teacher Education: New Expectations.* San Francisco: Jossey-Bass, 1992.

D'Souza, D. *Illiberal Education: The Politics of Race and Sex on Campus.* New York: Free Press, 1991.

Ducharme, E., and Agne, R. "Professors of Education: Uneasy Residents of Academe." In R. Wisniewski and E. Ducharme (eds.), *The Professors of Teaching.* Albany, N.Y.: State University of New York Press, 1989.

Eppenauer, P. A., and Smith, W. C. "Redefining a Knowledge Base: A Proposal for Reform in an Urban Setting." Paper presented at the annual meeting of the American Association of Teachers and Educators, Las Vegas, Feb. 1990.

Fields, C. "Poor Test Scores Bar Many Minority Students from Teacher Training." *Chronicle of Higher Education,* 1988, *35*(10), A1, A32.

Fortune Magazine. Special Issue. "Saving Our Schools." Spring 1990.

Gallegos, B. "Teachers for Chicago." *Phi Delta Kappan,* 1995, *76*(10), 782–785.

Garcia, E. "Educating Mexican American Students: Past Treatment and Recent Developments in Theory, Research, Policy, and Practice." In J. A. Banks and C. M. Banks (Eds.), *Handbook of Research in Multicultural Education.* New York: Macmillan, 1995.

Gollnick, D. "Multicultural Education: Policies and Practices in Teacher Education." In C. A. Grant (ed.), *Research and Multicultural Education: From the Margins to the Mainstream.* Bristol, Pa.: Falmer Press, 1991.

Gomez, M., and Tabachnick, B. R. "Telling Teaching Stories." *Teaching Education,* 1992, *4,* 129–138.

Goodlad, J. "Common Schools for the Common Weal: Reconciling Self-Interest with the Common Good." In J. Goodlad and P. Keating (eds.), *Access to Knowledge: An Agenda for Our Nation's Schools.* New York: College Entrance Examination Board, 1990.

Grant, C. A. "Urban Teachers: Their New Colleagues and Curriculum." *Phi Delta Kappan,* 1989, *70,* 764–770.

Grant, C. A. (ed.). *Research and Multicultural Education: From the Margins to the Mainstream.* Bristol, Pa.: Falmer Press, 1992.

Grant, C. A., and Gillette, M. "The Holmes Report and Minorities in Education." *Social Education,* 1987, *51,* 517–521.

Grant, C. A., and Secada, W. "Preparing Teachers for Diversity." In W. R. Houston, M. Haberman, and J. Sikula (eds.), *Handbook of Research on Teacher Education.* New York: Macmillan, 1990.

Grottkau, B., and Nickolai-Mays, S. "An Empirical Analysis of a Multicultural Education Paradigm for Preservice Teachers." *Education Research Quarterly,* 1989, *13*(4), 27–33.

Haberman, M. "More Minority Teachers." *Phi Delta Kappan*, 1989, *70*, 771–779.

Haberman, M. "Can Cultural Awareness Be Taught in Teacher Education Programs?" *Teaching Education*, 1991a, *4*(1), 25–31.

Haberman, M. "The Rationale for Training Adults as Teachers." In C. Sleeter (ed.), *Empowerment Through Multicultural Education*. Albany, N.Y.: State University of New York Press, 1991b.

Haberman, M. *Star Teachers of Children in Poverty*. West Lafayette, Ind.: Kappa Delta Pi, 1995a.

Haberman, M. "The Meaning of the Best and Brightest in Urban Schools." *These Times*, Jan.–Feb. 1995b, 26–28.

Hadaway, N., and Florez, V. "Diversity in the Classroom: Are Teachers Prepared?" *Teacher Education and Practice*, 1988, *4*(1), 25–30.

Heger, H., and Engelhart, J. "Using Predictor Tests to Strengthen Ethnic Diversity in Teacher Education." *Teacher Education and Practice*, 1991, *6*(2), 69–70.

Hilton, K. O. "California Here We Don't Come." *Black Issues in Higher Education*, Aug. 24, 1995, pp. 12, 14–16.

Hodge, C. "Educators for a Truly Democratic System of Schooling." In J. Goodlad and P. Keating (eds.), *Access to Knowledge: An Agenda for Our Nation's Schools*. New York: College Board, 1990.

Hollins, E. R. "Debunking the Myth of a Monolithic White American Culture; Or Moving Toward Cultural Inclusion." *American Behavioral Scientist*, 1990, *34*(2), 201–209.

Hollins, E. R. "Research, Culture, Teacher Knowledge, and Development." Paper presented at the annual meeting of the American Educational Research Association, San Francisco, 1995.

Holmes Group Report. *Teachers for Tomorrow's Schools*. East Lansing, Mich.: Author, 1986.

Howey, K., and Zimpher, N. "Professors and Deans of Education." In W. R. Houston (ed.), *Handbook of Research on Teacher Education*. New York: Macmillan, 1990.

Irvine, J. *Black Students and School Failure*. Westport, Conn.: Greenwood Press, 1990.

Kennedy, M., Jung, R., and Orland, M. *Poverty, Achievement, and the Distribution of Compensatory Education Services*. An Interim Report from the National Assessment of Chapter I. Washington, D.C.: Government Printing Office, 1986.

King, J. "Dysconscious Racism: Ideology, Identity, and the Miseducation of Teachers." *Journal of Negro Education*, 1991, *60*(2), 133–146.

King, J., and Ladson-Billings, G. "The Teacher Education Challenge in Elite Universities: Developing Critical Perspectives for Teaching in a Democratic and Multicultural Society." *European Journal of Intercultural Studies*, 1990, *1*(2), 15–30.

Kleinfeld, J., and Noordhoff, K. *Final Report to the Office of Educational Research and Improvement, U.S. Department of Education*. Fairbanks: Teachers for Rural Alaska Program, University of Alaska, 1988.

Kunjufu, J. *Developing Discipline and Positive Self-Images in Black Children*. Chicago: Afro-American Images, 1984.

Ladson-Billings, G. "Beyond Multicultural Illiteracy." *Journal of Negro Education*, 1991a, *60*, 147–157.

Ladson-Billings, G. *When Difference Means Disaster: Reflections on a Teacher Education Strategy for Countering Student Resistance to Diversity*. Paper presented at the annual meeting of the American Educational Research Association, Chicago, 1991b.

Ladson-Billings, G. *The Dreamkeepers: Successful Teachers For African American Children*. San Francisco: Jossey-Bass, 1994.

Ladson-Billings, G. "Multicultural Teacher Education: Research, Practice, and Policy." In J. A. Banks and C. M. Banks (eds.). *Handbook of Research on Multicultural Education*. New York: Macmillan, 1995.

Larke, P. "Cultural Diversity Awareness Inventory: Assessing the Sensitivity of Preservice Teachers." *Action in Teacher Education*, 1990, *12*(3), 23–30.

Lawrence-Lightfoot, S. *I've Known Rivers*. New York: Penguin Books, 1994.

Mahan, J., and Stachowski, L. "New Horizons: Student Teaching Abroad to Enrich Understanding of Diversity." *Action in Teacher Education*, 1990, *12*(3), 13–21.

Martin, R., and Koppelman, K. "The Impact of a Human Relations/Multicultural Education Course on the Attitudes of Prospective Teachers." *Journal of Intergroup Relations*, 1991, *18*(1), 16–27.

McCarthy, C. *Race and Curriculum*. Bristol, Pa.: Falmer Press, 1990.

McDiarmid, G. W., and Price, J. *Prospective Teachers' Views of Diverse Learners: A Study of the Participants in the ABCD Project*. Research Report 90–6. East Lansing, Mich.: National Center for Research on Teacher Education, 1990.

National Council for the Accreditation of Teacher Education. *NCATE Standards For the Accreditation of Teacher Education*. Washington, D.C.: Author, 1982.

Nava, A. "Toward a Model in Applied Cross-Cultural Education: CSUN/Ensenada Teacher Institute." *Social Studies Review*, 1990, *29*(3), 77–79.

Nelson, J. *Volunteer Slavery*. Chicago: Noble, 1993.

Nelson-Barber, S., and Mitchell, J. "Restructuring for Diversity: Five Regional Portraits." In M. Dilworth (ed.), *Diversity in Teacher Education*. San Francisco: Jossey-Bass, 1992.

Oakes, J., and Keating, P. "Access to Knowledge: Breaking Down School Barriers to Learning." Unpublished manuscript, prepared for the Education Commission of the States, Denver, and the College Board, 1988.

Olneck, M. "The Recurring Dream: Symbolism and Ideology in Intercultural and Multicultural Education." *American Journal of Education*, 1990, *98*, 147–174.

Olneck, M. "Immigrants and Education." In J. A. Banks and C. M. Banks (eds.), *Handbook of Research on Multicultural Education*. New York: Macmillan, 1995.

Olsen, L., and Mullen, N. *Embracing Diversity: Teachers' Voices from California's Classrooms*. San Francisco: California Tomorrow, 1990.

Ornstein, A. "The Need for Research on Teaching the Disadvantaged." *Journal of Negro Education*, 1971, *40*, 133–139.

Ornstein, A., and Vairo, P. (eds.). *How to Teach Disadvantaged Youth*. New York: David McKay, 1968.

Paine, L. *Orientation Towards Diversity: What Do Prospective Teachers Bring?* Research Report 89–9. East Lansing, Mich.: National Center for Research on Teacher Education, 1990.

Pan American University–Valley Schools. *Pan American University—Valley Schools Consortium Operative Plan*. Edinburgh, Tex.: Author, 1988.

Piscitelli, C. D. "Development of an In-Service Course to Assist Subject-Matter Teachers in Addressing the Unique Needs of Students Having Limited English Proficiency." Paper submitted for doctoral practicum, Nova University, 1990.

Rothenberg, P. "Integrating the Study of Race, Gender, and Class: Some Preliminary Observations." *Feminist Teacher*, 1988, *3*(3), 37–42.

Schlesinger, A. *The Disuniting of America: Reflections on a Multicultural Society*. Nashville, Tenn.: Whittle Direct Books, 1991.

Shulman, L. "Knowledge and Teaching: Foundations of the New Reform." *Harvard Educational Review*, 1987, *57*(1), 1–22.

Sleeter, C. "Doing Multicultural Education Across Grade Levels and Subject Areas: A Case of Wisconsin." *Teaching and Teacher Education*, 1989, *5*, 189–203.

Sleeter, C. *Keepers of the American Dream: A Study of Staff Development and Multicultural Education*. Bristol, Pa.: Falmer Press, 1992.

Sleeter, C. "How White Teachers Construct Race." In C. McCarthy and W. Crichlow (eds.), *Race, Identity and Representation in Education*. New York: Routledge, 1993.

Sleeter, C. "An Analysis of the Critiques of Multicultural Education." In J. A. Banks and C. M. Banks (eds.), *Handbook of Research on Multicultural Education*. New York: Macmillan, 1995.

Spring, J. (1989). *American Education: An Introduction to Social and Political Aspects*. White Plains, N.Y.: Longman, 1989.

Takaki, R. *A Different Mirror: A Multicultural History of the United States*. Boston: Little, Brown, 1993.

Tyack, D. *The One Best System: A History of American Urban Education*. Cambridge, Mass.: Harvard University Press, 1974.

Watson, B. C., and Traylor, F. M. "Tomorrow's Teachers: Who Will They Be, What Will They Know?" In J. Dewart (ed.), *The State of Black America*. New York: Urban League, 1988.

Wheeler, A. "Internationalizing the Curriculum Through Cooperation, Collaboration, and Commitment." Paper presented at the annual conference of the National Council of States on Inservice Education, Orlando, Fla., 1990.

Wilson, W. J. "'Jobless Ghettos': The Impact of the Disappearance of Work in Segregated Neighborhoods." In L. A. Daniels (ed.), *The State of Black America: 1998.* Washington, D.C.: The Nation Urban League, 1998.

Winfield, L. "Teacher Beliefs Toward Academically At-Risk Students in Inner Urban Schools." *Urban Review,* 1986, *18*(4), 253–268.

Womack, A. "Relevancy of Research Showcased in Effort to Thwart Budget Ax." *Black Issues in Higher Education,* Aug. 10, 1995, pp. 10–11.

Zeichner, K. "Teacher Education for Social Responsibility." Paper presented at the annual meeting of the American Educational Research Association, Chicago, 1991.

Zeichner, K. *Educating Teachers for Cultural Diversity.* Special Report. East Lansing, Mich.: National Center for Research on Teacher Learning, 1992.

Zimpher, N. "The RATE Project: A Profile of Teacher Education Students." *Journal of Teacher Education,* 1989, *40,* 27–30.

Zinn, H. *A People's History of the United States.* New York: HarperCollins, 1980.

PART TWO

RETHINKING TEACHER PROFESSIONAL DEVELOPMENT

CHAPTER FIVE

The Essentials of Effective Professional Development

A New Consensus

Willis D. Hawley and Linda Valli

A n almost unprecedented consensus is emerging among researchers, professional development specialists, and key policymakers on ways to increase the knowledge and skills of educators substantially. This new consensus calls for providing collegial opportunities to learn that are linked to solving authentic problems defined by the gaps between goals for student achievement and actual student performance. Although key stakeholders share a common vision of professional development, this vision differs radically from current practice in most schools.

The implementation of the consensus model will require major changes in how professional development is delivered, how schools are structured, and the culture and belief systems that perpetuate conventional educational processes, as well as the low status of professional development among educational priorities. Pursuing or effectively implementing these changes is unlikely, however, unless the forces that led to the new consensus are understood. We briefly describe these forces and then outline the eight characteristics of essential professional development embodied in both research studies and national policy reports.

We thank our two reviewers, Thomas Guskey and Mark Smylie, for their insightful critiques of an earlier draft of this chapter.

CONVERGING DEVELOPMENTS

The new consensus model for professional development is the product of four converging developments:

1. Research on school improvement that links change to professional development

2. Growing agreement that students should be expected to achieve much higher standards of performance, which include a capacity for complex and collaborative problem solving

3. Research on learning and teaching that reaches substantially different conclusions about how people learn from those that have shaped contemporary strategies for instruction and assessment.

4. Research that confirms the widespread belief among educators that conventional strategies for professional development are ineffective and wasteful and that provides support for the adoption of different ways to facilitate professional learning

The Link Between Professional Development and Substantial School Improvement

Teachers influence student learning in numerous ways. On the basis of a comprehensive review of research on alternative explanations for student achievement conducted for the U.S. Department of Education in the mid-1980s, Hawley and Rosenholtz (1984, pp. 3, 7) concluded:

> In virtually every instance in which researchers have examined the factors that account for student performance, teachers prove to have a greater impact than program. This is true for average students and exceptional students, for normal classrooms and special classrooms.
>   . . . There is an enormous amount of evidence that teachers have a significant impact on efforts to change schools and on the nature of the students' experience, whatever the formal policies and curricula of a school or classroom might be.[1]

Teachers modify curricula, intentionally or not. They keep the gates through which students must pass to gain access to the learning resources available. Teachers allocate and manage the students' time, set and communicate standards and expectations for student performance, and in a multitude of other ways enhance or impede what students learn. It follows that the improvement of schools requires the improvement of teaching.

One of the most persistent findings from research on school improvement is, in fact, the symbiotic relation between professional development and school improvement efforts. (See, for example, Bryk, Rollow, and Pinnell, 1996; Elmore, 1992; Evertson and Murphy, 1992; Fullan, 1993; Guskey, 1995; Hodges, 1996; Pink and Hyde, 1992.) The two processes are so tightly woven that their effects are almost impossible to disentangle. Taking his lead from Seymour Sarason (1990), Smylie (1995) observes that "we will fail . . . to improve schooling for children until we acknowledge the importance of schools not only as places for teachers to work but also as places for teachers to learn" (p. 92). School improvement cannot occur apart from a closely connected culture of professional development. Conversely, professional development flounders without a supportive school environment. Simply put, "Staff development cannot be separated from school development" (Fullan, 1991, p. 331).

Reports calling for comprehensive reform and improvement of schools from professional groups, foundations, and advocacy groups have begun to recognize this relationship. In contrast with such reports published in the 1980s, more recent reports have given greater emphasis to professional development and its integral role in continuous school improvement (Commission on Chapter 1, 1992; Consortium on Productivity in the Schools, 1995; National Commission on Teaching and America's Future, 1996; National Education Association, 1995). They essentially agree with the conclusion of the American Federation of Teachers (1995) that

> without professional development school reform will not happen. . . . The nation
> can adopt rigorous standards, set forth a visionary scenario, compile the best
> research about how students learn, change the nature of textbooks and assess-
> ment, promote teaching strategies that have been successful with a wide range
> of students, and change all the other elements involved in systemic reform. But,
> unless the classroom teacher understands and is committed to the plan and
> knows how to make it happen, the dream will come to naught [pp. 1–2].

The logic of investing in professional development, then, is straightforward: there is no more effective way to change schools substantially. But to appreciate more fully why professional development is essential to improving the capabilities of schools to enhance student learning, it seems important to understand that the core technology of schools is intensive. This piece of theoretical jargon is packed with meaning worth explaining. Organizations are ways of structuring, focusing, and facilitating collective human behavior. As such, organizations themselves can be described as technologies. In addition, some organizational processes, called *core technologies,* are more central to the organization than others. In schools, the core technology is teaching. If core technologies do not work well, other organizational processes will be relatively ineffective. Organizational technologies are intensive when one or more of the following conditions—all common to the tasks in which schools engage—are present (cf. Thompson, 1967):

- The relationship between the core technology and attainment of the goal one seeks to attain is uncertain. For example, the technology of teaching is uncertain because the effects of particular instructional practices depend, among other things, on many circumstances that practitioners cannot know about or even affect.

- The task to be performed varies greatly, and technologies must be adapted and modified continuously in response to their observed effects. For example, children vary in their readiness to learn from day to day and from subject to subject in ways difficult to predict.

- Desired outcomes are multiple, diffuse, and difficult to measure. What does it mean, for example, to "prepare students for democratic citizenship"?

For reasons that follow from their basic characteristics, the effectiveness of organizations with intensive technologies depends on (1) their flexibility, adaptiveness, and changefulness, (2) the quality of information they have about the tasks they must perform and the probable consequences of alternative ways to perform those tasks, and (3) the capabilities (such as competencies and judgment) of the people responsible for the core technology. These essential characteristics of intensive technology organizations are identified, in somewhat different terms, by Thompson (1967) and Senge (1990), among others.

Schools with these characteristics, sometimes called *learning-enriched schools,* support teacher learning. They are noted for their shared goals, teachers' sense of efficacy, collaborative cultures, and teacher commitment (Rosenholtz, 1989). The importance of these characteristics is invariably found in school effectiveness research. If innovations are to take root at the school level, colleagues must develop a shared understanding of the purposes, rationale, and processes involved in the innovation and believe that they can make a difference for students (Fullan, 1991). Teacher efficacy is enhanced when teachers have opportunities to see new strategies modeled, practice them, engage in peer coaching, acclimate students to new ways of learning, and use new teaching and learning strategies regularly and appropriately (NCRTE, 1991; Joyce and Showers, 1995). Being successful with new practices brings about a sense of confidence and willingness to participate in other change efforts (Guskey, 1995; Smylie, 1995).

Although collaborative cultures facilitate school improvement and teacher learning, most schools still isolate teachers from one another most of the time, providing little opportunity for purposeful social interaction. Lortie (1975) identified this as a primary source of teacher dissatisfaction twenty years ago. Teachers are too often asked to change their instruction in isolation and without support. But teachers need assistance from peer coaches or outside experts to support new instructional strategies (Little and McLaughlin, 1993). As Joyce and Showers (1995, p. 6) observe, "Without companionship, help in reflecting on practice, and instruction on fresh teaching strategies, most people can make very few changes in their behavior, however well-intentioned they are." Many teachers use a narrow range of instructional practices; they expand their repertoire only with carefully designed professional development (Borko and Putnam, 1995; Hodges, 1996; Joyce and Showers, 1995).

Because teaching is an intensive technology, teacher learning is essential to improved student learning. A school that fosters teacher learning will be one that (1) minimizes bureaucratic constraints and rules; (2) is clear about its multiple goals and the priorities it assigns to them; (3) provides teachers, students, and administrators valid and accurate measures of student performance and of the processes associated with differences in student performance; and (4) provides educators opportunities to learn collaboratively, practice what they learn, and evaluate the consequences in light of established goals. Senge (1990), among others, calls organizations with these characteristics "learning organizations."

Why Higher Standards for All Students Increases the Importance of Professional Development

As long as school improvement is defined as increasing the level and amount of facts and simple skills students must learn, the job of teaching can be seen as a fairly simple task of transmitting what the teachers know and texts explain. This view of teaching as telling or transmission is particularly reasonable when one does not expect all, or even most, students to achieve at relatively high levels. If teaching is believed to involve few technical pedagogical skills and is intuitively sensible, it can be learned in teacher preparation programs (if only they were good enough) and by experience. There would be little need for significant ongoing professional development. Moreover, traditional conceptions of teaching and learning assign the job of learning to students. This means that teachers can be seen largely as organizers of student activity and thus in need of limited new opportunities to improve their teaching (Borko and Putnam, 1995, p. 46).

Much higher standards for student learning have come with advances in knowledge. This involves much more than knowing more things and taking more difficult courses. (See, for example, the standards of the National Council of Teachers of Mathematics [NCTM], 1991.) As Borko and Putnam (1995) note, "Virtually all reform efforts are calling for changes in our education system that will help students to develop rich understandings of important content, think critically, construct and solve problems, synthesize information, invent, create, express themselves proficiently, and leave school prepared to be responsible citizens and lifelong learners" (p. 37). The character of the knowledge and skills—both intellectual and social—that students must have to participate in a culturally diverse democracy and an information-based economy is changing rapidly and coming to be defined in terms of criteria we have expected only some students to meet (Berryman, 1988; Johnston and Parker, 1987; Reich, 1991; SCANS, 1992; W. T. Grant Foundation, 1992).

Bereiter and Scardamelia (1987) have reviewed research on cognitive development and concluded that the linguistic and verbal reasoning abilities, literary standards and sophistication, and moral values and precepts traditionally associated with elites are within reach of most students (see also CCSSO, 1991; Gardner, 1991; Knapp, Shields, and Turnbull, 1992; Sherwood, Kinzer, Bransford, and Franks, 1987). But they also argue that whether this potential is realized will depend on the willingness and capabilities of teachers to approach the facilitation of learning in new ways. This will require professional development that deepens teachers' relevant knowledge systems (Borko and Putnam, 1995) and cultivates the belief that all students can achieve at high levels (Hodges, 1996).

As we learn more about how students learn and insist that students master more complex knowledge and develop greater capabilities for problem solving, "teaching by telling" is being replaced (or should be replaced) by "teaching for understanding." The latter is much more difficult for teachers but much more effective for students. In other words, schools—and teaching—matter more when we set our goals for learning higher (Resnick, 1987a; Resnick and Klopfer, 1989; Cognition and Technology Group at Vanderbilt, 1990; Murphy, 1991). It follows that professional development would be a more significant contributor to what students learn if it was more directly linked to students' mastery of complex knowledge and school improvement goals.

Research on Learning

Research on learning has significantly altered fundamental understandings of how and why people learn. Although those who do research on cognition differ on many issues (Anderson, Reder, and Simon, 1996), there are a number of core beliefs related to how people learn about which most researchers appear to be in considerable agreement (Rothman, 1991). Recently Alexander and Murphy (1998) have reviewed the relevant research and identified five learner-centered principles:

- "One's existing knowledge serves as a foundation of all future learning by guiding organization and representations, serving as a basis of association with new information, and coloring and filtering all new experiences" (p. 28). (the *knowledge base principle*)

- "The ability to reflect on and regulate one's thoughts and behaviors is essential to learning and development" (p. 28). (the *strategic processing principle*)

- "Motivational or affective factors, such as intrinsic motivation, attributions for learning, and personal goals, along with the motivational characteristics of the learning tasks, play a significant role in the learning process" (p. 33). (the *motivation/affect principle*)

- "Learning, ultimately a unique adventure for all, proceeds through common stages of development influenced by both inherited and experiential and environmental factors" (p. 36). (the *development principle*)

- "Learning is as much a socially shared undertaking as it is an individually constructed enterprise" (p. 39). (the *context principle*)

These research-based principles have important implications for professional development. First, they lead to approaches to teaching students that are very different from those that are commonly used in most schools and colleges (Resnick, 1987a; Bransford, Goldman, and Vye, 1991). This results in a need for substantial professional development through which educators can learn about research on learning and how to facilitate learning based on these five principles. Second, these principles explain why most professional development activities are relatively ineffective (Smylie, 1995). To use the motivational principle as an example, Hargreaves (1995) contends that staff development is often ineffective because it "does not acknowledge or address the personal identities and moral purposes of teachers, nor the cultures and contexts in which they work" (p. 14). One source of motivation for teachers is the conviction that their engagement in professional development will improve student achievement (National Foundation for the Improvement of Education, 1996). Another is teachers' need to resolve core dilemmas of teaching (Smylie, 1995). Third, if these principles of learning shaped the design of the opportunities to learn that are available to educators, professional development would look quite different than it does now. Some examples of such programs are the Cognitively Guided Instruction project and the Summer Math for Teachers program with follow-up support and supervision (Borko and Putnam, 1995).

Inadequacy of Conventional Approaches to Professional Development

Even when there is compelling evidence about the efficacy of a new strategy for improving schools, there are many advocates for the status quo. The result is that old and new beliefs exist side by side, yielding blurred visions and compromises that undermine the adoption of major changes. Professional development as we know it, however, has almost no defenders who argue that it substantially improves student learning. Indeed, a major reason that greater investments have not been made in professional development is that its presumed beneficiaries, teachers, have little positive to say about its usefulness (Bacharach, Bauer, and Shedd, 1986).

Shallow and *fragmented* are terms that critics commonly use to describe conventional approaches to professional development (Fenstermacher and Berliner, 1985). According to Fullan (1991), "Nothing has promised so much and has been so frustratingly wasteful as the thousands of workshops and conferences that led to no significant change in practice when teachers returned to their classrooms" (p. 315). In these workshops, which Fullan calls "the norm" for professional development, experts "exposed" teachers to new ideas or "trained" them in new practices. The success of these events "was typically judged by a 'happiness quotient' that measured participants' satisfaction with the experience" (Sparks, 1995, p. 2). Dissatisfaction with these approaches is evident in the rhetoric of paradigm shift. As can be seen by the following characterizations of the "old" paradigm, it ill suits adult learning needs and orientations.

Smylie and Conyers (1991) view the paradigm shift as moving from deficit-based to competency-based approaches, from replication to reflection, from learning separately to learning together, and from centralization to decentralization. Collinson (1996) sees eight shifting aspects of staff development, all of which would promote teacher inquiry. In the old paradigm, in-service workshops emphasize private, individual activity; are brief, often one-shot sessions; offer unrelated topics; rely on an external "expert" presenter; expect passive teacher-listeners; emphasize skill development; are atheoretical; and expect quick visible results. In contrast, in the new paradigm staff development is a shared, public process; promotes sustained interaction; emphasizes substantive, school-related issues; relies on internal expertise; expects teachers to be active participants; emphasizes the why as well as the how of teaching; articulates a theoretical research base; and anticipates that lasting change will be a slow process.

Sparks (1995) elaborates many of these themes and adds some new ones. He faults the old model for focusing on district-mandated, generic instructional skills of teachers "trained" as individuals by an outside "expert" away from their job site. Because this training is fragmented, piecemeal, and often based on current instructional fads, it is viewed as a frill, easily dispensed with during tough financial times. Perhaps most damaging, these workshops, although they often respond to expressed teacher needs, are seldom explicitly linked to what schools expect students to know and be able to do

In addition to the literature on paradigm shifts, literature on models of and outcomes for staff development provide further indications of the weakness of conventional approaches. According to Sparks and Loucks-Horsley (1990), five distinct models of staff development are commonly used. Each of these has different assumptions, theoretical underpinnings, procedures, and outcomes. Too often these models are implemented in ways that ignore some or all of the five learner-centered principles.

The *individually guided model* encourages professional development activity at the personal level. Teachers design their own learning experiences and determine their own goals. This approach might bring personal satisfaction and even professional growth, but it will do little to foster school improvement and student achievement if disconnected from teachers' daily practice and a coherent school improvement plan.

In the *observer/assessment model*, teachers receive feedback on classroom performance, usually from peer coaches. To be a powerful tool for professional development, coaches must be reliable sources of information about good teaching. Furthermore, multiple coaching sessions are necessary if learners are to use a new strategy effectively and consistently. Although this model is widely practiced, teachers sometimes view it with suspicion because of its association with evaluation. In a striking reversal to earlier claims, Showers and Joyce (1996) now recommend omitting verbal feedback because of its negative impact on collaborative activity. They claim that this omission does not depress implementation of new teaching approaches or student growth.

The *development/improvement process model* has teachers design curriculum or engage in a school improvement, problem-solving process. Participation in these activities is regarded, in and of itself, as a form of professional development. Obviously much would depend on the quality of the experience (Miller, 1992).

The *training model* is the one most people equate with staff development. It often occurs in "workshop-type sessions in which the presenter is the expert who establishes the content and flow of activities" (Sparks and Loucks-Horsley, 1990, p. 241). When it focuses on teacher thinking, explores theory, provides adequate demonstration and time for practice, and makes productive use of peers, it has the potential to change significantly teachers' beliefs, knowledge, and behavior and the performance of their students. Research supports this model of professional development more than the others; but, somewhat ironically, it has a number of characteristics associated with the old paradigm. It relies on outside experts as trainers, presumes that universal answers can be conceptualized external to the organization, emphasizes replication of practice, and treats teachers as recipients of knowledge transmitted by others (Eaker, Noblit, and Rogers, 1992). In the training model, "the key to professional knowledge and growth is held by someone other than teachers themselves" (Miller, 1992, p. 96).

In contrast, the last model, *inquiry,* resonates most with the new consensus model. Sometimes referred to as the *teacher-researcher model,* it "requires teachers to identify an area of instructional interest, collect data, and make changes in their instruction on the basis of an interpretation of those data" (Sparks and

Loucks-Horsley, 1990, p. 235). However, like the other models, this one can also be disconnected from a coherent plan for school improvement. It too can vary in quality depending on teachers' expertise in generating useful research questions and in analyzing and using data to improve practice.

The literature also specifies four possible outcomes for professional development: greater awareness, attitude change, skill development, and consistent and appropriate use of newly acquired knowledge (Joyce and Showers, 1995). But only the last outcome, using new knowledge, is linked to student achievement, and then only if the professional development content directly deals with curriculum, instruction, or technology. Unfortunately, much of what is offered for professional development ignores or gives only nominal attention to the use of new knowledge that is relevant to student learning.

Furthermore, decisions about appropriate use of new strategies are often complex. Too often instructional strategies are introduced in staff development sessions with little regard to conditional or contextual factors (Little and McLaughlin, 1993). It is not enough to know, for instance, what cooperative grouping is or how to use it. Teachers need to learn how to judge when cooperative grouping matches instructional goals, classroom context, student needs, and content demands. Using a variety of teaching strategies without a clear basis for choice is just as unreasoned as using the same strategy without variation. Neither one signals reflective or effective practice. When content and learning tasks are novel or particularly complex, professional development opportunities should incorporate well-rehearsed or familiar instructional strategies. And when instructional strategies are new to students, teachers should learn how to introduce them with familiar content.

The unwillingness of the nation to support continuing professional development of teachers is rooted, at least in part, in the fact that the most common forms of professional development have little chance to affect student learning. The clearer this has become, the greater has been the interest in identifying the characteristics of effective ways to enhance professional capacity. The case for increased investments in professional development depends, in other words, on making clear that such investments will not be made in traditionally weak forms of professional development and identifying viable and effective alternatives to business as usual.

DESIGN PRINCIPLES FOR EFFECTIVE PROFESSIONAL DEVELOPMENT

The convergence of research on learning, the growing recognition that teachers make a critical difference in what and how students learn, expectations that all students should attain higher academic standards, and the virtually unanimous agreement that educators' opportunities to learn are usually infrequent, poorly designed, and inadequately delivered has led to considerable attention being focused on the need for and characteristics of effective professional development as a key to school improvement. This attention has yielded new studies of professional development and several syntheses of research (Corcoran, 1995; Fullan, 1993; Gall and Vojtek, 1994; Guskey, 1995; Hargreaves, 1994; Little, 1993; McDiarmid, 1994; Miller, Lord, and Dorney, 1994; Wade, 1985).

Although these syntheses have somewhat different themes and purposes, their conclusions are consistent with respect to the characteristics of professional development that are most likely to lead to improvements in actions of educators that contribute to student learning. As these reviews of research have gained visibility, a number of reports have been issued at the national level that incorporate the central conclusions of the research (National Governors' Association, 1995; National Staff Development Council, 1994; U.S. Department of Education, 1995). The proposals made in these reports, like the conclusions of the research reviews, are remarkably congruent.

We have identified eight characteristics of effective professional development that cut across and embody the research syntheses and these recent calls for action. These eight design principles focus attention on professional development strategies that appear to be essential to improving students' learning over time. We provide illustrative, but not exhaustive, references to particular syntheses of research and to other studies that support each element of what we call the new consensus model of professional development. These principles are also supported by the more general research on learning.[2]

Much of this literature draws attention to the importance of the content of learning opportunities reflecting best demonstrated practice and, when relevant evidence is available, being research based. While this may seem obvious, professional development too often introduces educators to trendy but unproven ideas, as though these ideas were validated and likely to lead to improvements in student performance. This is worse than a waste of time; it undermines the motivation for professional learning and threatens the welfare of students.

Table 5.1 shows the relationship between the design principles for the new consensus model of professional development and the learning principles. Just as schools must be student centered, professional development opportunities for educators must be learner centered. They must account for educators' extant knowledge and beliefs, develop reflective capacities, attend to motivational and developmental issues, and build on social relations in the school context. We recognize the tension that exists among some of the principles. That is a necessary, perhaps even useful, part of the change process. Our claim is that professional development is more likely to result in substantive and lasting changes in the knowledge, skills, and behaviors of educators that strengthen student learning when it includes these characteristics.

Table 5.1. Relationships Between Research on Learning and the New Consensus Model of Professional Development.

Design Principles	Learning Principles				
	Knowledge Base	Strategic Processing	Motivation/ Affect	Development	Content
1. Driven, fundamentally, by analyses of the differences between (1) goals and standards for student learning and (2) student performance.	x	x	x		
2. Involves learners (such as teachers) in the identification of their learning needs and, when possible, the development of the learning opportunity and/or the process to be used.			x		
3. Is primarily school based and integral to school operations.			x		x
4. Provides learning opportunities that relate to individual needs but for the most part are organized around collaborative problem solving.	x		x		x
5. Is continuous and ongoing, involving follow-up and support for further learning, including support from sources external to the school.				x	
6. Incorporates evaluation of multiple sources of information on outcomes for student and processes involved in implementing the lessons learned through professional development.			x	x	
7. Provides opportunities to develop a theoretical understanding of the knowledge and skills to be learned.		x			
8. Is integrated with a comprehensive change process that deals with the full range of impediments to and facilitators of student learning.			x		x

Principle One: Goals and Student Performance

Professional development should be driven by analyses of the differences between goals and standards for student learning and student performance (Fullan, 1993; Howey and Collinson, 1995; Miller, Lord, and Dorney, 1994; Pink and Hyde, 1992). Such analyses will define what educators need—rather than want—to learn, make professional development student centered, and increase public confidence in the use of resources for professional development (American Federation of Teachers, 1995; Farkas and Friedman, 1995; National Foundation for the Improvement of Education, 1996). Educators can then use these analyses to explore the usefulness of alternative strategies for student learning and school improvement, paying close attention to the gains that diverse types of learners make.

The importance of this student-centered focus seems self-evident, but it has not been standard practice. Too often new teaching strategies, curricular approaches, or organizational designs, pursued as goals in and of themselves, have diverted attention from the school's central goal (Loucks-Horsley, 1995; Newmann and Wehlage, 1995). Moreover, school-level educators have often been prevented from developing analytic capacity for continual school improvement by bureaucratic structures. In an empirical study of a change effort in the Chicago public schools, for example, Bryk, Rollow, and Pinnell (1996) found diminished capacity in schools because the central school office assumed the functions of identifying problems, creating responsive programs, and evaluating their effectiveness.

Principle Two: Teacher Involvement

Professional development should involve learners (such as teachers) in the identification of what they need to learn and, when possible, in the development of the learning opportunity and the process to be used (Borko and Putnam, 1995; Little, 1993; Miller, Lord, and Dorney, 1994; Tillema and Imants, 1995). This engagement increases educators' motivation and commitment to learn (Hodges, 1996); affirms their strengths and enhances their sense of efficacy (Pink and Hyde, 1992); empowers them to take instructional risks and assume new roles and responsibilities (Pink, 1992; Barr, Anderson, and Slaybaugh, 1992); increases the likelihood that what is learned will be meaningful and relevant to particular contexts and problems (Pink and Hyde, 1992); improves instruction (Hodges, 1996); and makes the school culture more collaborative and improvement oriented (Pink, 1992). If teachers are denied input in their own professional development, they are likely to become cynical and detached from school improvement efforts and to reject what they experience as imposition (American Federation of Teachers, 1995; Guskey, 1995; Hargreaves, 1995). Lack of involvement also "significantly reduces the capacity of the school and district to understand and successfully manage the school change initiative" (Pink and Hyde, 1992, p. 268).

This principle, like the others, requires strong leadership at the school level. In a school where professional learning is integral to the implementation of the core technology leadership means being a facilitator of learning. Reform is short lived if it is led rather than facilitated by top leadership (Barr, Anderson, and Slaybaugh, 1992). Hierarchical authority creates learned conformity; more egalitarian authority relations "increase the likelihood that individuals will feel and be freer to engage in reflective practice and experimental learning" (Smylie, 1995, p. 99).

As indicated in Principle One, there are so many possibilities of learning so many things that school leaders must keep attention focused on what teachers need to learn in order to close the gap between school goals and school performance. For example, teachers are not likely to identify their need for subject matter knowledge or pedagogical content knowledge (Borko and Putnam, 1995). Professional credibility depends on teachers' "knowing" the material they teach students. Yet current understandings of mathematics, science, history, and the arts—and how to teach those subjects—have changed radically. School leaders must create organizational cultures in which everyone feels good about needing to learn. They must, however, protect teachers from unnecessary and unproductive involvement, unreasonable expectations, and burnout (Guskey, 1995).

Principle Three: School Based

Professional development should be primarily school based and integral to school operations (Feiman-Nemser, 1983; Grossman, 1992; Guskey, 1995; Little, 1993; Little and McLaughlin, 1993; Joyce and Showers, 1995; Louis, Marks, and Kruse, 1996; Smylie, 1995). This does not mean denying teachers access to out-of-school learning experiences through professional associations or networks, graduate study, or teacher centers. However, opportunities to learn in powerful ways are most often connected with the recognition of and solution to authentic and immediate problems. Hodges (1996) describes a large-scale staff development program in which "cohesiveness, transfer of training, and the resulting effect on student learning were—and continue to be—a direct function of the study teams teachers formed to establish norms of mutual support and inquiry into the learning process" (p. 229).

Motivation to learn and to engage in school change efforts also increases when these efforts are linked to improving and assessing daily practice. This is often referred to as *job-embedded learning*. As Loucks-Horsley (1995) claimed, "This direct connection between learning and application increases meaning for the teacher and potential impact on students" (p. 268). Smylie (1995) describes the optimal workplace as one in which learning arises from and feeds back into work experience, where learning is considered part of work.

Commenting on the mounting evidence about the efficacy of site-generated and -supported innovations, Pink (1992) argues for investment in school-level capacity building. One necessary investment is time. According to the National Foundation for the Improvement of Education (1996), teachers need a significant amount of instruction with follow-up days of technical assistance to develop new pedagogical skills. Such time can be built into the school day through flexible and creative scheduling or by extending the school year. The American Federation of Teachers (1995) urges that teachers have time during the workday for their professional growth.

Principle Four: Collaborative Problem Solving

Professional development should provide learning opportunities that relate to individual needs but for the most part are organized around collaborative problem solving (Fullan, 1991; Guskey, 1995; Hargreaves, 1994; Huberman, 1995; Little, 1993; Miller, Lord, and Dorney, 1994; Rosenholtz, 1989). But what exactly does collaborative problem solving look like? Activities can vary from interdisciplinary teaming (Whitford and Kyle, 1992) to curriculum development and critique (Bryk, Rollow, and Pinnell, 1996; Miller, 1992) to collaborative action research (Eaker, Noblit, and Rogers, 1992) to study groups (Hodges, 1996). In each case, educators working together to address issues of common concern facilitates the identification of both the causes and potential solutions to problems.

Although collaborative problem solving can result in potentially irreconcilable positions or merely perpetuate existing practice, when done skillfully, it leads to the clarification of learning needs and the sharing of knowledge and expertise. It breaks down teacher isolation (Bryk, Rollow, and Pinnell, 1996), collectively empowers teachers (Hargreaves, 1995), creates an environment of professional respect (Guskey, 1995), and develops a shared language and understanding of good practice (Little, 1982). Without collaborative problem solving, individual change may be possible, but school change is not. The inherent difficulties in implementing this principle are what make the following principle so critical.

Principle Five: Continuous and Supported

Professional development should be continuous and ongoing, involving follow-up and support for further learning, including support from sources external to the school that can provide necessary resources and an outside perspective (Fullan, 1993; Guskey, 1995; Hodges, 1996; Miller, Lord and Dorney, 1994; NCRTE, 1991; NEA, 1995; Pink and Hyde, 1992). As what is learned from professional development is implemented, learners often discover what they need to be effective. If that need for learning, resources, and support is not met, increased professional competence and student achievement are unlikely to be experienced and the motivation to engage in additional professional development will be affected. While most professional development should be school based, educators also need to enrich this learning with new ideas and knowledge gained from sources beyond the school (Lieberman, 1995). Innovations are constrained if they are informed only by those who share similar ideas and experiences (Smylie, 1995).

In a provocative example of the need for continuous learning, researchers found that a group of teachers who initially focused on learning pedagogical skills consistent with the new NCTM standards realized that a deeper problem was their understanding of mathematics (Prichard Committee, 1995). This type of change takes time, including time to establish trust and shared meanings with those inside and outside the school organization. In a study of student grouping, Barr, Anderson, and Slaybaugh (1992) found that district- and school-level educators took four years to deliberate and make changes. Describing a large-scale training program developed by Bruce Joyce and colleagues, Hodges (1996) concludes that "significant change in educational practice does not occur quickly but is the result of staff development programs designed with a 3- to 5-year time frame" (pp. 239–240). Ongoing support is especially critical in the first two years of implementation. Unfortunately the public expects to see quick changes in schools and concrete evidence of improvements in student achievement (Farkas and Friedman, 1995).

Principle Six: Information Rich

Professional development should incorporate evaluation of multiple sources of information on outcomes for students and processes that are involved in implementing the lessons learned through professional development (Little, 1993; Guskey, 1995; Tillema and Imants, 1995; NCRTE, 1991; Joyce and Showers, 1995). Teachers' knowledge and experience (Miller, 1992), as well as research studies and outside consultants (Barr, Anderson, and Slaybaugh, 1992), should be valued sources of information. The evaluation can be done by school-based educators, outside evaluators, or (and probably best) a joint team. It must be nonthreatening, be conducted throughout various stages of implementation, allow sufficient time for change to occur, assess change in teaching before assessing change in student learning, and help teachers think more carefully about their classroom practice (Hodges, 1996). Knowing the extent to which professional development has influenced student achievement contributes to the design of and incentives for further learning.

Principle Seven: Theoretical Understanding

Professional development should provide opportunities to engage in developing a theoretical understanding of the knowledge and skills to be learned (Eraut, 1995; Feiman-Nemser and Parker, 1992; Fullan, 1991; Joyce and Showers, 1995; McDiarmid, 1994; NCRTE, 1991; Tillema and Imants, 1995). Results of research, in comprehensible forms, need to be made accessible to teachers, who cite lack of understanding and limited access as reasons that they do not put theory into practice. Since teacher thinking and classroom behavior are influenced by their knowledge and beliefs, an important component of their professional development needs to be the expansion and elaboration of their professional knowledge base. Broadly this would include general pedagogical knowledge, subject matter knowledge, and pedagogical content knowledge, which address such areas as classroom management, conceptions of teaching a subject, and students' understandings and potential misunderstandings of subject matter (Borko and Putnam, 1995; Eraut, 1995).

New knowledge in itself does not effect change (NCRTE, 1991). Professional development must engage teachers' beliefs, experiences, and habits. Creating effective professional development opportunities means helping teachers (re)consider both their formal and their practical teaching knowledge (Fenstermacher, 1994). In reviewing three professional development programs based on a cognitive perspective, Borko and Putnam (1995) discuss the importance of teachers' being asked to reconsider fundamental beliefs, especially the belief that "they are the source of knowledge and that they have a responsibility to cover a specified amount of content" (p. 55). Such beliefs are difficult to change. Teachers must experience different types of learning themselves, spend time adapting their instruction, and see positive results in their students. However, since beliefs filter knowledge and guide behavior, significant transformations of teaching practice are unlikely to occur if they are ignored.

In addition to attending to teacher beliefs, professional development must attend to educators' needs to adapt their learning to their own students and contexts. This should help overcome suspicions that research is irrelevant to teachers' particular contexts and day-to-day responsibilities. Summarizing findings from case studies of professional development, Pink and Hyde (1992) stress the importance of "useful knowledge" for teaching. Teachers are more engaged participants when they see clear benefits between what they are learning and their own classroom situation. Such modification is more likely to be effective when it is informed by theory in which the educator involved has confidence.

Principle Eight: Part of a Comprehensive Change Process

Professional development should be integrated with a comprehensive change process that deals with impediments to and facilitators of student learning (Little, 1993; Smylie, 1995; Guskey, 1995). But as Guskey (1995) cautions, "There is no easier way to sabotage change efforts than to take on too much at one time. In fact, if there is one truism in the vast research literature on change, it is that the magnitude of change persons are asked to make is inversely related to their likelihood of making it" (p. 119). He recommends thinking big (having a comprehensive plan) but starting small (approaching change in a gradual, incremental manner). Small changes alone will not have a significant impact, but multi-faceted plans can be overwhelming.

Educators must practice what they learn. Too often they are asked to learn new things they cannot act on because there is no organizational commitment to continuous experimentation and improvement. Teachers need time and opportunities to investigate why some practices might be better than others, see models of such practices, and personally develop these practices. School- and district-level support are essential components of this process (AFT, 1995; NCRTE, 1991; Joyce and Showers, 1995). Some district-level types of support for comprehensive change efforts include adequate funding, technical assistance, sustained central office follow-through, avoidance of quick fixes, and providing teachers adequate time to learn, plan, and implement new practices (Hodges, 1996).

CONCLUSION

Of course, there are different ways of talking about these principles of effective professional development. And, to be sure, there could be (and should be) a variety of specific ways to implement the strategies implicit in these principles. The good news is that there is so much agreement about the essential elements of professional development that is likely to result in improvements in student learning. The bad news is that few of these principles are common to professional development programs in schools and colleges, and the cases where most, much less all, of the principles are being implemented simultaneously are rare indeed. The reasons for the discrepancy between knowledge and practice are no doubt multiple: institutionalized cultures, practices, and habits of mind; community concerns about taking teachers out of classrooms; lingering skepticism about the value of research and the need for change; poor experiences with previous in-service opportunities; and doubts about the feasibility of reform efforts. Each of these must be dealt with if the new consensus model is to become a reality.

The essential characteristic of effective professional development embedded in the eight principles is that it involves continuous teacher and administrator learning in the context of collaborative problem solving. When professional development is thought of as a program or a series of formal scheduled events, or is otherwise disconnected from authentic problem solving, it is unlikely to have much influence on teacher or student learning. This means that schools need to be structured in ways that provide educators with opportunities to learn as they collectively address the challenges embedded in the inevitable gap between high standards of learning for all students and actual student performance. Structuring schools as learning organizations is important to the development and maintenance of professional values and group norms that support continuous professional learning for educators. The much-discussed idea of a community of learners that involves students, faculty, and administrators is unlikely to be realized in the absence of such structures and cultures.

The design principles identified here, along with their rationale, may appear to suggest that professional development that is focused on individual needs and wants and takes place distant in form, time, and space from contextualized, collective problem solving would be inappropriate and unworthy of support. This would be a misreading of the research. Such individualized and "out-of-place" learning may be very productive for individuals. And if such learning is used by others in the school as a source of new ideas, critical evaluation, and expertise, it is likely to contribute much to school improvement. Implementing the principles of professional development identified here would substantially reduce the energy and resources now committed to developing the capabilities of individuals and rewarding teachers and administrators solely because of the number of courses, workshops, or conferences they attended.

If the new consensus on effective professional development has significant implications for the way professional development is conceptualized and provided for in schools, it also calls into question the role that colleges and universities have been playing in the continuing education of educators. Serious questions need to be raised about the content and processes that are embodied in college- and university-based programs for preparing teachers and administrators. But that is another story.

Notes

1. A host of recent studies come to the same conclusion. See, for example, Borko and Putnam (1995); Elmore (1992); Hargreaves (1994); Knapp, Shields, and Turnbull (1992); Putnam, Lampert, and Peterson (1990); Teddlie and Stringfield (1993).

2. These principles do not deal with the substantive content of professional development found in sources such as American Federation of Teachers (1995) and Loucks-Horsley, Stiles, and Hewson (1996).

References

Alexander, P. A., and Murphy, P. K. "The Research Base for APA's Learner-Centered Psychological Principles." In N. M. Lambert and B. L. McCombs (eds.), *Issues in School Reform: A Sampler of Psychological Perspectives on Learner-Centered Schools*. Washington, D.C.: The American Psychological Association, 1998.

American Federation of Teachers. *Principles for Professional Development*. Washington, D.C.: Author, 1995.

Anderson, J. R., Reder, L. M., and Simon, H. A. "Situated Learning and Education."

Educational Researcher, 1996, *25*(4), 5–11.

Bacharach, S. B., Bauer, S. C., and Shedd, J. B. *The Learning Workplace: The Conditions and Resources of Teaching: Organizational Analysis and Practice.* Washington, D.C.: National Education Association, 1986.

Barr, R., Anderson, C. S., and Slaybaugh, J. E. "Deliberations About Grouping in Crete-Monee." In W. T. Pink and A. A. Hyde (eds.), *Effective Staff Development for School Change.* Norwood, N.J.: Ablex, 1992.

Bereiter, C., and Scardamelia, M. "An Attainable Version of High Literacy: Approaches to Teaching Higher-Order Skills in Reading and Writing." *Curriculum Inquiry,* 1987, *17*(1), 9–30.

Berryman, S. *Education and the Economy: What Should We Teach? When? How? To Whom?* Occasional Paper No. 4. New York: National Center on Education and Employment, 1988.

Borko, H., and Putnam, R. T. "Expanding a Teacher's Knowledge Base: A Cognitive Psychological Perspective on Professional Development." In T. R. Guskey and M. Huberman (eds.), *Professional Development in Education: New Paradigms and Practices.* New York: Teachers College, Columbia University, 1995.

Bransford, J. D., Goldman, S. R., and Vye, N. J. "Making a Difference in People's Abilities to Think: Reflections on a Decade of Work and Some Hopes for the Future." In L. Okagaki and R. J. Sternberg (eds.), *Directors of Development: Influences on Children.* Hillsdale, N.J.: Erlbaum, 1991.

Bryk, A. S., Rollow, S. G., and Pinnell, G. S. "Urban School Development: Literacy as a Lever for Change." *Educational Policy,* 1996, *10*(2), 172–201.

Cognition and Technology Group at Vanderbilt (CTGV). "Anchored Instruction and Its Relationship to Situated Cognition." *Educational Researcher,* 1990, *19*(3), 2–28.

Collinson, V. "What Is in a Name? The Transition from Workshops to Staff Development for Sustained School Improvement." Unpublished manuscript, 1996.

Commission on Chapter 1. *Making Schools Work for Children in Poverty: A New Framework Prepared by the Commission on Chapter 1.* Washington, D.C.: American Association for Higher Education, 1992.

Consortium on Productivity in the Schools. *Using What We Have to Get the Schools We Need.* New York: Teachers College, Columbia University, 1995.

Corcoran, T. C. *Helping Teachers Teach Well: Transforming Professional Development.* New Brunswick, N.J.: Consortium for Policy Research in Education, Rutgers University, 1995.

Council of Chief State School Officers. *Higher Order Learning for All.* Washington, D.C.: Author, 1991.

Eaker, D. J., Noblit, G. W., and Rogers, D. L. "Reconsidering Effective Staff Development: Reflective Practice and Elaborated Culture as Desirable Outcomes." In W. T. Pink and A. A. Hyde (eds.), *Effective Staff Development for School Change.* Norwood, N.J.: Ablex, 1992.

Elmore, R. "Why Restructuring Alone Won't Improve Teaching." *Educational Leadership,* 1992, *49*(7), 44–48.

Eraut, M. "Developing Professional Knowledge Within a Client-Centered Orientation." In T. R. Guskey and M. Huberman (eds.), *Professional Development in Education: New Paradigms and Practices.* New York: Teachers College, Columbia University, 1995.

Evertson, C. M., and Murphy, J. "Beginning with Classrooms: Implications for Restructuring Schools." In H. H. Marshall (ed.), *Redefining Student Learning: Roots of Educational Change.* Norwood, N.J.: Ablex, 1992.

Farkas, S., and Friedman, W. *Professional Development for Teachers: The Public's View.* New York: Public Agenda for the National Foundation for the Improvement of Education, 1995.

Feiman-Nemser, S. "Learning to Teach." In L. S. Shulman and G. Sykes (eds.), *Handbook of Teaching and Policy.* White Plains, N.Y.: Longman, 1983.

Feiman-Nemser, S., and Parker, M. B. *Mentoring in Context: A Comparison of Two U.S. Programs for Beginning Teachers.* NCRTL Special Report. East Lansing, MI: National Center for Research on Teacher Learning, Michigan State University, 1992. ED 346 091.

Fenstermacher, G. D. "The Knower and the Known: The Nature of Knowledge in Research on Teaching." In L. Darling-Hammond (ed.), *Review of Research in Education.* Washington, D.C.: American Education Research Association, 1994.

Fenstermacher, G. D., and Berliner, D. C. "Determining the Value of Staff Development." *Elementary School Journal,* 1986, *85*(3), 281–314.

Fullan, M. *The New Meaning of Educational Change.* New York: Teachers College Press, 1991.

Fullan, M. *Change Forces: Probing the Depths of Educational Reform.* Bristol, Pa.: Falmer Press, 1993.

Gall, M. D. and Vojtek, R. O. *Planning for Effective Staff Development: Six Research-Based Models.* Eugene, Oreg.: ERIC Clearinghouse on Educational Management, University of Oregon, 1994. ED 025 786.

Gardner, H. *The Unschooled Mind.* New York: Basic Books, 1991.

Grossman, P. L. "Teaching to Learn." In A. Lieberman (ed.), *The Changing Contexts of Teaching: 91st Yearbook of the National Society for the Study of Education, Part I.* Chicago: University of Chicago Press, 1992.

Guskey, T. R. "Professional Development in Education: In Search of the Optimal Mix." In T. R. Guskey and M. Huberman (eds.), *Professional Development in Education: New Paradigms and Practices.* New York: Teachers College, Columbia University, 1995.

Hargreaves, A. *Changing Teachers. Changing Times: Teachers' Work and Culture in the Postmodern Age.* New York: Teachers College Press, 1994.

Hargreaves, A. "Development and Desire: A Postmodern Perspective." In T. R. Guskey and M. Huberman (eds.), *Professional Development in Education: New Paradigms and Practices*. New York: Teachers College, Columbia University, 1995.

Hawley, W. D., and Rosenholtz, S. "Good Schools: A Synthesis of Research on How Schools Influence Student Achievement." Special issue, *Peabody Journal of Education*, 1984, *4*, 1–178.

Hodges, H.L.B. "Using Research to Inform Practice in Urban Schools: Ten Key Strategies for Success." *Educational Policy*, 1996, *10*(2), 223–252.

Howey, K., and Collinson, V. "Cornerstones of a Collaborative Culture and Professional Development: Preservice Teacher Preparation." *Journal of Personnel Evaluation in Education*, 1995, *1*, 21–31.

Huberman, M. "Professional Careers and Professional Development: Some Intersections." In T. R. Guskey and M. Huberman (eds.), *Professional Development in Education: New Paradigms and Practices*. New York: Teachers College, Columbia University, 1995.

Johnston, W., and Parker, A. *Workforce 2000*. Indianapolis: Hudson Institute, 1987.

Joyce, B., and Showers, B. *Student Achievement Through Staff Development: Fundamentals of School Renewal*. (2nd ed.) White Plains, N.Y.: Longman, 1995.

Knapp, M., Shields, P., and Turnbull, B. *Academic Challenge for the Children of Poverty: Summary Report*. Washington, D.C.: U.S. Department of Education, 1992.

Lieberman, A. *The Work of Restructuring Schools: Building from the Ground Up*. New York: Teachers College Press, 1995.

Little, J. W. "Norms of Collegiality and Experimentation: Workplace Conditions of School Success." *American Education Research Journal*, 1982, *19*, 325–340.

Little, J. W. "Teachers' Professional Development in a Climate of Educational Reform." *Educational Evaluation and Policy Analysis*, 1993, *15*(2), 129–151.

Little, J. W., and McLaughlin, M. W. (eds.), *Teachers' Work: Individuals, Colleagues, and Contexts*. New York: Teachers College Press, 1993.

Lortie, D. *Schoolteacher: A Sociological Study*. Chicago: University of Chicago Press, 1975.

Loucks-Horsley, S. "Professional Development and the Learner Centered School." *Theory into Practice*, 1995, *34*(4), 265–271.

Loucks-Horsley, S., Stiles, K., and Hewson, P. "Principles of Effective Professional Development for Mathematics and Science Education: A Synthesis of Standards." *NISE Brief* (newsletter), 1996, *1*(1), 1–6.

Louis, K. S., Marks, H. M., and Kruse, S. "Teachers' Professional Community in Restructuring Schools." *American Educational Research Journal*, 1996, *33*(4), 757–798.

McDiarmid, G. W. *Realizing New Learning for All Students: A Framework for Professional Development of Kentucky Teachers*. East Lansing, Mich.: National Center for Research on Teacher Learning, Michigan State University, 1994.

Miller, B., Lord, B., and Dorney, J. *Summary Report. Staff Development for Teachers. A Study of Configurations and Costs in Four Districts*. Newton, Mass.: Education Development Center, 1994.

Miller, L. "Curriculum Work as Staff Development." In W. T. Pink and A. A. Hyde (eds.), *Effective Staff Development for School Change*. Norwood, N.J.: Ablex, 1992.

Murphy, J. *Restructuring Schools: Capturing and Assessing the Phenomena*. New York: Teachers College Press, 1991.

National Center for Research on Teacher Education. *Final Report: National Center for Research on Teacher Education*. East Lansing, Mich.: Michigan State University, 1991.

National Commission on Teaching and America's Future. *What Matters Most: Teaching for America's Future*. New York: Author, 1996.

National Council of Teachers of Mathematics (NCTM). *Professional Standards for Teaching Mathematics*. Reston, Va.: Author, 1991.

National Education Association. *KEYS. Keys to Excellence for Your Schools: An Interactive Startup Guide*. Washington, D.C.: National Center for Innovation, National Education Association, 1995.

National Foundation for the Improvement of Education. *Teachers Take Charge of Their Learning: Transforming Professional Development for Student Success*. Washington, D.C.: Author, 1996.

National Governors' Association. *Transforming Professional Development for Teachers: A Guide for State Policymakers*. Washington, D.C.: Author, 1995.

National Staff Development Council. *Standards for Staff Development*. Oxford, Ohio: Author, 1994.

Newmann, F. M., and Wehlage, G. G. *Successful School Restructuring*. Report to the Public and Educators by the Center on Organization and Restructuring of Schools. Madison, Wis.: University of Wisconsin–Madison, 1995.

Pink, W. T. "A School-Within-a-School for At-Risk Youth: Staff Development and Program Success." In W. T. Pink and A. A. Hyde (eds.), *Effective Staff Development for School Change*. Norwood, N.J.: Ablex, 1992.

Pink, W. T., and Hyde, A. A. "Doing Effective Staff Development." In W. T. Pink and A. A. Hyde (eds.), *Effective Staff Development for School Change*. Norwood, N.J.: Ablex, 1992.

Prichard Committee for Academic Excellence and Partnership for Kentucky School Reform. "Professional Development in the Service of Systemic Reform: Policy Action Research and Dissemination Project." Proposal submitted to the Pew Charitable Trusts, 1995.

Putnam, R. T., Lampert, M., and Peterson, P. "Alternative Perspectives on Knowing Mathematics in Elementary Schools." *Review of Research in Education*, 1990, *16*, 57–150.

Reich, R. B. *The Work of Nations: Preparing Ourselves for 21st Century Capitalism*. New York: Knopf, 1991.

Resnick, L. Learning in School and Out. *Educational Research*, 1987b, *16*(9), 13–20, 54.

Resnick, L., and Klopfer, L. "Toward the Thinking Curriculum: An Overview." In *Toward the Thinking Curriculum: Current Cognitive Research*. 1989 Yearbook of the Association for Supervision and Curriculum Development. Alexandria, Va.: ASCD, 1989.

Rosenholtz, S. *Teachers' Workplace: The Social Organization of Schools*. New York: Teachers College Press, 1989.

Rothman, R. "Pursuing a Vision Linking Study of Learning, Education Practice." *Education Week*, Special Report, Oct. 9, 1991, pp. 4–5.

Sarason, S. B. *The Predictable Failure of Educational Reform: Can We Change Course Before It's Too Late?* San Francisco: Jossey-Bass, 1990.

SCANS. *What Work Requires of Schools*. SCANS Report for America 2000. Washington, D.C.: U.S. Government Printing Office, 1992.

Senge, P. M. *The Fifth Discipline: The Art and Practice of the Learning Organization*. New York: Currency Doubleday, 1990.

Sherwood, R., Kinzer, C., Bransford, J., and Franks, J. "Some Benefits of Creating Macro-Contexts for Science Instruction: Initial Findings." *Journal of Research in Science Teaching*, 1987, *24*, 417–435.

Showers, B., and Joyce, B. "The Evolution of Peer Coaching." *Educational Leadership*, 1996, *53*(6) 12–16.

Smylie, M. A. "Teacher Learning in the Workplace: Implications for School Reform." In T. R. Guskey and M. Huberman (eds.), *Professional Development in Education: New Paradigms and Practices*. New York: Teachers College, Columbia University, 1995.

Smylie, M. A., and Conyers, J. G. "Changing Conceptions of Teaching Influence the Future of Staff Development." *Journal of Staff Development*, 1991, *12*(1), 12–16.

Sparks, D. "A Paradigm Shift in Staff Development." *ERIC Review*, 1995, *3*(3), 24.

Sparks, D., and Loucks-Horsley, S. "Models of Staff Development." In W. R. Houston (ed.), *Handbook of Research on Teacher Education*. New York: Macmillan, 1990.

Teddlie, C., and Stringfield, S. *Schools Make a Difference*. New York: Teachers College Press, 1993.

Thompson, J. D. *Organizations in Action*. New York: McGraw-Hill, 1967.

Tillema, H. H., and Imants, J. G. M. "Training for the Professional Development of Teachers." In T. R. Guskey and M. Huberman (eds.), *Professional Development in Education: New Paradigms and Practices*. New York: Teachers College, Columbia University, 1995.

U.S. Department of Education. *Building Bridges: The Mission and Principles of Professional Development*. Washington, D.C.: Government Printing Office, 1995.

Wade, R. "What Makes a Difference in In-Service Education? A Meta-Analysis of Research." *Educational Leadership*, 1985, *42*, 48–54.

Whitford, B. L., and Kyle, D. W. "Interdisciplinary Teaming as Staff Development: Initiating Change in a Middle School." In W. T. Pink and A. A. Hyde (eds.), *Effective Staff Development for School Change*. Norwood, N.J.: Ablex, 1992.

W. T. Grant Foundation. *The Forgotten Half*. New York: Author, 1992.

CHAPTER SIX

Teacher and Student Learning

Strengthening Their Connection

Gary Sykes

Teacher professional development (TPD) as a significant lever for educational improvement is an emergent interest. At the same time, however, the relationship between TPD and student learning is uncertain. The current system that organizes teacher learning appears to have relatively weak effects, and the path to improvement is unclear. An important agenda for the future, therefore, is to strengthen the relationship between teacher and student learning.

EDUCATIONAL REFORM AND TEACHER PROFESSIONAL DEVELOPMENT

Several developments in education give impetus to TPD as a crucial element in educational reform. One is the emergence of systemic reform (Smith and O'Day, 1991; Thompson and Zeuli, this volume) as a major educational policy initiative at federal and state levels. The term refers generally to the coordination or alignment of multiple policy instruments to effect more powerful and authoritative instructional guidance. Curriculum frameworks, student learning objectives and standards, instructional materials, and assessments should reinforce what learning is desired and to what level of attainment. So much seems obvious, but contemporary accounts of instructional guidance stress its fragmented, ill-coordinated character (Cohen and Spillane, 1992). Within this account, however, aligned instruments establish the conditions for learning but require implementation—a.k.a. learning—by teachers. Any form of instructional guidance relies on teacher understanding and action for its ultimate effectiveness. Teachers are not solely responsible for implementing systemic reform, and other actors, including administrators, parents, and community agencies, also are vital. But the central educational professional who works day in and out with students is the teacher, and to the teacher falls the major responsibility for fostering academic learning.

Whereas professional development initially was regarded as one among a number of coequal policy instruments for promoting change, it now is reckoned as the centerpiece. Early predictions that new forms of assessment, including high-stakes testing, new curricular mandates, more detailed and grade-specific curriculum frameworks, or teaching standards documents, might serve as the main stimulus for change have not been borne out. Such policy instruments are important, to be sure, but policymakers are aware that to effect significant changes in student academic learning will require substantial learning by teachers. Curricular change, like all other important changes in education, ultimately relies on teacher understanding, skill, and will. Consequently, while policymakers continue to press for systemic reforms, a key issue is what teachers are prepared to do in conjunction with policy-driven change.

A second argument supporting TPD reckons that advances in research-based instructional practice can exert influence only through the ways teachers are engaged with new knowledge, including their participation in producing such knowledge, as well as testing and implementing knowledge generated by others. In education as in other fields, new knowledge and technology are not self-implementing; they require the mindful work of professional practitioners engaged with particular groups of students in particular settings. Consequently teachers must engage in processes of knowledge production, testing, dissemination, and use as a fundamental aspect of educational research and development. How best to organize teacher involvement in these activities continues to perplex reformers, however, and several approaches are in evidence, ranging from local action research to technical training around validated innovations. It appears, though, that regardless of the approach, teachers require more sustained, in-depth involvement if changes in instructional practice are to reflect new knowledge.

Finally, and most important, TPD has become more critical for a third reason. In the face of new demands on education for more ambitious learning, a more diverse and demanding student body, and a nationwide commitment to educate all children to high levels of accomplishment, knowledge and skill demands in teaching have escalated dramatically, even within the short time span of this century's most recent reform wave. Basic skills continue to preoccupy many schools, but the future of education clearly presses beyond the basics to more demanding forms of academic learning. The new learning agenda has not yet taken hold fully in the public mind, but the trend is pronounced. Our society will need more highly educated citizens and workers, and its individual members will require more sophisticated education to get ahead. Basic equity goals now require that ambitious learning be extended not just to an elite but to all, at a time when minority and poor students make up an increasing proportion of the school-age population. The profound, converging implications of new learning, new standards, and new students scarcely have been reckoned in the support for teacher learning supplied through public policy, but one clear implication is that teachers in the future must be capable of far more sophisticated forms of practice than in any prior era. The stakes around their learning are now much higher.

These arguments are quite general, however, and do not point to any particular course of action for improving teacher learning. They also require refinement around the question of how improvements depend on teacher learning. Broadly speaking, reforms that depend either directly or indirectly on teacher learning may be distinguished from reforms that are largely independent of teacher learning, yielding three classes of reform. Consider a few examples of each kind. Efforts to test the National Council of Teachers of Mathematics (NCTM) standards require direct learning by teachers that likely includes attention to their knowledge of mathematics, of its teaching, and of how students learn this subject. Many of the new standards have direct implications for teaching and require considerable learning (and unlearning) by teachers in order to realize their visions. So one large class of reforms involves instructional interventions in which teachers may learn new practices or the use of new materials (technology comes to mind), or experiment in producing instructional innovations of their own. In cases of this kind, professional development may be the reform, for teacher learning is central to the reform idea itself and to its effects on students.

In the second class are a wide range of reforms that rely to some degree on teacher learning to realize their intent or fulfill their potential. The history of American education is filled with reforms of this kind, including school desegregation, mainstreaming special needs students into regular classrooms, and restructuring schools. The logic or theory of such reform does not centrally implicate teacher learning, but the reform cannot succeed unless teachers change some of their beliefs, practices, and ways of working with others. The move to team teaching, block scheduling, interdisciplinary curricula, detracking, schools within schools, or many other curricular or organizational reforms typically places a heavy burden of learning on teachers, where learning is associated with change of some kind—revising beliefs and values, acquiring new knowledge and skill, adapting to new patterns of work, and coping with conflict and disruption of familiar routines. In this large class of reform, success depends in substantial but indirect measure on teacher learning. The theory of the reform often identifies nonteaching factors as crucial but works through teachers to produce desired effects. The history of such reform, however, typically reveals meager support for teacher learning manifest in short time lines for implementation, a weak base of technical knowledge, the absence of material resources, and a lack of sustained leadership. Securing teachers' hearts and minds around organizational and curricular changes has been the Achilles heel of much reform.

Finally, certain educational reforms are relatively independent of teacher learning. School finance comes to mind, as do some forms of administrative decentralization or the introduction of school choice policies. In such system-altering reforms, the technical core of the enterprise—teaching and learning—is not the target of reform. Rather the institutional arrangements and resources that frame education broadly are regarded as the primary point of leverage. Advocates for system-altering reforms may regard the current status of teaching and learning as satisfactory or not, but their strategic assumption does not call for interventions in the technical core, even if the full chain of assumptions behind such reforms leads eventually to a favorable impact on student learning.

Teacher professional development, then, is not crucial to all forms of reform but is likely to constitute a critical element in the implementation of two of these three broad classes and so to be of major, even determining, influence. At the same time, however, teachers' learning needs associated with these first two classes have been underestimated consistently in the history of reform.

IMAGES OF TEACHER LEARNING

Efforts to create closer relationships between teacher and student learning take place within established institutional arrangements for professional development that set an enabling (or disabling) context. Three images together capture the salient features of the present system. In one, teachers operate as consumers within a quasi-regulated market structured by bureaucratic service provision. In another, teachers perform as independent artisans building up knowledge, skill, and materials around craft-based approaches to their work. In a third, teachers act as professionals who orient their work according to communal and collegial norms. Each of these images contains a partial truth about professional development today that is worth describing.

From one perspective, professional development has evolved toward a consumer or demand-driven delivery model, in which school districts and other service providers supply a menu of offerings for teachers. Incentives to participate include advancement on salary scales and, in many states, licensure renewal through accumulation of continuing education units. Service providers include district personnel, external consultants, and universities offering degree and nondegree programs. Such arrangements are widely institutionalized in state and district policy and procedures. The main features of the system are nearly everywhere the same, leading to a prediction that in major outline, the professional development available to teachers varies little from place to place. The delivery system may be characterized as quasi-regulated insofar as states and districts establish certain minimal rules and incentives for participation on both the supply and demand sides. For example, states set requirements for renewal of teaching licenses, and districts and states approve offerings that count toward renewal. Such professional development is centrally planned, uniformly provided, and regulated within hierarchically organized structures, all classic features of bureaucracy. Teachers are consumers within this model because many options are available to meet common requirements. Teachers may select which universities to attend, which district workshops to join (although some may be mandatory), and which other experiences to seek out. The image of the shopping mall, famously applied to the American high school (Powell, Farrar, and Cohen, 1985) fits teachers' professional development as well.

Interacting with this broadly institutionalized set of arrangements are many other initiatives that engage teachers in learning: school- and district-launched improvement activities; reform networks coalesced around new visions of schools, learners, subject matter, and other matters; local partnerships; policy-driven tasks such as mentoring new teachers or scoring student assessments; and others. In an era of intense, continuous reform, professional development is often locally initiated and highly dynamic. A visitor to almost any American school would soon discover that some or all of the teachers have been, are, or soon will be engaged in some form of school or professional development that places new learning demands on them. Schools can appear somewhat indiscriminate in the volume and pace of activity. At any given time, teachers may be trying out a new district-adopted textbook, attending workshops to learn about a new state curriculum framework, studying student test results as a basis for modifying instruction, participating in a school reform network promoted by the principal that requires school restructuring of some sort, attending classes at a local university or extended institutes in the summer, and tinkering with new materials and ideas in their own classrooms. Equally likely, teachers may choose not to participate in any or all of these activities, or to phase in and out of participation. Many options are available, but considerable discretion resides with individual teachers. In terms of their impact on teachers, the local, dynamic elements may well outweigh the institutionalized features. By this account, local contexts are extremely important, with considerable variation across all layers of the system: the state, district, school, and even subunits within schools may each contribute to teacher learning.

Moving closer still, teachers themselves exercise their discretion over professional development. They can choose what to become involved in and to what extent. And as studies (Huberman, 1993a) have revealed, teacher engagement is typically patterned by career stage and developmental trajectory. Teachers' voluntary participation in school and professional development varies over the course of careers in the classroom. Close-up case studies describe teachers, both individually and collectively, as actively constructing their own learning opportunities out of the variable elements available to them (see, for example, Spillane, 1995; McCarthey and Peterson, 1993).

Finally, what intervenes between the formal opportunities presented by the environment and the discretionary involvements of teachers is the culture and structure of the work organization. Some schools—and within them, some teacher clusters, departments, or other subgroups—elicit greater involvement over time as a function of leadership and the nature of professional community (Louis and others, 1995; Louis, Marks, and Kruse, 1996; Newmann and others, 1996; Talbert and McLaughlin, 1994). Associated with the construct of professional community are such school characteristics as the presence of shared norms and values cultivated through regular reflective dialogue; the deprivatization of practice, referring to open scrutiny of individual teachers' practice through dialogue, observation and feedback, and examination of student work; a schoolwide focus on student learning; and high levels of collaboration around such tasks as curriculum development, coordination of instruction, and assessment of student learning. Of equal importance to these process variables is the press toward academics in the school. Schools that offer demanding curricula and employ teachers whose educational expectations for students are high tend to produce higher levels of student achievement than schools that rank high on communitarian values but low on academic press (Battistich and others, 1995; Phillips, 1997; Shouse, 1996). Just as schools vary in the academic press they place on students, so they vary in the professional press toward continued learning that they place on teachers.

Taking into account the highly variable and discretionary nature of professional development activity, two contrasting images have emerged to characterize teacher responses (see also Thompson and Zeuli, this volume). One, proposed by Huberman (1993b), resorts to the analogy of the independent artisan developing craft knowledge, skill, and materials. The modal American teacher spends considerable time working alone in the classroom. Over time teachers gradually accumulate an instructional repertoire and construct a teacher identity around their interests, strengths, and dispositions. Change in practice resembles the gradual building up of repertoire, punctuated by episodes during which some teachers engage in more radical, discontinuous change. Within this imagery, the individual teacher serves as arbiter of new ideas, adopting or adapting some, rejecting others, and complying with surface features of still others. Learning is largely self-selected and self-directed, and in the main it is conservative. Teachers conserve those practices that make their work manageable, provide meaning to their professional identities, and bring success within their own terms (see Cuban, 1993). However, as the change literature reveals, many career teachers depart during certain stages of their work lives from the model of stable, gradually evolving practice to experiment with potentially transformative or revolutionary practices. These episodes have variable results. Teachers may transform their practices over time, or they may change the innovation to fit their existing practice (a process described as mutual adaptation in the early change literature), or the experiment may end in disillusionment and withdrawal from further adventures.

This model accommodates both continuity and change in teaching, while emphasizing its craftlike aspects together with the essential independence—some say, isolation—of the teacher. It also fits well with the image of the teacher as consumer in a professional development marketplace, free to choose among available opportunities. The rules and incentives structuring the market press on the teacher, but not too heavily. The system is loosely coupled, with much discretion residing in the craftsman-consumer.

The third image, however, complicates and challenges the fit between the other two by construing teachers as social beings working within particular school cultures. Schools as work organizations mediate transactions between individuals and environments, introducing an important source of variability—and of constraint. What can and sometimes does influence teacher response to opportunities supplied by the policy and market environments are collective norms and traditions, social relationships, and the organizational structure of the workplace. As a function of their cultural and structural properties, schools may be more or less collegial; more or less open to innovation and outside influence; more or less inclined to scrutinize practice and results, to involve participants in decision making, and to hold members of the school community to shared ideals, standards, norms, and values. These functions of the local community do not absolutely bind members, but they can exercise decisive influence through processes of selection (in and out), socialization, and training.

This orientation defines professional development not as a discrete, variable activity but as a fundamental disposition and responsibility encouraged, even enforced, through membership in a particular occupational community and work organization. In schools where professional community is strong, teacher learning is a regular, ongoing feature, with participation ensured through the socially constructed web of mutual obligations among colleagues. In such schools the professional practitioner, rather than the independent artisan, becomes the guiding metaphor for teacher learning. However, most accounts of schooling suggest that this model is relatively rare.

These three accounts may be fashioned into an explanatory framework for analyzing teachers' professional development. Learning opportunities are provided by environments structured by both policy and markets. *Environment* in this case is a covering term for what may be a bewildering array of activity influenced by many sources that include all levels of government together with a range of nongovernmental entities, such as professional associations, reform networks, and universities. Policy supplies formal sanctions and incentives in the form of pay increases, licensure renewal requirements, and others, with opportunities to learn about new policy developments. Local initiatives launched at district and school levels add further opportunities to the array. Participation, however, depends on responses from teachers. As various observers have noted, teaching long has been structured as individual work featuring strong, craftlike elements. Left to their own devices within traditionally organized schools, teachers will respond as independent artisans, honing their craft. But schools and extraschool agents also may create a sense of community that draws teachers into collective efforts.

This tripartite portrayal of teachers as independent artisans exercising choice in a loosely structured marketplace of offerings, variably influenced by characteristics of the school workplace, raises problems for reform even as it offers certain advantages. An enterprise so organized is open to many ideas and can respond rapidly to new initiatives. Its market-like organization obviates the need for and the problems associated with central planning. And it supplies the front-line workers (teachers) with considerable freedom in directing their own learning and development. At the same time, this way of organizing teacher learning has some serious liabilities. It is difficult to direct to organizational or policy priorities, it lacks accountability, and it appears largely ineffective in improving instruction in any systemic, widespread way. If TPD is to become a significant policy instrument for educational improvement, these three liabilities must be addressed.

Within the current provision, TPD is very difficult to mobilize for any focused priority. The market decentralizes priority setting to the consumer, while the system of suppliers made up of district personnel, itinerant consultants, university programs, and others are weakly related to any process of collective decision making. Loose jointed internally, TPD also is loosely coupled to other improvement processes as well. Systemic reform, for example, explicitly calls for the orchestration of such elements as learning standards, instructional materials, performance assessments, and TPD. If standards-based reform is to influence student learning, then these elements must be pursued in concert as the primary organizational focus. Current arrangements for TPD, however, do not naturally support such actions at either district or school levels.

A related liability, TPD lacks accountability. Few mechanisms exist to hold those responsible to account or to organize it productively. Absent accountability-oriented feedback, TPD as an institutionalized function will remain unchanged in fundamental respects. Teachers may be charged with the responsibility to continue their own learning, and the professional model supplies one basis on which to organize accountability. But an emphasis on individual responsibility alone is insufficient in the light of education's public purposes and its collective nature. Teacher learning is a critical organizational resource and as such must be well managed at school and district levels, where accountability also resides.

Finally, unhappiness with TPD reflects an assumption that it is largely ineffective in improving teachers' instructional practices and organizational capacities. It is probably more accurate to claim that TPD's impact is unknown rather than inadequate or meager, but few teachers or administrators express much confidence in it. In their testimony, teachers typically identify some powerful, consequential learning experiences while admitting that these isolated opportunities stand out from a mass of superficial, forgettable activity.

TPD's ineffectiveness may be attributed to resource inadequacies, particularly follow-up in teachers' classrooms, where assistance is most needed, but many analysts also suspect that existing resources are not used efficiently. In any event, there is little evidence that TPD is effectively mobilized at either school or district levels to improve student learning through effects on teacher learning.

STRENGTHENING THE CONNECTION

A familiar chicken-and-egg problem haunts efforts to improve TPD by strengthening its connection to student learning. Many reformers today argue that policy-initiated efforts must be pursued in concert to remedy education's ills. TPD cannot be reformed alone because it is embedded in a system some of whose other elements must be changed simultaneously if improvements in TPD are to produce student learning results. A brief example illustrates this problem of embeddedness. Results from the Third International Mathematics and Science Study (TIMSS) portray the U.S. elementary curriculum as suffering a number of critical defects in comparison with national curricula in other countries (Schmidt, McKnight, and Raizen, 1997). In the subject areas of mathematics and science, the U.S. curriculum contains far more topics than can be covered in the time available. Teachers and students alike can cover all the material represented in curriculum frameworks, instructional materials, and tests only by skimming the surface, treating knowledge as information that may be taught through "telling" and learned through memorization. "A mile wide and an inch deep" is the phrase the TIMSS team used to characterize the American curriculum in these content areas in comparison with other countries that produced superior student achievement. Such a curriculum may not reflect the preferences of American teachers, but it is deeply institutionalized in policy and practice.

TPD that pursues more ambitious learning goals, requiring, for example, conceptual understanding of subject matter or application of knowledge to novel problems and new situations of use, is unlikely to exert much influence even if the TPD itself is well designed and supported. State and district curriculum frameworks, instructional materials, tests, and, not least, longstanding traditions will combine to subvert teachers' efforts to change instructional practice. Similar influences will continue molding student efforts as well, so that student resistance to innovative teaching may be added to the list of impediments. Exemplary TPD, according to this argument, is unlikely to produce strong, desirable effects on student learning because other powerful elements in the equation linking the two remain unaltered.

A different assessment of the problem of embeddedness comes out of studies that describe the organization and operation of TPD within districts (Miller, Lord, and Dorney, 1994; Moore and Hyde, 1981; Schlechty and Whitford, 1983). These accounts portray staff development as fragmented organizationally, particularly in large urban districts, where funding, personnel, and authority tend to be spread across offices and poorly coordinated with any set of stable priorities. Delivery modes feature brief workshops, and overall levels of investment are both low and variable across districts. The range of investment in one study, for example, extended from 1.8 percent of the total operating budget ($1,755 per teacher) in one district to 2.8 percent ($3,528 per teacher) in another (Miller, Lord, and Dorney, 1994). Districts also vary in the extent to which staff development is centralized at the district level or decentralized to the school level, so that the organizational context for reform of this function is extremely variable. To the extent that such local, contextual factors will influence the impact of policy-driven reforms, results are likely to be highly uneven.

These portrayals yield a paradox. If TPD is to be successful, it must fit with the regularities in place, but if it fits, it is unlikely to exert much beneficial influence on teacher or student learning. Organized as an exchange relationship within a market, supplied through mechanisms with strong bureaucratic features, yet controlled ultimately by individual craftspersons variably influenced by characteristics of the local workplace, TPD is incapable of producing sustained, powerful effects on student learning through its effects on teacher learning. Yet these elements of market organization, bureaucratic provision, and local craft orientation are strongly institutionalized, hence resistant to wholesale change. Furthermore, TPD is unlikely to exert strong, independent influence on teacher and student learning absent connection to a yet wider set of reforms in school curriculum and district organization.

Taken as a whole, this analysis does not point ineluctably toward a solution of the TPD "problem," but it does suggest a tendency, a general direction. The strategic conclusion to be drawn comes in two parts. First, TPD must be treated not as an encapsulated function that may be reformed successfully without attending to related reforms at the same time. Centralized direction and coordination are necessary to overcome TPD's atomized, inconsequential character. The systemic reformers make a strong case for such an approach. Second, the content and character of TPD itself must feature more direct linkages between what students are to learn and what teachers learn. These twin leads may be elaborated in greater detail, beginning with the learning connection, then mapping out to needed supports in curriculum, organization, and policy.

Guidance for TPD

TPD as a function is currently distributed between school and district levels while also bringing external agents such as universities into play. While the formal coordination of TPD therefore involves administrators, the delivery of TPD may be provided by a wide range of agents, including teachers in particular. The configuration of agents will depend on local circumstances. An elementary school located in a centralized, urban district next to a large university faces prospects quite different from a rurally isolated school in a small district whose central office includes the superintendent and one or two additional professional staff. Some general guidance, however, may be identified to strengthen the teacher-student learning connection, which necessarily would be enacted quite differently in these contrasting situations. Five such leads are sketched out next:

- Use the teacher-student learning connection as a criterion for the selection and design of TPD.
- Embed TPD in the specific content of the student curriculum.
- Integrate examination of student learning, using multiple sources of evidence, into TPD.
- Include attention to student learning in TPD associated with the implementation of curricular and instructional innovations.
- Reference both formative and summative evaluation of TPD to student learning.

First and most obvious, the teacher-student learning connection should serve as a *criterion for selection of professional and school development activity*. Teachers' professional development appears weakly coupled to effects on students, in part as a function of decision making and choice processes. Whether it is university course work or the workshops provided by consultants, in-service planned by districts, schoolwide improvement plans, or teachers' voluntary activity, too often the relationship to improvement in student learning is remote to nonexistent. Teachers and schools pursue improvement activity for a range of legitimate reasons that extend beyond their direct effects on students, and there is probably no simple rule to follow in setting priorities. But it is possible to render judgments about whether on average and for the most part the current investment in teacher learning is related consistently and productively to student learning.

Regardless of the decision makers, TPD can be designed more explicitly with student learning in mind as proximate or ultimate outcome. This selection principle, however, need not overly constrain the nature of TPD. Rather, it requires two forms of planning and justification. One is that TPD designers have (and commit to test) a theory of the relationship between the learning opportunities provided to teachers and the eventual learning of students. The second is that they propose an argument, against competing alternatives, to justify their priorities, plans, and activities in terms of potential impact on student learning. A few examples will illustrate how TPD as theory and argument can serve to focus teacher learning opportunities on students.

A useful discipline in planning TPD is to develop in as much detail as possible a set of working hypotheses about how the particular learning opportunities to be supplied to teachers will come eventually to influence student learning. Theoretical leads may come from prior research on teacher or student learning, evaluations of past programs and investments, social science models, and experience-honed ideas of expert practitioners. The critical exercise, however, is to set forth in rigorous fashion the chain of causal reasoning that leads from interventions in teacher learning to effects on student learning.

Along these lines, a recent analysis by Hill and Celio (1997) is instructive. They gathered a set of the most prominent broad-based reforms that are being tried in the United States today (such as standards, decentralization, and teacher professional development) and unpacked the causal assumptions underlying each. They discovered that every reform they examined contains a "zone of wishful thinking," where the targeted reform is dependent for its system-transforming success on a large series of related changes over which the proposed reform has no control. Particular TPD initiatives do not possess the scope of omnibus reform ideas, but the practice of causal mapping helps to expose soft, underdeveloped assumptions in interventions at the outset that may be refined, firmed up, and specified in greater detail.

Consider next the injunction to treat the selection of TPD as an argument. District staff developers might face a choice between investing in workshops around the adoption of a new mathematics text series or a systematic training program that introduces the precepts of the Reading Recovery Program to regular classroom teachers. Each TPD activity arguably relates to the enhancement of student learning, so that a choice between them (or a phased combination of them) is not obvious. Selecting a course of action requires consideration of trade-offs among competing priorities, each of which may be anchored in student learning. A broad range of factors may be admitted into such arguments: comparison of student mathematics versus reading achievement, evidence of the efficacy of particular interventions, district priorities as established by the superintendent and school board, (re)learning requirements associated with the alternatives, and many others. The essential recommendation here, though, is to conceive TPD at the planning or design stage as an argument competing with other arguments about how best to improve student learning and as a theory or set of working hypotheses about the relationship.

Within such a discourse regime, decision makers could adopt a variety of rules for investing scarce resources in TPD. For example, schools or districts might decide to set 25 percent of TPD resources aside for activity that is not demonstrably related to student learning, but is compelling on other grounds. For example, the early stages of implementing Kentucky's omnibus school reform agenda has occupied many educators in learning about the details of the reforms. Such learning arguably is necessary but is tangentially related to student learning. Nevertheless, the new policy environment is a priority demanding some attention. What schools and districts must do is to establish and monitor resource allocation decisions more carefully, using as a prime criterion the effect that TPD is presumed to have on student learning.

A second guideline is to *embed TPD in the specific content of the student curriculum*. The idea here is relatively simple. Many teachers need greater opportunities to work directly with the content of the student curriculum considered in three, closely related ways. Teachers need to deepen (1) their own understanding of the subject matter and skills-related content, (2) the various ways of representing and conveying that content in instruction (frequently referred to as pedagogical knowledge or understanding of content), and (3) their understanding of how students learn the content. This triumvirate should form the heart of TPD as it comprehends the three commonplaces of the subject matter, the teaching, and the learning. Teachers need regular, rich opportunities to work on these commonplaces as referenced to the particular curriculum that their students are expected to master.

The rationale for this focus comes from a number of sources. One such source is the situated cognition perspective (Brown, Collins, and Duguid, 1989), which explores how knowledge acquisition and use is fundamentally indexed to situations that provide important cues to the learner. Although contested by some theorists (Anderson, Reder, and Simon, 1997), this perspective suggests that teachers as learners may need to work with the specifics of their curriculum, their school, and their students in order to acquire knowledge usable in their teaching.

Of these contextual factors, knowledge related to the teaching and learning of subject matters appears most critical. In a recent review of research that examined the impact of in-service education programs on student achievement in mathematics and science, Kennedy (1998) reports several provocative findings. Of the small set of studies that traced effects on student learning, the program with the greatest impact first developed a taxonomy of types of arithmetic problems and types of student learning difficulties associated with each. This material provided the content of the in-service program rather than any particular teaching strategies. Instead, teachers were encouraged to discuss among themselves alternative ways of teaching each type of problem to children. The researchers in this case offered no specific practices or curriculum materials for teachers to use (Carpenter and others, 1989).

This in-service approach yielded greater effect sizes on student mathematics achievement than did programs concentrating on either generic or subject-specific teaching behaviors. Furthermore, structural features of this set of interventions, such as total contact time, concentrated versus distributed contact hours, and presence or absence of in-class coaching produced no clear, dramatic effects by themselves. Kennedy concludes that while the rhetoric of TPD has long emphasized shortcomings in organizational factors, a critical element instead may be the content of the in-service. And the most potent content appears to be knowledge about how students learn specifics of the school curriculum.

Another suggestive research result along these lines comes from a survey study of California teachers' professional development opportunities in relation to new state standards and assessments (Cohen and Hill, 1997). The researchers found that when teachers' learning opportunities met several conditions—grounding in the curriculum that students study; reinforcement from several elements of teaching practice, that is, not only curriculum but assessment; and extended time to learn rather than single, brief workshops—then it is reasonable to expect significant change in many teachers' practices. More particularly, this study's results posit that teacher learning opportunities "may have to go one level deeper than just subject specificity. It seems to help change mathematics teaching practices if teachers have even more concrete topic-specific learning opportunities" (p. 14). The study further reveals modest but significant association with student achievement on the state mathematics assessment. Although the study issues appropriate cautions about limitations due to a small sample and a cross-sectional design, the tentative conclusion is provocative: "When teachers have significant opportunity to learn the content that their students will study, in ways that seem to enable them to learn more about teaching that material, and when assessments are linked to the student and teacher curriculum, teachers' opportunities to learn pay off in their students' performance" (p. 26).

Finally, this guideline also reflects professional development practices in many Asian countries, including Japan and China, where a primary form of teacher learning is the local study group that explores multiple ways of representing topics, ideas, and concepts to students in the light of typical or recurrent questions, misconceptions, and barriers to learning. What is most notable about this form of professional development is that it subsists within a widely shared national curriculum, it privileges knowledge generated by teachers themselves, and it is disseminated across schools through networks of teachers (for descriptions, see Paine, 1990; Shimahara and Sakai, 1995; Stigler and Stevenson, 1991).

The injunction to embed TPD in the specific content of the school curriculum has proved difficult to carry out for reasons that are not obvious. In his study of TPD associated with the Kentucky school reforms, for example, McDiarmid (1997) begins by citing a range of studies that stress the strong relationship between teachers' knowledge of subject matter and student achievement (Ferguson, 1991; Ferguson and Ladd, 1996). Then he notes the puzzling absence of attention to subject matter under conditions where teachers themselves control the content. In a stratified, random sample of seventy-seven schools in Kentucky, he found substantial attention to literacy, particularly writing portfolio activities, which was stimulated largely by changes in the high-stakes state assessment, but almost no concentration on the core academic areas of mathematics, literature, science, or social studies. He goes on to speculate as to why teachers themselves do not emphasize greater attention to subject matter. Recollecting their college courses, teachers may not believe that more subject matter knowledge will be helpful to their teaching, an attitude particularly prevalent among elementary teachers. They also do not perceive themselves as lacking subject matter knowledge, especially related to a school curriculum regarded as rudimentary. As well, McDiarmid argues that external factors play a role. Teacher evaluation in Kentucky pays little attention to subject matter knowledge, and the state's current emphasis on high-stakes testing has pressed teachers toward learning about the new assessments rather than about the standards and the curriculum that they reference. Furthermore, as more schools experiment with interdisciplinary curricula, "ways of knowing," "learning styles," and "multiple intelligences," the value of disciplinary knowledge is further eroded in the minds of many educators.

To focus teacher learning on the student curriculum also requires that there be a relatively stable and relatively shared school curriculum. These enabling conditions are supplied by the policy system, and frequently they are not well met. Where they are in place, however, then TPD can be organized around teacher interactions within and across schools as teachers share their wisdom, present problematic cases, and explore multiple approaches to the teaching of content. Absent a knowledge content anchor, it is difficult to see how teacher learning could be related reliably to student learning, given the situated, highly specific character of knowledge use in teaching. Consequently policymakers and administrators have an important role to play in creating conditions that are conducive to this connection, a point to be amplified below.

A third precept closely related to the second recommends that *the close examination of student learning, using multiple sources of evidence, be integrated into TPD.* The tradition of educational testing in the United States numbers among its disadvantages the thin feedback provided to teachers. A heavy reliance on standardized tests employed for external accountability fails to supply teachers with rich information about the course of student learning and development. Today, however, many schools and districts are experimenting with new forms of assessment and new practices for documenting children's learning. Teachers increasingly are engaged in designing "authentic" assessment tasks that purport to measure ambitious learning outcomes, creating scoring rubrics, evaluating student work samples contained in portfolios, and implementing assessment practices that feature public demonstrations and collectively developed standards for evaluation. Related practices involve teachers in keeping careful qualitative records of student development in such areas as literacy and mathematics, then using these records as the basis for evaluative conferences with students, parents, and other teachers.

Examples of new approaches to assessment and documentation of student learning are emerging in many locales. One of the oldest is the descriptive review of the child, pioneered by Patricia Carini and colleagues at the Prospect School in Bennington, Vermont. Founded in 1965, Prospect was a small, private school serving some sixty students aged four and a half to fourteen; although it closed in 1990, it had a broad impact on progressive education in the United States. The process engages teachers in developing holistic narratives of children's development, based on close examination of children's work, observation of their behavior in class, informal interviews with the student, and related evidence assembled over long periods of time. At Prospect descriptive reviews took on a collective dimension in that they formed the basis for conferences with parents, discussions among teachers, and an ongoing archive of children's work that supplied a permanent record of development for reference by the school community (Carroll and Carini, 1991).

Another example is the Primary Language Record (PLR), a process of documenting children's growth in literacy through the collection of qualitative evidence over time (for accounts of the PLR, see Darling-Hammond, Ancess, and Falk, 1995). Pioneered as an alternative assessment practice in England in the mid-1980s, the PLR spread to the United States, where it now is used in schools from New York City to California. The PLR involves teachers in assembling a body of evidence on an individual student using such sources as focused interviews with the child and the family, systematically recorded teacher observations, student work samples collected over time, and rating scales that describe progress along a variety of dimensions. Enacted as a collective practice in schools, the PLR serves as the basis for parent conferences and professional discourse among teachers. Its use helps teachers to learn about their students and individualize their instruction.

A final example from the high school level is the use of student work portfolios and year-end demonstrations at Central Park East Secondary School in

New York City. In this case, the assessment serves a summative purpose, to determine a student's readiness for graduation. This assessment practice evolved over a number of years and currently includes fourteen areas, from which students must make presentations in seven areas to a graduation committee of at least two faculty members, another adult of the student's choosing, and a student. Each student's postgraduation plan is the first of the fourteen portfolios and the centerpiece of the process. Evaluating the presentations and portfolios consumes considerable faculty and student time, is a high-stakes assessment that students begin preparing for from the seventh grade onward, and is one critical means through which the school's faculty enact their commitment to personalized education on one hand and high standards for all on the other (Meier, 1995).

These examples share certain critical features. Teachers engage in all aspects of assessment, including design of exercises, development of scoring rubrics and standards, administration of the assessments, scoring (or qualitative evaluation) of student performance, and reporting of results. The assessments themselves rely on multiple forms and kinds of evidence assembled over time. And the assessment process draws all members of the school community together around the close scrutiny of individual students' learning and development. Finally, these approaches to assessment and documentation serve not only as the basis for decision making but also as sites for teacher learning.

It is this last feature that warrants greater emphasis. The construction of assessment systems is a balancing act that counterposes external demands for accountability with internal demands for formative information useful to the improvement of teaching and learning. Coincident with the rise of standardized testing, the balance has involved commercially produced tests of achievement with classroom-bound assessments that individual teachers use (often based on the teacher guides accompanying textbooks). Together these approaches have left out assessments rich in qualitative detail, anchored in collective processes that serve to define standards of accomplishment in learning. This gap is now beginning to be filled. This line of thinking suggests that a critical accompaniment to improvements in TPD will be school- and district-based assessment that complements and supplements externally oriented testing. A hypothesis to be explored posits two reasons that TPD and assessment is a critical link. First, collective teacher engagement with student assessment in itself may promote professional learning related to student learning. Second, the assessments may be tied to other TPD, serving as one explicit point of reference in the design, implementation, and evaluation of professional development activity. Conversely, if schools and districts decouple assessment practice from TPD, then two opportunities are lost: to create teacher learning opportunities out of assessment-related tasks and to strengthen the focus of TPD on student learning.

A fourth guideline refers to professional development associated with skills training, program development, and the implementation of innovations. The guidance here calls for *explicit attention to student learning as an integral aspect of implementation*. Schools and school districts routinely implement new programs and practices stimulated by policy initiatives, professional networks, administrative leadership, and other sources. Too often, however, the training that accompanies implementation makes little or no reference to what students learn. Relatively few schoolwide innovations have been validated on the basis of their impact on student learning (Fashola and Slavin, 1998). Instead, they represent popular theories or ideological positions or partially tested programs in delimited settings that cannot be generalized with confidence. The reform impulse is strong in many American schools, leading to considerable openness to new ideas and practices. From one angle this is a very positive feature of American education, but from another angle, such responsiveness produces a restless, even shiftless, search for panaceas that results in the widely remarked tendency to faddism. One means for introducing greater discipline into the process of implementation is to build in more attention to effects on student learning as a means both to improve the process and test the program or innovation itself.

Carrying out this guidance could take many forms, including use of small-scale experiments, where teachers formally test samples of students using curriculum-specific assessments, design and administer new assessments based on the new program's learning objectives, conduct clinical interviews with selected students to explore qualitative dimensions of their learning, or engage in action research projects that focus on students. A common element in all these approaches is to specify what the innovation or program is expected to accomplish in terms of its effects on students, and then mount local, small-scale inquiries to probe for such effects. Another common element is the collective nature of such tasks, which require some form of social organization at school and district levels that implicates resources of shared time, collaborative work norms, and leadership—elements associated with the construct of professional community. And a third common element is a supportive ethos that favors critical scrutiny of new ideas and practices in terms of their effects on students.

Identifying these elements helps to reveal the challenges in this guidance. Many school cultures would be unreceptive to the collective dimensions of such work and the critical, inquiring stance that is required. Reform enthusiasts would have to temper their advocacy with analysis, a difficult feat when many reforms are contested and vulnerable to political opposition. Teachers would have to balance commitment to learn the innovation with dispassion in testing its effects, even during the early stages of implementation. And educators would need to be mindful of the "implementation dip" that typically accompanies the trial of new practices (Fullan, 1991), as teachers struggle to master new ideas, methods, and skills. Responsible attention to effects on students takes care not to dismiss the promise of fully mastered practice on the basis of early struggles in learning new practices.

Attending to student learning in the context of implementation has a deceptive simplicity that belies its transformative potential. In truth, following this injunction would require subtle but important changes in how schools operate. To identify a few controversial implications, administrators would be judged not on whether they had introduced an innovation but on how it affects students beyond the process of early adoption. And the decision making around program development would need to accept extended time lines and greater support in order to gauge effects on student learning. This might require districts to be more selective in adopting new practices, thereby concentrating resources on a small set of innovations or new practices over longer time spans. From this chapter's perspective, however, all of these changes would be desirable alterations in current patterns of TPD.

Finally, schools and districts can create firmer accountability by *referencing both formative and summative evaluation of TPD to student learning.* Admittedly this guidance is difficult to pursue. The causal chain that connects an in-service intervention to effects on teacher thinking and instructional practice, in turn yielding effects on student learning, is complex and hard to establish. The process unfolds slowly and uncertainly in the face of many contingencies that lie outside the control of both teacher and student learning. Furthermore, not all TPD aims to influence student learning. As already noted, proposed improvements that depend directly on teacher learning, such as new instructional policies, are but one class of reform that schools pursue. Consequently, good reasons abound to ignore improvements in student learning as an explicit outcome of TPD. Current evaluative practice typically does not even seek evidence that worthwhile and significant change in teaching practice has occurred as a result of TPD, for even this question is filled with complexities.

At the same time, it seems reasonable to argue that at least some evaluative resources should be devoted to this issue insofar as the rationale for much TPD includes at least implicit reference to student learning. Greater attention to student learning would have two other salutary effects as well. It would highlight the importance of maintaining an instructional priority long enough to expect an impact on student learning, and such evaluation would begin building a body of knowledge about effective TPD when judged against the ultimate criterion of student learning. The TPD agenda in most schools and districts tends to feature a rapid succession of topics, priorities, and targets so that no broad or deep influences on either teaching practice or student learning are very likely. Establishing student learning as an evaluative criterion for TPD forces organizational attention to the conditions necessary to produce such impact. And it creates new possibilities for knowledge production that arguably are the joint responsibility of the teaching profession and educational organizations that employ teachers. Teachers have a stake in defining the professional knowledge that underlies effective practice and so should participate in processes of creating such knowledge as one aspect of the meaning of teacher professionalism. At the same time, TPD as an organizational process implicates resource allocation decisions and so is a school management responsibility. These twin forms of accountability unite in requiring greater evaluative attention to the impact of TPD on student learning.

Concentration on this issue could take many forms, ranging from experimental interventions jointly designed by school and university-based collaborators to clinical case studies undertaken by teachers within school-based initiatives or cross-school networks. School-university partnerships, including collaboration in professional development schools and other shared sites, may be an especially promising context for joining the research expertise from the university to the wisdom of school practitioners. Longitudinal designs and projects in particular are warranted in order to establish firmly the complex relationship between teachers' opportunities to learn and student achievement.

Enabling the Reform of TPD

Any school or district might take up the practices just outlined in order to strengthen the learning connection between teachers and their students. A common element appears to be professional development focused on the specific content of what students are to learn, how they learn that content, and how it may be taught to diverse learners. At the same time this review has emphasized how conditions associated with the school curriculum itself, the organization of TPD, the culture of many schools, and the deeply learned preferences of schoolteachers constitute impediments to enacting this guidance. The fare that we eat is the analogy that springs to mind. Health mavens may prescribe diets that will help us feel better, lose weight, and live longer, but the culture provides an enormous mass of junk food together with powerful advertising to sell it, and we love it. The admonitions of dietitians may be scientifically validated, but their counsel is lost amid the powerful influences that shape what we eat. Yet to carry the analogy a step further, Americans can change overly determined cultural habits under the right circumstances. Witness the relatively successful efforts to encourage seatbelt use or to discourage smoking in public places. Underlying these large-scale shifts have been complex processes that combine social movements with scientific research, recourse to the law and to government regulation, mass media campaigns with grassroots organizing.

Using seatbelts and refraining from smoking in public places are relatively simple habits to change; they require little learning or relearning from large numbers of people. Strengthening the teacher-student learning connection on a widespread basis is a far more complex matter that requires support for local, teacher-led activities from the spheres of organization, management, and policy, even as the focus must be kept on learning opportunities that join teachers and students. To this end a number of leads may be proposed. One is to focus policy initiatives more directly on the content of TPD using the traditional instruments of mandates, inducements, and capacity building. In conjunction with ongoing state efforts to establish strong, parsimonious standards for student learning, there should be targeted efforts to support teacher learning around the content, the learning objectives, the ways students learn the content, and the instructional practices of effective teachers.

Policy provides the broad framework for teacher and student learning through the specification of content and learning standards coupled with assessments. As well, systemic reform emphasizes other elements to be orchestrated that include instructional materials and TPD. States vary widely in their coordination of these elements and in the role they assign to districts and schools in a federal system of governance. No single model of systemic reform could take hold across the diversity of state traditions and political cultures. Perhaps national standards and assessments will exert a beneficial standardizing influence over a long time span, but for the short term this appears unlikely. Nevertheless, the necessity is clear. States in partnerships of varying kinds with districts must create a framework of standards and assessments that sets the common ground for local efforts to connect student and teacher learning. As the TIMSS analyses make clear, the most critical, if politically difficult, task is to focus content standards on a delimited but powerful set of ideas that can genuinely guide learning, rather than the impossibly expansive and overly detailed lists of topics and skills that have been produced in many locales and from many professional sources.

In conjunction with standards policy, states can then use multiple policy instruments to focus TPD on the content. This is potentially a controversial recommendation, because it calls for states to be more directive about three related policy targets: (1) the content of preservice education for teachers, (2) the content of teacher licensure and induction, and (3) the content of continuing education and certification. These are the critical policy levers through which states can anchor teacher learning in state-sanctioned content related to student learning. However, in pursuit of tighter coupling between student learning, standards, and teacher learning, states have a range of policy options extending from capacity-building projects to voluntary guidelines, to incentives-based approaches, to mandates. And states could enlist districts and universities as partners in these policy developments by encouraging multiple local projects to emerge, networking among districts, and testing planned variations. What seems imperative at this juncture is to build spacious avenues, through state policy, between a strong, parsimonious set of student learning standards and teachers' learning that is anchored in the student standards.

Student assessment policy is another potent tool for concentrating teacher learning on student outcomes, but recent reports indicate it is a double-edged sword. Some research indicates that state-sponsored performance-based assessments can serve as a strong stimulus for teacher learning. Reports from both Vermont (Murnane and Levy, 1996) and Kentucky (Bridge, Compton-Hall, and Cantrell, 1997) point to positive effects on teacher learning and instructional practice as a result of introducing statewide assessments. In the Vermont case, teachers came together to score student responses on mathematics problems, in the course of which they reported learning a good deal about standards and student learning. In the Kentucky case, the state-mandated introduction of portfolio assessments that require students to write in a range of genres produced changes in both the amount and kind of writing that teachers featured in their instruction. Assessment policy, then, can serve as a relatively direct and powerful stimulus to instructional practices that in turn are related to student learning.

In Vermont, results on the new performance assessments were reported to districts for their own use, but the state did not attach high stakes to their results. In Kentucky, test results were linked to school improvement through the distribution of cash bonuses for high performance and the threat of sanctions for poor performance (schools can be assigned outside assistance and ultimately taken over for continuing failure). Some reports (Jones and Whitford, 1997) are beginning to document the adverse effects of linking performance assessments to high-stakes accountability. Among the adverse consequences, Kentucky's new testing regimen has narrowed attention to a de facto state curriculum in opposition to the expressed aim of encouraging greater site-based decision making, elevated stress for teachers and students alike, focused instruction too narrowly on only those learning outcomes that are easily measurable, and increased drill in test taking procedures.[1] Yet another study (Firestone, Mayrowetz, and Fairman, 1998), this one comparing the impact on mathematics curriculum and instruction of new assessments in Maine and Maryland, found modest influences amid continuation of traditional teaching practices. Contemporary research, then, ranges from accounts of positive effects, to negative effects, to few effects at all.

State-mandated performance assessments appear to produce variable outcomes, and their use is not easy to reconcile, for in most states political pressures press toward high-stakes testing that cannot easily serve double duty as a vehicle for school and instructional improvement. Educators must continue advocating for state testing systems that balance accountability with improvement; where accountability pressures are severe, however, efforts must be mounted to supplement external assessments with locally developed performance measures.

Other enabling developments in organization and management would need to unfold at district and school levels. Recent work has shed some doubt on the capacity of structural and governance reforms to exert impact on teaching and learning (Elmore, 1992). Consequently it may make sense to work in new ways within existing organizational structures and routines rather than launch major reforms as precursors to direct work on teaching and learning. (Note, though, that this strategic assumption may not hold in every locale; city school districts such as Chicago, New York City, and Philadelphia may require restructuring and governance interventions to unlock the potential for focused work on curriculum and instruction.) Several examples illustrate this approach. Most school districts engage in regular review and updating of instructional materials in the content areas, typically around textbook adoptions. This stable organizational routine involves teachers and administrators in reviewing new texts, comparing their contents to district standards and external assessments, and piloting innovative materials. Such commonplace activity, however, is often decoupled from district staff development, which is treated as a separate organizational routine. However, the potential to pursue teacher and student learning in the context of focused work on instructional materials is great.

In the context of such curriculum-related activity, teachers might pilot new materials with an eye to understanding their uses in various lesson formats, how they interact with other materials, how students learn from new materials, and related matters. Teachers could work on teams to design the texts that accompany new materials, supplementing what publishers typically produce by concentrating on such matters as student understanding of the concepts and "big ideas" involved, the tasks that might be used to engage student thinking, and the knowledge teachers need to use the materials in thoughtful ways with diverse students (see Ball and Cohen, 1996, and Ball and Cohen, this volume, for related ideas along this line). Many possibilities are available, but the main point is to note that schools and districts might better exploit the routine, professional activities of teachers to enhance their learning in conjunction with targeted work related to their students' learning.

A second site for TPD is districtwide and schoolwide work on student assessment, where schools develop methods that complement the external regime of testing emanating from higher levels of governance. Standardized testing is a powerful and stable feature of American education, but it does not well serve to guide teaching and learning in schools. Many schools disaggregate and study achievement test data as one basis for instructional decision making, and this is a useful collective activity. But schools also need to develop alternative assessments that engage teachers in a fuller range of assessment tasks. Local work on assessment, then, is a potentially valuable organizational activity that may be stimulated from the district level and carried out at the school or school cluster levels. In a recent study of restructuring schools, the investigators found that strong forms of accountability were rare, that external accountability did not have beneficial effects on schools' organizational capacities, and that strong internal accountability tends to augment local capacity (Newmann, King, and Rigdon, 1997).

In this analysis, "internal accountability" is present when "staff identified clear standards for student performance, collected information to inform themselves about their levels of success, and exerted strong peer pressure within the faculty to meet the goals" (p. 48). Standards and assessments must become the basis for local teacher-led work if they are to have a genuine impact on student learning. They are useful tools for focusing and directing instruction, but educators must use them in mindful ways if they are to exert influence. Encouraging such use must be an organizational priority if standards-based activity is to have widespread effects, so administrative action is needed to initiate such work, develop organizational capacity around standards and assessments, and link such work to external sources of guidance from both government and professional sources.

Yet a third organizational priority is to establish regular, ongoing connections between a school's faculty and outside sources of expertise and feedback. Huberman (1995) makes a powerful case for this recommendation, arguing that if innovations are to effect changes in teaching practice, then teachers must participate in cycles of activity that combine collective work internal to the school with interactions outside the school that supply conceptual inputs, technical consultations, observations and demonstrations, and other resources. What he calls the "open collective cycle" aims to produce change in teaching practices but does not include a link to student learning. A simple extension of this model, however, incorporates attention to student learning based on the guidance sketched above. The main point, though, is to create an organizational context for teacher learning that orchestrates a range of linked activities over time that combine internal work with external consultations. Such work is school and classroom centered while connecting with outside sources of expertise. Teachers play a central role, but district and school administrators can be critical in establishing and supporting the process. Equally important, however, is the focus on content and learning. Organizational process models can be used in relation to a wide range of innovations. Shachar (1996), for example, describes a case where cooperative learning is the focus, illustrating how schoolwide organizational processes can support and sustain instructional change in classrooms. But if the focus of teacher learning and change is to link directly to student learning, then the content of the intervention must focus on knowledge of the subject matter that students are to learn, strategies and approaches for teaching that subject matter, and understanding of how students learn that subject matter.

Finally, a largely unexplored strategy for enhancing TPD is to concentrate professional development for administrators on contemporary approaches to teaching and learning in the disciplines, in conjunction with standards-based education. District and school administrators serve as critical gatekeepers for instructional improvement. They can mobilize resources, direct attention, deflect diversions, and institute supportive organizational routines. Research that probes administrators' understanding of new ideas about teaching and learning reveals both how limited is their knowledge and how influential they can be in directing reform to what counts (see, for example, Spillane, 1998). Related work illustrates how administrator thinking about instruction may be modified based on relatively modest in-service education (Nelson, 1997; Nelson and Sassi, 1998). As many accounts of schooling suggest, administrators are powerful agents in school reform; they need to be drawn more directly into the study of teaching and learning so that they may better understand and manage the core enterprise of schooling.

CONCLUSION

This chapter has taken what might be termed an incremental approach to the reform of TPD by advocating guidance and principles that educators might act on directly, without first making large structural or governance changes. At the same time, the analysis acknowledges the embedded nature of the difficulties facing TPD. The school curriculum serves as the context for both teacher and student learning. Large-scale problems with this curriculum can be remedied only through policy actions from higher levels of governance, that is, state and federal levels. The organizational routines that frame and focus TPD have also been subjected to extensive criticism, together with repeated calls for structural reform, increased attention and resources, and the like. These calls are not misplaced, but they have so far not yielded substantial improvements. Recommending that the teacher workday be restructured to allow more collaborative time for professional learning is a sound structural recommendation that proves difficult to enact on a widespread basis. The regularities of schooling are deeply institutionalized.

Instead, the line of attack here emphasizes greater attention to the core relationship between what teachers learn and what students learn, building outward from this essential connection. Student learning is the ultimate justification for teacher learning and so should be brought more powerfully into the planning and evaluation of TPD for this reason. But equally, if TPD is to contribute to the effectiveness and efficacy of teachers, then its content should more directly be concerned with student learning. Finally, if teachers themselves tend to underestimate the nature and depth of subject matter knowledge that is useful to good teaching, then greater direction around this critical matter will be needed from the spheres of policy, organization, and management. Such leadership can be provided within the current system, even admitting its structural flaws. The implication of this argument is that policymakers, administrators, school board members, and other leaders must understand the centrality of the content of TPD and begin working out ways to emphasize this priority. In the competition for the precious resource of teacher time and attention, professional attention to student learning and the content of student learning should be the paramount consideration.

Note

1. At this writing, Kentucky policymakers have just replaced the six-year-old Kentucky Instructional Results Information System with the new Commonwealth Accountability Testing System. The details of the new test have yet to be worked out, but the thrust is to include a national, norm-referenced portion that matches the state's core curriculum and to reduce the written portion of the test.

References

Anderson, J., Reder, L., and Simon, H. "Situative Versus Cognitive Perspectives: Form Versus Substance." *Educational Researcher,* 1997, *26,* 18–21.

Ball, D., and Cohen, D. "Reform by the Book: What Is—or Might Be—the Role of Curriculum Materials in Teacher Learning and Instructional Reform?" *Educational Researcher,* 1996, *25,* 6–8, 14.

Battistich, V., Solomon, D., Kim, D., Watson, M., and Schaps, E. "Schools as Communities, Poverty Levels of Student Populations, and Students' Attitudes, Motives, and Performance: A Multilevel Analysis." *American Educational Research Journal,* 1995, *32,* 627–658.

Bridge, C., Compton-Hall, M., and Cantrell, S. "Classroom Writing Practices Revisited: The Effects of Statewide Reform on Writing Instruction." *Elementary School Journal,* 1997, *98,* 151–170.

Brown, J., Collins, A., and Duguid, P. "Situated Cognition and the Culture of Learning." *Educational Researcher,* 1989, *18,* 32–42.

Carpenter, T., Fennema, E., Peterson, P., Chiang, C.-P., and Loef, M. "Using Knowledge of Children's Mathematical Thinking in Classroom Teaching: An Experimental Study." *American Educational Research Journal,* 1989, *26,* 499–531.

Carroll, D., and Carini, P. "Tapping Teachers' Knowledge." In V. Perrone (ed.), *Expanding Student Assessment.* Alexandria, Va.: Association for Supervision and Curriculum Development, 1991.

Cohen, D., and Hill, H. "Teaching and Learning Mathematics in California." Paper presented at the American Educational Research Association annual meeting, Chicago, March 1997.

Cohen, D., and Spillane, J. "Policy and Practice: The Relations Between Governance and Instruction." In G. Grant (ed.), *Review of Research in Education,* Vol. 18. Washington, D.C.: American Educational Research Association, 1992.

Cuban, L. *How Teachers Taught: Constancy and Change in American Classrooms, 1880–1990.* (2nd ed.) New York: Teachers College Press, 1993.

Darling-Hammond, L., Ancess, J., and Falk, B. *Authentic Assessment in Action.* New York: Teachers College Press, 1995.

Elmore, R. "Why Restructuring Alone Won't Improve Teaching." *Educational Leadership,* Apr. 1992, pp. 44–49.

Elmore, R., Peterson, P., and McCarthey, S. *Restructuring in the Classroom: Teaching, Learning, and School Organization.* San Francisco: Jossey-Bass, 1996.

Fashola, O., and Slavin, R. "Schoolwide Reform Models: What Works?" *Phi Delta Kappan,* 1998, *79,* 370–379.

Ferguson, R. "Paying for Public Education: New Evidence on How and Why Money Matters." *Harvard Journal on Legislation,* 1991, *28,* 465–497.

Ferguson, R., and Ladd, H. "How and Why Money Matters: An Analysis of Alabama Schools." In H. Ladd (ed.), *Holding Schools Accountable.* Washington, D.C.: Brookings Institution, 1996.

Firestone, W., Mayrowetz, D., and Fairman, J. "Performance-Based Assessment and Instructional Change: The Effects of Testing in Maine and Maryland." *Educational Evaluation and Policy Analysis,* 1998, *20,* 95–114.

Fullan, M., with Stiegelbauer, S. *The New Meaning of Educational Change.* (2nd ed.). New York: Teachers College Press, 1991.

Hill, P., and Celio, M. "System-Changing Reform Ideas: Can They Save City Schools?" Unpublished manuscript, Brookings Institution and University of Washington, 1997.

Huberman, M. *The Lives of Teachers.* New York: Teachers College Press, 1993a.

Huberman, M. "The Model of the Independent Artisan in Teachers' Professional Relations." In J. Little and M. McLaughlin (eds.), *Teachers' Work: Individuals, Colleagues, and Contexts.* New York: Teachers College Press, 1993b.

Huberman, M. "Networks That Alter Teaching: Conceptualizations, Exchanges, and Experiments." *Teachers and Teaching: Theory and Practice,* 1995, *1,* 193–211.

Jones, K., and Whitford, B. L. "Kentucky's Conflicting Reform Principles: High-Stakes School Accountability and Student Performance Assessment." *Phi Delta Kappan,* 1997, *79,* 276–281.

Kennedy, M. "The Relevance of Content in Inservice Teacher Education." Paper presented at the annual meeting of the American Educational Research Association, San Diego, Calif., Apr. 1998.

Little, J. W. "Norms of Collegiality and Experimentation: Workplace Conditions of School Success." *American Educational Research Journal,* 1982, *19,* 325–340.

Louis, K. S., and others. *Professionalism and Community: Perspectives on Reforming Urban Schools.* Thousand Oaks, Calif.: Corwin, 1995.

Louis, K. S., Marks, H., and Kruse, S. D. "Teachers' Professional Community in Restructured Schools." *American Educational Research Journal,* 1996, *33,* 757–798.

McCarthey, S., and Peterson, P. "Creating Classroom Practice Within the Context of a Restructured Professional Development School." In D. Cohen, M. McLaughlin, and J. Talbert (eds.), *Teaching for Understanding. Challenges for Policy and Practice*. San Francisco: Jossey-Bass, 1993.

McDiarmid, W. "Teachers' Aversion to Subject-Matter Professional Development." Unpublished paper, 1997.

Meier, D. *The Power of Their Ideas*. Boston: Beacon Press, 1995.

Miller, B., Lord, B., and Dorney, J. *Staff Development for Teachers. A Study of Configurations and Costs in Four Districts*. Newton, Mass.: Education Development Center, 1994.

Moore, D., and Hyde, A. *Making Sense of Staff Development: An Analysis of Staff Development Programs and Their Costs in Three Urban School Districts*. Chicago: Designs for Change, 1981.

Murnane, R., and Levy, F. "Teaching to New Standards." In S. Fuhrman and J. O'Day (eds.), *Rewards and Reform: Creating Educational Incentives That Work*. San Francisco: Jossey-Bass, 1996.

Nelson, B. S. *Lens on Learning: How Administrators' Ideas About Mathematics, Learning, and Teaching Influence Their Approaches to Action in an Era of Reform*. Newton, Mass.: Center for the Development of Teaching, Education Development Center, May 1997.

Nelson, B. S., and Sassi, A. "Cultivating Administrators' Professional Judgment in Support of Mathematics Education Reform: The Case of Teacher Supervision." Paper presented at the annual meeting of the American Educational Research Association, San Diego, Calif., April 1998.

Newmann, F., and others. *Authentic Achievement: Restructuring Schools for Intellectual Quality*. San Francisco: Jossey-Bass, 1996.

Newmann, F., King, M. B., and Rigdon, M. "Accountability and School Performance: Implications from Restructuring Schools." *Harvard Educational Review*, 1997, *67*, 41–74.

Paine, L. "The Teacher Virtuoso: A Chinese Model for Teaching." *Teachers College Record*, 1990, *92*, 49–81.

Phillips, M. "What Makes Schools Effective? A Comparison of the Relationships of Communitarian Climate and Academic Climate to Mathematics Achievement and Attendance During Middle School." *American Educational Research Journal*, 1997, *34*, 633–662.

Powell, A., Farrar, E., and Cohen, D. *The Shopping Mall High School*. Boston: Houghton Mifflin, 1985.

Rosenholtz, S. *Teachers' Workplace: The Social Organization of Schools*. White Plains, N.Y.: Longman, 1989.

Schlechty, P., and Whitford, B. "The Organizational Context of School Systems and the Functions of Staff Development." In G. Griffin (ed.), *Staff Development*. 82nd Yearbook of the National Society for the Study of Education. Chicago: University of Chicago Press, 1983.

Schmidt, W., McKnight, C., and Raizen, S. *A Splintered Vision: An Investigation of U.S. Science and Mathematics.* Norwell, Mass.: Kluwer, 1997.

Shachar, H. "Developing New Traditions in Secondary Schools: A Working Model for Organizational and Instructional Change." *Teachers College Record,* 1996, *97,* 549–568.

Shimahara, N., and Sakai, A. *Learning to Teach in Two Cultures: Japan and the United States.* New York: Garland, 1995.

Shouse, R. C. "Academic Press and Sense of Community: Conflict, Congruence, and Implications for Student Achievement." *Social Psychology of Education,* 1996, *1,* 47–68.

Smith, M., and O'Day, J. "Systemic School Reform." In S. H. Fuhrman and B. Malen (eds.), *The Politics of Curriculum and Testing.* Bristol, Pa.: Falmer Press, 1991.

Spillane, J. "Constructing an Ambitious Pedagogy in Fifth Grade: The Mathematics and Literacy Divide in Instructional Reform." Paper presented at the annual meeting of the American Educational Research Association, San Francisco, Apr. 1995.

Spillane, J. "A Cognitive Perspective on the Role of the Local Educational Agency in Implementing Instructional Policy: Accounting for Local Variability." *Educational Administration Quarterly,* 1998, *34,* 31–57.

Stigler, J., and Stevenson, H. "How Asian Teachers Polish Each Lesson to Perfection." *American Educator,* 1991, *15,* 12–20, 43–47.

Talbert, J., and McLaughlin, M. "Teacher Professionalism in Local School Contexts." *American Journal of Education,* 1994, *102,* 123–153.

PART THREE

RETHINKING ORGANIZATIONS FOR TEACHER LEARNING

CHAPTER SEVEN

Teacher Recruitment, Selection, and Induction

Policy Influences on the Supply and Quality of Teachers

Linda Darling-Hammond,
Barnett T. Berry, David Haselkorn, and Elizabeth Fideler

Over the next decade the United States will need to hire 2 million teachers due to rising enrollments, growing retirements, and high rates of attrition for beginning teachers. Although only about half of those hired are expected to be newly prepared teachers (with the remainder from a reserve pool of teachers who are returning to the classroom), this period represents one of the largest increases in teacher demand in the past century. By 2002 America's schools will be serving more children (54 million) than ever before, and the total number of teachers will grow to over 3.3 million (up from 2.5 million in 1980). In some communities, especially in high-poverty urban and rural locations, schools already report difficulties in recruiting qualified teachers in critical subject areas such as physical science, mathematics, bilingual education, and special education, and across the nation there is a need for far more teachers of color to meet schools' desires for a teaching force that reflects the growing diversity of America (Darling-Hammond, 1994).

As a consequence of these trends, teacher recruitment is an increasingly important issue for school systems. Finding teachers, however, is just one aspect of the problem. If students are to be well served, schools must be able to recruit teachers who will be effective in the classroom and stay in teaching over the course of a career. None of these issues is nonproblematic in the United States. Research on teacher education, licensing, and hiring practices reveals the use of idiosyncratic criteria, highly variable standards, and cumbersome procedures that can discourage the selection and placement of the best candidates (Wise,

Darling-Hammond, and Berry, 1987; Darling-Hammond, Wise, and Klein, 1995). Similarly the degree to which newly hired teachers are supported and assessed in their initial years of teaching can determine whether they remain in teaching and whether they are able continuously to develop their knowledge, skills, and dispositions (Bolam, 1995). Research suggests, for example, that as many as 30 percent of new teachers leave within five years of entry (Darling-Hammond, 1997), yet high-quality induction and mentoring programs lower attrition rates for new teachers and can strengthen teacher effectiveness (Huling-Austin, 1990; Odell and Ferraro, 1992b).

Until recently policy responses to the issues of getting and keeping good teachers have rarely considered the many labor market and school district dynamics that influence teacher recruitment and retention. Much research has consisted of correlational studies that use rough proxies for teacher quality available in large-scale databases for examining the relationships among teacher characteristics, school practices, and student learning. These studies of the relationship between achievement or aptitude test performance and decisions to teach in various settings or at various wage levels are useful for understanding broad labor market trends, but they reveal little about how to attract, retain, prepare, select, or support teachers who will be successful with students in particular contexts (Hanushek and Pace, 1995; Ballou, 1996). Other studies that seek to open the black box of recruitment and retention decisions reveal the complexities of teacher markets, as well as the effects of various policies and practices on these markets. For example, some research has pointed out the mediating influence of working conditions on recruitment and retention (Murnane, 1991), and other work has demonstrated how teacher commitment is moderated by powerful intervening variables related to working conditions, such as collegiality, involvement in decision making, and opportunities for professional development (Rosenholtz, 1989).

Although the United States faces many challenges in terms of assuring qualified teachers for all of its communities, many promising programs for recruiting and retaining well-prepared teachers have been launched across the country. A variety of innovative programs have been developed for meeting classroom diversity challenges; scores of universities have created professional development school partnerships with local districts, offering markedly improved preparation for new prospective teachers; and a growing number of peer assistance and evaluation programs have been established for novice teachers. Research on these programs, described in this chapter, supplements other studies suggesting links between teacher quality and student achievement (Darling-Hammond, 1997; Ferguson, 1991; Greenwald, Hedges, and Laine, 1996; Sanders and Rivers, 1996).

As a nation, the United States excels at initiating innovative demonstration programs. However, useful experiments frequently remain exceptions to the norm rather than vehicles for broader reform. What has been lacking in most districts, states, and at the national level is a framework for policy that creates a coherent infrastructure of recruitment, preparation, and support programs that connect all aspects of the teacher's career continuum into a teacher development system that is linked to national and local education goals.

The National Commission on Teaching and America's Future (NCTAF) (1996) outlined the dimensions of this challenge, pointing to deficiencies in the way the nation develops education's human resources—its teachers and other education personnel: recruitment is ad hoc; teacher preparation is often unaligned with the needs of contemporary classrooms and diverse learners; selection and hiring are often disconnected from either specific school district goals or a more complex and rigorous image of quality teaching; induction and mentoring are frequently scattershot—and likely to be the first programs to be eliminated when districts cut their budgets. The commission argued that given growing teacher demand, changing student demographics, and ambitious school improvement goals, the country needs more thoughtful, sustained, and systemic approaches to teacher recruitment, development, and support.

Furthermore, by paying insufficient attention to the capacity, quality, cultural responsiveness, and diversity of its teaching force, the United States puts all of its various education reform and restructuring efforts at risk because improved student performance relies substantially on effective teaching by qualified, committed teachers who can address the needs of the students they serve. As standards for student performance rise, teachers will need to have mastered sophisticated content knowledge and pedagogical skills that can make difficult ideas accessible to a wide range of learners. And as America grows more diverse, so does the need for a more qualified, diverse, and culturally skilled teacher workforce. This is important not only to provide role models for students of color, but so that all students will be better prepared to live and work in a pluralistic, multicultural society and to negotiate the complex cultural transactions that will be required to thrive in that society.

In this chapter, we describe the demographic backdrop behind education's human resource imperative; summarize what is known about effective recruitment, selection, and induction programs; describe efforts underway across the country to create improved pathways to teaching careers; and provide a framework for evaluating what it will take to recruit, prepare, select, and induct a teaching force of excellence and diversity.

Achieving such results is likely to require revamped preservice preparation programs; more innovative and coordinated approaches to teacher recruitment, selection, and hiring; and induction at the institutional, district, state, and national levels. One aspect of creating a learning continuum for teachers involves tightening the linkages among the standards used to shape teacher education accreditation, teacher licensure, and advanced certification, using the same performance-based standards and assessments to assess teacher education programs as well as the quality of teachers prior to the issuance of a license and for recertification (NCTAF, 1996). Recruitment, selection, and induction policies and practices should be the subject of similar efforts to achieve coherence. Policies that reinforce well-grounded conceptions of teaching and means for acquiring the teaching knowledge they imply would allow policymakers and practitioners to develop and use shared standards and assessments in making decisions about who is sought, why they are hired, and how they are assessed and supported in their initial years of teaching. This might create the kind of coherent institutional structure that enables teachers to get from the places where they are prepared to the places where they are needed with the kind of knowledge and skills that enable them to succeed.

ISSUES IN TEACHER SUPPLY AND DEMAND

Historically policies that govern teacher hiring and the knowledge and skills required of teachers have been strongly influenced by supply and demand considerations. These have been framed by efforts to keep salaries relatively low and supply plentiful (Goodlad, 1990). With growing demand, questions have resurfaced as to whether teacher shortages actually exist. Those who argue yes and those who argue no are both correct. In times of high demand in a labor market that operates with a variety of barriers and inequalities, overall surpluses can exist side by side with local shortages. In spite of the fact that the United States annually produces more new teachers than its schools hire, significant apparent shortages exist by locality, subject field, school level, and quality (Boe and Gilford, 1992). Over the past decade many schools have reported difficulty hiring qualified teachers in bilingual education, special education, physics, chemistry, mathematics, and computer science; such difficulties predominate in inner cities with increasing numbers of immigrant children and in the rapidly growing South and West (Akin, 1989; Ingersoll, 1997a).

It also appears that these localized shortages can be addressed through proactive teacher recruitment policies. For example, Connecticut took significant strides to recruit and retain qualified teachers in the 1980s and virtually eliminated shortages and created surpluses of teachers by the 1990s (see Darling-Hammond and McLaughlin, this volume). Other states that have paid less attention to recruiting and preparing teachers have far less qualified teachers in the classroom (Darling-Hammond, 1994a). For example, Alaska and Louisiana, which have problematic labor markets and lack systemic teacher recruitment and retention policies, have strikingly large numbers of underprepared teachers, especially in high-demand fields. As just one indicator of the degree of disparity across states, while 84 percent of mathematics teachers in Wisconsin and Missouri held full-state certification and a major in 1994, only 39 percent met this standard in Alaska and only 59 percent did so in Louisiana (Darling-Hammond, 1997).

The issue of supply in teaching is not one of bodies, since most states are willing to lower standards to fill classrooms, but one of quality. Issues of supply and demand should be considered in the light of who enters, their characteristics, and whether they stay. In turn, these variables should be considered in terms of market forces and the demographic demands posed by the schools of today and tomorrow.

Who Enters Teaching, Who Stays, Who Leaves

Many studies conducted over the past two decades have identified who enters, stays in, and leaves teaching. Over the past few decades, trends have changed substantially. Whereas teaching was the field most frequently selected by college students in the 1960s and early 1970s, beginning in the late 1970s teacher demand slackened, and teaching became substantially less attractive as a career choice relative to other professions. Whereas teaching was once one of only a few fields open to women and people of color, the opening up of other occupations during the 1970s, combined with a decrease in teacher demand and teacher salaries in the late 1970s and early 1980s, led to changes in both the attractiveness of teaching as a career and the characteristics of those who pursued it.

Between 1966 and 1985, there was a 71 percent decline in the proportion of freshmen planning to pursue elementary or secondary teaching careers, from 21.7 percent in 1966 to 6.2 percent in 1985 (Astin, Green, and Korn, 1987). The number of college students who graduated with bachelor's degrees in education plummeted by more than 50 percent during this period, from more than 194,000 in 1972 to only 87,000 in 1987 (National Center for Education Statistics [NCES], 1989; American Council on Education [ACE], 1989). The declines were most pronounced for minority candidates, dropping by over 40 percent for Hispanic and Native American candidates between 1975 and 1987 and by two-thirds for African American candidates (NCES, 1989; ACE, 1989). By 1987 only 8,000 minority candidates received bachelor's degrees in education, representing 9 percent of all education degrees, a substantial drop from the 13 percent of a much larger number of degrees that had been awarded to minorities ten years earlier. Whereas interest in teaching grew for white candidates after 1985, the number of education degrees continued to decline for African American college students into the early 1990s.

Data collected and analyzed in the late 1970s and 1980s revealed that shrinking demand for new teachers and attractive jobs in other professions took their toll on indicators of teacher quality as well. For example, students who had high academic ability (as measured by Scholastic Aptitude Test scores) and those taking college preparatory course work in high school increasingly migrated to other college majors where economic rewards were greater and job prospects more secure (Schlechty and Vance, 1983; Darling-Hammond, 1984). These earlier studies indicated that while teacher education graduates were more academically accomplished than high school students who thought they would enter education, they tended to be less academically able than the average college graduate (Hanushek and Pace, 1995).

Since the late 1980s, however, there has been a steady increase in interest in teaching careers (Metropolitan Life, 1995). With rising demand for teachers, increases in teacher salaries, and school reforms that are changing the roles and working conditions of teachers, many highly able young people and older entrants from other careers are choosing to teach. In 1993 over 140,000 bachelor's degree recipients graduated with preparation for teaching, and about 20,000 prepared to teach in master's degree programs (Darling-Hammond, 1997). In 1996 about 10 percent of college freshmen indicated an interest in becoming teachers (Astin, 1996).

Academic standards for entering teacher education appear to be rising too, as many states and colleges required higher test scores and grade point averages (GPA) for teacher education students during the 1980s. By 1990 50 percent of newly qualified teachers had earned a GPA of 3.25, compared to 40 percent of all college graduates (Gray and others, 1993). A recent study in Kentucky, one of the many states that increased its teacher education standards and required accreditation of schools of education during this time, revealed that the state's teacher education students scored above the national average for all college-bound students on American College Testing assessment of cognitive achievement (Clements, 1998; see also Darling-Hammond and McLaughlin, this volume).[1]

Although these are positive trends in the attractiveness of teaching to academically able college students, it is too soon to tell how many of these recruits will stay in the profession. Studies of teacher attrition in the 1980s revealed that the more academically able candidates were most likely to leave the profession soonest. Research on candidates recruited during the late 1970s and early 1980s found that beginning and experienced teachers who scored higher on the National Teacher Examinations were more likely to leave teaching sooner and were less likely to return than their lower-scoring peers (Murnane and others, 1991; Schlechty and Vance, 1983). Similarly, beginning teachers with a disciplinary specialty in math, chemistry, and physics (all high-demand fields) were found to leave the profession at higher rates than novice teachers in other disciplines (Murnane, Singer, and Willett, 1989; Sclan, 1993). In addition, first-year high school teachers were more likely to leave teaching than were elementary and middle school teachers (Sclan, 1993).

A number of reasons have been advanced for these phenomena, including greater marketability of high-ability candidates, teachers with disciplinary degrees, and those in fields like mathematics and science (Murnane, Singer, and Willett, 1989). Some studies suggest that the ablest candidates have a lower threshold for accepting some of the bureaucratic routines and infantilizing expectations found in many public schools (Darling-Hammond, 1984; Johnson, 1990). These studies have become dated, however, and it will be important to see if such findings continue to hold up given the current attractions to and conditions of teaching.

In terms of labor market variables, salary can make a difference in terms of who enters and stays in teaching. Several studies conducted in the 1980s revealed that beginning salaries can make a difference in terms of teacher recruitment (Hanushek, 1989; Richards, 1988). In a study of New York State school districts, Jacobson (1988) found that higher beginning salaries resulted in the hiring of more experienced and more educated teachers. Bruno (1981) found that new teachers could be attracted to more challenging school environments if salary incentives were in place, an important finding given the evidence regarding where academically able teachers are more willing to teach. In separate studies of teacher and school characteristics and student achievement, Ferguson (1991) found that more academically able teachers were less likely to teach in lower-socioeconomic schools, and Ballou (1996) noted that teachers from selective colleges tended to work in schools with smaller percentages of poor students and higher percentages of those bound for college.

Other dimensions of teacher quality are important as well. For example, many new teachers are entering the field without adequate preparation for their jobs. A recent study revealed that about 11 percent of newly hired teachers in 1994 entered the field with no license, and an additional 16 percent had received a substandard license, indicating that they lacked full preparation in either their content field or in education courses or both. Most of these recruits were hired in low-income schools serving large numbers of students of color (Darling-Hammond, 1997; see also Oakes, 1990; Ingersoll, 1997a, Ballou, 1996). Contrary to some conventional wisdom, unlicensed recruits are less academically able than their licensed counterparts, achieving GPAs well below those of other college students, who in turn perform less well than teacher education graduates (Gray and others, 1993).

The disproportionate placement of underprepared teachers in disadvantaged schools is especially problematic given the mounting research evidence that fully qualified teachers—those who are more knowledgeable in subject matter, pedagogy, curriculum development, assessment, and learning theory—are more effective than those who do not possess this knowledge and skill, especially in contexts where skillful teaching is most needed (Darling-Hammond, 1997; NCTAF, 1996). A critical issue in today's schools is the bimodal distribution of teachers, which increasingly poses a national dilemma. While the fruits of reforms in the teaching profession are apparent in the increasingly impressive qualifications and abilities of teachers in advantaged communities, a large number of whom are entering with master's degrees from redesigned and much more effective teacher education programs, a countervailing trend is growing in inner cities and rural areas, where many underprepared candidates, who are armed with little knowledge about teaching and learning, are entering classrooms to teach the nation's most vulnerable students.

This situation reflects an ongoing tension between two contradictory policies toward entry into teaching: one approach attempts to upgrade educational standards and teacher knowledge to meet growing expectations of teachers. The other ignores such standards when recruiting unprepared individuals into classrooms where students are less powerful and resources are scarce. The policies that divide America's students in this way are rooted in the failure of the policy system and the profession to create incentives that ensure an adequate supply and appropriate distribution of qualified teachers. This is a failure that must be overcome by all members of the education community if America's schools and children are to meet the challenges they now face.

Current Challenges

Despite the overall surpluses of teachers in the United States, there are major problems in the distribution of teachers. Some areas and fields have great surpluses (for example, many states in the Midwest, and fields like English and social studies), and others have apparent shortages (for example, states with high levels of immigration and enrollment growth, and fields like mathematics and physical science). Among the structural barriers are the fact that some states— those with large numbers of teacher education institutions and/or those with lower levels of enrollment growth and turnover—produce many more teachers than they need, while other states produce many fewer teachers than they need to hire. Yet labor markets are still managed locally rather than nationally. There are no national mechanisms for projecting areas of teacher demand by field and location and no systematic mechanisms to provide information about vacancies or help in getting teachers from where they are prepared to where they are needed. There are also many barriers to teacher mobility in addition to lack of information: lack of reciprocity in licensing across states, lack of pension portability, unwillingness of districts to pay teachers for the experience they have accrued in other districts, and the like. In addition dramatic inequalities in revenues and spending across states and districts lead to vastly different salary schedules and working conditions for teachers, which make recruitment easy in some places and difficult in others. Without policy intervention, these differences can be expected to become increasingly problematic as demand increases in the coming years.

Historic changes in labor supply also matter. Whereas teacher shortages have occurred periodically in American education, the demand for teachers throughout much of this century was met by talented, well-educated women and minorities who had few alternative professional opportunities open to them. As we have noted, the opening of the labor market in the 1960s and 1970s removed much of this captive labor pool for teaching. When school enrollments grew and teacher shortages arose, special programs were created to attract different pools of individuals into the profession, by either devising incentives or lowering standards for teachers (Sedlak and Schlossman, 1986).

Incentives prevailed in the years when attention to raising student standards was most pronounced. For example, in the post-*Sputnik* years, highly focused teacher recruitment programs created new pathways for attracting and preparing teaching talent, among them the National Defense Education Act of the 1950s and the Education Professions Development Act of the 1960s. During the early 1970s, the federal Career Opportunities Program provided $129 million to support fifteen thousand teacher aides on pathways into teaching. National Science Foundation initiatives targeted the preparation and recruitment of mathematics and science teachers. Teacher Corps programs created preparation programs for those entering urban school systems.

At other times, however, increased investments in teachers were not the preferred policy response to shortages (Sedlak and Schlossman, 1986). Over the past decade or so, greater demand for math and science teachers, occurring when the many federally sponsored teacher recruitment programs had been disbanded, has led to a proliferation of emergency credentials and out-of-field placements. Only a few states have initiated recruitment incentives in the form of scholarships for preparation or other inducements to teaching to prevent shortages.

Another factor affecting teacher supply and demand is the current school reform movement. Efforts to restructure America's schools for the demands of a postindustrial, knowledge-based economy are redefining the mission of schooling and the job of teaching. Because the great masses of students now need to be educated for thinking work rather than low-skilled factory tasks and educational success is a necessity rather than a luxury for a chosen few, schools are being asked to restructure themselves to ensure higher levels of success for all. Rather than merely "offering education," schools are now expected to ensure that all students learn and perform at high levels. Rather than merely "covering the curriculum," teachers are expected to find ways to support and connect with the needs of all learners (Darling-Hammond, 1994). In addition teachers are expected to prepare all students for thinking work: framing problems; finding, integrating, and synthesizing information; creating new solutions; learning on their own; and working cooperatively.

The kind of teaching required to meet these demands for more thoughtful learning cannot be produced through teacher-proof materials or regulated curriculum. In order to create bridges between common, challenging curriculum goals and individual learners' experiences and needs, teachers must understand cognition and the many different pathways to learning. They must understand child development and pedagogy, as well as the structures of subject areas and a variety of alternatives for assessing and supporting learning (Darling-Hammond, Wise, and Klein, 1995; Shulman, 1987).

Educators are striving to attain more ambitious goals at a time when schools are more inclusive than they have ever been before. More students stay in school longer, and more students with special needs—many of them unserved several decades ago—are served in more mainstreamed settings. If all children are to be effectively taught, teachers must be prepared to address the substantial diversity in experiences that children bring with them to school—the wide range of languages, cultures, exceptionalities, learning styles, talents, and intelligences that require an equally rich and varied repertoire of teaching strategies. In addition, teaching for universal learning demands a highly developed ability to discover what children know and can do, how they think and how they learn, and to match learning and performance opportunities to the needs of individual children. This mission for teaching defies the single, formulaic approach to delivering lessons that has characterized the goals of much regulation of teaching, many teacher education and staff development programs, and a number of teacher testing and evaluation instruments.

Other challenges concern the characteristics of teacher recruits. Although the average new recruit is now slightly older than other college graduates (American Association of Colleges of Teacher Education [AACTE], 1991)—a consequence of the depressed teacher job market of the late 1980s, the growing prevalence of extended teacher preparation programs, and an increasing number of midcareer entrants to the profession—in other respects the teacher workforce appears virtually unchanged from the early part of the century: predominantly female (72 percent) and largely white (86.5 percent). The 13.5 percent of all current teachers who are persons of color compares to a student population that is nearly one-third minority. This proportion is increasing rapidly; African American, Latino, Asian, and Native American citizens accounted for 70 percent of the nation's population growth between 1985 and 1995 (Estrada, 1995). Children of color and language-minority students already comprise over 75 percent of the students in the nation's forty-seven largest urban school districts (Council of the Great City Schools, 1992). Currently 15 percent of students in teacher preparation are candidates of color, but if past trends hold true, only two-thirds of these will find their way into teaching (National Education Association [NEA], 1992).

At the same time, the difficulty of recruiting well-qualified teachers for inner cities and rural communities, where working conditions are poor and pedagogical demands far greater, has been well documented (Darling-Hammond and Sclan, 1996). With the exception of minorities, most prospective teachers want to teach near their original homes (Berry, 1985; Zimpher and Ashburn, 1992) and prefer not to teach in inner-city schools, even though that is where a disproportionate number of jobs are (Howey and Zimpher, 1993). The majority of teacher education students do not venture far when deciding where to enroll for their preparation; nearly three-fourths of preservice teacher education students commute to their college campuses (AACTE, 1991; Goodlad, 1990), and most hope to find jobs nearby.

Concerns for recruiting a diverse teaching force are shared by many school district officials. In a recent survey of personnel directors in twenty-eight major urban areas,[2] over 96 percent of the respondents reported what they viewed as a shortage of minority teachers in their school districts, 86 percent indicated a male teacher shortage, and 71 percent indicated a shortage of bilingual teachers (Recruiting New Teachers, 1996a). From the perspective of those staffing schools, current challenges include constructing a teaching force that can respond to the students and settings that schools now serve, as well as one that can meet the challenges of higher content standards for student learning.

Finally, many teacher education candidates have had little firsthand experience with cultural diversity. Many students, both white and minority, still attend schools that are substantially segregated by race (Orfield, Monfort, and Aaron, 1989), and 44 percent of all American schools have no minority teachers (NCES, 1992). To a large extent, these are the schools most future teachers attend. Although NCATE-accredited colleges must, as a condition of accreditation, seek to recruit diverse student bodies and attend to issues of cultural responsiveness in teaching, most schools of education are not accredited. Many continue to provide a curriculum and learning environment characterized by the cultural parochialism that mirrors the homogeneous environment in which future teachers grew up. In combination, these factors can leave teachers unprepared for the students and the settings where most job opportunities are and can exacerbate the recruitment and retention difficulties many urban school systems experience.

DIFFICULTIES IN PROJECTING TEACHER DEMAND AND SUPPLY

Despite the availability of increasingly sophisticated demographic projections, anticipating teacher supply and demand represents one of education policy's most complex puzzles. Historically demand projections were made using relatively simple demographic calculations of live births and the size of the current teacher workforce. Supply was calculated as a static share of the college-age population. Recently such projections have been called into question by a range of other factors that affect supply and demand, including immigration and migration; changing labor market trends; shifts in college enrollment patterns; fluctuations in the reserve pool; educational reform agendas affecting demand for teachers in different locations and fields; reforms of preparation, licensing, and induction; state fiscal policies; changing entry and retirement policies; and more. Furthermore, as we have noted, there are frequently surpluses in some places and shortages in others. Accordingly the literature on supply and demand often reflects contention rather than consensus.

Estimating Demand

There are three major components of teacher demand: pupil enrollments, pupil-to-teacher ratios, and turnover. Two of these components—enrollments and pupil-to-teacher ratios—are reasonably easy to forecast; the third and largest component—turnover—has been subject to much debate and is the source of substantial divergence in the numerical estimates used for projections. In all three cases, though, the signs point to significant increases in new demand for teachers.

Pupil enrollments have increased in recent years due to a rise in the annual number of U.S. births coupled with the largest wave of immigration the United States has experienced since the early 1900s. Immigration policies and trends obviously affect enrollments, as do shifts in childbirth trends. In addition school policies and practices affect enrollments. If substantial progress were to be made in stemming the high level of dropouts in American schools (currently about 20 percent of high-school-age youth), this would increase the demand for secondary-level teachers. Reform efforts to increase student course taking in particular subject areas, for example, mathematics, science, and foreign languages, also increase the demand for teachers in these areas. Pupil-to-teacher ratios have been declining slowly but steadily for many years (NCES, 1992). Recent reform initiatives, including some to lower class sizes further and provide additional special services to students, will likely cause this trend to continue, thus boosting teacher demand.

Important as these trends are, the demand for additional teachers in any given year is largely a function of turnover, which usually comprises two-thirds to three-fourths of total new demand. Because most published turnover estimates have been based on old data and few projections have taken teacher retirement trends into account, widely differing estimates of projected teacher demand are available. For example, the NCES in consecutive years published projected estimates of new teacher demand for the years 1988 to 1995 ranging from a total of 1.23 million (an average of 175,000 annually) to 2.021 million teachers (an average of 290,000 annually). In 1991 the number of newly hired teachers, excluding transfers, was about 230,000, just between the two estimates.

The lower of these estimates was implausible because it was based on the assumption that the turnover rates of the early 1980s, when retirements were at their lowest level in twenty years, would continue, despite an aging teaching force that would create steep increases in retirement. The higher estimate (which assumed a 7.5 percent turnover rate for elementary teachers and a 6.5 percent rate for secondary teachers) is more realistic for the longer haul, given the current age composition of the teaching force. Half of current teachers are age forty-two and over (NEA, 1992); 25 percent are over the age of fifty (Darling-Hammond, 1997). Given current retirement trends, virtually all of them will retire over the next twenty years, most during the next decade. Some analysts believe the aging of the teaching force—and the traditionally higher turnover rates of the young teachers who will be replacing those who retire—could boost turnover rates to as high as 9 or 10 percent in coming years (Grissmer and Kirby, 1987). At the same time, induction programs that reduce attrition rates for beginning teachers—rates that have recently averaged about 30 percent over the first five years of teaching, (Darling-Hammond, 1997)—could alter this revolving door feature of new teacher recruitment, offsetting anticipated turnover.

In sum, there is no doubt that teacher demand will continue to increase over the next decade. The most well-reasoned estimates would place the total demand for new entrants at 2 million to 2.5 million between 1998 and 2008, averaging over 200,000 entrants annually, some of them newly prepared teachers and some of them migrants or returnees from the reserve pool of teachers. And depending on policy decisions, the number who are unprepared entrants could grow substantially larger or smaller. In 1994 27 percent of all newly hired teachers had either no license or a substandard license in the field they were hired to teach (Darling-Hammond, 1997), indicating that they either had not prepared to teach or lacked one or more of the requirements for a license in the state in which they were hired. This number is substantially larger than a decade earlier due to rising demand with few policies in place to increase and manage supply.

Estimating Supply

In 1994 as in previous years, many more college students prepared to teach than were hired. Yet school districts hired large numbers of individuals who were not prepared to teach. Whereas more than 160,000 college students prepared to teach in bachelor's and master's degree programs, only two-thirds of them applied for teaching positions. Just over 100,000 newly prepared teachers were hired (about half of all newly hired teachers), while districts also hired at least 40,000 new and veteran teachers who were not fully licensed for their positions (Darling-Hammond, 1997). The unlicensed hires either had not undertaken teacher education, had not completed all of their state's course work or testing requirements, had prepared in one state but were hired in another with different licensing rules, or were hired in a field other than the one in which they prepared.

Clearly the overall problem is not shortages but an array of distributional and other labor market factors. Boe and Gilford (1992) suggest that rather than evaluating teacher supply in terms of gross numbers of teachers needed in relation to gross demand, it would be more fruitful to think in terms of specific qualifications and characteristics of the teaching force: subject matter knowledge, instructional skills, fluency in multiple languages, location, and demographic characteristics. In particular, they suggest that the prospect of teacher shortages must be examined in terms of the distribution of qualified teachers among schools of different characteristics and locations.

Wealthy districts that pay high salaries and offer pleasant working conditions rarely experience shortages. Districts that serve low-income students tend to pay teachers less and offer larger class sizes and pupil loads, fewer materials, and less desirable working conditions, including less professional autonomy (Darling-Hammond, 1997). For obvious reasons they have more difficulty recruiting and retaining teachers. States that produce large numbers of teachers or have slow enrollment growth have surpluses, and those with fewer teacher preparation programs and rapid enrollment growth must import teachers from elsewhere. In addition, states that equalize spending or salaries across districts experience fewer disparities in teacher qualifications.

Assumptions about who will teach should not remain static because supply pools are variable across time and labor markets. During the 1970s and early 1980s, it was assumed that most teachers hired would be returnees from the reserve pool (about two-thirds of all those hired in the 1980s), many of them women who had stopped out for child rearing. For example, 57 percent of the women who left teaching between 1970 and 1979 stayed out of the labor force in the following year, and 47 percent of them ultimately returned to teaching. However, most teachers who now have children continue to work without breaks in service. Those who leave generally go into other occupations. In contrast, only 30 percent of the women who left teaching between 1980 and 1986 were out of the labor force the following year, and only 36 percent of women defectors in the 1980s returned to teaching (Darling-Hammond, 1994; Murnane and others, 1991).

In general, recruitment from among the pool of former teachers has dropped substantially as the number of newly hired teachers has been increasing. Altogether, newly hired teachers increased from 11 percent of the teaching force in 1987–1988 to nearly 15 percent in 1993–1994. Meanwhile, the proportion of these newly hired teachers who had not taught before increased from 39 percent in 1987–1988 to 53 percent in 1990–1991, while those returning to teaching after a break in service decreased from 42 percent in 1987–1988 to 31 percent in 1990–1991. These are signs that the reserve pool for teaching was dwindling over this time period. A large majority of newly hired teachers in mathematics and science in 1990 were first-time teachers (Blank and Gruebel, 1993). This probably indicates a smaller reserve pool of potential reentrants in these particular fields than in others. This makes sense given the different labor market conditions for teachers in fields like mathematics and science, where alternative career opportunities are more available and are more financially attractive.

Another potential source of teachers is midcareer entrants from other fields. There have been many recent initiatives to attract such candidates, ranging from midcareer recruitment through teacher education programs at the graduate level (these are viewed as alternate routes in some states but are traditional or regular routes in others), to shorter-term alternative certification routes that reduce the requirements for state licensure, to emergency certificates that admit anyone. Most states' alternate routes aimed at recruiting nontraditional entrants into teaching are graduate-level programs structured to ensure that those who have already received other degrees do not have to repeat their undergraduate course work (Feistritzer, 1990). A few states, however, have authorized programs offered by school districts or the state itself; these require little formal preparation and rely instead on on-the-job supervision, which does not always materialize (Darling-Hammond, 1990). Studies of various preparation models find that the quick entry routes into teaching have such high attrition rates (50 to 60 percent within three years) that they are ultimately more costly per recruit than longer, more thorough preparation programs (Darling-Hammond, 1990; Darling-Hammond, Hudson, and Kirby, 1989).

The real issue, of course, is the supply of qualified teachers. Determining quality can be a sticky issue, because every state defines a licensed teacher quite differently, with varying requirements for knowledge of subject matter, pedagogy, curriculum, assessment, learners, and learning. For example, a number of states, including Arizona, Connecticut, and New York, require at least a master's degree on top of a strong subject matter degree for full professional certification; these requirements generally incorporate forty credits of professional education course work and a lengthy supervised practicum or internship in addition to subject matter preparation. On the other hand, New Jersey, Texas, and Virginia have reduced professional education course work to no more than eighteen credits at the undergraduate level, without requiring a master's degree or internship to compensate for the reductions in professional preparation. Thus, the meaning of a teaching license varies tremendously from state to state in terms of knowledge and skills represented (Darling-Hammond, 1990).

To make matters more complicated, a state can set high standards at the same time it creates loopholes for easy entry into classrooms through emergency licensing. Whereas some states do not admit any teachers who have not met licensing standards, others admit as many as half of their newly hired teachers on substandard or no licenses (Darling-Hammond, 1997). And schools often assign teachers outside the field in which they have prepared. In 1994, for example, 22 percent of English teachers, 28 percent of math teachers, 55 percent of physical science teachers, and 52 percent of history teachers had not taken the equivalent of a college minor in the subject areas they were teaching (Ingersoll, 1997a).

The prognosis for teacher supply is complicated. On the one hand, heightened demand usually produces a lagged increase in supply. This is occurring now, and current recruitment initiatives may further support this effect. Salary hikes for teachers during the late 1980s and early 1990s helped to increase the attractions to teaching. On the other hand, these recent increases raised teachers' salaries to about the levels they had previously reached in 1972 (after the last major round of teacher shortages), leaving them 25 percent below those of other college graduates and 30 to 50 percent below those of graduates in scientific and technical fields (Gray and others, 1993). Of the 1990 college graduates working full time in 1991, teachers' earnings were near the bottom. Annual salaries ranged from $18,400 for those in service jobs and $19,100 for those in education, to $31,000 for health professionals and $32,000 for engineers (Gray and others, 1993). Without further substantial boosts in both the financial and nonpecuniary attractions to teaching, it is likely that teaching will have difficulty competing in the contest for college-educated workers, at least in some fields.

Thus, the teacher supply and demand equation is complex, affected by a variety of state and national policy considerations, local labor market conditions, institutional practices, and overall societal attitudes toward teaching. In the long run, much depends on policies currently being proposed—or yet to be formulated—in response to existing and emerging needs. While the supply and academic ability of new teacher education candidates are increasing, the capacity and willingness of these new recruits to remain in teaching and to teach the range of children they will find in their classrooms remains a question. The changing composition of the school-age population has added diversity as a central integer in the teacher recruitment and development equation, begging for new responses by the colleges and universities that seek and prepare teachers and the school districts that hire and support them.

RECRUITMENT AND SELECTION
INTO TEACHER EDUCATION

Why do people teach? Some researchers have observed that "eased entry" into the profession has played a major role in the social construction of teaching (Lortie, 1975). Goodlad (1990) has noted that until recently, almost anyone could enter a teacher education program at almost any time, charging that admission to teacher education has been viewed more as a right than a privilege. This has changed in recent years with the establishment of higher standards for admission to preparation programs in many states and mandates for competency tests for teachers in forty-seven states. Nonetheless, the quality and rigor of standards for entering teaching through either traditional routes or emergency or alternate routes remain highly variable across states.

Even where standards for entry have been increasing, some critics believe that traditional standards do not measure all of the important qualities of teachers. Policy reforms of the 1980s and early 1990s tended to focus on criteria such as grades and test scores in overhauling admissions standards, due to concerns about the lower levels of academic preparation of teacher education recruits in the early 1980s. Haberman (1995) claims that although such criteria may be important, they may ignore other important considerations, like dispositions toward and capacity for teaching children of color and those who live in low-income communities. Only some teacher education programs seek to screen for these dispositions or for what Fullan (1993) calls the sense of "moral stewardship" associated with teaching—that is, the disposition to take responsibility for the learning of all children. Richburg (personal communication, 1995) also contends that once a threshold of subject matter knowledge has been met, what distinguishes effective from ineffective teacher candidates is a "focus on students and desire to teach all of them."

What matters for teaching? Basic academic competence appears to factor into future teacher success (Kennedy, 1990), although correlations between basic skills test scores and measures of teacher performance are typically low (Guyton and Farokhi, 1987). Some studies have found that teacher verbal ability is correlated with student achievement; however, research on the relationship between scores on tests of general academic ability or subject matter knowledge (for example, the SAT or the National Teacher Examinations) and measures of teacher effectiveness has found mixed results, with both positive and negative correlations, usually insignificant (Wise, Darling-Hammond, and Berry, 1987). This may be as much a function of the tests studied as of the importance of the qualities they seek to measure.

Other research indicates that teachers who know their subjects well and possess the pedagogical skills and ability to translate that knowledge into effective instructional strategies in the classroom are more effective than those without these qualifications (McDiarmid, Ball, and Anderson, 1989; Hawk, Coble, and Swanson, 1985; Guyton and Farokhi, 1987; Evertson, Hawley, and Zlotnick, 1985). There is evidence that subject matter knowledge is a predictor of effectiveness up to a threshold level. Beyond that level, additional content knowledge seems to matter less to enhanced effectiveness than knowledge of teaching and learning (for a review, see Darling-Hammond, Wise, and Klein, 1995). In addition, qualities like flexibility, creativity, and adaptability have consistently been found to be important predictors of teaching effectiveness (Wise, Darling-Hammond, and Berry, 1987). Haberman (1995) has found that factors such as cultural familiarity, comfort, and commitment, as well as knowledge of a school community's characteristics, problems, and resources are important in predicting teachers' capacity to work in inner-city schools that primarily serve poor and minority children.

Encouraged by new professional accreditation standards that track enrollment diversity, admissions standards, and placement records, along with a growing awareness of the changing settings for teaching, preparation programs increasingly are developing criteria for selecting candidates based on their commitments, prior experiences with children, and dispositions to teach in diverse communities, as well as their academic ability and subject matter knowledge. Less attention has been paid thus far to correcting imbalances in the supply of teachers by teaching field, given the decentralized nonsystem of higher education and training that exists in the United States. Many schools and colleges of education continue to produce too many teachers in fields that have oversupplies, while school districts continue to seek specific teachers in areas of high demand. A recent study concluded that surpluses of elementary, social studies, and physical education teachers continue to be produced while school districts need many more mathematics, science, and special education teachers (American Association for Employment in Education, 1996).

Finally, many institutions of higher education—driven by funding formulas that reward gross numbers of teaching candidates and unaided by information on incentive to address demand—continue to produce as many teachers as possible in whatever fields are popular among the candidates, irrespective of need. Some teacher education students, particularly those in large four-year undergraduate programs, do not intend to teach, while others in high-demand fields are ultimately recruited by industry, where salaries are higher and working conditions far more attractive. Still others cannot find teaching jobs where they want to teach and do not know where vacancies are located. The upshot is that many new teachers are prepared who will not teach. Meanwhile, many states and districts have shortfalls of qualified teachers in specific fields.

By some estimates, of the students who enter four-year teacher education programs, only 50 to 70 percent of them actually graduate with degrees in education; of these, only 60 to 70 percent enter teaching in the year after graduation; and only about 70 percent are still teaching three to five years later (Andrew, 1990; Andrew and Schwab, 1995; Richburg, in press; NCTAF, 1996). Thus, from a pool of 1,000 individuals on whom some teacher education resources were spent, only 200 to 350 enter and remain in teaching a few years after they have graduated from college. By contrast, recent studies of extended teacher education programs (five-year programs that begin in undergraduate school and continue with a year of graduate-level teacher education) have found that their graduates are not only more satisfied with their preparation and are viewed by their colleagues, principals, and cooperating teachers as better prepared, they are much more likely to enter and stay in teaching than their peers prepared in traditional four-year programs (Andrew, 1990; Andrew and Schwab, 1995; Arch, 1989; Denton and Peters, 1988; Dyal, 1993). Estimates suggest that of those who participate in such programs, over 90 percent enter teaching and 85 to 90 percent are still teaching after three to five years. Thus, for every 1,000 individuals who prepare in the more extensive programs, 750 to 850 can be expected to remain in teaching, a ratio more than twice that of the large four-year college example cited earlier. Even with the greater time and money spent on preparation for extended program graduates, the National Commission on Teaching estimated that when differential entry and attrition rates are factored into the equation, such programs cost substantially less per career teacher than traditional routes and even less per career teacher than short-term alternative routes described below.

LEADING-EDGE RECRUITMENT EFFORTS

As more educators and policymakers are recognizing the complexity of the teacher recruitment challenge, they are responding with a range of innovative programs to expand the pool and improve the pipeline into teaching. Such efforts fall roughly into five categories: (1) precollege recruitment initiatives, (2) programs to improve recruitment and retention in traditional four-year and redesigned five-year university-based programs, (3) programs to develop pathways for students in community colleges, including articulation agreements between two- and four-year colleges, (4) initiatives that tap the substantial pool of school paraprofessionals and teacher aides, and (5) programs to attract midcareer candidates and other college graduates into teaching through postbaccalaureate programs.

Precollegiate Teacher Recruitment

Although many factors motivate young people to stay in school, graduate, and enroll in an institution of higher learning, some studies suggest that career choices are often made at a much younger age than previously thought (Page and Page, 1982; Metropolitan Life, 1989) and that teachers play an important role in determining whether young people consider entering the teaching profession (Lortie, 1975; Berry, 1985). Partly as a result of these findings, literally hundreds of programs have been initiated by school districts, colleges, professional associations, regional collaboratives, and states to interest young people in teaching. These offer teaching, tutoring, and mentoring experiences in a variety of settings. Many are designed to identify high-ability students and promising students of color in order to interest them in teaching careers. Many directly confront images of teaching as low status by developing messages that emphasize the importance as well as the intellectual complexity of teaching.

A 1995 national survey of precollegiate teacher recruitment efforts located 253 programs serving over 50,000 students, 64 percent of whom were young people of color (Recruiting New Teachers, Inc., 1996b). Although few of these programs had been evaluated, those that were studied in a previous survey found that the most successful (defined by students' positive views of teaching, college-going rates, and rates of choosing teaching as a career) possessed some common characteristics (Recruiting New Teachers, Inc., 1996a):

- Clear entrance requirements and high expectations for participants
- Apprenticeship-style activities to prepare and motivate students for teaching
- Curriculum that taught and modeled a conception of the teaching profession emphasizing teacher leadership and school reform
- A long-term commitment to their students
- Help for prospective teachers to make the transition to college and teacher education
- The capacity to monitor their students and submit the program to ongoing evaluation

Among the more well known of these precollegiate teacher recruitment programs are South Carolina's Teacher Cadet Program (TCP), Teach Boston, and the Summerbridge National Project. The TCP, a high school program that recruits academically able students and then engages them in a year-long, college credit–bearing course focused on teaching and learning and the future of the teaching profession, is one of the few programs that has been in existence for more than a decade and has been intensively evaluated.

The TCP was initiated in 1986 in four high schools. Today more than 122 high schools and 19 partner colleges serve nearly eighteen hundred academically able high school juniors and seniors, who enroll in a year-long credit-bearing course that in most schools is part of the school's social studies curriculum. Cadets participate in seminars and group projects as well as in discussions with professionals in the field of education. They study education-related content that includes educational history, principles of learning, child development, and pedagogy. They visit classrooms to observe teachers and students, construct lesson plans, tutor other students, and teach practice lessons. Depending on the relationship that the high school has with its college partner, college credit may be granted to some students. A four-hundred-page curriculum was developed for use in all participating programs and has served as a model for programs in at least six other states.

The TCP evaluation studies have studied the factors that encourage (or discourage) the program's participants to enter and remain in teaching. Approximately 23 percent of the identifiable 1987–1988 high school senior cohort of former cadets were certified to teach in South Carolina by 1993. Of these, 66 percent were actually teaching—about 30 percent of them in rural locations and 29 percent in a critical shortage area (Whatley, Ren, and Rowzie, 1993). (It is not known how many might have gone on to teach in other states.) Although these statistics mean that fewer than 15 percent of the original participants were teaching in South Carolina two years after most would have graduated from college, another study of several cohorts identified other potential benefits of the program, including reports from the participants that the program helped them appreciate teaching, understand its requirements, and better prepare them for college in general. Eighty-seven percent of a random sample of cadets claimed that the program "helped them think about being a teacher," and 59 percent claimed that as a direct result of the program, they were more likely to become a teacher (Rowzie, 1992). In 1993, 25 percent of twelfth grade participants said that they intended to teach when they initially enrolled in the program. By the end of the year-long course, 36 percent of the cadets reported that they intended to teach (Whatley, Ren, and Rowzie, 1993).

Although the TCP studies have been more sophisticated than other investigations of precollegiate recruitment programs, they lacked adequate controls, tended to rely too heavily on self-reported data, and were not able to track longitudinally a sufficient sample of former participants into their later teaching and nonteaching careers. These design flaws reflect evaluation costs that few of these fledgling programs can afford to meet (J. Poda, personal communication, 1997).

College-Based Teacher Education Recruitment Strategies

During the 1960s and 1970s the federal government created a wide array of recruitment initiatives to entice college students into teaching. These included scholarships and forgivable loans for students who prepared to teach, along with innovative preparation programs, such as the Urban Teachers Corps and master of arts in teaching programs, to help them do so. Although the funding for these programs was discontinued in the early 1980s, some states created their own recruitment incentives when demand for teachers began to grow again in the late 1980s.

One such initiative that has maintained outcome data is the North Carolina Teaching Fellows program. Funded by the North Carolina state legislature at $8 million a year, the program provides $20,000 in service scholarships to each of four hundred high-ability high school seniors a year who enroll in intensive four-year teacher education programs throughout the state. The fellows do not have to pay back their scholarship if they teach for at least four years in North Carolina schools. The average combined Scholastic Aptitude Test score of the fellows is over 1100, and their average college GPA is 3.5. Over 20 percent of the fellows are racial minorities.

The Fellows Program consciously seeks to prepare a new breed of teacher for North Carolina, ready to think in new ways about teaching, school organization, and working relationships with other educators and parents. During their teacher preparation, fellows visit a variety of schools, investigate pertinent public education issues in monthly seminars, and take courses addressing issues of leadership, at-risk students, and cultural diversity (among other topics). Early and extensive field experience is another distinctive feature of the teacher education program. In summer months, teaching fellows travel across North Carolina to learn about the state's schools, regions, cultures, and economy. They attend conferences and participate as a cohort in a variety of other preparation and enrichment experiences.

Currently 75 percent of all fellows have completed their four-year obligation and are still teaching in the North Carolina public schools. Some are teaching in other states. Of more than fifteen hundred teaching fellows who had completed the program when it was recently studied, one is national board certified, nine are now in the state's principal fellows program and 112 are in graduate school (J. Norris, personal communication, 1998).

In a recent evaluation of the program, principals claimed that the fellows' first-year classroom performance far exceeded that of other new teachers in every area assessed. The fellows viewed themselves as innovative teachers committed to helping their students understand, apply, and analyze information. They had high expectations about making schools a better place for children to learn and felt that, for the most part, their teacher education programs had prepared them for the multiple and demanding roles they play as teachers. Fellows had far more extensive preparation than most other new teachers in areas relating to student diversity and assessment. They pointed to the importance of this preparation and also noted their desires for additional learning opportunities (Berry, 1995).

Despite their promising entry into teaching—including the fact that more fellows complete their preparation and enter the classroom than is typical of other undergraduate teacher education programs—surveys indicate that when compared to other new teachers nationwide, fellows are less likely to indicate an intention to remain in teaching. This troubling comparison recalls the finding of higher attrition rates among more academically able students. It should also be noted that North Carolina's salaries fall well below the national average (although new legislation—passed in 1997—is beginning to change this) and that teachers in the state feel they have less control over instructional decision making than the norm (Darling-Hammond, 1997, Appendix B); both factors have been found elsewhere to contribute to teacher attrition. On the other hand, recruits' plans to leave the classroom could reflect intentions to assume other leadership roles in education, as is true for graduates of other programs that prepare candidates for such broader responsibilities. Whatever the reason for these reports, both preparation and teaching context appear to matter to candidates' views of the future. Fellows are more likely to report that they plan to stay in teaching when they feel they have experienced better preparation and on-the-job support systems. In addition reported work commitment is higher for those who report more professional working conditions, including participation in decision making (Berry, 1995).

Several other states have instituted similar scholarship programs, and at least sixteen other states offer some form of loan forgiveness to prospective teachers. A few offer added incentives, such as shorter payback periods or specifically earmarked scholarships, for those who prepare to teach in high-need fields or in high-need locations. Little research has been conducted in most states to evaluate the effectiveness of these different models for meeting recruitment goals.

Another important aspect of recruitment into preparation is the design and quality of the teacher preparation program itself. It does little good to recruit candidates into programs if they do not enter and remain in teaching. As we noted earlier, some recent evidence suggests that extended programs, like the recently developed five-year models in some universities, show high rates of entry into and retention in teaching. Analyses of these programs indicate that one of the factors important to this outcome may be the year-long student teaching experience coupled with interwoven course work, which allows candidates to develop greater levels of skill and experience a much less traumatic first year of teaching (Breidenstein, 1998; Andrew and Schwab, 1995).

Another important part of the current redesign of teacher preparation includes efforts to create more systematic approaches to mentoring and team teaching within restructured school settings. A growing number of education schools are working with school systems to create institutions like professional development schools and internship sites that allow new teachers to learn to teach with teams of colleagues in ways that prepare them for current school reforms. Some evidence suggests that prospective teachers' excitement about preparing to teach in restructured schools and the more positive experience of teaching in schools that feature state-of-the-art practice and a more collegial structure may serve as recruitment incentives as well as enhancements of training (Darling-Hammond, 1994; Harris, 1995).

Community College Articulation Programs

There are many sources of prospective teachers aside from students who are currently entering or are enrolled in four-year undergraduate colleges. For example, approximately 5 million students are enrolled in the nation's community colleges, 23 percent of whom are students of color and most of whom are first-generation college attendees, a traditional source of recruits into teaching. This represents 40 percent of the nation's postsecondary enrollment. Given the numbers of two-year college students and the rather meager policy attention directed toward this potential pool of teachers, it is not surprising that community colleges have been called "a missing rung" on the teacher education ladder (Anglin, Mooradian, and Hamilton, 1993).

In several states four-year colleges have worked to create articulation agreements with community colleges so that students can begin taking some of the appropriate course work for a teaching credential in their first two years of college and be assured that it will apply to their college degree when they transfer. Such programs may include a special sequencing of course work (including basic skills, subject matter content, and introductory education courses) and on-the-job training. Much more needs to be known about the characteristics and outcomes of such programs and about strategies associated with successful models. Among some strategies that seem to have substantial payoffs are pathways that help paraeducators complete two- and four-year degrees while becoming certified for teaching.

Paraeducator Pathways into Teaching

The nation's nearly 500,000 paraeducators, commonly known as teachers' aides, represent a promising source of prospective new teachers who are representative of and rooted in the communities in which they serve. A 1995 survey identified more than 149 programs for preparing paraeducators for teaching nationwide. Of nearly 9,000 current participants, 67 percent were prospective teachers of color. This figure represents nearly half the number of minority teachers hired annually in the United States and nearly as many minority recruits as the nation's annual production of minority bachelor's degrees in education (Recruiting New Teachers, Inc., 1996c).

Paraeducator programs appear to attract highly motivated individuals already familiar with challenging classroom environments. Programs provide their candidates with a range of supports required to help them succeed in collegiate programs, ranging from tuition aid and stipends to mentoring, advisement, and tutoring assistance. Some bridge the community college to the four-year college divide. Others operate within the context of traditional undergraduate programs. Still others carry candidates from college through graduate-level teacher education programs. Perhaps because these graduates possess a high degree of readiness, are already involved in schools, and are well supported, they are highly likely to enter and stay in teaching. The paraeducator programs identified exhibit significantly lower rates of attrition than many traditional teacher education programs. Attrition estimates from traditional undergraduate preparation programs can range between 30 and 50 percent; the median attrition rate from paraeducator programs is only 7 percent (Richburg, Knox, Carson, and McWhorter, forthcoming).

Nearly half of the surveyed programs indicated a significant focus on special education, and almost two-fifths reported bilingual teacher preparation as an area of focus—two fields in which many schools report shortages of qualified candidates. Three-quarters of all paraprofessional programs serve urban school systems, where the demand for a more qualified, diverse, and culturally responsive teaching force is particularly acute.

One example of a promising paraeducator pathway program is the Latino Teacher Project (LTP), designed to increase the number of Latino teachers by creating a career track for practicing teacher assistants in the Los Angeles Unified School District. In 1996 the LTP enrolled approximately eighty-one paraeducators. These participants must be above-average students, are prepared in a cohort of peers in a mix of school- and university-based experiences, and are assigned a mentor. They also receive a small stipend. This program emphasizes several key factors associated with effective teacher education by selecting teacher candidates on the basis of their prior success with students and extending preparation through an "elongated teaching practicum" (Hentschke, 1995).

Alternative Preparation

Finally, over the past decade there has been a dramatic increase around the country in the number of alternative preparation pathways, which function outside the parameters of the traditional four-year undergraduate teacher education program. Typically such programs are designed to expedite the licensure process for teacher candidates who already have bachelor's degrees and subject matter expertise. Requirements can range from a few weeks of training in the summer before full-time teaching to a full master's degree with extensive supervision and support in learning how to teach. More than forty states had implemented alternative certification programs by 1998. Using a broad definition that includes certification through graduate-level master's programs, transcript review for teachers trained in one state who move to another, and school districts' own programs, Feistritzer (1990) estimated that forty thousand individuals were certified through alternative routes between 1985 and 1992 (a full twenty thousand between 1990 and 1992), indicating the rapid growth of these programs (National Center for Education Information [NCEI], 1992).

Most states' alternative routes are graduate-level teacher education programs (these are dubbed alternate routes in some states but are traditional or regular routes in others). These are usually aimed at recruiting nontraditional entrants into teaching are actually university-based master's degree programs structured to ensure that those who have already received other degrees do not have to repeat their undergraduate course work (Feistritzer, 1990). A few states—notably New Jersey, Texas, and Califonia—have created or authorized shorter-term alternative certification programs that reduce the requirements for a state license. Some "alternatives" are indistinguishable from long-standing emergency hiring practices that fill vacancies with individuals who have not met standard teaching requirements. Short-term alternatives typically require only a few weeks of formal preparation and rely instead on on-the-job supervision. However, studies of such programs have found that this supervision rarely materializes as intended, so that many such recruits must learn to teach by trial and error largely on their own (Darling-Hammond, Hudson, and Kirby, 1989; Gray and Lynn, 1988; Smith, 1990a, 1990b, n.d.; Wright, McKibbon, and Walton, 1987).

Obviously such wide variations in program design reflect very different conceptions of knowledge for teaching. Using the distinctions offered by Darling-Hammond, Hudson, and Kirby (1989), *alternate routes* into teaching are those that provide options to the traditional undergraduate teacher education program without lowering existing standards. Such routes seek to meet teacher licensure requirements through more flexible preparation at the postbaccalaureate level that takes into account the existing knowledge and experience of recruits and efficiently provides the additional training needed to meet full standards. *Alternative certification,* on the other hand, reduces the standards for entry and allows individuals to assume roles as teachers even though they have not completed many of the requirements for a license in either the study of subject matter or of teaching and learning. Many alternative certificates are awarded after only a few weeks of formal training. Most such programs serve urban areas, such as Los Angeles, Houston, Dallas, and Newark.

In a RAND Corporation study of nontraditional recruits into teaching, the experiences of candidates from these two types of alternatives were compared. In the first category were graduate-level preservice preparation programs, usually resulting in a master's degree, targeted to the needs of midcareer entrants, including course work focused on teaching and learning combined with an intensive supervised internship or student teaching experience of nine to twelve months. In the other category were short-term programs of four to eight weeks, which then placed recruits directly into classrooms as teachers of record with varying expectations for ongoing course work or supervision. Recruits in the extended university-based programs were more likely to be midcareer professionals with more extensive work experience in higher-level technical jobs (such as chemical engineer) than the alternative certification candidates, who were younger and tended to have been employed in less-skilled jobs (as lab technician or service employee, for example). The RAND study, like others, found that the candidates who were prepared in the more extensive programs were much more satisfied than those in the short summer programs with the amount and quality of preparation they received, reported fewer difficulties when they entered classroom teaching, and were more likely to say they planned to stay in the profession (Darling-Hammond, Hudson, and Kirby, 1989).

Project Promise, a ten-month alternate route program for midcareer professionals, is one example of such an extended program. The program recruits career changers from fields ranging from engineering and the health professions to journalism and the liberal arts. Candidates bring bachelor's degrees and substantial professional experience in other careers to a program that emphasizes participant selection based on specific dispositions and values and experiential learning. Project Promise's competency-based program requires forty-five semester credits of course work and field experiences, and successful candidates must demonstrate readiness to teach in four different settings: a middle school, a rural K–12 school, and urban and suburban high schools. Four college faculty work with approximately twenty program participants, who are regularly assessed by mentor teachers in the schools and college faculty alike. An integrated approach to theory and practice is emphasized, and college faculty regularly visit (and coach) program graduates in their initial teaching assignments, creating an extended preparation and induction period that is both school and university based. Evidence suggests that virtually all of the program's graduates readily find teaching jobs, their evaluations are remarkably strong, and virtually all have remained in the profession (Richburg, Knox, Carson, and McWhorter, forthcoming).

By contrast, studies of teachers admitted through quick-entry alternatives frequently note that their generally high attrition rates are partly a function of the lower commitment to teaching required by such programs and partly caused by inadequate preparation that causes many candidates to find teaching too stressful (Darling-Hammond, Hudson, and Kirby, 1989; Lutz and Hutton, 1989; Roth, 1986; Stoddart, 1992). Among recruits to Los Angeles' Teacher Trainee Program, a state evaluation found that 20 percent dropped out before completing the training, 20 percent left within the first two years, and 20 percent more were not deemed ready for employment within two years (Wright, McKibbon, and Walton, 1987). Of those who entered teaching, 53 percent had left within six years of program operation (Stoddart, 1992). In an evaluation of Dallas's alternative certification program, only 54 percent of recruits had successfully become full-fledged teachers after their first year as interns, and only 40 percent of these interns said they planned to stay in teaching, as compared to 72 percent of traditionally trained recruits (Lutz and Hutton, 1989). Similarly, statistics from the Teach for America (TFA) program that sends college graduates into urban classrooms after several weeks of summer training show that of those who started in New York City in 1990, 58 percent had left by the third year. The Maryland State Department of Education reported that 62 percent of TFA members who started in Baltimore in 1992 had left within two years.

Recruits from short-term alternative certification programs have been found to have difficulty with curriculum development, pedagogical content knowledge, teaching methods, classroom management, and student motivation (Lenk, 1989; Feiman-Nemser and Parker, 1990; Grossman, 1989; Mitchell, 1987). Compared to beginners who have completed a teacher education program, teachers who enter without full preparation are less aware of students' needs and differences, less able to plan and redirect instruction to ensure learning (and less aware of the need to do so), and less skilled in implementing instruction (Bents and Bents, 1990; Bledsoe, Cox, and Burnham, 1967; Copley, 1974; Grady, Collins, and Grady, 1991; Grossman, 1989; Rottenberg and Berliner, 1990). They are less able to anticipate students' knowledge and potential difficulties and less likely to see it as their job to do so, often blaming the students if their teaching is not successful.

These findings are reflected in a study of alternative certification candidates in New Hampshire, who receive three years of on-the-job training in lieu of college preparation. The study found they were rated by their principals significantly lower than university-prepared teachers on instructional skills and instructional planning, and they rated their own preparation significantly lower than did the university candidates. Similarly, several evaluations of the TFA program found that the recruits lack instructional skill and tend to engage in practices that are developmentally and cognitively inappropriate for their students (Grady, Collins, and Grady, 1991; Roth, 1993; Texas Education Agency, 1993).

These difficulties affect teachers' students as well. Gomez and Grobe's (1990) study of the performance of alternative certification candidates in Dallas who were prepared in a summer program prior to entering teaching found that candidates were rated lower than traditionally trained new teachers on such factors as their knowledge of instructional techniques and instructional models. A much greater share—from two to sixteen times as many—were rated poor on each of the teaching factors evaluated. (The proportions of these candidates rated poor ranged from 8 percent on reading instruction to 17 percent on classroom management.) The effects of this unevenness showed up most strongly on students' achievement in language arts, where the achievement gains of students of alternatively certified teachers were significantly lower than those of traditionally trained teachers.

Not surprisingly, some studies have shown a disinclination on the part of school district personnel officials to hire alternatively licensed candidates (NCEI, 1992). Current teachers are also skeptical about the advisability of this approach; most think the hiring of teachers who have not met full licensing standards has a negative effect on teacher quality (Harris, 1995). The general public strongly disapproves of this practice as well (Recruiting New Teachers, Inc., 1998), preferring strategies that increase incentives to teaching rather than strategies that lower standards.

A recent analysis of a national sample of teachers who entered teaching through alternate routes during the early 1990s underscores these concerns and the equity issues noted earlier: those who entered teaching through short-term alternative certification programs tended to have lower academic qualifications than those who entered through other routes. They were less likely to stay in teaching but more likely to be teaching in inner-city schools that serve more economically disadvantaged students (Shen, 1997). Other analyses have found similar results. Nationally, unlicensed entrants to teaching have significantly lower levels of academic achievement than most college students and far lower achievement levels than those who prepare to teach (Gray and others, 1993). Alternative certification recruits in fields like mathematics and science have lower GPAs than those from schools of education and are much more likely to say they entered teaching because jobs were available than because they wanted to work with children (Natriello, Zumwalt, Hansen, and Frisch, 1990; Stoddart, 1992).

Alternative routes to teaching represent a significant policy challenge and opportunity. On the one hand, thoughtfully designed postbaccalaureate and mid-career entry programs have proved successful in attracting a talented and diverse cadre of new recruits into teaching. Many are developing extended clinical preparation tightly linked to critical course work for teaching and offer examples of improved induction. On the other hand, alternative licensure programs that short-circuit much of the course work and supervised clinical experience needed to learn to teach may ultimately undermine both the retention of teachers and their ability to teach well. Policymakers should select program models carefully to secure the benefits of new alternatives without suffering from the shortcomings of lower-quality options.

SCHOOL DISTRICT SELECTION AND HIRING

School districts' hiring processes have an equally important influence on the quantity and quality of teachers in the labor market and on the distribution of teachers to different types of school systems. The most successful efforts to prepare high-quality teachers may be undermined by inefficiency in the hiring process coupled with lack of attention to important professional qualifications.

Hiring Practices

Surprisingly, much hiring of underqualified teachers is a function of hiring practices rather than labor market shortages (NCTAF, 1996). School districts do not always hire the most qualified and highly ranked teachers in their applicant pools due to inadequate management information systems and cumbersome hiring procedures that discourage good applicants by large numbers of steps in the application process, demeaning treatment, unreturned telephone calls, and lack of timely action (Wise, Darling-Hammond, and Berry, 1987). Some prospective teachers report that they decided not to enter teaching at all after having their files lost, experiencing interviews in which their qualifications were barely reviewed, failing to receive responses to repeated requests for information, and receiving late notification of job availability.

These are particular problems in large urban districts. Reports of vacancies and information on candidates are not always accessible to recruits or to district decision makers. Hiring procedures are cumbersome and bureaucratic, sometimes including as many as fifty or more discrete steps and taking many months to complete. Late budget decisions from state or local funders and union contracts requiring placement of all internal teacher transfers prior to hiring of new candidates can delay hiring decisions until late August or September, when well-qualified candidates have since decided to take other jobs. As a result of these inefficiencies, large urban districts often lose good candidates to other districts and to nonteaching jobs. Thus, many districts that might have successfully recruited outstanding candidates do not hire them, resulting in a loss of the very teachers they so desperately need (NCTAF, 1996; Wise, Darling-Hammond, and Berry, 1987; see also Pflaum and Abrahamson, 1990).

Other state and school district practices can also undermine high-quality teacher recruitment and development—for example:

- Many districts pay less attention to qualifications than costs and connections, preferring to hire unqualified candidates who are cheaper (or who may be patronage appointees) over better qualified and more experienced candidates.

- Most districts impose a cap on the salaries they offer experienced candidates; as a consequence, highly educated and experienced teachers are forced to take a cut in pay if they move to a new locality and want to continue to teach. Many choose instead to change professions.

- States maintain varying requirements for licensure, and few allow for reciprocity in licensing or the transfer of pension benefits.

- Few districts provide reimbursement for travel and moving expenses.

- Many districts place beginning teachers in the most difficult schools with the highest rates of teacher turnover, the greatest numbers of inexperienced staff, and the least capacity to support teacher growth and development. Without induction supports, many new teachers leave quickly.

Case studies of districts that are successful in hiring the teachers they most want and need have found that they have developed the following techniques (Snyder, in press; Wise, Darling-Hammond, and Berry, 1987):

- Outreach systems for recruiting from local colleges and from other regional and national sources

- Streamlined personnel systems that use sophisticated information technology to make information about vacancies available to candidates and information about candidates readily available to decision makers, systems for projecting vacancies and making offers early in the spring

- Strategies for ensuring that those who receive offers are made to feel welcome, wanted, and well inducted into the school district

Selection Procedures

A system's capacity to attract and keep desired candidates is strongly influenced not only by the pool of available teachers but also by the methods used to assess prospective teachers, collect and distribute information to decision makers about them, and interact with candidates during the hiring process. Some studies have noted that some districts appear to perceive teaching as "routine" (not "smart") work and manage teacher selection practices accordingly (Wise, Darling-Hammond, and Berry, 1987). In addition, districts and schools have different and often competing operational definitions of the "good teacher." Despite superficial similarities, there are substantial differences in the criteria embodied in selection tools that districts use (such as interview guides, tests, certification standards, and evaluation of credentials); the weights placed on different indicators of teaching ability; the extent to which selection processes are centralized or decentralized; and the manner in which candidates are treated before and after hiring.

Schlechty argues that specific criteria for recruitment into teaching are essential for developing a distinctive occupational identity and socializing members so that they are likely to adopt that identity. He and others have noted, however, that many districts select teachers more on the basis of their ready availability and perceived ability to fit in than on the basis of their academic and teaching qualifications. A host of factors—including political agendas, ability to perform extracurricular activities, and perceived personality traits—appear to be equally important determinants of who is chosen to teach (Browne and Rankin, 1986; Johanson and Gips, 1992; Pflaum and Abrahamson, 1990; Wise, Darling-Hammond, and Berry, 1987). In a survey of secondary school principals, Johanson and Gips (1992) found that intellectual capacity was rated as the least important factor in the selection of teachers. In another study, Ballou (1996) noted that although college GPA—as a measure of academic ability—is related to the probability of a teacher's obtaining a job, the overall quality (that is, the selectivity) of the college attended appears to matter little to district administrators. Some analysts suggest that patronage still plays a significant role in district hiring policies, especially in certain urban (Haberman, 1995) and rural systems (J. Poda, personal communication, 1995).

Selection Tools

Most large districts have adopted some standardized procedures to rationalize the hiring process. Initial procedures tend to screen candidates on the basis of generally applicable qualifications such as academic achievement and interpersonal skills. Later hiring processes screen candidates on characteristics more specific to the vacancy or the hiring school's particular needs. However, as applicants are progressively screened, the data used to evaluate teacher candidates get progressively more expensive to obtain. Gleaning qualifications from transcripts and the certification record is less costly than administering a test or conducting an interview. Classroom observations and performance assessments are more expensive, but are likely to offer far more valid performance indicators for decision makers. However, most districts trade off the benefit of a classroom observation against its added cost and end up relying heavily on individual interviews in selection and hiring decisions.

One attraction of most interview instruments is that they provide a high degree of standardization and thereby offer some semblance of objectivity and therefore a presumably equitable candidate review. Unfortunately an overreliance on interviews may be misplaced (Webster, 1988; Braun, Green, Williams, and Brown, 1990; Rinehart and Young, 1990). Pflaum and Abrahamson (1990) raise cautions about depending on the "gut reactions" that are common in teacher interviews, noting their inherent unreliability. Industrial and organizational psychologists have been studying employment interviews for over six decades in an effort to determine their predictive validity. Reviews of the literature offer a decidedly mixed assessment of their validity and reliability (Arvey and Campion, 1982; Reilly and Chao, 1982; Niece, 1983; Young, 1984).

Nonetheless, the popular educational literature is replete with references to the importance of the selection interview and with five-step formulas for better teacher selection (Pawlas, 1995). This penchant for cookbook-type prescriptions is, of course, easily derided. Most thoughtful practitioners claim no more than that the interview—if properly structured—can yield useful information when combined with other forms of candidate review (E. Arons, personal communication, Nov. 13, 1995; Richburg, personal communication, 1995).

One of the most popular commercially available teacher selection interview instruments is the Gallup organization's Teacher Perceiver, one of the many selection instruments Gallup has developed for a wide range of occupations and professions. This instrument consists of sixty dichotomous questions organized around twelve "life themes," such as mission, empathy, rapport, and individualized perception. Teacher candidates are assessed by their answers, which Gallup claims indicate propensities predictive of teaching dispositions associated with each life theme. Gallup recommends that the interview, which can take as little as thirty minutes, be used in concert with other screening procedures and criteria, such as college grades and references (H. Dyas, personal communication, Oct. 15, 1995), an appropriate recommendation given its inconclusive effects. The correlations between teacher interview scores and later administrative ratings of teaching effectiveness have ranged from .50 in one study to .13 in another (Gallup Organization, 1990, 1994). The connection to student outcomes is a missing link in these validation studies and those for other selection tools, as are dependent measures that address whether teachers who score high on a particular instrument possess the knowledge, skills, and dispositions necessary for success with diverse learners.

If selection interviews and standard measures of academic ability are inadequate predictive proxies for future teacher success, how can districts improve their ability to choose the best possible candidates? Braun, Green, Williams, and Brown (1990) suggest portfolios that include biographical information, credentials, letters from members of the community for voluntary service projects, letters of professional recommendation, lesson or unit plans, and videotapes of teaching experiences as potentially powerful tools for giving decision makers a more complete picture of a candidate's teaching abilities. A growing number of colleges routinely engage teaching candidates in preparing portfolios for purposes of guiding, assessing, and documenting their teaching, and these are increasing informed by professional standards such as those developed by the National Board and the Interstate New Teacher Assessment and Support Consortium (INTASC) (Darling-Hammond, forthcoming). Perhaps in time this strategy will become a complement to others that provide glimpses of the knowledge and skills of beginning teachers, enabling a more productive and accurate selection process.

Unfortunately human resource development in education lags behind personnel management in many other industries, particularly high-performance companies in knowledge-intensive fields. Applying greater knowledge to the reform of teacher selection practices will require more sophisticated processes for assessing teachers in ways concomitant with the new standards for teaching and with evidence about what matters for effectiveness in the classroom. Keeping such well-recruited and well-selected teachers in the profession will require approaches to beginning teacher induction that support their efforts to learn to teach well.

INDUCTION PROGRAMS:
IMPROVING THE TRANSITION TO TEACHING

The roles of the resident in medicine, the intern in architecture, and the associate in a law firm illustrate the importance other professions place on an extended clinical preparation period that carefully guides novices into growing responsibilities and increasingly more complex practice. In these and other professions, novices continue to hone their knowledge and skills under the watchful eyes of more knowledgeable and experienced practitioners. At the same time, the novices, fresh from their studies, bring the latest research and theoretical perspectives to bear on their practice, where it is shared and tested by novice and veteran practitioners alike.

The normative conditions of teaching are far from this utopian model. Traditionally new teachers have been expected to sink or swim with little support and guidance. Overburdened principals charged with the supervision and evaluation of all teachers, along with their other responsibilities, have typically been unable to provide the intensive mentoring and oversight that novices require. In addition to the fact that this leaves new teachers with little daily help, it has also meant that decisions about continuation and tenure have typically been pro forma because they are based on little data (Wise, Darling-Hammond, McLaughlin, and Bernstein, 1984).

Over the past decade, however, induction and mentoring programs for new teachers have become far more prevalent. In 1994 slightly more than one-half of all public school teachers with five or fewer years of experience reported that they had participated in some kind of induction program (Darling-Hammond, 1997). The proportions, however, ranged from 15 percent in some states to over 80 percent in others. An increasing number of states and school districts have developed policies and programs specifically designed to support, assess, and evaluate the performance of novices and experienced teachers who are new to a school district or certification area.

The growing literature about such programs suggests that these programs offer widely varying supports, most of them fairly minimal (Odell and Ferarro, 1992a; Huling-Austin, 1990; Adelman, 1991; Gold, 1996). Many rely on periodic workshops designed to provide new teachers information about the school district and how to obtain needed resources and materials pertinent to the curriculum to be taught, advice on instructional processes and strategies, emotional support, classroom management tips, support pertaining to the physical environment of the classroom, and straightforward procedures for presenting lessons (Odell, 1986, 1989). Few take into account the differing needs of recently minted teachers and those new to a school system or state (Odell, 1986).

These programs often focus on orientation to the work environment and classroom management tactics, which are among the felt needs many new teachers report (see, for example, Veenman, 1984). However, a focus on generic strategies to help the novice teacher to cope with classroom discipline may neglect the real needs of novices for subject-specific pedagogical strategies that will work with the increasingly diverse learners they teach (Gold, 1996). When novices do not have an adequate grounding in content and teaching methods so that they can make the translations necessary for their students, they often clamor for surface-level strategies to manage and discipline students who are not engaged in classroom work. In turn, many induction programs address the symptoms, not the cause, of disengagement and suboptimal learning, offering a litany of workshops offering formulaic discipline strategies as a form of novice teacher triage.

States often initiate teacher induction initiatives as part of their licensure systems, seeking to ensure teacher quality through a more formalized assessment component. A recent report indicated that of twenty-one state-supported programs, fifteen focused on assessment and assistance, five focused solely on assessment, and six focused just on assistance (AACTE, 1994). Some analysts have found that widely used assessment protocols focused on generic skills and simplistic teaching formulas can inhibit teacher quality by discouraging attention to content concerns and preventing the use of context-sensitive strategies that are more responsive to student needs (MacMillan and Pendlebury, 1985; Darling-Hammond and Sclan, 1996). Particularly when assistance and assessment components are tightly intertwined, the support new teachers receive may be narrowly geared to meeting standardized teaching behaviors that frequently do not enhance student learning and do not develop teachers' skills and dispositions for assessing student needs and pursuing new solutions to problems of practice.

Less standardized approaches have their own problems. A 1992 report on the California New Teacher Project criticizes the state's more laissez-faire approach to beginning teacher assessment as seriously flawed (California Commission of Teacher Credentialing, 1992). Too often, the study concluded, assessments were conducted by unqualified assessors using unreliable, unrealistic, subjective criteria that were rarely used in planning future support for inductees. These and other authors advocate moving toward more developmentally staged supervision, assistance, induction, and evaluation models. However, they acknowledge that further research is needed to determine what methods are most appropriate and reliable in providing information on new teachers' competence and professional growth. In this regard, the new assessment protocols being developed for beginning teachers by the Interstate New Teacher Assessment and Support Consortium and for experienced teachers by the National Board for Professional Teaching Standards may provide more robust alternatives that are grounded in actual classroom practice, responsive to concerns for both subject matter and student learning, and evaluated by expert teachers who are trained for the assessments.

Relatively few state-mandated induction programs provide funding for trained mentors who work closely with beginners in their teaching field on the development of their practice (see Berry, 1995; Darling-Hammond, 1997). An exception is Connecticut's Beginning Educator Support and Training Program, which has created a content-based performance assessment of teaching modeled on the portfolio assessments of the National Board for Professional Teaching Standards to be used as the basis for granting a professional license. Mentoring supports for beginners are provided by teachers in the same teaching field or level who are trained in the use of this assessment.

A similar but more intensive approach is featured in the beginning teacher mentoring programs sponsored by several school districts, including Columbus, Cincinnati, and Toledo, Ohio; Rochester, New York; and Seattle, Washington. These programs assign highly expert consulting (or master) teachers, selected jointly by the union and administration and released from all or part of their teaching loads, to assist all new teachers and evaluate their performance at the end of the year. Consulting teachers work in the same subject area as those whom they are assisting. They visit, observe, and consult with the beginning teachers at least weekly, and they meet regularly with one another to develop their skills as mentors and to share resources and ideas. In all of these districts, beginning teacher attrition has fallen sharply as a result of this program. In every case, first-year teachers leave at rates of no more than 5 percent—and generally because they have been discontinued as a result of the evaluation process rather than because they have become discouraged and defeated. Some of the districts previously experienced first-year teacher attrition rates as high as 30 percent or more (NCTAF, 1996).

A number of studies have found that well-designed mentoring programs improve retention rates for new teachers along with their attitudes, feelings of efficacy and control, and range of instructional strategies (California Commission of Teacher Credentialing, 1992; Karge and Freiberg, 1992). A recent analysis of a large-scale national teacher survey revealed that where teachers report receiving high-quality assistance, they are also more likely to indicate that they are committed to the profession (Ingersoll, 1997b).

Other successful induction programs involve collaboration between school districts and local schools of education (Debolt, 1992; Wisniewski, 1992; MacIssac and Brookhart, 1994). In many states and districts, these partnerships are framed by professional development schools (PDSs)—schools that, like teaching hospitals in medicine, can blur organizational lines between preservice teacher training, beginning teacher induction, and ongoing professional development. PDSs are usually partnerships between schools and universities that focus simultaneously on professional preparation for prospective and novice teachers, professional development for veteran teachers, and praxis-based research on school and instructional improvement in settings that seek to model state-of-the-art practice for teaching all children in ways that lead to high levels of achievement (Holmes Group, 1990).

An example of how professional development schools can transform beginning teacher preparation and induction is the configuration of the internship year in the University of Cincinnati's five-year teacher education program. In collaboration with the university, the Cincinnati public schools established nine professional practice schools and created a special intern designation at half-pay in the salary schedule. During their fifth year of training, interns teach half-time in one of the professional practice schools under the direct supervision of a team of expert veteran teachers who hold adjunct status with the university. The interns also complete course work and in-school seminars coplanned by school- and university-based faculty. The interns systematically learn the complexities of effective teaching under close supervision. Following their internship year, those who are hired in the Cincinnati Public Schools experience the additional advantages of the larger mentoring and peer review process described earlier.

As of 1996, more than six hundred institutions called themselves professional development schools, although they were at quite different stages of development and exhibited different concepts of what a PDS might be (Clark, 1997). States like Ohio, Minnesota, Maryland, and North Carolina have begun to create policy supports for establishing PDSs as part of the reform of teacher education and induction. In PDSs, entering teachers can be supported in learning how to apply complex knowledge in practice within settings that model highly competent teachers for a range of learners, rather than encouraging counterproductive teaching and coping strategies (Darling-Hammond, 1994). If fully developed, PDSs could institutionalize the process of professional improvement across the career continuum.

RECOMMENDATIONS

We have argued that a central issue for the United States as it enters the 21st century is the development of its human capital. Ironically, although schools are the front line for meeting this challenge, the nation has historically paid scant attention to the development of education's own human resources: its teachers and administrators. In virtually every profession, the ways in which members are recruited, selected, and inducted send a powerful message as to what is valued and intended. Teaching is no exception. It is through these processes that states and school systems signify how they value teachers, define best practices, and heighten or reduce their chances of constructing a teaching force that will be successful in promoting student learning. Despite the conventional wisdom that everyone knows a good teacher when she sees one and the common assumption that such judgments value the same qualities, very different conceptions of the "good teacher" are actually expressed in recruitment, selection, and induction processes. These differing conceptions, along with a patchwork of incompatible state and district policies left over from the day when teacher labor markets were local, have led to a fragmented system of teacher development nationwide.

Today, however, the twin imperatives of demographic change and educational reform make it essential that the nation adopt new and more effective strategies to recruit, select, hire, and induct its teacher workforce. Without such improved practices, it is unlikely that the nation will build the qualified, diverse, and culturally sensitive teacher workforce that classrooms demand. Meeting the challenges of demography and reform, however, will require serious confrontation with long-standing barriers to both effective practice and policy.

Demand for Teachers

With the number of school-age children increasing dramatically and the teacher workforce getting older, there is an unparalleled opportunity to reshape the composition of the teaching force. Although there are overall surpluses of teachers, surges in demand in an unmanaged labor market are making it more difficult to hire well-qualified teachers in all fields and communities. Interest in the teaching profession is on the rise, but there is still a need to expand the pool of prospective teachers, particularly among those who can teach effectively in urban classrooms and in high-need curriculum areas like mathematics, physical science, and special education. In addition, as America's school-age population becomes more multicultural and multilingual in composition, schools need teachers from diverse language and cultural backgrounds to bring their knowledge and life experiences to the challenges of teaching and learning and to serve as role models for children of all ethnic and cultural backgrounds.

Governments are not powerless in the face of these challenges. The federal government can provide high-leverage incentives to recruit and train individuals for the fields in which they are needed as it did for teaching in the 1960s and 1970s and for medicine and the military for the past thirty years. A key element of such an initiative could be service-linked college scholarships for highly capable candidates who prepare to teach. A large share of these scholarships can be targeted for teachers who prepare to teach in high-need teaching fields and agree to serve in hard-to-staff school locations. Federal and state governments can also provide incentives, through training grants to institutions, to encourage schools and universities to build on the more successful efforts to create new pathways into teaching for midcareer entrants, paraprofessionals, and other nontraditional recruits, as well as college students. And all parts of the education system can engage in outreach efforts that counter the common myth that "anyone can teach" and market teaching as a valuable, knowledge-based profession.

Demand for Improved Teaching Practice

Nearly every aspect of the current reform movement—new educational goals and standards, curriculum changes, performance assessment, site-based management, cooperative learning, and enhanced use of technology—expands the types of skills expected from teachers. At the same time, teachers encounter a range of classroom and social conditions—multilingual classrooms, increased mainstreaming of special education students, growing numbers of students in poverty and from single-parent families, persistent levels of school and social violence, and drug use—that compound an already complex set of professional challenges. Given these new challenges, schools need access to talented, well-prepared teachers committed to helping all students succeed, and teachers need much greater access to knowledge about teaching and learning before and during their careers.

In contrast to most other industrialized societies, which ensure a common, rigorous preparation for their teachers substantially funded by their national governments, the United States currently leaves to chance or to the proclivities of individual candidates and schools how much education, and of what kind and quality, teachers will acquire. This tradition, which appears to assume that teacher knowledge is an individual rather than a social good, is no longer supportable given the demands of schooling and its centrality to individual and societal success. A set of policies that would ensure access to a core of knowledge for all teachers would include mandatory accreditation for schools of education to ensure that they offer a comprehensive professional curriculum, required preparation for all candidates to ensure that they encounter the knowledge their students need for them to have mastered, and incentives to draw individuals into the field, including subsidies for preparation and reasonably competitive salaries. As the National Commission report (NCTAF, 1996) demonstrated, such investments are possible if funds are reallocated from the nonteaching functions that dominate the budgets of American schools to functions that support teacher recruitment and investments in expertise.

Demand for Greater Clarity in Identifying Good Teachers

Teachers need subject matter knowledge as well the ability to employ multiple teaching and assessment strategies for diverse learners. The classrooms of today and tomorrow need teachers who have a willingness and ability to learn and to figure out how others who learn differently can be taught to meet high academic standards. This type of ability cannot be determined solely by looking at academic transcripts, standardized test scores, or correct answers to structured interview formats. More comprehensive measures that sit closer to actual teaching practice and are validated in terms of student learning will be needed to aid colleges in evaluating their students' progress, states in evaluating prospective entrants to teaching, and school districts in evaluating potential hires.

A useful starting point is the linked set of professional standards created by INTASC and the National Board. These undergird systematic evidence of practice assembled in a highly structured portfolio that can be assessed by standardized evaluation methods based on the standards. Teachers may keep copies

of their portfolios while submitting them for evaluation to the relevant professional boards for the licensing or certification decision. Some colleges have
begun to develop similar portfolios for their students that the students can carry
with them into the hiring process. These sources of evidence can provide rich,
standards-based data for hiring and licensing decisions. Assessments of this kind
can also guide the induction process, so novices are encouraged to continue
their work and learning along a clearer continuum of professional practice. Also
needed is continued research on the links to effective teaching practice and ultimately to student learning of these and other measures of teacher knowledge
and skill.

Demand for Good Teacher Education Programs and Their Graduates

For the most part, there is not a substantial market for high-quality teacher education programs. Few states require programs to meet high standards in order
to operate. Prospective college students do not have much information that
would allow them to separate high-quality from low-quality programs, and parents of elementary and secondary students who will be taught by graduates
have even less. Most school districts do not place much premium on where a
prospective teacher was prepared. Because candidates bear most of the costs of
training in the United States (in contrast to many other countries where governments subsidize the preparation of teachers), the incentive for many is to
find a program that will provide a credential for the lowest possible cost in time
and money, regardless of how effectively it prepares participants to teach. Colleges and universities have many incentives to prepare as many low-cost teacher
candidates as possible in order to generate enrollments and tuition payments,
which tend to support other degree programs. Even for those consumers and
clients who would like to locate high-quality programs and their graduates, a
lack of attention to quality indicators in teacher education has undermined the
ability to do so.

To create a market for high-quality teacher education, educators, and policymakers, we need to develop both indicators of quality and incentives for universities and schools to pursue it. The development of more rigorous,
performance-based assessments of teaching, through the efforts of INTASC and
the National Board, may provide some indicators of quality. The proposed use
of these indicators in the accreditation process by the NCATE may begin to raise
them to the attention of the public, or at least make them salient to universities
in states that require or encourage accreditation. School districts need both
greater information about the content and quality of teacher education programs, which they often treat as a black box, and incentives to hire more fully
prepared teachers. These could include both information services about the nature and quality of programs, like the Barron's guide to colleges, and data from

research, currently just being launched, about the student outcomes associated with the efforts of differently prepared teachers.

Need to Reduce Barriers to Entry

Too often the most promising teacher candidates are frustrated by a byzantine maze of requirements and obstacles to career entry, from inaccessible teacher education programs and insufficient financial aid to lack of license and pension portability and underfunded, cumbersome, and inefficient district recruiting and hiring practices. Budget cutbacks have sometimes compounded these problems by reducing the funding for staff and technology in personnel offices needed to handle inquiries, offer candidates the information they need, provide candidate information to local schools, and employ performance-based selection tools that can better measure the qualities of prospective teachers.

States and districts can surmount these problems by working to adopt common licensing standards that allow cross-state reciprocity for an increasingly mobile teacher workforce and to create pension systems like TIAA-CREF for higher education faculty that allow for pension portability. States and local governments can aid school districts in making more timely hiring decisions by setting annual budgets earlier in the year. With assistance from the business community, school districts can also put in place new technological tools to make hiring procedures more efficient and friendly. School districts can offer salary credit for previous experience and knowledge if they value teaching expertise.

Need to Increase Information

There is much to be learned about effective teacher recruitment, selection, and induction practices. For example, each of the pathways to teaching described here offers some promise for the future, but designing new program models requires more detailed and comprehensive evaluation of various teacher recruitment and preparation initiatives. These studies are important not only to inform those practitioners who implement programs but also for policymaking bodies that must support and sustain them.

In addition the United States has experienced chronic mismatch between labor market needs and teacher preparation in particular fields. Neither the federal nor most state governments routinely project demand by field and location, and colleges rarely set enrollment targets in response to labor market trends. Only anecdotal information is available to prospective teachers regarding which fields and geographic locations need greater numbers of teachers. On a state-by-state basis, there has been little systematic collection and analysis of information on what kinds of teachers are needed[3] and no incentives for schools of education to seek out, prepare, and provide teachers for high-need fields and locations. The effects of this nonsystem are made more problematic by the fact that some "export" states produce far more teachers than they need, while "import" states produce far fewer than they need. Teachers must find their way by luck and word of mouth from where they are prepared to where they are needed.

An effort to launch a national data system and clearinghouse would enable federal and state policymakers and administrators of schools and colleges to understand and better manage the supply, demand, and distribution of prospective teachers. A clearinghouse could also enable prospective teachers to obtain information about where their skills are needed and, perhaps, assistance in transmitting a common application form to districts with needs that match their skills.

CONCLUSION

More intensive research regarding teacher recruitment, retention, selection, and induction is needed to inform the policymaking process and the development of successful programs during this critical era of growing teacher hiring. It is also important to make more accessible to practitioners and policymakers what is already known about effective practices. As we have suggested, a comprehensive understanding of the factors influencing teacher supply, demand, and distribution should be accompanied by a strategic framework for identifying and pursuing high-quality teachers and teaching, so that the issues of supply and quality are always considered and addressed in tandem. Assembling and targeting the resources needed to produce the well-prepared, diverse, and culturally sensitive teacher workforce classrooms demand is likely to rest on a recognition of the fact that teaching is the profession that shapes America's future. Few other tasks are of greater importance to the nation.

Notes

1. Despite these findings, there is still limited evidence as to the relationship between simple measures of academic ability (as indicated by standardized tests and college GPAs) and future teachers' long-term effectiveness (Ashton, Crocker, and Olejnik, 1987).

2. Responding districts were Atlanta, Dade County, San Diego, Broward County, Minneapolis, Fresno, Norfolk, Rochester, Dallas, Long Beach, Milwaukee, Los Angeles, Birmingham, Phoenix, San Francisco, District of Columbia, Indianapolis, Detroit, St. Paul, Dayton, Buffalo, Toledo, Portland, Pittsburgh, Memphis, Nashville-Davidson, Houston, and Denver.

3. Each year the Association of School, College and University Staffing (ASCUS) surveys its members with respect to regional demand for new teachers. Results are published annually in ASCUS's *Job Search Handbook for Educators.* While useful, data are based on the opinions of college placement officials and school district recruiters and not on actual hiring data.

References

Adelman, N. *Preservice Training and Continuing Professional Development of Teachers*. Washington, D.C.: Policy Studies Associates, 1991.

Akin, J. N. *Teacher Supply and Demand in the United States: 1989 Report*. ASCUS Research Report. Addison, Ill.: Association for School, College and University Staffing, 1989.

American Association for Employment in Education. *Teacher Supply and Demand in the United States: 1996 Report*. Evanston, Ill.: Author, 1996.

American Association of Colleges of Teacher Education (AACTE). *Teacher Education Policy in the States: A 50-State Survey of Legislative and Administrative Actions*. Washington, D.C.: Author, 1991.

American Association of Colleges of Teacher Education (AACTE). *Teacher Education Policy in the States: A 50-State Survey of Legislative and Administrative Actions*. Washington, D.C.: Author, 1994.

American Council on Education. *Eighth Annual Status Report on Minorities in Higher Education*. Washington, D.C.: Author, 1989.

Andrew, M. "The Differences Between Graduates of Four-Year and Five-Year Teacher Preparation Programs." *Journal of Teacher Education*, 1990, *41*, 45–51.

Andrew, M., and Schwab, R. L. "Has Reform in Teacher Education Influenced Teacher Performance? An Outcome Assessment of Graduates of Eleven Teacher Education Programs." *Action in Teacher Education*, 1995, *17*, 43–53.

Anglin, L. W., Mooradian, P., and Hamilton, A. "A Missing Rung of the Teacher Education Ladder: Community Colleges." *Action in Teacher Education*, 1993, *15*(1) 8–13.

Arch, E. C. "Comparison of Student Attainment of Teaching Competence in Traditional Preservice and Fifth-Year Master of Arts in Teaching Programs." Paper presented at the annual meeting of the American Educational Research Association, San Francisco, Calif., April 1989.

Arvey, R. D., and Campion, J. E. "The Employment Interview. A Summary and Review of Recent Research." *Personnel Psychology*, 1982, *35*, 281–322.

Ashton, P., Crocker, L., and Olejnik, J. "Teacher Education Research: A Call for Collaboration." Paper presented at the meeting of the Southern Regional Consortium of Colleges of Education, Nashville, Tenn., 1987.

Astin, A. W. *The American Freshman: National Norms for 1996*. Higher Education Research Institute. Los Angeles: UCLA Graduate School of Education, 1996.

Astin, A. W., Green, C. C., and Korn, W. S. *The American Freshman: Twenty Year Trends*. New York: American Council of Education, 1987.

Ballou, D. "Do Public Schools Hire the Best Applicants?" *Quarterly Journal of Economics*, Feb. 1996, pp. 97–133.

Bents, M., and Bents, R. "Perceptions of Good Teaching Among Novice, Advanced Beginner and Expert Teachers." Paper presented at the annual meeting of the American Educational Research Association, Boston, Mass., April 1990.

Berry, B. *Understanding Teacher Supply and Demand in the Southeast: A Synthesis of Qualitative Research to Aid Effective Policy Making.* Research Triangle Park, N.C.: Southeastern Regional Council for Educational Improvement, 1985.

Berry, B. *Keeping Talented Teachers: Lessons Learned from the North Carolina Teaching Fellows.* Commissioned by the North Carolina Teaching Fellows Commission, Raleigh, N.C.: Public School Forum, 1995.

Blank, R. K., and Gruebel, D. *State Indicators of Science and Mathematics Education 1993.* Washington, D.C.: Council of Chief State School Officers, 1993.

Bledsoe, J. C., Cox, J. V., and Burnham, R. *Comparison Between Selected Characteristics and Performance of Provisionally and Professionally Certified Beginning Teachers in Georgia.* Washington, D.C.: U.S. Department of Health, Education, and Welfare, 1967.

Boe, E., and Gilford, D. (eds.). *Teacher Supply, Demand and Quality—Policy Issues, Models, and Databases.* Washington, D.C.: National Press Academy, 1992.

Bolam, R. "Teacher Recruitment and Induction." In L. W. Anderson (ed.), *The International Encyclopedia of Teaching and Teacher Education.* New York: Elsevier Science, 1995.

Braun, J. A., Green, K., Williams, A., and Brown, M. "Getting a Job: Perceptions of Successful Applicants for Teaching Positions." *Action in Teacher Education,* 1990, *12,* 44–54.

Breidenstein, A. "A Comparative Analysis of the Perceptions of Four-Year and Extended Program Teacher Education Graduates Regarding Their Teacher Education and Teaching Experiences." Unpublished doctoral dissertation, Teachers College, Columbia University, 1998.

Browne, B. A., and Rankin, R. J. "Predicting Employment in Education: The Relative Efficiency of National Teacher Examination Scores and Student Teacher Ratings." *Educational and Psychological Measurement,* 1986, *46*(1), 191–197.

Bruno, J. "Design of Incentive Systems for Staffing Racially Isolated Schools in Large Urban Districts." *Journal of Education Finance,* 1981, *7,* 149–167.

California Commission of Teacher Credentialing. *Success for Beginning Teachers: The California New Teacher Project 1988–92.* Sacramento: California State Department of Education, 1992.

Clark, R. *Professional Development Schools: Policy and Finance.* Washington, D.C.: American Association of Colleges for Teacher Education, 1997.

Clements, S. *Kentucky Status of Teaching Report.* Report prepared for the Oversight Committee for Kentucky's Partnership with the National Commission on Teaching and America's Future, 1998.

Copley, P. O. *A Study of the Effect of Professional Education Courses on Beginning Teachers.* Springfield, Mo.: Southwest Missouri State University, 1974. ED 098 147.

Council of the Great City Schools. *National Urban Education Goals: Baseline Indicators, 1990–1991.* Washington, D.C.: Author, 1992.

Darling-Hammond, L. *Beyond the Commission Reports. The Coming Crisis in Teaching.* Report R-3117-RC. Santa Monica, Calif.: RAND, 1984.

Darling-Hammond, L. "Teaching and Knowledge: Policy Issues Posed by Alternative Certification for Teachers." *Peabody Journal of Education,* 1990, *67*(3), 123–154.

Darling-Hammond, L. *Professional Development Schools: Schools for Developing a Profession.* New York: Teachers College Press, 1994.

Darling-Hammond, L. *Doing What Matters Most: Investing in Quality Teaching.* New York: National Commission on Teaching and America's Future, 1997.

Darling-Hammond, L. "Teacher Quality and Student Achievement: A Review of State Policy Evidence." *Educational Evaluation and Policy Analysis,* forthcoming.

Darling-Hammond, L., Hudson, L., and Kirby, S. N. *Redesigning Teacher Education: Opening the Door for New Recruits to Science and Mathematics Teaching.* Santa Monica, Calif.: RAND, 1989.

Darling-Hammond, L., and Sclan, E. "Who Teaches and Why." In J. Sikula, T. Buttery, and E. Guyton (eds.), *The Handbook of Research on Teacher Education.* New York: Macmillan, 1996.

Darling-Hammond, L., Wise, A. E., and Klein, S. P. *A License to Teach: Building a Profession for 21st Century Schools.* Boulder, Colo.: Westview Press, 1995.

Debolt, G. *Teacher Induction and Mentoring: School-Based Collaborative Programs.* Albany, N.Y.: SUNY Press, 1992.

Denton, J. J., and Peters, W. H. *Program Assessment Report: Curriculum Evaluation of a Non-Traditional Program for Certifying Teachers.* College Station, Tex.: Texas A&M University, 1988.

Dyal, A. B. "An Exploratory Study to Determine Principals' Perceptions Concerning the Effectiveness of a Fifth-Year Preparation Program." Paper presented at the annual meeting of the Mid-South Educational Research Association, New Orleans, La., 1993.

Estrada, L. "The Four D's of Demography." Paper presented at the Third National Symposium in Precollegiate Teacher Recruitment, Pasadena, Calif., 1995.

Evertson, C., Hawley, W., and Zlotnick, M. "Making a Difference in Educational Quality Through Teacher Education." *Journal of Teacher Education,* 1985, *36*(3), 2–12.

Feiman-Nemser, S., and Parker, M. B. *Making Subject Matter Part of the Conversation or Helping Beginning Teachers Learn to Teach.* East Lansing, Mich.: National Center for Research on Teacher Education, 1990.

Feistritzer, E. C. *Profile of Teachers in the United States.* Washington, D.C.: National Center for Education Information, 1990.

Ferguson, R. "Paying for Public Education: New Evidence on How and Why Money Matters." *Harvard Journal on Legislation,* 1991, *28,* 465–498.

Fullan, M. *Change Forces.* Bristol, Pa.: Falmer Press, 1993.

Gallup Organization. *SRI Teacher Perceiver.* Lincoln, Neb.: SRI Gallup, 1990.

Gallup Organization. *Gallup SRI Teacher Perceiver Updated Research.* Lincoln, Nebr.: Author, 1994.

Gold, Y. "Beginning Teacher Support: Attrition, Mentoring, and Induction." In J. Sikula, T. J. Buttery, and E. Guyton (eds.), *The Handbook of Research on Teacher Education* (2nd ed.). New York: Macmillan, 1996.

Gomez, D., and Grobe, P. "Three Years of Alternative Certification in Dallas: Where Are We?" Paper presented at the annual meeting of the American Educational Research Association, Boston, 1990.

Goodlad, J. I. *Teachers for Our Nation's Schools.* San Francisco: Jossey-Bass, 1990.

Grady, M., Collins, P., and Grady, E. "Teach for America: Evaluation Report 1991 Summer Institute." Unpublished report, 1991.

Gray, L., and others. *New Teachers in The Job Market. 1991 Update.* Washington, D.C.: U.S. Department of Education, Office of Educational Research and Improvement, 1993.

Gray, D., and Lynn, D. H. *New Teachers, Better Teachers: A Report on Two Initiatives in New Jersey.* Washington, D.C.: Council for Basic Education, 1988.

Greenwald, R., Hedges, L. V., and Laine, R. D. "The Effect of School Resources on Student Achievement." *Review of Educational Research,* 1996, *66,* 361–396.

Grissmer, D. W., and Kirby, S. N. *Teacher Attrition: The Uphill Climb to Staff the Nation's Schools.* Santa Monica, Calif.: RAND Corporation, 1987.

Grossman, P. L. "Learning to Teach Without Teacher Education." *Teachers College Record,* 1989, *91*(2), 191–208.

Guyton, E., and Farokhi, E. "Relationships Among Academic Performance, Basic Skills, Subject Matter Knowledge and Teaching Skills of Teacher Education Graduates." *Journal of Teacher Education,* Sept.–Oct. 1987, pp. 37–42.

Haberman, M. "Selecting Star Teachers for Children and Youth in Urban Poverty." *Phi Delta Kappan,* June 1995, pp. 778–781.

Hanushek, E. The Impact of Differential Expenditures on Student Performance. *Educational Researcher,* 1989, *18*(4), 45–52.

Hanushek, E., and Pace, R. "Who Chooses to Teach (and Why)?" *Economics of Education Review,* 1995, *14*(2), 101–117.

Harris, L. *The American Teacher, 1984–1995, Metropolitan Life Survey. Old Problems, New Challenges.* New York: Louis Harris and Associates, 1995.

Hawk, P., Coble, C. R., and Swanson, M. "Certification: It Does Matter." *Journal of Teacher Education,* 1985, *36*(3), 13–15.

Hentschke, G. *Paraeducators: New Plumbing in the Teacher Education Pipeline.* Los Angeles: University of Southern California, School of Education, 1995.

Holmes Group. *Tomorrow's Schools: Principles for the Design of Professional Development Schools: A Report.* East Lansing, Mich.: Author, 1990.

Howey, K., and Zimpher, N. "Patterns in Prospective Teachers: Guides for Designing Preservice Programs." Unpublished paper, 1993.

Huling-Austin, L. "Teacher Induction Programs and Internships." In W. R. Houston (ed.), *The Handbook of Research on Teacher Education.* New York: Macmillan, 1990.

Ingersoll, R. "Out of Field Teaching in the United States." Paper prepared for the National Commission on Teaching and America's Future. New York: Teachers College, Columbia University, 1997a.

Ingersoll, R. *Teacher Professionalization and Teacher Commitment: A Multilevel Analysis*. Washington, D.C.: U.S. Department of Education, Office of Educational Research and Improvement, 1997b.

Jacobson, S. "The Effects of Pay Incentives on Teacher Absenteeism." *Journal of Human Resources,* 1988, *24,* 280–286.

Johanson, G. A., and Gips, C. J. "The Hiring Preferences of Secondary School Principals." *High School Journal,* 1992, *16,* 1–16.

Johnson, S. *Teachers at Work. Achieving Success in Our Schools*. New York: Basic Books, 1990.

Karge, B. D., and Freiberg, M. R. "Beginning Special Education Teachers: At Risk for Attrition." Paper presented at the annual meeting of the American Educational Research Association, San Francisco, 1992.

Kennedy, M. *Trends and Issues in Teachers' Subject Matter Knowledge*. East Lansing, Mich.: National Center for Research on Teacher Education, 1990.

Lenk, H. A. *A Case Study: The Induction of Two Alternate Route Social Studies Teachers.* Unpublished doctoral dissertation. Teachers College, Columbia University, 1989.

Lortie, D. C. *Schoolteacher: A Sociological Study*. Chicago: University of Chicago Press, 1975.

Lutz, F. W., and Hutton, J. B. "Alternative Teacher Certification: Its Policy Implications for Classroom and Personnel Practice." *Educational Evaluation and Policy Analysis,* 1989, *11*(3), 237–254.

MacIssac, D., and Brookhart, L. "A Partnership Approach to New Teacher Induction." Paper presented at the annual meeting of the American Association of Colleges of Teacher Education, Chicago, 1994.

MacMillan, J. B., and Pendlebury, S. "The Florida Performance Measurement System: A Consideration." *Teachers College Record,* 1985, *87,* 69–78.

McDiarmid, G. W., Ball, D. L., and Anderson, C. W. "Why Staying One Chapter Ahead Doesn't Really Work: Subject-Specific Pedagogy." In M. C. Reynolds (ed.), *Knowledge Base for the Beginning Teacher*. Washington, D.C.: American Association of Colleges of Teacher Education, 1989.

Metropolitan Life. *The American Teacher 1989: Preparing Schools for the 1990s.* New York: Author, 1989.

Metropolitan Life. *Survey of the American Teacher: 1995.* New York: Louis Harris and Associates, 1995.

Mitchell, N. *Interim Evaluation Report of the Alternative Certification Program* (REA87-027-2). Dallas, TX: DISD Department of Planning, Evaluation, and Testing, 1987.

Murnane, R. J. "The Case for Performance-Base Licensing." *Phi Delta Kappan,* 1991, *73*(2), 137–142.

Murnane, R. J., and others. *Who Will Teach?* Cambridge, Mass.: Harvard University Press, 1991.

Murnane, R. J., Singer, J. D., and Willett, J. B. "The Influences of Salaries and Opportunity Costs on Teachers' Career Choices: Evidence from North Carolina." *Harvard Educational Review,* 1989, *59*(3) 325–346.

National Center for Education Information (NCEI). *Alternative Teacher Certification: A State-by-State Analysis.* Washington, D.C.: Author, 1992.

National Center for Education Statistics (NCES). *The Condition of Education, 1989 Edition.* Vol. 2. Washington, D.C.: U.S. Department of Education, 1989.

National Center for Education Statistics (NCES). *High School and Beyond: Fourth Follow-up.* Washington, D.C.: U.S. Department of Education, Office of Educational Research and Improvement, 1992.

National Commission on Teaching and America's Future (NCTAF). *What Matters Most: Teaching for America's Future.* New York: Author, 1996.

National Education Association (NEA). *Status of American Public School Teacher 1990–91.* Washington, D.C.: Author, 1992.

Natriello, G., Zumwalt, K., Hansen, A., and Frisch, A. "Characteristics of Entering Teachers in New Jersey." Revised version of a paper presented at the 1988 annual meeting of the American Educational Research Association, April 1990.

Niece, P. "The Interview and Personnel Selection: Is the Process Reliable and Valid?" *Clearing House,* 1983, *56,* 232–255.

Oakes, J. *Multiplying Inequities: The Effects of Race, Social Class, and Tracking on Opportunities to Learn Mathematics and Science.* Santa Monica, Calif.: RAND Corporation, 1990.

Odell, S. "Induction Support of New Teachers: A Functional Approach." *Journal of Teacher Education,* 1986, *37*(1) 26–29.

Odell, S. J. "Developing Support Programs for Beginning Teachers." In L. Huling-Austin, S. J. Odell, P. Ishler, R. S. Kay, and R. A. Edelfelt (eds.), *Assisting the Beginning Teacher.* Reston, Va.: Association of Teacher Educators, 1989.

Odell, S. J., and Ferraro, D. P. "Collaborative Teacher Induction." In G. DeBolt (ed.), *Teacher Induction and Mentoring: School-Based Collaborative Programs.* Albany, N.Y.: SUNY, 1992a.

Odell, S., and Ferraro, D. P. "Teacher Mentoring and Teacher Retention." *Journal of Teacher Education,* 1992b, *43*(3), 200–204.

Orfield, G. F., Monfort, F., and Aaron, M. *Status of School Desegregation: 1968–1986.* Alexandria, Va.: National School Boards Association, 1989.

Page, F. M., and Page, J. A. "Perceptions of Teaching that May Be Influencing the Current Shortage of Teachers." *College Student Journal,* 1982, *16*(4), 308–311.

Pawlas, G. "The Structured Interview: Three Dozen Questions to Ask Prospective Teachers." *National Association of Secondary School Principals Bulletin,* 1995, *79*(567) 62–65.

Pflaum, S. W., and Abrahamson, T. "Teacher Assignment, Hiring, and Preparation." *Urban Review,* 1990, *22*(1), 17–31.

Recruiting New Teachers, Inc. *The Urban Teacher Challenge: A Report on Teacher Recruitment and Demand in Selected Great City Schools.* Belmont, Mass.: Author, 1996a.

Recruiting New Teachers, Inc. *Breaking the Class Ceiling: Paraeducator Pathways to Teaching.* Belmont Mass.: Author, 1996b.

Recruiting New Teachers, Inc. *The Essential Profession: A Public Opinion Poll.* Belmont, Mass.: Author, 1998.

Reilly, R. R., and Chao, G. T. "Validity and Fairness of Some Alternative Employee Selection Procedures." *Personnel Psychology,* 1982, *35,* 1–62.

Richards, C. "State Regulation of Entry Level Teacher Salaries: Policy Issues and Options." *Educational Policy,* 1988, *2,* 307–322.

Richburg, R. W. "How Much Does It Cost to Train World-Class Teachers?" *International Journal of Innovative Higher Education,* in press.

Richburg, R., Knox, K., Carson, S., and McWhorter, B. "Adding Power to Our Ability to Develop Outstanding New Teachers." *Journal of Teacher Education,* forthcoming.

Rinehart, J. S., and Young, I. P. "Teacher Selection: Research and Applications." *High School Journal,* 1990, *73*(3), 176–179.

Rosenholtz, S. *Teachers' Workplaces: The Social Organization of Schools.* New York: Longman, 1989.

Roth, R. A. "Alternate and Alternative Certification: Purposes, Assumptions, Implications." *Action in Teacher Education,* 1986, *8*(2), 1–6.

Roth, R. "Teach for America 1993 Pre-Service Summer Institute: Program Review." Unpublished report, Summer 1993.

Rottenberg, C. J., and Berliner, D. C. "Expert and Novice Teachers' Conceptions of Common Classroom Activities." Paper presented at the annual meeting of the American Educational Research Association, Boston, Mass., 1990.

Rowzie, G. *Assessing the Teacher Cadet Program: The 1992 Study.* Columbia, S.C.: South Carolina Educational Policy Center, University of South Carolina, 1992.

Sanders, W., and Rivers, J. C. *Cumulative and Residual Effects of Teachers on Future Student Academic Achievement.* Knoxville: University of Tennessee Value-Added Research and Assessment Center, 1996.

Schlechty, P., and Vance, V. "Recruitment, Selection and Retention: The Shape of the Teaching Force." *Elementary School Journal,* 1983, *83*(4), 469–487.

Sclan, E. "The Effect of Perceived Workplace Conditions on Beginning Teachers' Work Commitment, Career Choice Commitment, and Planned Retention." *Dissertation Abstracts International,* 1993, 54–08A.

Sedlak, M., and Schlossman, S. *Who Will Teach? Historical Perspectives on the Changing Appeal of Teaching as a Profession.* (R-3472). Santa Monica, Calif.: RAND, 1986.

Shen, J. "Has the Alternative Certification Policy Materialized Its Promise? A Comparison of Traditionally and Alternatively Certified Teachers in Public Schools." *Educational Evaluation and Policy Analyses,* 1997, *19,* 276–283.

Smith, J. M. "School Districts as Teacher Training Institutions in the New Jersey Alternate Route Program." Paper presented at the annual meeting of the Eastern Educational Research Association, Clearwater, Fla., February 1990a.

Smith, J. M. "A Comparative Study of the State Regulations for and the Operation of the New Jersey Provisional Teacher Certification Program." Paper presented at the annual meeting of the American Educational Research Association, Boston, Mass., April 1990b.

Smith, J. M. *Supervision, Mentoring and the "Alternate Route."* (Mimeograph.), n.d.

Snyder, J. *New Haven Unified School District: A Comprehensive Approach to Assuring Teacher Quality.* New York: National Commission on Teaching and America's Future, in press.

Stoddart, T. "An Alternate Route to Teacher Certification: Preliminary Findings from the Los Angeles Unified School District Intern Program." *Peabody Journal of Education,* 1992, *67*(3).

Texas Education Agency. *Teach for America Visiting Team Report.* (Meeting Minutes, Appendix B). Austin: Texas State Board of Education, 1993.

Veenman, S. "Perceived Problems of Beginning Teachers." *Review of Educational Research,* 1984, *54*(2) 143–178.

Webster, W. J. "Selecting Effective Teachers." *Journal of Education Research,* 1988, *81*(4), 245–253.

Whatley, W., Ren, J., and Rowzie, G. *Assessing the Teacher Cadet Program: The 1993 Study.* Columbia: South Carolina Educational Policy Center, University of South Carolina, 1993.

Wise, A. E., Darling-Hammond, L., and Berry, B. *Effective Teacher Selection: From Recruitment to Retention.* Santa Monica: RAND Corporation, 1987.

Wise, A. E., Darling-Hammond, L., McLaughlin, M. W., and Bernstein, H. T. *Effective Teacher Evaluation.* Santa Monica, Calif.: RAND, 1984.

Wisniewski, R. "On Collaboration." *Teacher Education and Practice,* 1992, *7*(2), 13–16.

Wright, D. P., McKibbon, M., and Walton, P. *The Effectiveness of the Teacher Trainee Program: An Alternate Route into Teaching in California.* Sacramento: California Commission on Teacher Credentialing, 1987.

Young, I. P. "The Effects of Interpersonal Performance Style in Simulated Teacher Selection Interviews." *Journal of Research and Development in Education,* 1984, *17,* 43–51.

Zimpher, N., and Ashburn, E. A. "Countering Parochialism in Teacher Candidates." In M. E. Dilworth (ed.), *Diversity in Teacher Education: New Expectations.* San Francisco: Jossey-Bass, 1992.

CHAPTER EIGHT

Organizing Schools
for Teacher Learning

Judith Warren Little

There is a certain elegant simplicity to the problem of organizing schools for teacher learning. As one celebrated school leader puts it, "At the very least, one must imagine schools in which teachers are in frequent conversation with each other about their work, have easy and necessary access to each other's classrooms, take it for granted that they should comment on each other's work, and have the time to develop common standards for student work" (Meier, 1992, p. 602). Such a description speaks to elemental habits of professional practice and to the organization that will support them.

In this and similar portraits, teacher learning arises out of close involvement with students and their work, shared responsibility for student progress, sensibly organized time and space, access to the expertise of colleagues inside and outside the school, focused and timely feedback on one's own work, and an overall ethos in which teacher learning is valued. Yet such portraits remain largely at odds with the organization of the ordinary school or the life of the ordinary teacher. Despite some well-documented and widely acclaimed exceptions, we find relatively few schools demonstrably organized to support and influence teacher learning. Teachers report that they find little satisfaction in episodic "inservice training," but are otherwise often thrust on their own resources in what

This chapter was adapted from a longer essay of the same title, prepared for the National Commission on Teaching and America's Future.

233

Michael Huberman (1995) has termed a "lone wolf scenario." This most common scenario remains one in which teachers labor on their own to decide what instruction works, what standard of student work is good enough, and what additional knowledge, skill, or insights would best serve them and their students. Further, they do so in the crowded interstices of the day and week. Huberman elaborates: "It is probable that this version of private, self-administered inservice, with whatever tools and expertise lie nearby, is the modal one across most school settings and at most points of the career. Both the architectural and social organization of schooling make it difficult to work otherwise" (p. 207).

In Huberman's analysis, the usual exception to the lone wolf scenario arises in the context of ambitious programs of innovation that supply favorable conditions for professional development: collaborative work among peers, external assistance, a new infusion of materials and technologies, sustained inquiry into problems of student learning in specific subjects, and the close evaluation of experiments in curriculum and instruction. "The problem," Huberman maintains, "is that such moments come rarely in the professional life span; we can expect, in a 30-year career, four or five such episodes, each lasting three to four years at their peak" (p. 207). Intensive, sustained learning experiences may come often enough to a few but rarely or not at all to others.

We have here the makings of a fundamental dilemma. By most accounts, teaching is extraordinarily demanding of teachers' expertise, energy, and enthusiasm, and it is becoming more so. The learning demands that inhere in that work cannot be fully anticipated or met by preservice preparation, even when that experience is stellar. Nor does it seem probable that more uniformly high levels of student achievement can be accomplished by teachers' working alone. It is an established sociological tenet that complex tasks require the development of strong lateral relations. Parallels are readily evident: piloting a large ship in a crowded harbor, diagnosing and treating serious illness, staging an opera. To acknowledge this necessary interdependence does not require that we dismiss the independent, creative role that talented and well-prepared individuals play, but it does suggest more deliberate supports for what I have termed *joint work* among teachers.

This chapter investigates the proposition that schools can and should play a far more powerful and consequential role in integrating teacher development more fully into the ongoing work of teachers. I concentrate on the ordinary contexts of teaching—first and foremost on the architectural and social organization of schooling that teachers encounter on a daily basis, and additionally on the ways in which the boundaries of the school might be made more permeable, joining teachers more readily to other sources of professional community and professional development. I posit that teacher learning will more assuredly be supported in schools that do the following:

- Emphasize teachers' individual and collective responsibility for student achievement and well-being, and make inquiry into student learning a cornerstone of professional development.

- Organize time, teaching responsibilities, and other aspects of teachers' work in ways that demonstrably enhance opportunities for teacher learning, both inside and outside the school.

- Employ staff development resources in ways that increase teachers' ability to make well-informed use of ideas, materials, and colleagues.

- Conduct staff evaluation and program or school reviews in a manner consistent with teacher learning.

- Embrace an ethos genuinely conducive to teacher development.

To some extent, this is speculative work. Assertions about the relationship between school organization and teacher learning rest in large part on theoretical work in the area of social and organizational learning, studies of the implementation of innovation, and studies of the workplace conditions of teacher efficacy and adaptability. Because we have not yet made serious comparative and longitudinal studies of schools as learning environments for teachers, we know relatively little about the relative salience of selected workplace features or about their combined effects. The available evidence points consistently to an emerging agenda in which practical action and research might productively be joined.

TEACHER LEARNING AND A COLLECTIVE FOCUS ON STUDENTS

Schools might profitably be organized to capitalize more fully on what and how teachers learn through their work with students. They might enable teachers to investigate, rather than merely respond to, the learning demands and learning resources that reside in classroom experience. Perhaps one of the most powerful and least costly occasions of teacher learning is the systematic, sustained study of student work, coupled with individual and collective efforts to figure out how that work results from the practices and choices of teaching. Learning from, with, and about students is more likely when schools supply teachers with the resources for inquiry into student experience and learning, teachers share responsibility for student well-being and achievement, and organizational scale enables sustained exchange regarding student learning.

Inquiry into Student Learning

Vivian Paley (1986) recalls her early experience as a kindergarten teacher in which "I . . . wanted most of all to keep things moving with a minimum of distraction. It did not occur to me that the distractions might be the sounds of children thinking." Paley relates her story of coming to be curious about children and their learning, spurred first by her children's unexpected response to a visiting science teacher and then by a speech (on teacher expectations) that jarred her out of classroom complacency. Soon, with the help of a tape recorder, "the act of teaching became a daily search for the child's point of view accompanied by the sometimes unwelcome disclosure of my hidden attitudes. . . . I began using the tape recorder to try to figure out why the children were lively and imaginative in certain discussions, yet fidgety and distracted in others. . . . Several phenomena emerged. Whenever the discussion touched on fantasy, fairness, or friendship (the three F's I began to call them), participation zoomed upward" (p. 79).

In this excerpt, as throughout Paley's other chronicles, one finds a thread of surprise—the assumption challenged, the unanticipated discovery. Paley's classroom inquiries are not unique, especially in a period of expanding support for teacher research, but they remain relatively uncommon. Most teachers say they learn from their students, describing processes of instructional trial and error or the occasional insights yielded by special events or relationships. Few say they have the time, knowledge, or resources to pursue structured inquiry. Few teach in circumstances where their own observations of students and their explanations of student progress matter to anyone else or form part of an ongoing school-level assessment of teaching effectiveness.

A school organized for teacher learning would promote the systematic study of teaching and learning in at least two ways. First, the school would support teachers in investigating questions, problems, and curiosities that arise in teaching. A writing workshop formed by teachers in one elementary school met weekly after school to "get smarter" about helping children become good writers. Teachers started by examining samples of their own students' work and gradually branched out to other resources. Other schools have supported teacher research projects—studies of the full inclusion classroom, the meaning that students attach to good work, students' experience of detracked classrooms, or the effects of an interdisciplinary house structure on high school students' attendance and performance. These inquiries exemplify a burgeoning teacher research movement made increasingly visible through conferences, journals, and published collections of teachers' research. Their principal significance, however, lies in their power to inform teachers' own practice (Burnaford, Fischer, and Hobson, 1996; Cochran-Smith and Lytle, 1993; Hollingsworth and Sockett, 1994).

Second, a school would promote the study of teaching and learning by developing the organizational habit of shared student assessment, employing a range of evidence that might span standardized tests, student portfolios, performances or exhibitions, periodic schoolwide writing prompts or open-ended math problems, and the like. School improvement and professional development initiatives have increasingly made assessment of student work a central component of their activities. Some provide a structured process for describing, analyzing, and reporting on student progress. An example is the Primary Language Record (Darling-Hammond, Ancess, and Falk, 1995). In this and other such ventures, teachers begin with samples of students' work or classroom experience (for example, student-produced texts in various writing genres or videotaped excerpts from math lessons on a common topic). Using samples of student work as a point of departure, teachers begin to investigate the relationships among the academic work students are asked or invited to do, the support they are given to do it, and the actual work they produce (see also Falk and Ort, 1997; Sheingold, Heller, and Storms, 1997).

Schools organized along these lines are growing in number, fueled by interest in school restructuring, teacher research, and student assessment. Schools funded by one state-sponsored school restructuring initiative have been urged to develop a structure and process for analyzing student work. In one example, an urban elementary school has developed an electronic portfolio system that enables teachers to profile students' work in language arts. All teachers participate in providing portfolio entries that accord with their agreed-on scheme for collecting student work—specific kinds of work each semester at each grade level—and entries are assessed in accordance with the scoring and feedback rubrics established collectively by the teachers. Scoring criteria are backed by accompanying "anchor papers" and periodically reexamined. The school has archived the student data by scanning student work into computerized templates and assembling year-long schoolwide samples for use on CD-ROM.

Schools like this one speak of embracing a "culture of inquiry," but report that giving life and substance to that image proves difficult amid the press of everyday activity. Teachers and others have been known to joke that it is far easier to achieve a culture of inquiry at conferences—in the "hotel learning community"—than to cultivate it on home ground. At the elementary school just described, the electronic portfolio has served principally to organize reports to parents and to guide teacher planning, but its resources have not yet been marshaled in the service of school-level inquiries or organized teacher learning. The relevant questions proliferate rapidly: What does an individual child's development look like over a three-year period? What does the process of learning to write look like among second-language learners? Do students show evidence of certain common problems with particular kinds of writing?

What kinds of classroom assignments and activities seem to yield the strongest response from students?

These two avenues of inquiry into student learning—subsidized teacher inquiry and shared assessment of student work—permit learning that is closely tied to the classroom and responsive to the histories and contexts that teachers bring to the discussion. Both stand to benefit the school as well as the individual participants. Both lend themselves to cross-school as well as within-school activity. And both might readily be enhanced by still other approaches: conventional course work or special institutes; partnerships with colleges, specialized nonprofit organizations, or individuals; or participation in teacher research or student assessment collaboratives. In whatever form, the main idea here is to mobilize the school's resources to place inquiry into student learning at the heart of teachers' professional development.

Shared Responsibility

Sustained and widespread inquiry into students' learning experiences and learning outcomes seems more likely to form an ongoing, central part of school work life—rather than an infrequent exercise—where teachers assume shared responsibility for students. Although formal configurations of shared responsibility might seem to be more readily achieved at the upper grades, where students typically receive instruction from more than one teacher, shared responsibility entails the same conditions at all levels: a symbolic embrace of the principle, combined with specific mechanisms by which teachers contribute to one another's success with students.

Although research is sparse, available evidence suggests that students' academic achievement is greater in schools where teachers report high levels of collective responsibility for student learning (Lee and Smith, 1996). Of course, this relationship may be attributed to factors quite independent of teacher learning—for example, to uniformity of expectations, coordination of effort, a plentiful supply of information about individual students, or effective recruitment and hiring. However, there is also a plausible case to be made that the effect on student achievement is the result of conditions that clarify professional development needs, expand the pool of curricular ideas available to each teacher, help teachers collect and interpret relevant information about students, and create a shared sense of obligation for student achievement. That is, shared responsibility for students may intensify teachers' incentive for professional growth and define a professional community whose members have reason to learn from and with one another.

Fostering shared responsibility for student well-being presents a leadership challenge and a learning problem for both schools and individuals. Traditional arrangements of "cellular" classrooms, individualized teaching assignments, and occupational norms of personal autonomy tend to obscure both the commonalities and the differences among teachers, and to place both structural and cultural constraints on teacher communication. Structures that create genuine interdependence among teachers (small schools, houses, teams, other school-within-a-school arrangements) make each teacher's contributions to student learning more visible. Such structures also give teachers a common basis for discussion, planning, assistance, and assessment—and thus a focus for teacher learning. Both the need for teacher learning and the resources for learning are likely to be more evident.

Such structural alternatives constitute an important organizational resource, but prove insufficient to produce a collective commitment to students or engender teacher learning. In seeking to modify constraints or foster communication, teachers and administrators routinely encounter tensions between personal autonomy and common commitments, between desirable scope for individuality and legitimate press for collectively held values and principles (Hargreaves, 1991, 1993; Huberman, 1993; Little, 1990b; Nias, Southworth, and Yeomans, 1989). In some schools organizational charts indicate houses, families, or teams—those arrangements formally designed to expand teacher interactions and organize shared responsibility for students—but observers may find little evidence that these are meaningful features of teachers' work. Procedures for student placement and teacher assignment remain unchanged, classrooms widely scattered, teachers' planning times uncoordinated. Such examples attest to the fact that structure alone will not ensure student benefit or an environment for teacher learning. However, the expanding case literature on restructuring schools offers numerous examples from both elementary and secondary schools that demonstrate the power of shared responsibility for students where structure and culture reinforce one another (Darling-Hammond, 1997; Lieberman, 1995a; Louis and Kruse, 1995; Peterson, McCarthey and Elmore, 1996).

Small Scale

Large schools and school districts supply teachers with a large pool of colleagues, but otherwise exacerbate the problem of teacher learning in several ways. First, large scale makes it less likely that teachers will share responsibility for the same students, and thus have a reason for looking closely together at student learning and related classroom practice (although simply teaching the same kinds of students, the same grade, or the same subject may also provide an impetus to do so). Second, large scale creates anonymity among teachers, making it less likely that teachers will know one another well enough both personally and professionally to contribute meaningfully to one another's learning. Finally, large scale and its attendant bureaucratization tend to multiply the sheer number of activities associated with the school and the range of nonteaching responsibilities borne by each teacher; time available for joint work among teachers competes at a disadvantage with other demands on teacher time and attention.

Although the benefits of small scale for teacher learning have not been specifically tested, testimonials abound in which teachers credit small school size, teams, study groups, or special projects with opening their eyes to new ideas and instilling new confidence in themselves and their students, even while they also testify to the occasional strains of working closely together. Selected case studies in small-scale environments—including small schools, small teacher teams, and sustained study groups or close networks—suggest that the advantages for teacher learning may be substantial, although not always easily realized. As in other aspects of teachers' work and workplace, structures alone prove insufficient to create professional community.

TEACHER LEARNING IN THE ORGANIZATION OF DAILY WORK

The mundane circumstances of work and workplace signal a school's or district's organizational stance toward teacher learning. In crucial ways, teachers discover the incentives and resources for professional development in the teaching assignments they acquire, the material and informational resources at their disposal, and the routine organization of professional time.

Significance of Teacher Assignment

Policies and practices of teacher assignment operate in three ways to strengthen or diminish the preparation that teachers bring to the classroom: the fit they achieve with existing (and growing) teacher competence, the scope of the teaching assignment and the demands it places on teachers for new learning, and the resulting school- or team-level configuration of staff talent and interest. Teaching assignments might thus be judged by criteria of fit, stretch, and community.

A first measure of teaching assignment is good fit at the individual classroom level, making the most of an individual teacher's existing knowledge, experience, and interest. Fit matters. Teachers have been shown to teach more conservatively, didactically, and inflexibly when they are not confident in the content they are expected to teach or in their ability to teach a particular group of students (Ball and Lacey, 1984; Little, 1990a; McLaughlin and Talbert, in press; Sedlak, Wheeler, Pullin, and Cusick, 1986). Yet studies of teacher induction consistently confirm that schools routinely assign inexperienced teachers to the most difficult-to-teach classes. Studies of teacher assignment show how assignment practices dominated by seniority or internal school politics may take little account of teachers' expertise and experience and thus exacerbate inequalities among students (Finley, 1984; Gehrke and Sheffield, 1985; Neufeld, 1984; Talbert, 1990). Recent teaching efficacy studies challenge the view that efficacy is a stable individual trait, showing its sensitivity to teacher assignment (Raudenbush, Rowan, and Cheong, 1992). Finally, studies of organizational culture and professional community suggest that schools may address problems of fit in reactive or proactive ways. In one example of the latter, a high school math department responded to a shortage of math specialists by growing its own—subsidizing teachers who were underprepared in math to acquire substantially more math expertise (Yu and Talbert, 1994).

Each of these lines of research implicates teacher assignment as a contributor to the quality of teaching, and each suggests organizational routes to good-fit assignments. Among the assignment-related factors subject to school leadership and organizational policy are the number and level of subjects taught; stability of classroom assignments in the first few years of teaching; composition of classes; availability of mentors, consultants, and other sources of expertise; and traditions and norms surrounding assignment to advanced or remedial classes.

A second measure of appropriate teacher assignment is the prospect for stimulation or "stretch" that resides directly in the classroom assignment or in related teaching responsibilities. The underlying idea is that teacher learning arises from assignments that tap existing teacher expertise while also stretching teachers' understanding and skill (Sprinthall and Thies-Sprinthall, 1983; Borko and Putnam, 1995). Schools may create conditions for stretching in various ways, and what gains acceptance in one school may feel like exploitation in another. For example, some high school departments have found that agreed-on rotation in teaching assignments broadens and deepens the staff's capacity to teach all the school's students and to teach across the school's program. It also offers a school greater "bench strength," minimizes the politics of course assignment, and ensures that the least experienced teachers are not consistently assigned to the lowest-achieving students. However, not all subject areas or staffing configurations lend themselves well to such a strategy. At the elementary school, shifting grade levels can be a major undertaking, especially between primary and intermediate grades, but may also be a source of renewal. The point is to discover and then act on the ways in which teaching assignments stimulate new learning or relieve creeping stagnation.

Finally, teaching assignments configure teachers' relationships with colleagues in particular ways. They may preserve well-protected fiefdoms or the prerogatives of seniority—or they may configure a staff in ways that provide a basis for professional exchange, mutual support, or shared inquiry. They may plunge beginning teachers into an ordeal of survival, or provide them with well-supported entry into teaching. One restructuring elementary school created three K–6 teams, each supporting multiage classrooms in grades 1–2 and 3–6. The small teams provided continuity in teaching for a cohort of students and supplied each teacher with a group of colleagues with whom to figure out the new demands of multiage teaching. In a large high school English department, teaching assignments were made in accordance with a departmental policy that each teacher should be prepared to teach any of the departmental offerings and that no one should "own" particular courses. The result was that teachers felt a common stake in the development and success of courses. Beginning teachers found a ready supply of advice, materials, exchange, and feedback as the stuff of course content and classroom activities overflowed into lunchtime conversations and department meetings.

Teacher assignments cannot carry the full burden of teacher development and community building, but they play an important part in supplying the ground and substance for teachers' professional intercourse—and particularly, in reinforcing either a competitive or collaborative climate among colleagues. A school strengthens its ability to use teacher assignments in this way by depoliticizing teacher assignment, moving to a collectively held set of criteria for individual assignment within the school, and creating a shared stake in teachers' success in their assignments.[1]

Access to Information, Materials, and Technology

Schools most conducive to teacher learning supply as rich a soup as possible of information, consultation, and materials both inside and outside the school. Insularity—from useful information, stimulating alternatives, competing ideas, or productive criticism—constitutes the major threat to productive professional learning. Yet physical space alone remains at a premium in many schools, even recently constructed ones. Some schools boast roomy department or team offices; others have none. Many teachers, forced to share classroom space with others, cannot count on the empty classroom as a place to work when they are not teaching. Staff lounges or dining rooms are often and quite reasonably dedicated to more casual exchange.

More serious than the absence of space is the relative scarcity of materials to work with—books, journals, reference materials, access to a telephone, computers, or to the informational riches of the Internet. At one extreme are schools where the library, staff workroom, or office spaces constitute curriculum resource centers. Examples of student and teacher work are plentiful, and journals and books abound. The library combines print materials with computers and media resources for teachers and students to use. At other extremes, far more numerous, curriculum resources reside only in individual classrooms, workrooms are poorly equipped, and staff rooms are devoid of any reading beyond the notices on the bulletin board.

Arguably a school landscape barren of professional and other intellectual resources retards teacher development; the situation worsens when teachers cannot readily seek those resources outside the school. Urban and suburban teachers are more likely than rural teachers to have access to colleges and universities, museums, and libraries. Experienced teachers are more likely than beginning teachers to have the discretionary dollars with which to subsidize travel to conferences, computer equipment, and journal subscriptions. Such disparities in the resources for teacher learning might reasonably be the focus of policy and resource choices at the school level.

Advances in computer technology present a special case. Researchers have only begun to turn their attention to the impact of computer technology and other technologies on teachers' professional development needs and resources. Meanwhile, teachers routinely claim that technology-related professional development lags behind hardware and software purchases. Schools supportive of teacher learning could thoughtfully undertake teachers' preparation to make ambitious, creative, well-informed use of computers and other technology in the classroom and in teacher planning, student assessment, and other professional communications. An additional possibility for technology is its use directly in the service of professional development. For example, teachers who participate in "video clubs" view and discuss taped excerpts of their own classrooms; by focusing on student performance in an environment of collegial support and curiosity, teachers arrive at insights into practice and at decisions to experiment that they might not achieve in more formal feedback settings (Frederiksen, Sipusik, Gamoran, and Wolfe, 1992; Gamoran, 1996).

School board members or parents may argue that such material expenditures for teachers must take second place to expenditures for children—at the extreme, that the need for computer software or journal subscriptions pales in the face of leaking roofs and outdated history texts. Yet the major investment in children's learning is the teacher. Overall we do far less than we might at the school level to supply teachers with what they need to remain well informed and well prepared to teach.

Organization and Use of Teacher Time

Schools expand opportunity for teacher learning by expanding the amount of discretionary (out-of-classroom) teacher time available and linking its organization and expected use in part to professional development. Without discounting all the ways in which teachers learn on their own, both in and out of school, the central argument here is that the school's contribution to teacher learning comes largely in the form of regularly scheduled common time among teachers who share responsibility for students or who otherwise have reason to work with one another.

Attending closely to the resources of teacher time challenges the expectation that professional development or in-service is something done after or apart from regular teaching responsibilities. A crucial test of adequate time for teacher learning is the simple ratio of in-class to out-of-class time during the salaried work schedule. Schools differ dramatically in the sheer volume of concentrated out-of-class time they make available for professional development or other joint work during the salaried day, week, and year. Allocations of out-of-class time in U.S. schools are relatively modest overall by comparison to other nations, in part due to staffing plans that increase teaching workloads by reducing teachers as a proportion of total staff (Miles, 1995; Darling-Hammond, 1997). Further, time allocations have varied across levels and communities—and sometimes even within schools. Secondary schools are more likely than elementary schools to provide teachers with personal planning time during the school day. Some districts preserve an even more elaborate hierarchy of personal planning time, with primary grade teachers having the least. The more out-of-class consultation time is available, the more likely it is that time will be used for activities beyond the rudiments of personal preparation (copying handouts, phoning a parent, or simply getting to the bathroom). Although the optimum ratio of in-class to out-of-class time is not clear, the ratio that is common now is arguably stacked unfavorably with regard to teacher development.

Schools engaged in some form of restructuring or "reinventing" have begun to demonstrate the feasibility of alternative time configurations and suggest the benefits that may accrue to students and teachers. Efforts to organize students differently for learning both justify and facilitate new time arrangements for teachers. Over the past decade, critics have stepped up their assaults on "schedules that bind" (Cushman, 1989; also Canady and Rettig, 1995), and educators have begun to document the advantages of schedules that permit more curricular coherence and greater personalization (Raywid, 1995). In one comparison of a traditional high school with two redesigned "small high schools," Darling-Hammond (1997, p. 184) charts substantial differences in the use of professional resources; the traditional high school allots teachers forty-five minutes per week (outside personal planning time) for joint planning or professional development, compared to a maximum of seven and a half hours available in the two small high schools. The small high schools also achieved smaller class sizes and more favorable ratios of teacher time per student. Teachers in some elementary schools have created blocks of time for their collaborative work by rearranging the instructional week, "banking" time on four longer days in preparation for one day in which students begin school later or leave school earlier; others have scheduled students' time with specialists in physical education, art, or music in ways that permit grade-level or cross-grade teams to meet together. Certainly the schools' effects on student performance cannot be attributed solely to investment in teacher time, but qualitative evidence is persuasive that teachers view such time as a critical contributor.

Noninstructional teacher time carries a special burden of justification. Administrators, school board members, and parents express concern that teachers will fail to make productive use of time outside the classroom. Oddly enough these groups fret far less about productive use of in-class time and devote far fewer organizational resources to scrutiny of classroom practice. To resolve the concern over noninstructional time, administrators tend to press for concrete indicators of productivity (such as a binder of curriculum materials to display the results of teachers' collaborative work). Ironically the emphasis on rapidly generated "products" may do more to inhibit than to foster teachers' learning. In one school English and social studies teachers met in interdisciplinary, grade-level teams on a monthly basis and for a full day once a semester. From the perspective of the teachers, the point of meeting was to investigate and test new ties between English and social studies. From the perspective of the administrators, the point was to produce interdisciplinary curriculum (units, lesson plans, assessments). To the teachers, the proposal for a curriculum binder signified a level of agreement they had not reached, assumed a correspondence across disciplines they knew to be oversimplified, and bypassed the kind of discussion and debate that they found frustrating but eye opening. Further, it treated the work of the group as if it were short-term product building rather than an ongoing process of inquiry into curriculum and instruction. Rather than starting with the development of new curriculum, the teachers began by examining the purposes, concepts, and skills embedded in materials already in use. In successfully resisting the requirement of the binder, however, the teachers also incurred an obligation to demonstrate in other ways to administrators and parents that they were engaged in "responsible" practice. In this instance, intensive teacher exchange during out-of-classroom time, organized by focused inquiry into curriculum, instruction, and assessment, generated precisely the kind of close investigation into classroom practice so often absent from teachers' work.

Admittedly out-of-classroom time has a large appetite, and there is much in the daily experience of schools to feed it. Creatively and consistently used, blocks of noninstructional time foster learning—and satisfy public demands for accountability—by enabling teachers to examine ideas and practices and to contribute to one another's teaching success. Poorly exploited, that time may prove simply inconsequential (no one participates and nothing happens) or time is devoted to routine matters. Three case study schools that Peterson, McCarthey, and Elmore (1996) investigated illustrate the range of time configurations associated with school restructuring and link the uses of time and team relationships specifically to teacher learning. All three schools had formally introduced teacher teams supported by scheduled team meeting time. In one school, "team meetings generally served as a place for discussion of school routines and procedures rather than for discussion or sharing of ideas about curriculum and learning" (p. 132). At a second school, where team structures and time schedules also facilitated interaction, teachers were "beginning to discuss ways to implement curriculum and to talk about individual students," and in a third, "teachers met together to discuss individual students' learning and to give ideas to other staff members about how to help the student. Teachers and the principal took advantage of these meetings to connect teaching practice and student learning and to develop a deeply shared vision" (p. 149). The researchers sum up their discoveries as emergent hypotheses that are specifically relevant to questions of time allocation and use:

> School structures can provide opportunities for the learning of new teaching practices and new strategies for student learning, but structures, by themselves, do not cause the learning to occur. . . . Successful relations occur among school structure, teaching practice, and student learning in schools where, because of recruitment and socialization, teachers share a common point of view about their purpose and principles of good practice. School structure follows from good practice not vice versa [pp. 148, 149].

ALTERNATIVES IN THE USE OF STAFF DEVELOPMENT TIME AND DOLLARS

Professional development is still typically described and envisioned as something external to the ongoing work of teaching, something that one "does" or that is "provided" in the form of activities or events. Elsewhere I have argued for professional development more closely tied to the actual contexts of teaching and the histories and capacities of teachers (Little, 1993). McLaughlin (1994) also sets us on this course when she argues for a conception of professional development "not as a special project or scheduled event but as a locally constructed product of an active professional community that is responsive to teachers' immediate professional concerns as well as their professional identity" (p. 31). Such an "active professional community" takes form both within and beyond the school (see also Elmore, this volume).

Proposals for changes in the content, form, and context of professional development have coincided with other moves toward site-based decision making—whether for reasons of professionalization or as a response to overall resource declines. As control over professional development resources moves more consistently to the school level, schools are well positioned to make choices that constitute a substantial advance over the widely criticized "one-shot" and "one-size-fits-all" modes of in-service education. This is not to say that school-based decision making ensures that professional development will be more meaningfully tied to teachers' needs and interests or that it will take new forms. Among the three restructuring schools described above (Peterson, McCarthey, and Elmore, 1996), one school was "virtually over-run with brief, one-shot workshops covering a variety of topics" (p. 147). In the second school, teachers focused their efforts on writing, but enjoyed limited access to outside resources or inside discussion and study. Only in one school were teachers connected to "several supportive communities" both inside and outside the school. The last school provided very little conventional or formal professional development, but it "established the norm that every teacher should have a consuming intellectual interest to pursue; and they formed both internal and external communities of like-minded professionals who were available to discuss problems of practice" (p. 148).

Schools have ventured beyond traditional in-service in several ways. Virtually all of these alternatives supply teachers with more authority and resources to take charge of their own learning. Typically they enable teachers to mine each other's expertise more fully within the school and at the same time engage them in more sustained, focused contact with resources outside the school. To organize the school for teacher learning in part is to supply more deliberate support for independent pursuits—in effect, acknowledging and modifying the lone wolf scenario by facilitating teachers' access to relevant resources of time, money, and expertise. It is also to strengthen the supports for teacher community in ways that make the school's walls more permeable, forming stronger links with external groups, organizations, and other sources of teacher development. Some of these alternatives require a shift in the way that dollars are spent; others require no dollar investment but do call on school leaders and teachers to make different use of time or to engage in different kinds of interaction with one another.

Teacher Research and Teacher Study Groups

Schools have begun to view teacher-initiated research as a form of professional development and have allocated professional development funds to the support of teacher research groups in the form of individual or team mini-grants. In some cases, teachers are encouraged to frame research topics tied to school goals, priorities, or problems; in other instances, they are afforded complete independence in deciding what to investigate. At their most vigorous, teacher research groups meet regularly, conduct or share their research in partnerships or teams, and may review their discoveries at conferences of fellow teacher researchers.

Student Assessment Events

In some schools, regularly scheduled time has been devoted to teachers' participation in a range of student assessment events: the design of portfolio requirements, review and scoring of actual portfolios, participation in student exhibitions and panel interviews, examination of the results of schoolwide writing or math assessments, the interpretation of data from standardized tests or teacher-designed classroom assessments, and the routine perusal of student work that results from a range of classroom assignments. Such activity arguably makes a stronger mark where it is embedded in the ongoing work of planning and teaching. An annual in-service to consider student work may be stimulating and intriguing, but is unlikely to stimulate the kind of ongoing discussion and debate that leads people to reconsider their own practice. Of all the alternatives listed here, this one constitutes the greatest test of professional community, as colleagues confront differences in their expectations or judgments of student work.[2]

Consultation and Planning Days

Concentrated blocks of time enable teachers to make good on the promise of collaboration. Such days do not replace common planning time during the work week; rather, they enable people to investigate a topic or brainstorm solutions to a problem in ways that are impossible in short daily bursts of conversation during preparation time, over lunch, or in the halls. Teachers who spend entire days focused on a single problem or topic discover what they have to offer one another and define more clearly what resources they must draw on from the outside.

Staff Retreats

Schools that have instituted regularly scheduled staff retreats maintain that there is no substitute for an uninterrupted block of time in which to evaluate overall school performance and consider long-term goals. The ethos of inquiry is evident in one teacher's explanation of why retreats are important: "We have a foundation on which we've built and I see us constantly going back to that foundation . . . 'Is this what we really meant when we said we wanted all children to have a relationship with a particular teacher?' 'Is that what we really meant by interdisciplinary teaching?' Teachers in other sites also speak to the role of retreats in building professional community, especially as new teachers join the staff: 'Without it, it's hard to establish continuity with new people as they come in.'"

Classroom and School Visitations

Observing and being observed remains rare. Even teachers who report frequent collaboration with colleagues tend to find that it stops at the classroom door. In a survey of teachers completed for California's staff development policy study (Little and others, 1987), teachers who were observed and who observed others frequently rated such activity as having a strong impact on their own development—but very few teachers actually did it. In a more recent survey undertaken by the National Education Association in partnership with researchers at George Washington University (Holmes, Futrell, Christie, and Cushman, 1995), 86 percent of teachers reported some form of professional development involving peer collaboration during school hours, and more than three-quarters expressed faith in observation as a way to sustain reform—but fewer than half (47 percent) said they had actually participated in any form of peer observation. Nonetheless, classroom and school visitations figure prominently in teachers' accounts of getting started with new ideas—especially when teachers are able to visit several different classrooms (or visit one classroom on several occasions) and spend time talking with the colleagues whom they have visited.

Computer and Video Technology for Teacher Development

Technology is a relatively underexamined resource for teachers' professional learning. Computer technology promises to aid teacher learning by easing access to information (Internet and CD-ROM searches) and facilitating communication with others. Some schools have encouraged teachers' computer use and interaction among teachers by setting aside space and computers for teacher use (adjacent to the staff lounge or the library and equipped with Internet access and software useful for curriculum development). Teacher networks and collaboratives have established electronic networks as a way to encourage more frequent exchange among their members. As noted above, video clubs demonstrate the benefit that teachers derive from a series of conversations focused on video excerpts from their classes. Split-screen video permits them to monitor two angles on the classroom simultaneously, thus watching their own actions and those of students. Available research provides testimony to teachers' unexpected discoveries and to the strong ties established among the participants (Frederiksen, Sipusik, Gamoran, and Wolfe, 1992; Gamoran, 1996).

Subsidized Participation in Summer Institutes

Teachers often reserve high praise for specialized summer institutes ranging from one to three or more weeks, typically focused in the teaching of specific subject areas (writing or literature, math, science, the arts) and often involving a mix of staff from schools, universities, or private industry. Such institutes permit the kind of depth and professional exchange that are rarely possible in other kinds of workshop settings. In some schools, teacher participation is subsidized only when two or more teachers attend as a team or when there is an explicit plan for how the expertise the participants acquire will be made available to those who did not attend. For such ripple effect plans to work well requires a compatible school culture.

Subject Matter Networks and Collaboratives

Among the greatest challenges for elementary and secondary schools is ensuring that teachers acquire expertise that joins subject knowledge with a solid grasp of pedagogical challenges and possibilities. Subject-specific teacher collaboratives and networks have grown in size, visibility, and influence over the past two decades. Examples have become almost too numerous to record. Perhaps the most long-lived and widely effective exemplar is the Bay Area Writing

Project (which over time has expanded to become the National Writing Project), but other well-documented examples exist in science, math, the humanities, and the arts. Some collaboratives supply individual teachers with rich sources of expertise and consultation outside the school, while others operate through links with school-based teams.

The subject collaboratives occupy an important niche in teacher development, providing an opportunity for teachers to deepen and broaden their subject expertise in a context that is specifically attentive to the context of classroom teaching. Lieberman and Miller (1996) posit that networks fill a need created "because schools are organized in ways that often do not encourage the kind of frank discussion that is necessary for inventing new modes of working with students" (p. 14). In these "intentional" but "borderless" learning communities, outside their own bureaucracies, teachers "find it easier to question, ask for help, or 'tell it like it is,' rather than be fearful that they are exposing their lack of expertise in a given area" (p. 15; see also Lord, 1994).

Other Partnerships, Networks, or Special Projects

Other kinds of networks and partnerships similarly join members who share interests and problems in common. Schools have begun to take more deliberate action to establish external ties, using school resources to subsidize teachers' participation in external professional communities and organizations. These include teacher-to-teacher networks, university-school partnerships, school networks, and special projects that join teachers with knowledgeable colleagues and inform them about new possibilities of import to their teaching (Lieberman and Grolnick, 1996; Lieberman and McLaughlin, 1992). Professional development schools provide a model intended to link school improvement with preservice and continuing teacher education (Darling-Hammond, 1994). Participants in the Coalition of Essential Schools and other reform networks serve as "critical friends" for one another—posing tough questions, introducing new possibilities, but also attesting to accomplishments.

It should be evident that this inventory of alternatives places a premium on opportunities for professional exchange and consultation, especially the obligation and opportunity to reach outside the school's walls. Schools are busy places that easily become insular places. Such insularity may work to the disadvantage of students even when teachers are well intentioned and hard working, as demonstrated by the sharp differences between modal practice and ambitious standards of teaching and learning in the core academic areas. Communities outside the school offer more than a broader pool of experts and materials to draw on; they also provide the stimulation and sometimes the intellectual push needed to consider possibilities beyond those a school would come up with independently. Meier (1992) urges:

[Teachers] need frequent and easy access to the kind of give-and-take with professionals from allied fields that is the mark of a true professional. They need opportunities to speak and write publicly about their work, attend conferences, read professional journals, and discuss something beyond what they are going to do on Monday. There must be some kind of discomfiture and support—focused always on what does and does not have an impact on children's learning [pp. 602–603].

Meier's words resonate in the experience of a high school math teacher who found new sources of stimulation and expertise in a math collaborative in a large urban area:

I have much more curiosity about mathematics. I want to learn more and more mathematics right now. I'm looking into areas of mathematics I've never studied before. I've become a student of mathematics again. I'm expanding my own understanding of mathematics, but I'm also trying to expand the students' understanding. So there's a vitality [Little and McLaughlin, 1991, p. 4].

FEEDBACK ON TEACHING AND SCHOOL EFFECTS

Neither teacher development nor school improvement seems likely in the absence of valid, plentiful, and timely feedback on performance: Is this the right thing to do? Are we doing it well? The quality and quantity of such feedback is likely to be greatest where teacher evaluation policy and practice are demonstrably and credibly linked to teacher learning and teachers participate in well-designed systems of school-level review and accountability.

Staff Evaluation

Observers have documented the largely perfunctory and inconsequential practice of teacher evaluation in American school systems, while advocates of reform have urged a system that more credibly joins the evaluation and improvement of teaching (McLaughlin and Pfeifer, 1988). Although individual schools are constrained by state and district requirements and by the provisions of bargained contracts, some schools have made highly productive use of traditional evaluation schemes, mainly by ensuring that judgments are well grounded in observed practice and that the evaluation process affords plenty of opportunity for dialogue and consultation. Districts have begun to adopt alternative forms of teacher evaluation for experienced teachers, including the use of portfolios or documented success with special projects.

Two developments seem especially consistent with expanded support for teacher learning: the portfolio- and interview-based methods of the National Board for Professional Teaching Standards and more widespread use of peer review. Both entail the shifting of teacher evaluation away from exclusive reliance on administrator ratings and in the direction of methods of evaluation more genuinely reflective of the actual work of teaching (Snowden, 1993; see also Peterson, 1984).

The National Board model yields multiple sources of evidence that more fully capture the depth and breadth of a teacher's work in the classroom and tap other aspects of professional maturity (such as contributions to the work of colleagues). In particular, its portfolio and interview components reveal far more of teachers' knowledge, insight, and disposition than do most extant models based on administrator ratings of isolated classroom performances.

Evaluation processes consistent with those of the National Board directly implicate the worth and feasibility of peer review. One could not reasonably make good on the technical advances of the National Board without peer involvement; it is both too labor intensive and too expertise dependent to be handled by individual administrators. Innovative teacher induction programs in several states have established a sound precedent for peer review, culminating in guidelines published by the Interstate Teacher Assessment and Support Consortium. By intensifying support in the first two years, review teams steepen the learning curve for beginning teachers; by linking support and assessment, they improve the chances that the tenure decision will be a well-informed one. Despite controversies over teachers' participation in teacher evaluation, there is no reason to believe that extending peer review to all teachers would not broaden the opportunities and obligations for teacher learning and would not strengthen personnel decisions in cases of promotion or dismissal.

Together these developments point toward teacher evaluation policies and practices built on a teacher's ongoing inquiry into his or her own knowledge and practice, in company with colleagues, tested in part against the achievements of students.

Program Evaluation and School Review

Most schools periodically undergo some form of overall review. The terms *accountability* and *review* may appear to gibe poorly with images of teacher learning, especially when reviews are widely spaced, criteria seem poorly juxtaposed to school priorities, and reviewers command little knowledge of the school's history and context. Even the most gutsy, cohesive, and capable staff can tell of being deeply discouraged by a school review gone awry. A teacher in a charter school describes the misfit between his school and the regional accreditation process: "The school is divided into cross-departmental learning communities, but was forced to evaluate itself departmentally because the accreditation tool had not caught up with the reforms" (Fecho, 1996, p. 2). Increasingly, however, state-level reviews and regional accreditation processes seem attentive to advances in school reform.

The learning potential of the school review experience resides partly in the form and content of the review itself: the visions it conveys, the questions it poses to staff, its ability to accommodate differences in school organization, the process by which the review proceeds, the timeliness of review, and its sensitivity to local school history and context. New York State's Program Quality Review combines a school self-study with a week-long visit by a team of reviewers; its aim is to shift from traditional compliance monitoring to a form of external review that is responsive to local school culture, yet sufficiently rigorous and comprehensive to stimulate inquiry and change. (For a thorough and insightful description of one elementary school's review experience, and for guidelines for conducting an external review, see Ancess, 1996.) California's Program Quality Review process similarly engages teachers and administrators in the indepth analysis of student work and classroom practice in at least one core subject area selected by the school, and it incorporates a multiday visit by a team of external reviewers. At the high school level, regional accreditation now emphasizes schoolwide criteria in place of the standard departmental self-study and places greater emphasis on students' experience of the school.

The learning potential of external reviews also rests on the internal capacities and habits of the staff: the degree to which the collection, analysis, and use of data on teaching and learning constitute central routines of school life. Establishing such capacities and habits presents three kinds of challenges: building the technical knowledge necessary for systematic assessment (for example, "What counts as evidence?" or "We've got tons of stuff but don't know how to interpret it"); creating a structure and process for effectively conducting the work of self-study; and reinforcing a school culture that values such assessment and can weather conflict and uncertainty over its interpretation or implications. The introduction of the Primary Language Record at P.S. 261 in New York City enabled that school's staff to meet all three of those challenges (Darling-Hammond, Ancess, and Falk, 1995). Anticipating the same challenges among California's demonstration restructuring sites, the California Center for School Restructuring (CCSR) enlisted more than twenty schools in developing a protocol focused on "examining student work for what matters." Although schools report variable success in using this tool, it has quite clearly helped to keep the restructuring discussion focused on student learning. The learning demands on teachers, administrators, and others remain correspondingly more visible than they might otherwise.

SCHOOL ETHOS IN SUPPORT OF TEACHER LEARNING

Finally, none of the structural supports for teacher learning will succeed without compatible values, beliefs, and norms—an overall ethos that supports a vital professional community among teachers and a strong service ethic in relation to students and their parents. Teachers form a disposition toward their own learning in the fabric of daily school work. That fabric is tightly woven in the brief exchanges and small moments that make up enduring patterns of professional life. It does not take a newcomer long to take stock of whether the school's values, norms, and relationships are consistent with learning: respect and encouragement, support for help seeking and help giving, celebration of struggle and accomplishment, principled and well-informed debate, and open consideration of alternative views.

Numerous studies have confirmed the power of workplace norms to shape teacher development. Throughout the 1980s school workplace ethnographies illuminated the relations between conditions of work and professional learning. These ethnographies identified within- and across-school variations in those modal organizational and occupational conditions that privilege personal autonomy and suppress advice giving and initiative on matters of practice. Little (1982) discovered that schoolwide "norms of collegiality and experimentation" were characteristic of schools that had achieved greater success and demonstrated greater adaptability during a period of court-ordered desegregation. The same study showed that comparably sound models of staff development had greater effect in schools with well-established collegial norms than in schools where teachers worked and learned on their own (Little, 1984). Rosenholtz (1989) later distinguished "learning-enriched" from "learning-impoverished" school workplaces by their relative support for collaboration and innovation, while other observers usefully elaborated the constituent dimensions of collegiality (Smylie, 1989) and identified the characteristics of "collaborative cultures" (Lieberman, 1988; Nias, Southworth, and Yeomans, 1989).[3]

Central to distinctions between collaborative and individualistic cultures or between learning-enriched and learning-impoverished schools is the question of educational benefit: whether the circumstances of teachers' work enable them to learn in ways that demonstrably strengthen teaching and enhance benefits to students. Based on his comprehensive review of the workplace learning literature, Smylie (1995) concludes, "We should not assume that all teacher learning is necessarily conducive to promoting student learning and development" (p. 94). It is, after all, possible to acquire conceptions and practices that are rich and deep, or shallow and static. Teachers' experience may engender or reinforce beliefs that are conducive to children's well-being, or detrimental to it. What does the school environment lead teachers to learn from and about teaching? Do teachers find reason, in the very course of their work, to ask tough questions of themselves, or do they find themselves pressed toward simplistic interpretations and expedient solutions? Do their colleagues and administrators stimulate those questions or stifle them?

Research over the past decade dwells increasingly on the question of the intellectual and moral qualities of teachers' professional relationships and on their import for student experience of schooling. This emerging body of work confirms the significance of vigorous professional communities within the school, successfully establishing links to student achievement. Nonetheless, it also shows that benefits to students and teachers do not follow automatically in the wake of teacher collaboration or general staff camaraderie. Not all strong teacher communities stimulate and support teacher learning, nor are all such communities committed to an ethic of service to students. Based on studies conducted by Stanford's Center for Research on the Contexts of Teaching (CRC), researchers have demonstrated how professional communities vary in the service ethic they embrace (McLaughlin and Talbert, in press; Talbert, 1995). For example, some groups of teachers are bound together by shared views of a subject area, curriculum priorities, and favored instructional approaches but tend to admit little in the way of collective responsibility for student learning. Other groups with equally strong "technical culture" bonds treat questions of curriculum and instruction flexibly and display a strong collective responsibility for all students. The CRC researchers posit that genuine teacher learning communities—those with a demonstrable effect on teaching and learning—are those that question and challenge teaching routines when they prove ineffective with students and that routinely examine new conceptions of subject and teaching.

The formation of teacher learning communities is arguably more assured when schools solve the problem of the closed classroom door and displace the norm of "noninterference." As teachers eloquently affirm, a "deprivatized" school is one in which the aims and practices of teaching are frequently and forthrightly examined. Staff must be able to put forward new ideas and critically evaluate ideas as they are tried out in practice. They must tolerate informed dissent and urge a healthy skepticism—but also live with one another through the messiness of genuine discovery. Where a culture of inquiry thrives, one might expect to find experienced teachers routinely observing and co-planning with beginning teachers, or teachers at a grade level comparing examples of student writing, or members of an interdisciplinary group trying to determine authentic links between subjects.

More centrally, the ethos of the school speaks to the stance taken by its adults as educated members of a democracy. For a school to engage seriously in a culture of inquiry, teachers must be able to initiate open and critical discussions that extend to fundamental educational matters—and to do so in ways that are resolutely public, even when the issues seem unresolvable. Deborah Meier (1995) recalls the efforts of staff at Central Park East Secondary School to deal with the "thorny underbrush" of racism and other "supercharged" social and educational issues:

> There's no pretending that we don't need to do this, or that once we clear it
> all up we can get on to other things. We must deal with this issue over and
> over. . . . [Yet] because our adult debates are not hidden from our students, there
> is no sharp dividing line between "staff development" activities and student
> educational activities. The deep immersion in a value system that places mutual
> respect first and encourages a climate of diversity and disagreement becomes
> enormously powerful over time, and not just for staff [pp. 57, 58–59].

By what they do and say in the classroom, staff room, and hallway—and in the community beyond the school—teachers illuminate for students and for one another what it means to be educated.

CONCLUSION

The central motivations and occasions of teacher learning are closely linked to the actual work of teaching and the circumstances in which teachers work. From this follows a substantial public interest in the ways in which schools strengthen or erode teachers' motivation and opportunity to learn.

How schools satisfy that public interest follows directly from the images that teachers, administrators, parents, and members of the public hold of teaching—the kind of work it is and how teachers learn to do it well. The most common organization of schools—independent classrooms linked by a common parking lot—leaves one with the impression that teaching is a relatively straightforward activity, bolstered as needed by outside course work and other occasional in-service activities. Such an impression is readily dashed by virtually all other evidence, whether it comes from the journals of practicing teachers, the recorded observations of teacher-student interactions, comparisons of expert and novice teachers, or the in-depth study of children's classroom experience. Teaching is more complex and difficult than we would be led to believe by looking at the typical organization of teachers' work. Nor can its complexities be fully anticipated or resolved by whatever prior preparation teachers bring to the classroom. Teaching requires continual discovery and judgment.

The classroom and the school occupy a crucial place in teachers' professional growth. It matters how the school organizes and promotes teachers' work and teacher learning. As a matter of public and professional interest, attending to how schools shape teacher learning is not a luxury but a necessity. Nor is this public interest satisfied simply by assembling the right set of programs or shifting professional development funding to the school site; rather, it requires a deliberate consideration of the ways in which all the elements of the workplace bear on teachers' expertise and engagement in their work. Teachers' immediate surroundings supply them with learning resources of several crucial sorts, resources that may prove rich or poor—a standard of substantive expertise, a pool of available ideas and technologies, a disposition toward students and what they can achieve, a pattern of collegial relationships, and the capacity to connect easily (or not) with colleagues or other assistance outside the school.

The aspects of school life examined in this chapter arguably enhance or diminish teachers' motivation, opportunity, and resources to learn. Culled largely from research on the workplace contexts of teaching, they take account of how context matters in shaping the practices of teaching and the perspectives of teachers. They form neither a simple checklist by which schools might be rated nor a template that can be translated uniformly into formal policy. Broadly conceived they embrace a set of obligations, opportunities, and resources for teacher learning. Some of them (the organization of teacher time, for example) lend themselves to formal decision making better than others (for example, the overall ethos of a school). Inevitably they bear the stamp of local school history and circumstances.

For much of their history, public schools have taken little direct responsibility for the quality of the teacher workforce beyond initial hiring and routine staff evaluation, the limitations of which have been well documented. In Susan Moore Johnson's (1990) words, "Schools are in the business of promoting students' learning and growth. . . . Ironically, public schools are not in the business of promoting teachers' learning and growth" (p. 249; see also Bird and Little, 1986). Professional development has typically been an individual responsibility and prerogative, with teachers advancing on the salary schedule through the accumulation of salary credits.

With the escalation in school improvement initiatives and the emphasis on the school as a unit of change has come the push for more school-based professional development and greater school-level autonomy in the allocation of professional development resources. In certain important respects, schools work within the constraints of external policy and practice—for example, in constructing a productive teacher evaluation system or ensuring adequate time for teacher consultation and study during the salaried work week and year. As one moves away from an emphasis on discrete staff development activities or programs and toward a view of a school's organizational capacity to support teacher learning, certain external constraints become more visible, and so do the possibilities that lie within reach of teachers and schools. It has been the thrust of this argument that we might do more to realize those possibilities and make them widely known.

Notes

1. I have concentrated here on strategies that are directly under the control of schools. Teacher assignment is also subject to certain external controls and influences, including contract provisions affecting hiring and internal transfer, state licensure and assignment provisions, and legislative and policy constraints on teacher mobility. State policy instruments may prove effective in protecting against extremes of misassignment, but are too blunt and too distant to ensure that teacher assignment is a resource for teacher learning at the school level.

2. This problem goes almost completely unaddressed among the challenges outlined in the emerging literature on teachers' responses to alternative assessment. For one exception, see Darling-Hammond, Ancess, and Falk (1995, pp. 21–82).

3. Although school ethnographies of the 1970s, 1980s, and 1990s have not always directly targeted questions of teacher learning, many of them vividly illuminate the intersections of organizational context, teaching career, and professional development. Among them, in addition to those cited in the text, are Little (1981); Metz (1978); Ball (1981); Sikes, Measor, and Woods (1985); McNeil (1986); and Bruckerhoff (1991).

References

Ancess, J. *Outside/Inside, Inside/Outside: Developing and Implementing the School Quality Review*. New York: NCREST, Teachers College, Columbia University, 1996.

Ball, S. J. *Beachside Comprehensive*. New York: Cambridge University Press, 1981.

Ball, S. J., and Lacey, C. "Subject Disciplines as the Opportunity for Group Action: A Measured Critique of Subject Subcultures." In A. Hargreaves and P. Woods (eds.), *Classrooms and Staffrooms: The Sociology of Teachers and Teaching* (pp. 232–244). Milton Keynes: Open University Press, 1984.

Bird, T., and Little, J. W. "How Schools Organize the Teaching Occupation." *Elementary School Journal,* 1986, *86*(4), 493–511.

Borko, H., and Putnam, R. T. "Expanding a Teacher's Knowledge Base: A Cognitive Psychological Perspective on Professional Development." In T. R. Guskey and M. Huberman (eds.), *Professional Development in Education: New Paradigms and Practices* (pp. 35–65). New York: Teachers College Press, 1995.

Bruckerhoff, C. *Between Classes: Faculty Life at Truman High*. New York: Teachers College Press, 1991.

Burnaford, G., Fischer, J., and Hobson, D. *Teachers Doing Research: Practical Possibilities*. Hillsdale, N.J.: Erlbaum, 1996.

Canady, R. L., and Rettig, M. D. "The Power of Innovative Scheduling." *Educational Leadership,* 1995, *53*(3), 4–10.

Cochran-Smith, M., and Lytle, S. L. *Inside/Outside: Teacher Research and Knowledge*. New York: Teachers College Press, 1993.

Cushman, K. "Schedules That Bind." *American Educator,* Summer 1989, pp. 35–39.

Darling-Hammond, L. (ed.). *Professional Development Schools: Schools for Developing a Profession*. New York: Teachers College Press, 1994.

Darling-Hammond, L. *The Right to Learn: A Blueprint for Creating Schools That Work*. San Francisco: Jossey-Bass, 1997.

Darling-Hammond, L., Ancess, J., and Falk, B. *Authentic Assessment in Action: Studies of Schools and Students at Work*. New York: Teachers College Press, 1995.

Elmore, R., and Burney, D. "Staff Development and Instructional Improvement: Community District 2, New York City." Paper commissioned by the National Commission on Teaching and America's Future, 1996.

Falk, B. and Ort, S. "Sitting Down to Score: Teacher Learning Through Assessment." Paper presented at the annual meeting of the American Educational Research Association, Chicago, 1997.

Fecho, R. "Chip Off the Old Block: Rethinking Collegiality in an Urban Secondary School." Paper presented at the annual meeting of the American Educational Research Association, New York, 1996.

Finley, M. K. V. "Teachers and Tracking in a Comprehensive High School." *Sociology of Education,* 1984, *57,* 233–243.

Frederiksen, J. Sipusik, M., Gamoran, M., and Wolfe, E. *Video Portfolio Assessment: A Study for the National Board for Professional Teaching Standards.* Princeton, N.J.: Educational Testing Service, 1992.

Gamoran M. "The Nature and Dynamics of Teachers' Content Knowledge." Unpublished doctoral dissertation, University of California, Berkeley, 1996.

Gehrke, N., and Sheffield, R. "Are Core Subjects Becoming a Dumping Ground for Reassigned High School Teachers?" *Educational Leadership,* 1985, *42*(8), 65–69.

Hargreaves, A. "Contrived Collegiality: The Micropolitics of Teacher Collaboration." In J. Blase (ed.), *The Politics of Life in Schools: Power, Conflict, and Cooperation.* Thousand Oaks, Calif.: Sage, 1991.

Hargreaves, A. "Individualism and Individuality: Reinterpreting the Teacher Culture." In J. W. Little and M. W. McLaughlin (eds.), *Teachers' Work: Individuals, Colleagues, and Contexts.* New York: Teachers College Press, 1993.

Hollingsworth, S., and Sockett, H. (eds.). *Teacher Research and Educational Reform.* 93rd Yearbook of the National Society for the Study of Education. Chicago: University of Chicago Press, 1994.

Holmes, D. H., Futrell, M. H., Christie, J. L., and Cushman, E. J. "School Restructuring: Meeting Teachers' Professional Development Needs." Paper presented at the annual meeting of the American Educational Research Association, San Francisco, 1995.

Huberman, M. "The Model of the Independent Artisan in Teachers' Professional Relations." In J. W. Little and M. W. McLaughlin (eds.), *Teachers' Work: Individuals, Colleagues, and Contexts.* New York: Teachers College Press, 1993.

Huberman, M. "Professional Careers and Professional Development: Some Intersections." In T. Guskey and M. Huberman (eds.), *Professional Development in Education.* New York: Teachers College Press, 1995.

Johnson, S. M. *Teachers at Work: Achieving Success in Our Schools.* New York: Basic Books, 1990.

Kruse, S. D., Louis, K. S., and Bryk, A. S. "An Emerging Framework for Analyzing School-Based Professional Community." In K. S. Louis and others (eds.), *Professionalism and Community: Perspectives on Reforming Urban Schools* (pp. 23–42). Thousand Oaks, Calif.: Corwin Press, 1995.

Lampert, M., and Ball, D. L. "Aligning Teacher Education with Contemporary K–12 Reform Visions." Paper prepared for the National Commission on Teaching and

America's Future. East Lansing: College of Education, Michigan State University, 1995.

Lee, V. E., and Smith, J. "Collective Responsibility for Learning and Its Effects on Gains in Achievement and Engagement for Early Secondary School Students." *American Journal of Education,* 1996, *104*(2), 103–147.

Lieberman, A. (ed.). *Building a Professional Culture in Schools*. New York: Teachers College Press, 1988.

Lieberman, A. *The Work of Restructuring Schools: Building from the Ground Up.* New York: Teachers College Press, 1995a.

Lieberman, A. "Practices That Support Teacher Development: Transforming Conceptions of Professional Learning." *Phi Delta Kappan,* Apr. 1995b, 591–596.

Lieberman, A., and Grolnick, M. "Networks and Reform in American Education." *Teachers College Record,* 1996, *98*(1), 7–45.

Lieberman, A., and McLaughlin, M. W. "Networks for Educational Change: Powerful and Problematic." *Phi Delta Kappan,* 1992, *73*(9), 673–677.

Lieberman, A., and Miller, L.. *Transforming Professional Development: Understanding and Organizing Learning Communities*. Washington, D.C.: National Education Association, 1996.

Little, J. W. *School Success and Staff Development: The Role of Staff Development in Urban Desegregated Schools*. Boulder, Colo.: Center for Action Research, 1981.

Little, J. W. "Norms of Collegiality and Experimentation: Workplace Conditions of School Success." *American Educational Research Journal,* 1982, *19*(3), 325–340.

Little, J. W. "Seductive Images and Organizational Realities in Professional Development." *Teachers College Record,* 1984, *86*(1), 84–102.

Little, J. W. "Conditions of Professional Development in Secondary Schools." In M. W. McLaughlin, J. Talbert, and N. Bascia (eds.), *The Context of Teaching in Secondary Schools: Teachers' Realities* (pp. 187–223). New York: Teachers College Press, 1990a.

Little, J. W. "The Persistence of Privacy: Autonomy and Initiative in Teachers' Professional Relations." *Teachers College Record,* 1990b, *91*(4), 509–536.

Little, J. W. "Teachers' Professional Development in a Climate of Educational Reform." *Educational Evaluation and Policy Analysis,* 1993, *15*(2), 129–151.

Little, J. W., and McLaughlin, M. W. *Urban Mathematics Collaboratives: As the Teachers Tell It*. Stanford, Ca.: Center for Research on the Contexts of Secondary School Teaching, Stanford University, 1991.

Little, J. W., and others. *Staff Development in California: Public and Personal Investment, Program Patterns, and Policy Choices*. San Francisco: Far West Laboratory for Educational Research and Development, 1987.

Lord, B. "Teachers' Professional Development: Critical Colleagueship and the Role of Professional Communities." In N. Cobb (ed.), *The Future of Education: Perspectives on National Standards in America* (pp. 175–204). New York: College Board Publications, 1994.

Louis, K. S., and Kruse, S. D. *Professionalism and Community: Perspectives on Reforming Urban Schools.* Thousand Oaks, Calif.: Corwin Press, 1995.

McLaughlin, M. W. "Strategic Sites for Teachers' Professional Development." In P. P. Grimmett and J. Neufeld (eds.), *Teacher Development and the Struggle for Authenticity: Professional Growth and Restructuring in the Context of Change* (pp. 31–51). New York: Teachers College Press, 1994.

McLaughlin, M. W., and Pfeifer, R. S. *Teacher Evaluation: Improvement, Accountability, and Effective Learning.* New York: Teachers College Press, 1988.

McLaughlin, M. W., and Talbert, J. E. *High School Teaching in Context.* Chicago: University of Chicago Press, in press.

McNeil, L. M. *Contradictions of Control: School Structure and School Knowledge.* New York: Routledge and Kegan Paul, 1986.

Meier, D. "Reinventing Teaching." *Teachers College Record,* 1992, *93*(4), 594–609.

Meier, D. *The Power of Their Ideas: Lessons for America from a Small School in Harlem.* Boston: Beacon Press, 1995.

Metz, M. H. *Classrooms and Corridors: The Crisis of Authority in Desegregated Secondary Schools.* Berkeley: University of California Press, 1978.

Miles, K. H. "Freeing Resources for Improving Schools: A Case Study of Teacher Allocation in Boston Public Schools" *Educational Evaluation and Policy Analysis,* 1995, *17*(4), 476–493.

Neufeld, B. "Inside Organization: High School Teachers' Efforts to Influence Their Work." Unpublished doctoral dissertation, Harvard University, 1984.

Nias, J., Southworth, G., and Yeomans, R. *Staff Relationships in the Primary School: A Study of Organizational Cultures.* London: Cassell, 1989.

Paley, V. G. "On Listening to What the Children Say." *Harvard Educational Review,* 1986, *56*(2), 122–131.

Peterson, K. "Methodological Problems in Teacher Evaluation." *Journal of Research and Development in Education,* 1984, *17*(6), 62–70.

Peterson, P. L., McCarthey, S. J., and Elmore, R. F. "Learning from School Restructuring." *American Educational Research Journal,* 1996, *33*(1), 119–153.

Raudenbush, S. W., Rowan, B., and Cheong, Y. F. "Contextual Effects on the Self-Perceived Efficacy of High School Teachers." *Sociology of Education,* 1992, *65,* 150–167.

Raywid, M. *The Subschools/Small Schools Movement—Taking Stock.* Madison: Center on Organization and Restructuring of Schools, University of Wisconsin, 1995.

Rosenholtz, S. *Teachers' Workplace.* New York: Longman, 1989.

Sedlak, M. W., Wheeler, C. W., Pullin, D. C., and Cusick, P. A. *Selling Students Short: Classroom Bargains and Academic Reform in the American High School.* New York: Teachers College Press, 1986.

Sheingold, K., Heller, J. I., and Storms, B. "On the Mutual Influence of Teachers' Professional Development and Assessment Quality in Curricular Reform." Paper presented at the annual meeting of the American Educational Research Association, Chicago, 1997.

Sikes, P., Measor, L., and Woods, P. (ed.). *Teacher Careers: Crises and Continuities*. Bristol, Pa.: Falmer Press, 1985.

Smylie, M. A. "Teachers' Collegial Learning: Social and Psychological Dimensions of Helping Relationships." Paper presented at the annual meeting of the American Educational Research Association, San Francisco, 1989.

Smylie, M. "Teacher Learning in the Workplace: Implications for School Reform." In T. R. Guskey and M. Huberman (eds.), *Professional Development in Education: New Paradigms and Practices* (pp. 92–113). New York: Teachers College Press, 1995.

Snowden, C. D. *Preparing Teachers for the Demands of the 21st Century: Professional Development and the NBPTS Vision*. Detroit: National Board for Professional Teaching Standards, 1993.

Sprinthall, N. A., and Thies-Sprinthall, L. "The Teacher as Adult Learner: A Cognitive-Developmental View." In G. Griffin (ed.), *Staff Development: Eighty-Second Yearbook of the National Society for the Study of Education* (pp. 13–35). Chicago: University of Chicago Press, 1983.

Talbert, J. *Teacher Tracking: Exacerbating Inequalities in the High School*. Stanford: Center for Research on the Context of Secondary Teaching, Stanford University, 1990.

Talbert, J. "Boundaries of Teachers' Professional Communities in U.S. High Schools: Power and Precariousness of the Subject Department." In L. S. Siskin and J. W. Little (eds.), *The Subjects in Question: Departmental Organization and the High School* (pp. 68–94). New York: Teachers College Press, 1995.

Wise, A., Darling-Hammond, L., McLaughlin, M. W., and Bernstein, H. *Teacher Evaluation: A Study of Effective Practices*. Santa Monica, Calif.: RAND Corporation, 1984.

Yu, H. C., and Talbert, J. E. *Labor Force Conditions of High School Math Departments: Inequalities and the Mediating Effects of Teacher Community*. Stanford, Calif.: Center for Research on the Contexts of Teaching, Stanford University, 1994.

CHAPTER NINE

Investing in Teacher Learning

Staff Development and Instructional Improvement

Richard F. Elmore and Deanna Burney

There is growing consensus among educational reformers that professional development for teachers and administrators lies at the center of educational reform and instructional improvement. We know a good deal about the characteristics of successful professional development: it focuses on concrete classroom applications of general ideas; it exposes teachers to actual practice rather than to descriptions of practice; it offers opportunities for observation, critique, and reflection; it provides opportunities for group support and collaboration; and it involves deliberate evaluation and feedback by skilled practitioners with expertise about good teaching. But although we know a good deal about the characteristics of good professional development, we know a good deal less about how to organize successful professional development so as to influence practice in large numbers of schools and classrooms.

This chapter describes and analyzes one school district's use of staff development to change instruction on a systemwide basis. The subject of the chapter is Community School District 2 in New York City. Its superintendent, district

This chapter was prepared for the National Commission on Teaching and America's Future. Earlier parts of the research were supported by the Consortium for Policy Research in Education (CPRE) and the Center on Restructuring Schools, under grants from the Office of Educational Research and Improvement of the U.S. Department of Education (CPRE Grant RllG10007).

The quotations from Anthony Alvarado in this chapter are taken from personal interviews conducted by the authors.

staff, principals, and teachers have a growing reputation for sustained attention to school improvement through professional development. District 2 is an exemplar not so much because it engages in specific professional development activities that other districts do not, but because it does a variety of things in a uniquely systematic way. The lessons from District 2 are as much lessons about how to organize and manage professional development around the objective of instructional change as they are about specific professional development activities.

This chapter is neither an evaluation of District 2's professional development efforts nor an attempt at a definitive account of what works in the use of professional development for instructional change. The chapter has a much simpler purpose: to document, describe, and analyze a single attempt to use professional development to mobilize knowledge in the service of systemwide instructional improvement. In this sense this case can be seen as an "existence proof" that it is possible for local districts to be agents of serious instructional improvement. It can also be seen as a source of ideas for practitioners in other settings to use in thinking about their own school improvement efforts.

THE DISTRICT CONTEXT

District 2 is one of thirty-two community school districts in New York City that have primary responsibility for elementary and middle schools. District 2 has twenty-four elementary schools, seven junior high or intermediate schools, and seventeen so-called Option Schools, which are alternative schools organized around themes with a variety of different grade configurations. District 2 has one of the most diverse student populations of any community district in the city. It includes some of the highest-priced residential and commercial real estate in the world, on the Upper East Side of Manhattan, and some of the most densely populated poorer communities in the city, in Chinatown in Lower Manhattan and in Hell's Kitchen on the West Side. The student population of the district is twenty-two thousand, of whom about 29 percent are white, 14 percent black, about 22 percent Hispanic, about 34 percent Asian, and less than 1 percent Native American. About 20 percent of students use English as a second language, and recent immigrants have come from about one hundred different countries. About 50 percent of students come from families whose incomes are officially classified as below the poverty level; a slightly higher proportion of students in elementary schools are classified as poor than in junior high schools. About two hundred students reside in temporary shelters, and about two thousand students receive special education services.

The proportion of students living in poverty is between 70 percent and 100 percent in fourteen of the district's schools, with five of those schools having proportions of poor children between 95 percent and 100 percent. At the other extreme, nine schools have proportions of poverty at 25 percent or below. District 2 has a thriving, diverse, middle-class population of families who take public education seriously, but who are also willing to make financial sacrifices to send their children to readily available private schools if they find the quality of public schools lacking. Principals speak consistently of having to win the loyalty and allegiance of middle-class parents through providing high-quality education. The schools and classrooms of District 2 are a virtual United Nations of diversity (the UN is actually in the district); every school has substantial racial, ethnic, and cultural diversity, even when the student population is predominantly of one race or ethnicity. Most schools have substantial diversity of social class.

Anthony Alvarado became superintendent of District 2 in 1987, after spending ten years as community superintendent in District 4, in Spanish Harlem, immediately adjacent to District 2 above Ninety-Sixth Street on the north, and after an eighteen-month stint as chancellor of the New York City public school system. Among Alvarado's earliest initiatives in District 2 was to exercise a strong hand in personnel decisions. In his first year, he recruited and hired a deputy superintendent, Elaine Fink, whose experience and job description emphasized direct work with schools rather than central office administration. Later he hired Bea Johnstone, whose credentials were also primarily in work with schools, to oversee staff development. Alvarado communicated to principals early in his tenure that he expected them to play a strong role in instructional improvement in their schools. "We expected principals to have a clear vision of what they wanted to have happen in teaching and learning in their schools and to be willing to question themselves and their capacity to deliver," Alvarado said. Some principals found Alvarado's expectations congenial; others did not. Over the first four years of Alvarado's tenure, he replaced twenty of the district's thirty or so principals; most were "counseled out" and found jobs in other districts; three retired. At the same time he was exercising influence over the appointment of principals, Alvarado created seventeen Option Schools, small alternative programs with distinctive themes, and staffed them with "directors," a title he had invented earlier in District 4, whose role is a hybrid of senior teacher and principal.

At the same time he was changing the leadership of District 2 schools, Alvarado was working on the transformation of the teaching force. District staff estimate that they have replaced about 50 percent of the district's teachers in the eight years of Alvarado's tenure. He communicated the expectation that principals and school directors were to take an active role evaluating teachers in their buildings, establishing networks with other principals and with higher education institutions to recruit student teachers and new teachers, and working with district personnel to ease the transition of ineffective teachers out of the district and prevent the transfer of ineffective teachers into the district.

Alvarado's early personnel decisions at the level of the central office, school leadership, and the teaching force sent a strong signal that his priorities were focused on instructional improvement. These decisions also communicated that instructional improvement depends heavily on people's talents and motivations. These combined efforts seem to have worked.

In 1987 Community School District 2 ranked tenth in the city in reading and fourth in mathematics out of thirty-two districts. In 1996, it ranked second in reading and second in mathematics. These gains occurred during a time in which the number of immigrant students in the district increased and the student population grew more linguistically diverse and economically poor. Many of the immigrants entering school came with less education and linguistic development than had previously been the case. Yet improvements in the quality of teaching have proved more powerful than these challenges to the achievement of students.

Over the eight years of Alvarado's tenure in District 2, the district has evolved a strategy for the use of professional development to improve teaching and learning in schools. This strategy consists of a set of organizing principles about the process of systemic change and the role of professional development in that process; and a set of specific activities, or models of staff development, that focus on systemwide improvement of instruction.

ORGANIZING PRINCIPLES: MOBILIZING PEOPLE IN THE SERVICE OF INSTRUCTIONAL IMPROVEMENT

Central to Alvarado's strategy in District 2 is the creation of a strong belief system, or a culture, of shared values around instructional improvement that binds the work of teachers and administrators into a coherent set of actions and programs. Like most other belief systems, this one is not written down, but it is expressed in the words and actions of people in the system. I have reduced this complex set of ideas to seven organizing principles that emerge from the ideas and actions of people in the district.

It Is About Instruction, and Only About Instruction

The central idea in District 2's strategy is that the work of everyone in the system, from central office administrators to building principals, to teachers and support staff in schools, is about providing high-quality instruction to children. This principle permeates the language that the district leaders use to describe the purposes of their work, the way district staff manage their relationships with school staff, the way principals and school directors plan their own work, the way they interact with district staff, and the way professional development is organized and delivered. Most school systems purport to organize themselves to support good instruction; few carry this principle as far as does District 2.

Alvarado describes the district's commitment to instruction in this way:

Our time is precious when we visit schools and when we work with people in schools. We try to communicate clearly to principals and school directors that we're not interested in talking to them about getting their broken windows fixed or getting the custodians to clean the bathrooms more often. Not that those things aren't important, but there are ways of dealing with them that don't involve our spending precious time that could be focused more productively on instruction. So when principals and school directors raise those issues with us, we say quite firmly that we're there to talk about what they are doing specifically to help a given teacher do a better job of teaching reading. We try to model with our words and behavior a consuming interest in teaching and learning, almost to the exclusion of everything else. And we expect principals to model the same behavior with the teachers in their schools.

Alvarado describes the genesis of this idea from his previous experience as community superintendent in District 4:

My strategy there was to make it possible for gifted and energetic people to create schools that represented their best ideas about teaching and learning and to let parents choose the schools that best matched their children's interest. We generated a lot of interest and a lot of good programs. But the main flaw with that strategy was that it never reached every teacher in every classroom; it focused on those who showed energy and commitment to change. So after a while, improvement slowed as we ran out of energetic and committed people. Many of the programs became inward looking instead of trying to find new ways to do things. And it focused people's attention on this or that "program" rather than on the broader problem of how to improve teaching and learning across the board. So when I moved to District 2, I was determined to push beyond the District 4 strategy and to focus more broadly on instructional improvement across the board, not just on the creation of alternative programs.

Instructional Change Is a Long, Multistage Process

Teachers do not respond to simple exhortations to change their teaching, according to District 2 staff. Bea Johnstone, director of educational initiatives and coordinator of the district's professional development activities, describes the process of instructional change as involving at least four distinct stages:

- Awareness, which consists of providing teachers with access to books, outside experts, or examples of practice in other settings as a way of demonstrating that it is possible to do things differently

- Planning, which consists of working with teachers to design curriculum and create a classroom environment supportive of that curriculum

- Implementation, which consists of trying out new approaches to teaching in a setting where teachers can be observed and can receive feedback

- Reflection, which consists of opportunities for teachers to reflect with other teachers and with outside experts on what worked and what did not when they tried new practices and to use that reflection to influence their practice

At any given time, Johnstone says, groups of teachers are involved in different activities at different stages of development. They may be immersed in implementation and reflection in reading and literacy while they are in the early stages of awareness in math. Johnstone describes the process as a gradual softening up of teachers' preconceptions about what is possible, introducing new ideas in settings and from people who have credibility as practitioners, adapting new ideas to teachers' existing practice under the watchful eye of someone who is a more accomplished practitioner, and reflecting on the problems posed by new practices with peers and experts. Hence, the district's strategy is to engage teachers and principals in a variety of instructional practices that move them through the stages of the process in different domains of practice.

Shared Expertise Is the Driver of Instructional Change

The enemy of instructional improvement, according to District 2 staff, is isolation. Alvarado describes the problem this way:

> There is a tendency for teachers and principals to get pulled down into all the reasons why it is impossible to do things differently in their particular setting—and there are lots of reasons why it is difficult. What we try to do is to get a pair of outside eyes, not involved in the maelstrom, to bring a fresh perspective to what's going on in a given setting.

Shared expertise takes a number of forms in District 2. District staff regularly visit principals and teachers in schools and classrooms, as part of a formal evaluation process and an informal process of observation and advice. Within schools principals and teachers routinely engage in grade-level and cross-grade conferences on curriculum and teaching. Across schools principals and teachers regularly visit other schools and classrooms. At the district level staff development consultants regularly work with teachers in their classrooms. Teachers regularly work with teachers in other schools for extended periods of supervised practice. Teams of principals and teachers regularly work on districtwide curriculum and staff development issues. Principals regularly meet in each others' schools and observe practice in those schools. Principals and teachers regularly visit schools and classrooms within and outside the district. And principals regularly work in pairs on common issues of instructional improvement in their schools. The underlying idea behind all these forms of interaction is that shared expertise is more likely to produce change than individuals' working in isolation.

Focus on Systemwide Improvement

The enemy of systemic change, according to District 2 staff, is the "project." Whether projects take the form of special programs for selected teachers and students or categorical activities focused on students with specific needs, they tend to isolate and balkanize new ideas. Systemic change in District 2 means operationally that every principal and every teacher is responsible for continuous instructional improvement in some key element of their work. Instructional improvement is not the responsibility of a select few who operate in isolation from others, but rather a joint, collegial responsibility of everyone in the system, working together in a variety of ways across all schools.

At the same time, District 2 staff recognize that change cannot occur in all dimensions of a person's work simultaneously. So although they create the expectation that instructional improvement is everyone's responsibility, they also focus improvement efforts on specific parts of the curriculum and specific dimensions of teaching practice.

District 2 staff do not say exactly what they regard as the ideal end state of systemic instructional improvement, but presumably it is not a stable condition in which everyone is doing some version of "best practice" in every content area in every classroom. Rather, the goal is probably something like a process of continuous improvement in every school, eventually reaching every classroom, in which principals and teachers routinely open up parts of their practice to observation by experts and colleagues, in which they see change in practice as a routine event, and where colleagues participate routinely in various forms of collaboration with other practitioners to examine and develop their practice. This is clearly not an end state in any static sense, but rather a process of continuous instructional improvement unfolding indefinitely over time.

Good Ideas Come from Talented People Working Together

Alvarado says,

> Eighty percent of what is going on now in the district I could never have conceived of when we started this effort. Our initial idea was to focus on getting good leadership into schools, so we recruited people as principals who we knew had a strong record of involvement in instruction, and we tried to create a lot of reinforcement for that by the way we organized around their work. Then we wanted to get an instructional sense to permeate the whole organization, so we said, "Let's pick something we can all work on that has obvious relevance to our community and our kids." So we settled on literacy. Since then, we've built out from that model largely by capitalizing on the initiative and energy of the people we've brought in. They produce a constant supply of new ideas that we try to support.

A focus on people working together to generate new ideas permeates the managerial language of District 2 staff. Alvarado's descriptions of his and his staff's work are peppered with examples of specific principals or schools that are either exceptional or in need of improvement in some respect, and the efforts district staff make to put the former together with the latter. He speaks with pride about gradually increasing control at the district and school levels over recruitment and assignment of teachers and deflecting the reassignment of teachers to District 2 who have been released from other districts. The district staff organizes its time around work with specific schools, based on its assessment of their unique problems, and often asks principals pointed questions about the progress of specific teachers within their schools. This emphasis on attracting, selecting, and managing talented people in relation to one another is a central tenet of District 2's view of how improvement occurs.

Set Clear Expectations, Then Decentralize

District 2's strategy emphasizes the creation of lateral networks among teachers and principals and the selection of people with a strong interest in instructional improvement. A corollary of these principles is the idea of setting clear expectations and then decentralizing responsibility. Each principal or school director prepares an annual statement of supervisory goals and objectives according to a plan set out by the district, and in the ensuing year each principal is usually visited formally twice by the deputy superintendent, Elaine Fink, and often by Alvarado himself. The conversation in these reviews turns on the school's progress toward the objectives outlined in the principal's or director's plan. Over time schools have gained increasing authority over the district's professional development budget, to the point where most of the funds now reside in the budgets of the schools.

Although Alvarado and the district staff generally favor decentralization, they are pragmatists. "If the teachers really own teaching and learning," Alvarado says, "how will they really need or want to be involved in governance decisions? Our instincts are to push responsibility all the way down, but they may not want it, and it may get in the way of our broader goals of instructional improvement."

Collegiality, Caring, and Respect

"Our vision of instructional improvement," Alvarado says, "depends heavily on people being willing to take the initiative, to take risks, and to take responsibility for themselves, for students, and for each other. You get this kind of result only when people cultivate a deep personal and professional respect and caring for each other. We have set about finding and hiring like-minded people who are interested in making education work for kids. We care about and value each other, even when we disagree. Without collegiality on this level you can't generate the level of enthusiasm, energy, and commitment we have." According to Alvarado, "The worst part of bureaucracy is the dehumanization it brings. We try to communicate that professionalism, and working in a school system, is not a narrowed version of life; it is life itself, and it should take into account the full range of personal values and feelings that people have."

Alvarado, Fink, and Johnstone articulate this broad conception of collegiality with extraordinary fervor. In their view, improvements in practice require exceptional personal commitment on the part of every person in the organization, not just to good instruction but also to meeting the basic needs of the human beings involved in creating good instruction—their need for personal identification with a common enterprise, their need for help and support in meshing their personal lives with the life of the organization in which they work, and their need to feel that they play a part in shaping the common purposes of the organization.

Alvarado worries that District 2's approach to instructional improvement will be seen by outsiders as a collection of management principles rather than as a culture based on norms of commitment, mutual care, and concern. Implementing the principles without the culture, he argues, will not work because management alone cannot affect peoples' deeply held values. He also worries that emphasizing managerial principles at the expense of organizational culture makes it appear that district administrators can change practice, when in fact the process of changing practice has to originate with teachers, students, administrators, and parents as they work out difficult problems together in a web of shared expectations. The effectiveness of district-level management, he argues, is determined by the level of commitment and mutual support among those responsible for instruction.

SPECIFIC PROFESSIONAL DEVELOPMENT MODELS

Most school systems see professional development as a discrete activity, organized and managed as one specialized function among many, usually from the central office. In this view, professional development is an activity or service provided to schools as one of a number of centrally organized administrative functions. The priorities that drive the content and delivery of professional development are a combination of district- and school-level goals for improvement of curriculum, teaching, and school organization. Typically what emerges is a menu of discrete professional development activities, usually focused on specific content issues (a new way to teach math, for example) or pressing issues in the daily conduct of schooling (discipline policy, for example). These activities are often organized and delivered centrally, so that school personnel participate in training that is designed and conducted in isolation from their work setting. The theory behind this way of organizing staff development, if there is one, stresses the economies of scale that are achieved by organizing and delivering staff development at the district level and the importance of exposing teachers and principals to new ideas in their field, so that they can take these ideas back to their schools and classrooms and apply them.

In District 2 professional development is a management strategy rather than a specialized administrative function. Professional development is what administrative leaders do when they are doing their jobs, not a specialized function that some people in the organization do and others do not. Instructional improvement is the main purpose of district administration, and professional development is the chief means of achieving that purpose. Anyone with line administrative responsibility in the organization has responsibility for professional development as a central part of his or her job description. Anyone with staff responsibility has the responsibility to support those who are engaged in staff development. It is impossible to disentangle professional development from general management in District 2 because the two are synonymous for all practical purposes.

Consequently District 2 personnel do not see professional development as a discrete set of activities centrally provided in a particular place at a particular time on a particular subject. Nor do they see the purpose of professional development as providing useful ideas that can be taken back to the school or classroom. Instead professional development permeates the work of the organization and the organization of the work. It pops up in several forms in the course of a day for a given teacher or principal. It insinuates itself into the way teachers do their jobs and the way they relate to each other in the workplace. Professional development sometimes occurs in settings apart from the schools where people work. But most professional development is delivered in the actual settings where it is designed to be used: in schools and classrooms. Staff developers, district administrators, and principals never expect ideas generated in settings outside the classroom to be taken back and applied. Rather, the prevailing theory is that changes in instruction occur only when teachers receive more or less continuous oversight and support focused on the practical details of what it means to teach effectively.

I have grouped District 2's professional development models into five major categories. These categories include most, but by no means all, of what District 2 regards as professional development. They represent the implementation of the organizing principles outlined in the previous section. The models constitute a broad agenda for professional development that is constantly shifting in response to learning in the system and initiatives from teachers and principals, rather than a fixed menu.

The Professional Development Laboratory

One example of how professional development permeates the organization of District 2 is the Professional Development Laboratory (PDL). The design of the PDL is relatively simple and ingenious. The district staff designate an experienced practitioner as a resident teacher, in collaboration with principals, school directors, and the head of the PDL. A resident teacher agrees to accept a certain number of teachers as visitors in her classroom. These teachers are called visiting teachers; they apply for this designation with the consent of their principals or school directors. Each visiting teacher spends three weeks of intensive observation and supervised practice in the resident teacher's classroom. While the visiting teacher is working with the resident teacher, an experienced and highly qualified substitute teacher, called an adjunct teacher, takes over the visiting teacher's classroom. The adjunct teacher spends considerable time observing and practicing in the resident teacher's classroom. The adjunct teacher then spends one week with the visiting teacher before the visiting teacher's time with the resident teacher in order to acclimate to the visiting teacher's classroom. The adjunct also spends one week with the visiting teacher after he or she returns to the classroom to support the development of new practices learned in the resident's classroom. Resident teachers follow up with visits to the visiting teacher's classroom after the visitors have finished their three-week rotation to consult on issues of practice.

There are six possible three- to four-week rotations of visitors with residents during the school year. In any given year, ten to twelve teachers are designated as residents. If the PDL were running at full capacity, it could handle somewhere in the neighborhood of seventy teachers per year, but residents typically do not accept visitors in every cycle, so in a typical year about sixteen to twenty visitors receive PDL training. The main cost of the PDL, after the initial training of residents, is the substitute teachers' compensation paid to the adjuncts who cover the visiting teachers' classrooms. This cost is budgeted in the individual school's professional development plan and paid out of the school's professional development allocation.

The PDL has been in operation for five years and originated from a collaborative proposal between District 2, New York University, and the United Federation of Teachers to the Morgan Foundation. The PDL operates in at least one other New York community district. According to Barbara Schneider, the current coordinator of the PDL, the idea grew out of a site visit that she and a group of parents and teachers made to the Schenley High School in Pittsburgh, a school specifically designed to be both a working school and a site for staff development. They adapted the model in District 2 by locating professional development activity in several schools under the guidance of resident teachers.

According to Bea Johnstone, the PDL is "explicitly not designed on the deficit model"; that is, visiting teachers apply to the program and are chosen based on the school's staff development priorities rather than being judged to be in need of remediation. Schneider says that she explicitly had to resist the deficit model in the early years of the PDL because principals wanted to use it to deal with their weakest teachers. Although the PDL is not designed for remediation, Schneider says, she and the principals have become increasingly flexible in their decisions about whom to accept and are more willing now to accept a few less experienced and weaker teachers. The focus of the PDL on promoting quality instruction and encouraging good teachers makes it a valued experience that carries status among teachers who participate and creates demand for participation among teachers who have not yet participated.

Instructional Consulting Services

District 2 invests heavily in professional development consultants who work directly with teachers individually and in groups at the school site. Over time the district has developed two main types of consulting arrangements. The first type relies on outside consultants, experts in a given instructional area who are employed under contractual arrangements, sometimes with universities and sometimes as independent consultants. The second type relies on district consultants, typically recruited from the ranks of district personnel, paid directly on the district budget, and given an assignment to work in a given instructional area. Principals and school heads play a key role in assessing the needs of the school and brokering consulting services.

The district's first instructional improvement initiative, which began soon after Alvarado's arrival in the district eight years ago, relied exclusively on outside consultants and was focused on literacy, reading, and writing. Through the district's early involvement with Lucy Calkins and the Writing Project at Teachers College, Columbia University, the staff began to inquire about who had the expertise to work directly with teachers on a broad scale to develop skills focused on the teaching of writing and the use of literature in the development of students' literacy. The district identified Diane Snowball, an Australian educator, and hired her through a contractual arrangement with Teachers College for a one-year consulting arrangement. This has subsequently grown into a large-scale, multiyear agreement, involving several Australians, who have taken up residence in New York and provide consulting services to a number of schools in the district and in the city at large.

Snowball's approach to consulting, which has become the norm for external consultants, is to establish close working relationships with small groups of teachers in several schools. School schedules are typically constructed to allow common planning time by grade level, so that all the first-grade teachers, for example, have a designated common time available to work together on instructional issues. The understanding among principals, teachers, and district personnel is that some amount of this common planning time will be used for teachers to meet with professional development consultants. In addition, Snowball works with individual teachers in their classrooms, either at the invitation of the teacher or the encouragement of the principal. This classroom-based consultation involves observation of a teacher working with students, demonstration lessons given by Snowball herself, and debriefings with individual teachers.

Finally, Snowball occasionally works with larger groups of teachers, from either one school or a number of schools, to introduce them to the ideas of process writing and literature-based reading instruction. These larger professional development sessions were seen as ways of creating demand for consulting services rather than as sufficient in themselves to change teachers' instructional practice.

Over time this external consulting practice in District 2 has grown to the point where in the 1995–1996 school year, eleven contract consultants were working across a number of content areas. Each consultant typically works one-on-one with eight to ten teachers for blocks of three to four months each, and in addition works with grade-level teams and larger groups of teachers during planning time, at the lunch hour and after school. Consultants are frequently involved in intervisitations (joint visits by teachers, principals, and consultants to observe practice in other schools). The district negotiates a broad agreement with the consultants for a certain specified amount of services delivered to schools, and principals in schools make arrangements for consultants to work with specific teachers according to the goals outlined in their annual professional development plans. Most of the external consulting services are paid for out of schools' professional development budgets.

As this external consulting model has developed, the district has adapted and modified it for use with district staff developers, who provide consulting services but are employees of the district rather than outside contractors. The emergence of the district staff development model took place around the introduction of instructional improvement in mathematics. When the district decided to expand its improvement efforts from literacy to mathematics, it contracted with Marilyn Burns, a California mathematics professional development consultant, to provide summer workshops. These summer workshops are offered in four levels, so by the fourth year of the mathematics initiative, a cadre of teachers had completed four consecutive summers of mathematics professional development. In 1993 the district hired one of Burns's staff development consultants, a senior teacher from California, to provide external consulting services. In the spring of 1995 the district designated a full-time mathematics consultant, Lucy Mahon, an elementary school administrator with extensive training in mathematics professional development, whose first job was to work during the summer and the next school year with the cadre of teachers who had completed all four levels of summer math professional development. Some of these teachers are becoming the district's math consultants, working in conjunction with Mahon to provide consulting services to teachers in math instruction.

Overall the District 2 professional development consulting model stresses direct work by external consultants and district staff developers with individual teachers on concrete problems related to instruction in a given content area; work with grade-level teams of teachers on common problems across their classrooms;

consultation with individual teachers who are developing new approaches to teaching in their classrooms that other teachers might use; and work with larger groups of teachers to familiarize them with the basic ideas behind instructional improvement in a given content area. Change in instructional practice involves working through problems of practice with peers and experts, observation of practice, and steady accumulation over time of new practices anchored in one's own classroom setting.

The consulting model is labor intensive, in that it relies on extensive involvement by a consultant with individuals and small groups of teachers, repeatedly over time, around a limited set of instructional problems. Connecting professional development with teaching practice in this direct way requires making a choice at the district level to invest resources intensively rather than using them to provide low-impact activities spread across a larger numbers of teachers. The approach also implies a long-term commitment to instructional improvement in a given content area. In order to reach large numbers of teachers with the District 2 consulting model, district- and school-level priorities for professional development have to stay focused on a particular content area—in this case literacy and math—over several years, so that consultants have the time to engage teachers repeatedly across a number of schools in a year and then expand their efforts to other schools in successive years.

Intervisitation and Peer Networks

A third form of professional development in District 2 is a heavy reliance on peer networks and visits to other sites, inside and outside the district, designed to bring teachers and principals into contact with exemplary practices. Intervisitation, as it is called in the district, and peer consultations are routine parts of the district's daily life. Teachers often visit other classrooms in conjunction with consultants' visits, either to observe one of their peers teaching a lesson or a consultant teaching a demonstration lesson. And groups of teachers often visit another school, inside or outside the district, in preparation for the development of a new set of instructional practices. Usually principals initiate these outside visits and travel with teachers.

In addition principals engage in intervisitations with peers in other schools. New principals are paired with "buddies," who are usually more senior administrators, and they often spend a day or two each month in their first two years in their buddy's school. Groups of teachers and principals working on district initiatives travel to other districts inside and outside the city to observe specific instructional practices. And monthly districtwide principals' meetings are held on site in schools, and often principals observe individual teachers in their peers' schools as part of a structured agenda for discussing some aspect of instructional improvement. Principals are encouraged to use visits and peer advising as management strategies for teachers within their buildings. A principal who is having trouble getting a particular teacher engaged in improvement might be advised by the district staff to pair that teacher with another teacher in the building or another building in the district. And principals themselves might be encouraged to consult with other principals on specific areas where they are having difficulties.

Intervisitations and peer advising as professional development activities tend to blend into the day-to-day management of the district. The district budgets resources to support about three hundred days of professional time to be allocated to intervisitation activities. Many such activities are not captured by these budgeted resources, since they occur informally among individuals on an ad hoc basis.

A specific example serves to illustrate how professional development and management blend together around peer advising and intervisitation. An elementary principal who is in the last year of her probationary period and is considered to be an exemplar by district personnel described off-handedly that throughout her probationary period, she had visited regularly with two other principals in the district. She is currently involved in a principals' support group that meets regularly with three other principals, and she provides support to her former assistant principal, who was recruited to take over another school as an interim acting principal. In addition this principal has led several groups of teachers from her school to observe teaching of reading and writing in university settings and in other schools in the city. She has attended summer staff development institutes in literacy and math with teachers from her school, and in the ensuing school year, she taught a series of demonstration lessons in the classrooms of teachers in her school to work out the complexities of implementing new instructional strategies. She speaks of these activities as part of her routine administrative responsibility as a principal rather than as specific professional development activities.

Another example of how peer advising and intervisitation models come together in the routine business of the district is the monthly principals' conferences. Most districts have regularly scheduled meetings of principals, typically organized by elementary and secondary levels. These routine meetings usually deal primarily with administrative business and rarely with specific instructional issues. In District 2, in contrast, regular principals' meetings—frequently called principals' conferences—are primarily organized around instructional issues and only incidentally around routine administrative business, and they often take place in the schools. At one recent principals' conference, which took place in a school, the meeting principals were asked to visit classrooms, observe demonstration lessons, and use a protocol to observe and analyze classroom practice. Another recent principals' conference convened at New York's Museum of Modern Art. The theme was the development and implementation of standards for evaluating students' academic work. The conference consisted of a brief introductory discussion of District 2's activities around standards by Alvarado; an overview of standards work by the standards coordinator, Denise Levine, and a principal, Frank DeStefano, who has taken a leadership role in developing standards in his school; a series of small group discussions of an article about standards by Lauren Resnick; an analysis by small groups of participants of a collection of vignettes of student work around standards; and an observation of the museum's education programs. Discussion of routine administrative business occupied less than thirty minutes at the end of the seven-hour meeting.

Off-Site Training

District 2 offers extensive off-site training in the summer and during the school year. This form of training is most like what school districts typically think of as professional development, although it is distinctive in the way it is organized and delivered. A typical array of summer institutes during the summer of 1995 included three levels of mathematics training for elementary teachers, training in elementary social studies, sessions on the development and implementation of standards and curriculum frameworks, mathematics and literacy institutes for middle school teachers, and an advanced literacy institute for experienced teachers.

Much of the planning that precedes off-site training occurs at the school level. Each school receives money to plan its staff development agenda for the coming year. School staffs work out an agenda for summer staff development and integrate it with support for teachers during the school year. In the words of Bea Johnstone, "Summer institutes don't make any sense unless you have the resources to support direct assistance to teachers during the school year."

The district looks at its off-site training as a continuous investment in a few strands of content-focused training over a long term, designed to have a cumulative impact on teachers within the district. The largest proportion of funds spent on off-site training goes to district initiatives that have been in place over a number of years—at least eight years in literacy and four or five years in math. Focusing on the same content areas over multiple years means that progressively greater numbers of teachers are introduced to new conceptions of teaching in specific content areas and that these teachers, along with their principals, who also attend the training, create the demand for more intensive consulting services and for other forms of professional development like peer advice and intervisitation. The central idea, then, is not to provide training in the innovation du jour, or whatever the prevailing new instructional idea is in any given year, but to provide continuous support for larger and larger numbers of teachers to learn to teach new content at increasingly higher levels of complexity in a few select areas.

A final distinctive feature of District 2's use of off-site training is that participation in summer institutes involves a complex balancing of district and school-site priorities. Staff development funds, including money for off-site training, are officially allocated to schools to be spent in accordance with school site professional development plans. Yet off-site services are contracted for and provided by the district, so decisions about what kind of content to offer at what level for what target populations of teachers involve a complex byplay between school and district personnel. The district sets the overall priorities for what content areas will be the focus of off-site professional development, and it does so in accordance with a multiyear strategy for involving progressively greater numbers of teachers in content-focused training. In any given year, schools are asked to estimate the level of demand they will have for summer programs as part of their professional development planning, and the district uses these estimates to decide how much of which kind of training to provide in that summer.

Oversight and Principal Site Visits

A final element of District 2's professional development strategy is routine oversight of schools. Alvarado and Fink form a team whose primary focus is continuous monitoring of schools' progress toward instructional improvement. Fink and Johnstone spend at least two days each week visiting schools, and often more when special problems need to be addressed. They make at least one formal review of each school in the district at least once each year. Alvarado maintains a schedule with the goal of visiting each school at least once each year, in addition to the many occasions when he is in schools for regular events like principals' conferences.

The centerpiece of oversight and performance review is the supervisory goals and objectives process. Each year each principal completes a plan that lays out his or her objectives for the year and specific plans and activities for achieving those objectives. These plans form the basis for the performance reviews and school visits. District staff set the structure for the plans, which focuses almost exclusively on instructional improvement in specific content areas: literacy, science, math, interdisciplinary studies, bilingual/English as a Second Language, and parental involvement. Most of the content of the plans deals with the use of various forms of professional development to meet instructional goals. In effect, the plans are a description of how professional development will be deployed in the school around the principal's instructional objectives.

Alvarado and Fink's formal visits to schools constitute the other major component of oversight and performance review. The visits are usually, but not always, announced in advance. They consist of a conversation with the principal about specific issues in the school, a walk-through and a visit to several classrooms, a debriefing discussion with the principal that focuses on specific actions, and a letter from Fink that describes the results of the visit and the agreed-on actions.

In addition to these formal visits, Fink and Johnstone make myriad informal visits to schools. In schools where there are interim acting principals (principals who are filling temporary vacancies) or recently appointed principals, Fink and Johnstone often visit frequently and pay special attention to orchestrating intervisitations and mentor relationships. Schools that for one reason or another are seen as problematic get more informal attention than those that are seen as doing well.

Alvarado says of this process, "I think it has had a substantial effect on getting our philosophy of instructional improvement across. If you contrast the principals' plans of four years ago with the plans they did this year, the thing that stands out is how much more detail there is about specific instructional improvement and how much more sophisticated the principals are in the strategies they're using." Indeed there is substantial evidence in the plans that principals are focusing much of their time and energy on decisions about how to use professional development to meet their instructional objectives. There is also evidence that the emphasis on specific content areas in the planning document has the effect of focusing principals' attention on how to improve instruction rather than on general goals having to do with the structure and climate of the school. In other words asking principals what they are doing about the improvement of instruction has the effect, not surprisingly, of focusing their attention on instruction.

Another effect of the oversight and performance review process is that district staff get to know a lot about schools. Alvarado says,

> After you've been at this for several years, you know who the particularly
> strong or weak teachers are, or the teachers who are on the verge of big changes
> in their practice, and you can make a beeline for those classrooms when you
> visit. A lot of this comes from the principals themselves; they tell us where their
> problems and successes are in order to get help in figuring out what to do. So
> we get to know a tremendous amount about what's going on inside schools, and
> that is very helpful in shaping our ideas about what we need to do at this level
> to support instructional change.

HOW THE STRATEGY DEVELOPED AND WHERE IT IS GOING

Although the development of this strategy involved a great deal of improvisation and opportunism, a few stable themes emerge. One important theme that has implications for other systemic change efforts is the phased introduction of instructional changes, organized mainly around content areas. District 2's approach began with reading and writing because this focus provided a readily available way for the district to demonstrate improvement in academic performance in an area that was important on citywide assessment measures and because literacy was important in the context of the district's linguistic and ethnic diversity. As district staff, consultants, and principals learned how to change teaching practice through the literacy initiative, Alvarado began a parallel effort in mathematics, adapting the same model to learning from the literacy initiative and the fiscal realities of the district. Recently the district has begun another set of initiatives, including the development of middle schools and the development of standards to be used in assessing student work. These activities assume most of the characteristics of earlier improvement efforts and reinforce their organizing principles.

This approach stems from the recognition that systemic change cannot occur simultaneously in all parts of the system at once. Nor is it possible to ask teachers to change their practice simultaneously on all dimensions—for example, reading, writing, math, science, and social studies. The strategy suggests, however, that it is possible to create the expectation that systemwide changes can occur in certain domains and that these changes can reach progressively more content areas and more teachers over time. The strategy also suggests that people in the system will learn important lessons about how to change teaching practice in the early stages that they can use to work more effectively in the later stages. What is systemic about the strategy is not that it tries to change all dimensions of teaching practice at once, but that it sets in motion a process for making changes in teaching practice, and it creates the expectation that these changes will reach deeply and broadly in the system.

Another major theme in the development of the strategy is the intentional blurring of the boundaries between management of the system and the activities of staff development. In District 2 management is about marshaling resources in support of instructional improvement, and staff development is the vehicle by which that occurs. Accountability within the system is expressed in terms of teachers' and principals' objectives for instructional improvement, and the idiom of management is instruction. Principals write their annual objectives in terms of specific attempts to improve instruction in specific content domains, not in terms of generalized ideas about such matters as improving school climate, keeping the hallways clean, and keeping parents happy. District- and school-level budget priorities are expressed in terms of expenditures on instructional consultants, substitute teachers, and access to workshops that lead to changes in instruction rather than in terms of general line items or functional categories. In other words, management is operationally defined as helping teachers to do their work better, and work is defined in terms of teaching and learning.

A third theme of the strategy is a complex and evolving balance between central authority and school site autonomy. Alvarado has pushed steadily to lodge more and more budget and administrative responsibility at the school level, largely in the hands of principals. At the same time his strategy of instructional improvement requires principals and teachers to share a common view that their jobs are fundamentally about improving instruction and to accept some discipline in the way resources get focused on specific content areas and issues. In the absence of this discipline, the strategy would consist of schools' improvising on the theme of instructional improvement with little or no cumulative systemwide impact on teaching and learning in specific content domains. Alvarado and his district staff walk a fine line between exerting discipline and focus on districtwide instructional priorities, on the one hand, and encouraging principals and teachers to take the initiative in devising their own strategies and plans, on the other.

A fourth theme in the development of the strategy is that district administrators are unapologetic about exercising control in areas that are central to the success of the strategy. The most prominent example of this theme is the way Alvarado and his staff have handled the replacement of principals. In order for a decentralized strategy for instructional improvement to work, and in order for principals to accept a view that management equals the improvement of instruction, the system had to be able to select, hire, and retain principals on the basis of their aptitude for and agreement with the district's overall strategy. Alvarado and his staff have focused what would be seen in most school systems as an inordinate amount of attention on recruiting principals, grooming emerging leaders within the district for principalships, creating support networks for acting and probationary principals, and creating norms that principals are to participate along with teachers in staff development activities dealing with content-focused instruction. The reason for this attention is that Alvarado sees the principalship as the linchpin of his systemic strategy, and he recognizes that if he cannot influence who becomes a principal in the system, he cannot decentralize and get the results he wants.

This attitude toward the centrality of personnel decisions has begun to permeate principals' attitudes toward the hiring of teachers. Most of the principals we interviewed in the system said without any prompting by us that the key determinant of their capacity to meet their school-level objectives is the quality of their teachers and that they had learned how to exercise more influence on the process of recruiting, hiring, nurturing, retaining, and firing, or counseling out, of teachers in their schools.

Another example of the theme of central control of key elements of the strategy has to do with external consultants. A central part of the district's strategy for instructional improvement is finding expertise that is consistent with the strategy and bringing it into the system. In a highly decentralized system, schools would make their own judgments about the specific consultants they would use to meet their objectives. District 2's strategy evolved along different lines. District staff recruit and select external consultants and evaluate their performance on the basis of how well they are able to work with principals and teachers. School staff select from the available array of consultants and deploy them according to their internal priorities. This use of central authority is calculated to lend focus, coherence, and discipline to a relatively decentralized process.

A fifth and final theme of District 2's strategy is consistency of focus over time. Most districts' staff development activities reflect district priorities in any given year, and these priorities often shift in response to changes in policy at the local or state level, curricular fads or fashions of the moment, and the multiple demands of various school- and district-level constituencies. The logic of District 2's strategy requires a long-term focus on a few important instructional priorities. The strategy depends on reaching teachers directly in their classrooms through a labor-intensive consulting model and using routine processes of management and oversight to educate principals and teachers to the centrality of their role in instructional improvement.

Alvarado and his staff see at least three major themes emerging for the future of professional development and instructional improvement in the district. The first of these centers on standards and assessment. District 2 was recently selected by the Pew Charitable Trust to participate in a national network of school systems engaged in systemic reform and, as part of that effort, to participate in the piloting of standards for student learning and new forms of student assessment. In addition the district has formed an alliance with the University of Pittsburgh's new Institute for Learning, which also has as its focus the introduction of standards-based curriculum and assessment.

Alvarado sees this emerging emphasis on standards as a logical extension of his past efforts at instructional improvement. "At some point in the process," he says, "you have to begin to ask the question, 'How do we know we're doing well by the kids?' and the only way you can answer that question is by getting agreement on what kids should know and be able to do and starting to assess their learning in some systematic way." Alvarado thought that introducing the standards and assessment issue before principals and teachers who had extensive experience with instructional improvement would have been a mistake. "You can kill a lot of the learning that you need in the system by insisting that it all has to line up with some item on a test," he says. On the other hand, he thinks standards and assessment are logical extensions of his heavy emphasis on professional development as a mechanism of instructional improvement. "Professional development costs a lot of money, and sooner or later we're going to have to say what we've gotten for what we've invested in people," he says. "I want to have some control over the terms on which we make that judgment."

The second theme for future development is dealing with schools that, for one reason or another, have lagged behind others in the district in instructional improvement. In some cases, district staff observe, schools lag because their principals are not fully engaged in the districtwide agenda. In some cases they lag because they do not have access to the right array of resources to meet their needs. And in some cases the schools have recently organized new leadership, and teachers are adapting to new expectations. In the 1995–1996 school year, district staff formed a network within a district of the seven schools that have the highest number of children performing in the lowest quartile of the citywide reading test. These schools receive extra scrutiny and support from the district, and their principals convene to share ideas about instructional improvement.

A third theme for future development is moving the instructional improvement strategy more explicitly into the middle grades. Because the district strategy initially formed around the improvement of literacy in the early grades, the schools that were most intensely involved at the outset were elementary schools with high proportions of poor and language-minority children. As the strategy expanded to include more and more schools, it focused again at the elementary level. Now the system is coming to terms with the fact that cohorts of children moving into the middle grades have had a distinctive kind of instruction in the elementary grades and the junior high schools are not necessarily prepared to capitalize on these children's knowledge and skills. About two years ago, the district started to emphasize instructional improvement in the middle grades and to develop middle schools, grades 6 through 9, and to emphasize instructional improvement in the middle grades. District staff admit that this part of the strategy is developing slowly and that they are still learning about the unique conditions for instructional improvement in the middle grades.

FINANCIAL RESOURCES

Staff development requires money. Finding money to support professional development is usually difficult, since state and local policymakers often see training as an expendable budget item when they are struggling to cover increasing salary and facilities costs in the face of constant or declining revenues. Under conditions of scarce resources, policymakers are probably inclined to view professional development more as a professional perquisite than as a major force for improving performance of teachers and students. District 2 probably spends more money on staff development per capita than other districts and probably allocates a larger share of its district budget for this purpose, although it is impossible to prove this conjecture since districts do not maintain comparable data on their staff development expenditures. How much does District 2's strategy cost? Where do the resources come from? How are they spent? District 2 does a better job than most other school systems of keeping track of what it budgets for professional development, although, it is still difficult to estimate the exact costs of the strategy. In fiscal years 1994 through 1996, professional development consumed roughly 3 percent of the total budget.

These budgeted costs covered direct expenditures on salaries, contracts, and materials related to the delivery of professional development, but not the time the principals and teachers spend during the regular instructional day working with each other or with consultants on the improvement of teaching, the networking activities that principals engage in as part of their regular administrative duties, and much of the district-level overhead associated with administering the strategy. Committing a specific proportion of the budget has the effect of communicating the importance of professional development to key constituencies in the district.

To generate the revenue required to meet this commitment, Alvarado and his staff engage in what is called in administrative circles "multipocket budgeting," that is, orchestrating multiple sources of revenue around a single priority to produce the maximum amount of revenue available for that purpose. In effect District 2 staff treat revenue from a variety of sources—including local tax revenues, federal categorical programs (Title 1, special education), and state categorical programs (magnet schools)—as being available for use in the district's professional development strategy, as long as the uses of the money are consistent with the requirements of the program.

This money is spent on the following items (see Table 9.1):

- Teacher compensation—the on-budget costs of the compensated time teachers spend in professional development activities and compensation for substitute teachers who replace teachers in the classroom while they are engaged in professional development activities

- Contracted services—consulting services for direct delivery of instructional support to teachers or for summer workshops

- The Professional Development Laboratory—administrative costs for oversight of the program and compensation for adjunct teachers who replace visiting teachers while they are with resident teachers

- Materials purchased for use by teachers directly in training

Table 9.1. Budgeted Expenditures by Function, Fiscal Years 1994–1996.

	FY 1994	FY 1995	FY 1996
Teacher compensation	$1,100,605	$787,733	$234,118
Contracted services	$259,500	$933,910	$1,279,532
Professional Development Lab	$233,860	$275,000	$225,000
Materials	$98,676	$98,045	$34,628

The district has shifted costs toward consulting services and away from summer workshops by opening up participation in summer workshops to teachers from other districts, which in effect subsidizes the participation of District 2 teachers.

THE VIEW FROM THE SCHOOLS

District 2's strategy involves a complex and evolving set of relationships between central administrators and school staff. On the one hand, Alvarado places a high priority on shifting major responsibilities for budget and instructional decisions to the school level. Over three years, for example, he moved from a system of central office control over all professional development expenditures to one in which schools are allocated a lump sum for professional development that they decide how to spend in accordance with a school site plan. District 2's approach to management and oversight of principals also stresses the central role that principals play in developing and implementing their own priorities. On the other hand, the district maintains a strong hand in certain domains that are central to the success of the strategy. The district identifies the contract consultants who will deliver instructional support services. District personnel oversee and review principals' priorities and pay regular visits to schools and classrooms to review principals' progress. And the district has developed a strategy for focusing attention on instructional improvement in low-performing schools. So the District 2 strategy has elements of both decentralization and centralization. On the decentralization side, the strategy has a heavy focus on school site decision making related to specific decisions about which teachers will receive training and support, which content areas will receive attention, and which consultants will be employed over a specific period, and on orchestrating professional networks around specific school issues. On the centralization side, the strategy places major responsibility with central staff for deciding which instructional areas will receive priority attention, maintaining the focus on these areas, forming and maintaining relationships with consultants who deliver training and support in these priority areas, and keeping school site decisions focused on districtwide priorities.

Not surprisingly, such a complex division of labor produces a variety of responses from school staff. One response might be characterized as "hearing footsteps." Principals are acutely aware that they are responsible for professional development and instructional improvement in their schools and that this responsibility runs to making assessments of individual teachers' competencies and capacities and matching these teachers with available resources. Principals are also aware that district staff pay attention, often in detailed ways, to what they are doing in their schools to foster instructional improvement. They perceive that some principals receive greater attention and scrutiny than others, but those who receive less scrutiny still give high visibility to district-level priorities. Visits from district staff are often viewed with some trepidation. More experienced principals often coach less experienced ones about how to prepare for and participate in the walk-through that district staff conduct periodically in schools. Principals report feeling challenged by district staff—sometimes unfairly, they feel—about the practices of specific teachers in their schools. Most principals view these walk-throughs and their accompanying reviews and debriefings by district staff as constructive; some view them as less than helpful; all view them unambiguously as influential in shaping their thinking about their work.

Principals also respond in a variety of ways to the increased control over professional development funds they are receiving. Many of the principals we spoke with saw little real difference between the previously centralized approach and the more recent decentralized approach. They argue that they always negotiated with district staff about how to spend budgeted resources and how to get extra resources for activities they wanted to pursue that were not budgeted. This negotiation continues, they say, and they feel they generally get what they need from it. A few principals chafe at what they regard as a contradiction in the district's strategy: Principals have discretion over professional development funds as long as they focus on district-approved activities and priorities, but they do not have discretion if they propose to spend the money on activities that district staff feel do not fall within their priorities. In most instances, though, principals understand that they have considerable latitude as long as they have a reasonably clear set of priorities in their annual plans and can demonstrate that they are making progress with individual teachers in line with those priorities. They also understand that if they take advantage of the professional networks available to them in the district and the opportunities available to interact with Alvarado and his staff, they will gain access to the opportunities they need to demonstrate success in their schools. The District 2 strategy sends a strong signal to principals that if they work in concert with others rather than in isolation, they will get access to the resources necessary to do their jobs well.

For the most part, school staff did not report being overwhelmed by district initiatives, as school people are in many districts with aggressive, entrepreneurial leaders. They report feeling pressure to perform well and to demonstrate what they are doing. They report feeling that they are held to much higher expectations for performance than their peers in other districts, although usually without seeing these expectations as negative. They sometimes report experiencing difficulty in meeting the expectations that district staff communicate and sometimes feeling that district staff do not demonstrate sufficient appreciation of the special problems of their schools. But they do not report being confused about district priorities, receiving conflicting or mixed signals about which specific activities they should be focusing on, or getting sideswiped or ambushed by shifting district priorities.

Most principals and teachers with whom we spoke reported that they were gratified, energized, and generally enthusiastic, if sometimes a bit intimidated, by the attention they receive through District 2's professional development strategy. They report attending professional development activities outside the district or conducting visits to other schools and districts and being impressed with the amount of attention that teaching and learning receive in District 2. Teachers from outside the district who attend District 2–sponsored summer professional development activities often report that they have heard that the district is the place for teachers who are interested in good teaching, and they comment favorably on the range of professional development activities available to District 2 teachers and principals. Outsiders also comment on the (to them) unusual practice of principals' attending content-centered professional development activities with teachers from their schools. For the most part, then, teachers seem to be aware that District 2 provides a range of opportunities that would not be available if they were teaching elsewhere, and they seem to value those activities.

LESSONS AND ISSUES

District 2 provides compelling evidence that local districts can play an active and influential role in mobilizing resources to support sustained improvement in teaching practice. Furthermore, it demonstrates that local districts may have certain natural advantages in supporting sustained instructional improvement through professional development. Districts can achieve economies of scale in acquiring the services of consultants; they can introduce strong incentives for principals and teachers to pay attention to the improvement of teaching in specific domains; they can create opportunities for interaction among professionals that schools might not be able to do by themselves; and they can make creative use of multipocket budgeting to generate resources to focus on instructional improvement. District 2 can be seen as proof that local districts can play a strong role in instructional improvement through staff development, perhaps a role that other entities cannot play with the same effectiveness.

What seems to distinguish District 2 from many other districts is, first, that it has a specific strategy focused on the improvement of teaching; second, that the strategy has as its goal the sustained improvement of teaching practice, and not just in a few select places; and third, that the strategy permeates all aspects of the district's organization, including routine management and oversight, budgeting and resources allocation, and district policy. What distinguishes District 2's strategy is that it makes instructional improvement through staff development the central purpose and rationale for the district's role. Beneath this over-arching commitment lie myriad specific decisions about the organization of district staff, the creation of a set of operating principles, the development of specific activities that demonstrate these principles, and the development of a managerial and budgetary infrastructure that supports and reinforces the principles and activities. The specific principles, activities, and supporting structures could, one imagines, differ considerably from one setting to another, depending on the skills, resources, and constraints that operate in any given setting. What seems important for District 2 is the willingness of Alvarado and his staff to follow the implications of their interest in instructional improvement into a specific set of principles, activities, and structures and to inspire a lot of problem-solving activity in the district around these ideas. It may be less important for other districts to imitate what District 2 is doing than for them to shift the purposes and activities of the system to focus more centrally on instructional improvement and sustain that commitment long enough for people in the system to begin to internalize it and to start engaging in problem-solving consistent with it.

There are, to be sure, special circumstances in District 2 that might not apply in other school districts: Alvarado's experience, energy, and tenacity; the district's relatively small scale and relatively focused responsibility for only elementary and junior high schools; the extraordinary diversity and resources of the community surrounding the district; and the special circumstances that allowed the district to replace most of its principals and a large proportion of its teachers over a relatively short period. But there are also other circumstances that make District 2 an instructive case for other districts: the extraordinary diversity of its student population, its resource levels and revenue sources, and its relatively conventional governance and administrative structure. It seems unlikely that any other district will confront circumstances identical to those that Alvarado confronted in District 2, but it also seems plausible that any district could engage in something like the process of bringing district resources into alignment around instructional improvement that occurred in District 2. It is less the context that distinguishes District 2 from other districts than it is what Alvarado and his staff have done to mobilize the resources and authority available to them to shape the district's purposes, activities, and structures.

Among the issues that the District 2 strategy poses is how systemic change occurs. District 2 has focused its efforts on changing teaching practice in specific content areas and then expanding the scale of its efforts by increasing the number of content areas and grade levels as well as expanding the number of teachers exposed to new practices.

It is unclear from observing District 2 how long it will take to reach all teachers and principals in all areas of the curriculum. In the literacy area, where the district has about eight years' experience with the strategy, there is ample anecdotal evidence that it has had extensive effects on teaching practice in virtually all elementary schools. It is less clear what the district would regard as a satisfactory level of practice and what proportion of teachers have reached that standard of practice. The same issue arises in mathematics, where the strategy has been under way for only two or three years, and teachers are only beginning to grapple with the implications of new ways of teaching. Finally, there are certain areas of the curriculum—social studies, for example—where only small amounts of activity have occurred. What seems clear, then, is that although District 2's strategy poses a reasonable solution to the problem of systemic change of teaching practice, the district has a long way to go to meet its goal of systemwide continuous improvement of practice.

A second issue arises out of the increasing necessity for Alvarado and his staff to justify their emphasis on ambitious, relatively expensive, and labor-intensive approaches to instructional improvement in the face of increasingly scarce resources. District 2 staff are addressing this issue by beginning to develop standards for evaluating student work that are consistent with the changes in instruction that the district is promoting, participating in a network of school districts that is working on using new forms of student assessment, and developing the district's capacity to assess changes in practice and their relationship to changes in student performance. It seems apparent that as teachers, parents, board members, and external policymakers begin to understand how much sustained attention it takes to engage in systemic, continuous improvement, they will gain the ability to ask harder questions about whether the costs can be justified in terms of improved student performance and whether the improvements are taking place fast enough in enough classrooms and schools to make systemwide improvement a plausible goal. These expectations have to be met head-on with new forms of information about changes in teaching practice and their relationship to student learning. Otherwise the district will have difficulty justifying the strategy.

A third issue has to be with continuity and stability over time. The story of educational reform in the United States is, for the most part, a story of nervous movement from one fad to another, with little enduring effect on teaching practice (Tyack and Cuban, 1995; Elmore, 1993). Most schools and school districts have adapted to this view of change by adopting whatever the innovation is at any given moment, investing their resources in spreading it among schools and classrooms without serious attention to its effect on the fundamentals of teaching practice, and then abandoning it when the next fad comes along. District 2 has taken a much different approach by focusing on the fundamentals of teaching practice in a few select content areas and using staff development to reach directly into classrooms and schools in a sustained way that is designed to influence how teachers and students interact around content. In order for this approach to work on a systemic scale, the school district has to stay focused on a few content areas with an evolving set of staff development activities for a long period. This commitment to sustained change requires district policymakers and high-level administrators to sustain an unusual degree of focus and to buffer the district from external influences that make it difficult to stay focused. District 2 seems to have demonstrated that focus is possible over a period of time in which most districts would have switched reform agendas two or three times. Whether the district can stay focused long enough to reach all classrooms and schools across all content areas remains to be seen. Continuity and depth of district leadership, the creation of enduring networks and structures that connect teachers and principals, stability in the commitment of resources to key professional development activities, and attention to demonstrating the impact of changes in teaching practice on student performance are all factors that could contribute to stability and focus over time.

References

Elmore, R. "The Role of Local Districts in Instructional Improvement." In S. Fuhrman (ed.), *Designing Coherent Education Policy: Improving the System.* San Francisco: Jossey-Bass, 1993.

Tyack, D., and Cuban, L. *Tinkering Toward Utopia.* Cambridge, Mass.: Harvard University Press, 1995.

CHAPTER TEN

Networks and Reform
in American Education

Ann Lieberman and Maureen Grolnick

Networks as an organizational form are becoming increasingly important to the reform movement in American education. They have become a way of engaging school-based educators in directing their own learning and, by allowing them to sidestep the limitations of institutional roles, hierarchies, and geographic locations, are encouraging them to work together with many people outside their schools. Participants have opportunities to grow and develop in a professional community that focuses on their development, providing ways of learning in keeping with their lived professional lives (McLaughlin and Talbert, 1993).

TOWARD A DEFINITION OF NETWORKS

Although many educators have observed and participated in educational reform networks for some time, little is known about how such networks are formed, what they focus on, and how they are sustained. Much of what we do know about these networks is anecdotal or drawn from studying single networks that have their own particular context and purpose (Sirotnik and Goodlad, 1988).

This chapter is adapted from Lieberman, A., and Grolnick, M. "Network and Reform in American Education." *Teachers College Record,* 1996, *98*(1), 7–45. Reprinted by permission of Blackwell Publishers.

The most important general study of networks, done by Allen Parker (1977, p. 25), described five key ingredients drawn from studying over sixty networks organized for educational improvement more than twenty years ago:

- A strong sense of commitment to the innovation
- A sense of shared purpose
- A mixture of information sharing and psychological support
- An effective facilitator
- Voluntary participation and equal treatment

A key insight for Parker was that members "have a sense of being part of a special group or movement" (p. 7). Parker's key ingredients and his observation about the role that networks play in helping people work outside the system served as the basis for an initial working definition as we began to inquire into the nature of contemporary educational reform networks.

WHOM DID WE TALK TO AND WHAT DID WE ASK?

At the National Center for Restructuring Education, Schools and Teaching (NCREST) at Teachers College,[1] we have been learning more about educational reform networks while helping to support and, in some cases, organize them. After extended discussions with the leaders of three of the networks organized by NCREST, we recognized that these reform networks, unlike more permanent institutions, were intentionally constructed without rigid borders, buildings, or permanent structures and embedded in a complicated web of connections, events and relationships. These interviews led us to seek answers to such questions as these: How do these networks evolve and take shape, and how do they build commitment to common purposes? Who leads these networks, and what is the nature of their work and their learning? What activities bind people together in these networks, and how are they organized? What tensions and dilemmas do they face in the process of developing and sustaining these entities?

We expanded our inquiry to gain additional information from other educational reform networks that had been in existence for enough time to have a history, were made up of a variety of organizational forms, and linked people together who were of different status and played many roles (see Table 10.1 for complete list). In addition to interviewing the leaders, we collected their newsletters and other print materials to expand our understanding and gain insight into these seemingly improvisational arrangements, effective in practice but hard to characterize theoretically or conceptually.

Table 10.1. Purposes and Participants of Networks Studied.

Network	Participants	Purposes	Contents
Breadloaf Rural Teacher Network	Secondary school English teachers and their students	Ease the isolation of teachers in rural schools across the country	National, electronic
Center for Collaborative Education	New York City public schools; teachers and directors	Promote education reform and school restructuring based on the successful practices of member schools	New York City affiliate, Coalition of Essential Schools
Consortium for Educational Change	Districts that, in conjunction with the National Education Association union leadership, commit to involvement—superintendents, school boards, union leaders and, increasingly, community members	Build trust and collaboration between the teachers' union and district and school administrators	Regional
Diversity and Excellence Working for the Education of Youth (DEWEY)	Eight school districts selected because of their increasingly diverse student populations; administrators, teachers, and university-based educators	Share and support practices that promote diversity and excellence	Regional (Westchester and Rockland counties in New York)
Four Seasons	Teachers	Collaboration among three networks to build knowledge about how teachers learn, use, and shape authentic assessment	National, electronic
Foxfire Teacher Outreach Network	Secondary school English teachers	Support individual teachers who have adopted the Foxfire approach to the teaching of writing and learning and to integrate that approach into the life of the school	National
Harvard Principals' Center	Public school principals in the greater Boston area	Provide a professional support network for principals committed to school improvement	Regional

Name	Membership	Purpose	Scope
(Harvard) Teachers' Center	Teachers from the greater Boston area	Provide teachers committed to their own professional growth and to school improvement opportunities to learn and share with like-minded colleagues	Regional
Institute for Literacy Studies—Elementary Teachers' Network	Primarily elementary teachers	Promote effective literacy instruction using the primary language record as the focus	Regional (New York City)
Mission Valley Consortium	All members of the Mission Valley school community	Review and revise curriculum in participating districts and build a sense of shared ownership and commitment to curriculum reform	Regional
National Network for Educational Renewal	School-university partnerships	Promote the simultaneous renewal of schools and the education of educators	National
Network of Progressive Educators	Teachers, teacher educators, parents, public and private schools, child advocacy organizations	Provide a professional nework for people who share the same values and beliefs about progressive education	National
North Dakota Study Group	Educators committed to the principles of progressive education who have been invited to join	Bring together educators from across the country who are committed to progressive education, support democratic schools, and are interested in assessment	National
Program for School Improvement—League of Professional Schools	Schools committed to shared governance, instructional initiatives, and action research	Help create schools that are driven by internal decisions based on the school's own criteria for success—"democratic schools"	Regional, national
Professional Development Schools	Professional development school partnerships, university- and school-based educators	Share support and build knowledge about professional development schools (school-university partnership)	National
Southern Maine Partnership	School districts	Help schools reflect on their own practice and move toward restructuring and help the university reflect on and restructure its preparation of educators (evolved over time)	Regional

ORGANIZATIONAL THEMES

We found five descriptive organizational themes woven into the fabric of all sixteen networks that we studied, as well as five tensions that were a source of recurring negotiation. These organizational themes and tensions that we observed provided the frame we used to understand the practices, structure, and culture of these networks (Miles, 1978, p. 49).

Theme 1: Purposes and Directions

Central to the start-up of networks are the myriad ways organizers rally prospective participants to a particular cause, idea, or set of connections, and the ways in which those connections grow to encompass larger goals. As one network founder stated, "You've got to have a compelling idea . . . a dust particle around which to coalesce. But it must be compelling to the potential coalescees."

Because educators belong to a variety of organizations that have tremendous claims on their time, it would seem that reform networks must somehow demonstrate a compelling reason to convince people to participate in, what is yet another activity (Schön, 1977, p. 28). In practice we found that the reasons for the creation of networks were often embedded in the particulars of the contexts out of which they emerged. Some began with informal conversations that led to broader and deeper purposes, while others, starting with lofty purposes, had to develop practical ways of engaging people in understanding what these ideas might mean on a day-to-day basis. Still others were begun by charismatic leaders, and the networks were organized around the vision associated with a particular person, as the following examples show:[2]

> The partnership started with conversations. In the beginning we had as many as seventeen different groups. These conversations led to a linkage between teacher development and school development.

> We began in one rural school where the principal wanted to change. Another school heard about our discussions. Then seven or eight other schools eventually came to a meeting and said, "Let's form a league, looking at schools as democratic institutions."

> In the first wave, we began eight school-university partnerships and had the postulates as a guide representing the purposes of the network. In the second wave we reinvented the process.

Although the networks evolved from different starting points—some from conversations, courses, or consultations (examples are the League of Professional Schools and the Southern Maine Partnership) and others with high purpose and then figuring out how to engage their membership in working toward the goals (examples are the National Network for Educational Renewal, the Consortium for Educational Change, the Mission Valley Consortium, and Foxfire)—the idea or focus of the network founders eventually became a superordinate goal for the group. Ideas were usually broadly formulated in ways that left much room for learning, teaching, shaping, and inventing. A strong sense developed in the group that working together in this way would be of mutual importance to its members and the institutions from which they came (for example, school-university educators, cross-role groups, groups of districts, people of like mind in geographically distant places).

The networks developed in a number of different ways. For some it was a slowly evolving process in which one activity gave rise to another and eventually led to the need for a more systematic way of connecting. For example, Foxfire began teaching summer classes to teachers from a variety of school settings. As it became clear over time that these teachers needed support during the year, the Foxfire Teacher Outreach Network was created. In contrast, the National Network for Educational Renewal originated with the explicit purpose of linking the restructuring of schools with the simultaneous renewal of teacher education. It was this goal itself that necessitated the formation of partnerships between teacher education institutions and schools. In an example of a third pattern we observed—where strong leaders were able to attract and bring together people who were willing to follow their vision—the League of Professional Schools began with Carl Glickman's passion to develop schools as democracies. A relationship began with one school seeking a consultation with Glickman, but eventually grew to encompass over one hundred schools that embraced his democratic vision. A fourth pattern, where networks were formed to support educators as they tried to develop and support their reform ideas in a hostile environment, is illustrated by the Center for Collaborative Education in New York City. This network was organized to protect and support several alternative elementary and secondary schools that were multiaged, student centered, heterogeneously grouped, and developing strong school-based accountability measures within a large urban, highly bureaucratized system. Table 10.1 captures the variety of the purposes, participants, and contexts of the reform networks we studied.

Theme 2: Building Collaboration, Consensus, and Commitment

Networks derive great power and energy from the possibility that they offer members a voice in creating and sustaining a group in which their professional identity and interests are valued. Norms of participation and leadership support agendas that are responsive to the members and their particular needs in ways that most educational institutions are not, yet the very egalitarian quality that draws people to networks can be a source of tension. Most educators have spent their professional lives in school organizations that expect self-sufficiency in the classroom but dependence on outside sources for expertise. The transition to working interdependently is not always easy. In the Four Seasons Network, for example, teachers listened to the ideas of experts concerning assessment as if the experts could provide them with all the answers. When those same teachers began to organize regional conferences on assessment, however, they recognized that their own peers also had a significant contribution to make to the understanding of assessment practices. As one teacher commented, "When I was first in Four Seasons, I thought the gurus were the only ones who knew anything. It took a while before I felt that I had something important to say and that I was an expert too."

The ways in which people are brought together affects the interplay between participants' developing relationships with each other and with the ideas that will form the basis of their work. Collaborative relationships build trust, essential to the development of ideas, and ideas build network interest and participation as they themselves are transformed by the participants and fed back into the network (Schön, 1977). In the process, people become committed to each other and to larger ideas and ideals that expand their world and their work.

As some participants commented:

For several years we met once a month over dinner. University professors would find an appropriate article, and the groups would eat and discuss ideas. There was no attempt to prescribe anything. People would take the ideas and the format back to their school and create similar discussions.

Regional networks grew out of a real need to provide a support system for teachers after they have taken a summer course on the Foxfire way of teaching and learning. These became a lifeline for the teachers.

Regardless of how these networks evolved, the initial relationships seemed to involve meetings, conversations, or activities that created opportunities for people to gain information while receiving psychological support (Parker, 1979). Whether original purposes were broad or narrow, focused or only loosely defined, seems of less importance than the fact of people being brought together who felt that what they were doing was worthwhile and productive. This contrasts with many conventional professional development efforts because of the nature of the activities that are mounted, the relationships among the participants, their participation in shaping the network's work, and the perceived opportunities for personal and professional development afforded by the network.

Theme 3: Activities and Relationships as Important Building Blocks

The activities that a network sponsors are designed to serve the collaborative's purposes, which include building relationships among participants. At the DEWEY leadership academy, members not only listened to experts but presented their own work to peers and made connections with participants from other districts who shared their problems and concerns. The summer workshops, sponsored by Four Seasons, offered presentations by experts, but also built the substance of the conference experience around work that the participants did together. Professional Development Schools (PDS) based the shape of its collaboration on work done in problem-solving sessions attended by the representatives of their school-university partnerships.

Activities like these serve different levels of interrelated purposes. Speakers provide information and inspiration, conferring a sense of validation by an outside authority. But because the design of collaborative activities is driven by participants' needs and interests, they can also focus on their own particular issues by giving people alternative ways of thinking and acting. In this process activities build identification with a larger group of colleagues and commitment to purposes beyond one's own classroom, school, or district. They support the sort of reciprocity that motivates members to contribute to the larger project, believing that it will be helpful to their individual work as well (Kadushin, 1976, p. 36).

Most problems in education are not solved by the mechanical application of simplistic schemes or panaceas. Peer presentations have the advantage of offering insights into the complexities of the process from colleagues who share comparable goals and constraints. (Four Seasons teachers found collaboration essential to their progress on assessment work; the PDS network had a much better vision statement after the contribution of all of its participants.)

But the effects of collaboration extend in many directions. Working actively with others strengthens the investment that participants have in the network; the work becomes quite literally their own. Connecting with other members across schools, institutions, roles, and geography enables participants to develop more complex views of the issues they are concerned about and encourages them to take different perspectives and different ways of knowing into account (Granovetter, 1973). One leader commented, "What the schools were seeing and hearing from each other was more powerful than any facilitation. It opened up worlds to people. There were things they never thought about and had never imagined."

Collaboration within the network develops the skills of communication, negotiation, and accommodation that members need to translate their ideas into proposals for school change outside the network. While participating in the many connecting activities that are involved in this work, they develop relationships that bind them more closely to the goals of the larger group; for a network is built on its relationships.

As some network leaders said:

You really have to focus on relationships first, then create structures. All this is part of creating an environment that has multiple entry points.

Reading *Experience and Education* [Dewey, 1938] together turned out to be the most valuable thing we did because it engaged teachers in the "whys," not just the "hows." This speaks to teachers' personal values as well as what they do in their class.

Engaging educators in activities in which they learn to work interdependently, reflect on their practice, value their own expertise, play leadership roles, and respond flexibly to unanticipated problems and opportunities is as central to the purposes of networks as it is to the processes of school reform.

Sometimes the gap between the norms of the network and the professional expectations of the schools can be the source of some tension. Educators, accustomed to meetings and staff development activities for which someone else provides the agenda and leads the session, may initially perceive the more open-ended style of network gatherings as too loose or unstructured. Activities that draw on participants rather than experts for professional knowledge may be experienced as "sharing ignorance." Networks try to transcend these perceptions and provide meaningful professional experiences that are based on collaboration. But who facilitates the changes in norms and expectations? How do the activities get organized? Who makes it all happen?

Theme 4: Leadership—Cross-Cultural Brokering, Facilitating, and Keeping the Values Visible

Two network leaders described the way the perceive their role.

I really strive to operate democratically. The organization is never dependent on a single person. The leadership function is to articulate the values and help people work through how to express them.

I keep my ear to the ground. I'm a teacher! I see the network as a big class. I spend a lot of time with personal relationships fighting to protect the emergent, reciprocal stance that has become normative.

Leadership may be one of the least-studied aspects of networks, coalitions, and partnerships. Although Parker (1977) speaks about a facilitator of a network, he gives few details as to what this means and what facilitators actually do. As federal programs concerned with education increased during the 1970s, there was talk about linking schools with universities in ways that anticipated a form many networks are taking today. In these arrangements the leadership role was often defined as a person who was what Crandall (1977) called a "linking agent."

Leadership appears to be important in ways that are sometimes not readily apparent to the network constituency, perhaps because of the subtle quality of what leaders do, as well as what they encourage others to do. The functions of leadership include both backstage and onstage work in the development of collaborative arrangements and activities that help stimulate the network and move it forward. Brokering, facilitating, and organizing are functions common to the leaders of the networks we studied, but the styles and particulars varied by network. We discovered how layered the leadership role is and how tied it is to relationships, activities, and setting.

At times facilitating networks appears to be about making telephone calls, raising money, establishing connections, forming groups, finding places to meet, and brokering resources and people. However, it is also about creating public spaces in which educators can work together in ways that are different in quality and kind from their institutions, as well as from much that is considered standard professional development. It may be building structures that encourage a respectful dialogue between and among school and university personnel, or modeling more collaborative stances toward learning and support, enunciating important ideals (as in the National Network for Educational Renewal, Foxfire, and the League of Professional Schools), or leaving room for emergent goals (as in the Southern Maine Partnership, the Breadloaf Rural Teacher Network, and the Consortium for Educational Change). As five of our network leaders put it, it is about "providing a challenge, not a delivery of services"; "figuring out how to push people along and give them what they want at the same time"; "understanding the tension between the values of the network and the problems of the field"; "facilitating teachers' work outside, so that they can make changes inside"; and "keeping the focus on the partnership way of doing work." It is also about figuring out how to sustain these networks and help them develop and deepen their work while the education dollar continues to shrink.

Theme 5: Dealing with the Funding Problem

Of the sixteen networks studied, fourteen received significant or complete support from private or corporate foundations. The two that did not were started by constituents in the public school system (the Mission Valley Consortium and the Consortium for Educational Change, the former initiated as a collaboration among three school districts and the latter by a regional branch of the Illinois National Education Association). Those networks with sources of support in addition to foundations received money from universities (six networks), the U.S. Department of Education (two networks), the National Education Association (one network), and participating school systems (two networks).

Three-fourths of the network representatives who contributed to the study affirmed that the struggle to find funding was an important part of their story. In some instances the pursuit of funding helped to create the network because it encouraged prospective constituents to share available moneys more broadly by forming a network. (The Elementary Teachers' Network in New York City is an example.) Alternatively funders built networking into the conditions of the grant (as with the funding of the DEWEY network).

Foundation funding can also produce great tensions for networks. Matthew Miles's (1978, p. 33) admonition of twenty years ago—that finding primary funding outside the collaboration can be "fatal"—still stands. The Network of Progressive Educators struggled over its very name, with many members arguing that the word *progressive* would be unappealing to prospective funders. (It might indeed have contributed to the difficulty of getting funds.) In another instance, a funder felt entitled to exert ongoing influence on the emphasis a network placed on each of its multiple goals. Often the needs of many foundations for an assessment that documents outcomes can be at odds with the process-oriented work of many networks. One interviewee said, "No one wants to pay the bill for a network. The problem is wired in. It's not clear to anyone who the beneficiaries of a network are and what the outcomes should be. All the data are soft."

Learning in networks can be powerful, but it is often indirect: a result of new commitments and friendships, the exposure to new ideas, contacts with and observation of others' work, long-term involvement with many kinds of educators, growing cosmopolitanism, and openness to ideas. This view of learning presents a measurement and evaluation problem that has not yet been solved in ways that satisfy the expectations of many funders or confirm the concrete experiences of those who view reform networks as the most appropriate forms for professional growth and learning.

THE POWER AND FRAGILITY OF NETWORKS: NEGOTIATING THE TENSIONS

Tensions occurred consistently within all of these networks. From our perspective the dynamics inherent in these tensions appeared to be central to the process of how networks organize, build new structures, learn to collaborate, and develop a sense of community. Although the resolutions to these tensions were heavily influenced by the context and character of each network—sometimes obscuring their similarities—the tensions themselves were common to all of them.

The tensions included negotiating between the purpose of the network and the dailiness of the activities that constitute network work; dealing with the balance between inside knowledge and outside knowledge; creating a structure to resolve contradictions between centralization and decentralization; moving from informality and flexibility to more formal and rigid forms as the network grew; and making decisions about how inclusive or exclusive membership policy should be. We look at each of these.

1. *Meaningful or Emergent Purpose or Compelling Activities*. Initially networks attract participants who agree with their stated purposes, which in some cases may represent lofty ideals or long-standing aspirations. Examples are the National Network for Educational Renewal, which focuses on the simultaneous renewal of teacher education and the restructuring of schools, and the League of Professional Schools, dedicated to creating democratic schools. Alternatively compelling purposes can be driven by ideas that promise to transform classroom practice in specific ways. The Four Seasons network focused on assessment, and the Breadloaf Rural Teacher Network focused on the writing process and literacy. Educators with shared philosophies often form networks. The Network of Progressive Educators and the North Dakota Study Group are made up of members committed to the principles of progressive education; educators in the Center for Collaborative Education are bound together by a commitment to child-centered education.

Other networks, made up of several different groups with different roles or perspectives, may decide to work together in the interests of improving schools before they have developed an all-embracing philosophy. The Consortium for Educational Change links school district administrators with the teachers' union, while the Mission Valley Consortium brings teachers and administrators together across building and district lines. Some networks have a single focus. Foxfire's commitment is to developing literacy teaching, while Harvard's Principals' Center[3] provides primary support to building administrators. There are networks that have a more systemic mission. Both the DEWEY network and the National Network for Educational Renewal are committed to a model of school reform that engages them with the institution at every level.

However, no matter what the purpose of the network, the nature of the activities and the growth of relationships within the group appear to be the crucial elements in cementing the commitment of the participants. Activities have to be compelling enough to keep people coming back, no matter how meaningful or well intentioned the purposes of the network.

2. *Inside Knowledge and Outside Knowledge.* Whatever their purpose, networks must take a stance on what and whose knowledge should inform the work of the network. This is particularly true for educational reform networks, which are often trying to forge connections between communities and different role groups that encompass a variety of perspectives and have different ways of knowing, developing, and using knowledge (Lytle and Cochran-Smith, 1992). Teacher and principal knowledge developed in the context of their work is of a

different order from the knowledge of university researchers or that of outside experts. Simply reading and studying outside knowledge may fail to help participants make connections to the world of practice as they experience and live it in their particular contexts. But while networks have to find ways to accommodate these different ways of knowing, a network that deals only with experiential or context-specific knowledge may cut itself off from knowledge that inspires new ideas, expands personal and professional vision, or helps teachers and administrators invent new techniques and processes for improving their practices. In the worst of situations, participants might "just be sharing ignorance."

Most networks try to embrace both inside and outside knowledge. The synthesis is affected by what the purposes are, how participants are involved with practical and conceptual ideas, and where the knowledge and ideas come from. As interviewees said:

> The work must be driven by questions of practice. A few times we have sought out "experts" but this was only when we got started. Students and teachers have become their own experts.

> For awhile the postulates focused the work, but the dilemma is when to push for further success on values or when to accept a practical adaptation.

One of the fundamental differences between networks and conventional professional development activities is that the content knowledge of school-based educators and outside knowledge are both acknowledged as important sources for agenda building. How and when these resources are used has to do with the purposes, the context, and the organizational arrangements of the network's central governing group and its participants. Juggling inside and outside knowledge to keep the agenda in creative tension is a hallmark of networks that learn to sustain their members' interest and commitment.

3. *Centralization and Decentralization.* Some networks are loose federations of people who come together to support, discuss, and learn together (for example, the Network of Progressive Educators and the International Network of Principals' Centers); others create tighter structures and build norms of membership by working to internalize explicit goals (such as the League of Professional Schools and National Network for Educational Renewal). Some form for specific—even local—purposes, subsequently broadening their agendas as the networks' roots take hold (examples are Breadloaf, Foxfire, and Harvard Principals' Center).

Each organizational tendency suggests a complementary style of organization: centralized, decentralized, or what we might call evolving. The forms are not always rigidly adhered to, however, since their effectiveness might be reduced. For example, a typical "district office" approach might be very efficient, but fail to involve the membership in helping to shape the work. A totally grass-roots approach, on the other hand, might promote a committed membership but fail to link with other partners who have different perspectives, different knowledge bases, or different ways of working. An effective network organization creates ways to engage participants directly in the governance and leadership of the organization, while maintaining the flexibility to organize complex and potentially far-reaching operations.

4. *From Informality and Flexibility to Formality and Rigidity.* Because networks are not tied to district specifications and particular in-service days, they are freer to create informal mechanisms to bring people together—serving food at meetings, perhaps, or meeting over dinner; they can also set aside whole days for conferences or convene retreats in more isolated settings. Networks develop their own ways of working, depending on context or character, often designing unique and informal ways of communicating and meeting that become particularly associated with their network work. For many years the core activity of the Network of Progressive Educators has been an annual meeting with inside and outside speakers who legitimate and support progressive education practices while intellectually challenging the membership. Additionally, the National Network for Educational Renewal creates task forces, sponsors special regional conferences, and, where appropriate, makes use of the expertise of consultants. The League of Professional Schools began by organizing a congress to represent its member schools, and the Southern Maine Partnership started with an activity it calls "dine and discuss." The tension arises as the network matures: trying to sustain the flexible forms of work that are a source of its strength, the network central office or leadership often tries to institutionalize them so that they will endure. To give conferences, money must be raised, people must be hired, and rooms must be rented. To develop collaboration across schools, districts, or role groups, activities must be organized and facilitated, and work must be coordinated. The energy, initiative, peer support, and trust developed informally within each network are often threatened as the organization seeks ways to stabilize and expand (Miles, 1978, p. 43). The more success that networks experience, the more they reach out to other areas and the more pressure they feel to expand their bureaucracy. Protecting what makes a network special becomes more difficult as it grows, requiring time, effort, and, most of all, creative solutions to the problems of success.

5. *Inclusivity and Exclusivity of Membership.* At different times in a network's life, criteria are established for membership that are explicitly or implicitly shaped by the purposes of the network. Is the central purpose of a network to bring together like-minded people who will develop and expand members' knowledge? Such a group might restrict membership to educators who already share a particular perspective. Is it to provide a way of talking across districts to share resources and improve schools? In such a network efforts would be made to enlist

the broadest possible base of participation. Should anyone who wants to join be allowed to become a member? In a network intended to induct the uninitiated into new ways of thinking about education, membership is actively recruited. All networks have to determine who should be included in their membership and how expansive the network feels about recruiting new members.

These decisions lead to dealing with the problem of how to socialize new members into the network. Some provide specific activities for new members (League of Professional Schools, Breadloaf) that help to define membership, while others provide activities that are always open to new members (South Maine Partnership, Consortium for Educational Change). Regional networks often reach a point where size becomes a problem; sometimes instead of growing larger, they encourage the formation of new networks that share their vision and purpose, thereby gaining new organizational partners.

WHAT WE HAVE LEARNED:
UNDERSTANDINGS AND QUESTIONS

Although each of these networks, partnerships, and coalitions is unique, growing out of the specifics of its context, purpose, and participants, they all have to deal with similar themes and tensions in their formation and development (Miles, 1978; Rosenbaum, 1977; Goodlad, 1977; Parker, 1977; Peterson, 1977). Our interviewees, in reconstructing many years of experience, spoke not only of their successes but with great candor about the fragility of their networks and the problems that were a part of the process of creating and sustaining them. However, despite acknowledging the problems, they stressed their perception of the powerful effects these networks have on their members.

First, teachers and administrators are given opportunities to label, articulate, and share the tacit knowledge that they have developed through their work. Networks encourage the sharing of this knowledge, which gives their members greater access to "just-in-time learning"—learning that is tied to the actual work educators do. This also has the effect of dignifying and giving shape to the substance of what teachers share: dailiness of work that may be invisible to outsiders but binds insiders together. Networks are particularly good at helping school-based educators reveal and work on current problems, even as they are learning new ideas and building new relationships.

Second, networks have the flexibility to organize activities first, letting the structures needed to support those activities follow, instead of the other way around. This does not mean that networks are necessarily loose or structureless, but rather that they are not locked into permanent mechanisms. Several interviewees spoke about how they had originally organized conversations, task forces, or study groups that were very popular for awhile and then ceased to be of interest to their members. They were dropped, but often reappeared a year or so later in a new iteration. This kind of responsiveness to the network participants provides for a more developmental approach to member learning, empowers its members to voice their approval or disapproval (giving them the feeling that the network is responsive to their perspective), and encourages a more personal and professional connection to their own learning.

Third, we found that these networks were attempting to shift the meaning of adult learning away from prescription toward challenging involvement and problem solving. They tried to achieve goals of participant learning and professional competence by modeling different modes of inquiry, supporting the formation of teams to create and write school-based plans for change, finding mechanisms to encourage cross-role groups to work together, focusing deeply on particular topics, and inviting the participants to help shape the agenda in their own terms. This shift is significant in many ways, not least because it gives voice to those who have usually been the recipients of the agendas of others.

Fourth, although each of the networks we studied had a formal leader, there were numerous opportunities for members to take leadership roles. They could do this formally—as site coordinators, regional directors, partnership associates, and network coordinators—or informally—as teacher scholars, proposal writers, organizers, and experts in newly acquired knowledge. Where leadership roles are possible for many network members regardless of their status, different norms and roles emerge that serve to strengthen the commitment of members to the network, broaden their vision of its roles and possibilities, and enlarge the scope of their personal and professional associations.

Fifth, networks provide numerous examples of collaboration among their members. Learning to work across role groups has never been easy. Schools, as they are currently organized, do not give people many opportunities to work collaboratively; networks almost always expect participants to collaborate. Indeed expectations and opportunities to learn how to work together may be the reason many of these networks become so compelling to their members (McLaughlin and Talbert, 1993). They provide authentic examples of professional community built around shared work, shared interest, and shared struggle. The League of Professional Schools requires that member schools form a school site planning committee made up of teachers, administrators, and parents. Breadloaf expects teachers to share their work and learn from one another. The Principals' Center expects principals to frame problems, share strategies, and learn from one another as a result of their network participation. Such communities legitimate a search for alternative solutions to complex educational problems that have no simple or universally agreed-on answers (Little, 1983; Lieberman, 1995; Darling-Hammond and McLaughlin, 1995).

Sixth, when networks, coalitions, and partnerships last long enough to create ongoing learning communities, cultures based on mutual knowledge, learning, and collaboration replace the transmission of knowledge from one institution to another. These cultures, focused on critical issues of school reform, place educational practice at their center, providing the kind of social and professional nourishment that leads many members to invest time, effort, and commitment far beyond what they give to the usual professional development opportunities. Networks encourage large visions, and their flexibility, reliance on more egalitarian relationships, and norms of collaboration can make them seem more like movements than mere organizations. At a time when schools are not well supported yet under tremendous pressures to do more and do it better, these collaborative cultures offer their members social support, the sharing of knowledge, and the mobilization of collective resources (Rosenbaum, 1977, p. 5).

QUESTIONS FOR FURTHER STUDY

It is in the nature of exploratory work that new questions emerge as information is gathered and analyzed. We briefly discuss some of these that require further study.

Prominent Leadership

Over half the leaders we interviewed are well known and of great importance to people concerned with educational practice and improvement. Some networks, although they have an official name, are even known to their members by their leader's name. This suggests more than a casual attachment to the founders and the difficulty of building structures that will last after they leave. Institutionalizing routines and structures may seem to be the antithesis of what makes networks work, but can a network maintain itself without building some kinds of structures? How can a network keep the core of what makes it special when its founder leaves? Are networks leadership dependent, even though their purpose is to work toward more egalitarian relationships and shared leadership responsibilities?

Temporary Systems or New Models for Professional Community?

Are reform networks and partnerships temporary systems that exist only as effective ways to influence change in education, or are they new models of professional communities that can have a life of their own? Some of the networks we studied were over twelve years old and still growing and changing. A number of them were able to take advantage of funding opportunities to deepen their work as they matured. (Breadloaf and Southern Maine Partnership are involved in the Annenberg Rural Challenge and are recognized as having expertise in organizing rural networks.) Some networks were content to remain a loose coalition of like-minded participants, and others languished as their influence diminished over time. Are the professional communities that last somehow better suited to a different paradigm for learning and school reform, as some contemporary scholars suggest (Little, 1983; Lytle and Cochran-Smith, 1992; McLaughlin and Talbert, 1993)?

Funding

Fifteen of the sixteen networks we studied sought and received external funding. Those with university connections often had to fight to convince the university to pay its share and support the network, even when the network was meeting or exceeding its goals. Some interviewees complained that funders wanted to use the network for purposes that distorted what made the network special to its members (for example, using schools in the network for a research study not initiated by the network). How does a network maintain its integrity if it has problems pleasing its primary funders? And alternatively, how does a parent organization support a network that does not always follow its direction?

Single Focus–Single Role versus Systemic Focus–Multiple Roles

Our sample included single-focused networks with participants who were either teachers or principals (Foxfire, Principals' Center, Breadloaf) and networks that embraced larger communities of schools, districts, and other multiple institutions where participants were from all levels of the organization. Single-focused networks seemed easier to mount and run, and even to spread more rapidly. They are strong on what their participants learn, sometimes providing transformative experiences, yet because of their lack of breadth, they may fail to provide adequate support for their membership on their return to their own institution; even with this support, returning teachers rarely effect change beyond their own classroom. Networks that are made up of schools, entire districts, or interinstitutional relationships must struggle with how to make their network powerful, not just for one role group but for many. This makes the agenda, leadership, and focus far more diffuse and complicated. When it works, the whole system is involved and moving in the same direction. In stark terms the choice is this: Should effort be put into forming a network with a manageable agenda and a workable single-focused idea, or into a network with a complicated systemic agenda—difficult to manage and lead—involving people who play multiple roles, in situations where new learning and authentic change has a greater chance to affect whole institutions? Perhaps single-focused networks can expand their focus and work toward systemic changes, or maybe networks can come together, deepening their individual and collective work. Several of these choices are already happening in a few instances.

Measuring the Impact of Network Participation

Are principals more effective? Are teachers teaching better? Are students learning more? These are the bottom-line questions that funders ask when they give money to support networks. Yet as we have seen, network activity and success must be measured by understanding and tracking the connections among member involvement, learning, and active participation, as well as by observing changes in practice. Since it is always difficult to measure the relationships between cause and effect in school improvement, how can network participation and changed practice be documented to assure funders, politicians, and the public that this is a worthwhile investment?

Scaling Up or Losing Focus

If a network is successful, why not make it available and accessible to all those who seek membership? Often what makes networks special to their members are the norms, activities, and relationships that allow people to feel that they have had a significant part in shaping the work. Personal identification with and commitment to the network's purposes, and to one's own professional development, are the defining characteristics of successful networks. Some networks protect what is special about their group with clearly defined socializing experiences for new members (such as school site plans, six-week summer sessions, or a beginning course that introduces members to the core values of the network). Others count on slow-growing norms of participation that have a unique staying power of their own (such as "the partnership way" and "democratic schools"). How far can these ideas be spread without losing the power of what they mean to their members? How much do people need to experience to feel that they are a part of a network? The larger the network, the more organization-like the problems and the less network-like the participation. Where is the breaking point?

PROFESSIONAL DEVELOPMENT IN TRANSITION

The study of these sixteen networks has allowed us to explore how networks take shape and develop and to delineate the issues that crop up in organizing and maintaining them. Our look across networks helps us to understand their strong contextual nature, their infinite variety of purpose and character, and their similar organizational tensions. Regardless of their individual differences, they appear to have in common the ways in which they bring people together and organize their work: agendas that are more often challenging than prescriptive; learning that is more indirect than direct; formats for work more collaborative than individualistic; attempts at change more integrated than fragmented; approaches to leadership more facilitative than directive; thinking that is more multiperspective than uniperspective; valuing both context-specific knowledge and generalized knowledge; and structurally and philosophically more movement-like than organization-like. At a time when schools are reinventing themselves to serve a changing society, these problematic yet powerful third spaces are becoming an important force for reform in American education.

Notes

1. Both of us have had a great deal of experience in educational reform networks as participants and creators of networks. One of us is the codirector of NCREST and the other has been a long-term member of a national network for secondary school change. We came to this inquiry with experience, hunches, and a strong interest in understanding how to think about and frame what educational networks are and why they are so difficult to describe.

2. All quotations are from network leaders we interviewed.

3. The Harvard Principals' Center is based at Harvard University and made up of school principals from the Boston area. The International Network of Principals' Centers grew out of the Harvard organization, but is now quite distinct. As a network of networks, its geographic neighborhood is boundless.

References

Crandall, D. C. "Training and Supporting Linking Agents." In N. Nash and J. Culbertson (eds.), *Linking Processes in Educational Improvement* (pp. 189–274). Columbus, Ohio: University Council for Educational Administration, 1977.

Darling-Hammond, L., and McLaughlin, M. "Policies That Support Professional Development in an Era of Reform." In *Practices and Policies to Support Teacher Development in an Era of Reform* (pp. 21–39). New York: NCREST, 1995.

Dewey, J. *Experience and Education.* New York: Collier Books, 1938.

Goodlad, J. I. "Networking and Educational Improvement: Reflections on a Strategy." Paper presented for the Networking Conference, NIE's School Capacity for Problem Solving Group. Washington, D.C.: National Institute on Education, Mar. 1977.

Granovetter, M. S. "The Strength of Weak Ties." *American Journal of Sociology,* 1973, *78*(6), 1360–1380.

Granovetter, M. S. "The Strength of Weak Ties: A Network Theory Revisited." *Sociological Theory,* 1983, *1*(2), 201–233.

Kadushin, C. "Introduction to the Theory of Macro-Network Analysis." Unpublished manuscript. New York: Columbia University, 1976.

Lieberman, A. "Practices That Support Teacher Development: Transforming Conceptions of Teacher Learning." *Phi Delta Kappan,* 1995, *76*(8), 591–596.

Lieberman, A., and McLaughlin, M. "Networks for Educational Change: Powerful and Problematic." *Phi Delta Kappan,* 1992, *73*(9), 673–677.

Little, J. W. *Teachers' Professional Development in a Climate of Educational Reform.* NCREST Reprint Series. New York: NCREST, 1983.

Lytle, S. L., and Cochran-Smith, M. (eds.). *Inside-Outside: Teacher Research and Knowledge.* New York: Teachers College Press, 1992.

McLaughlin, M. W., and Talbert, J. *Contexts That Matter for Teaching and Learning.* Stanford, Calif.: Center for Research on the Context of Secondary School Teaching, 1993.

Miles, M. "On Networking." Unpublished manuscript. Washington, D.C.: National Institute of Education, Center for Policy Research, 1978.

Nash, N., and Culbertson, J. (eds.). *Linking Processes in Educational Improvement.* Columbus, Ohio: University Council for Educational Administration, 1977.

Parker, A. "Networks for Innovation and Problem Solving and Their Use for Improving Education: A Comparative Overview." Unpublished manuscript. Washington, D.C.: National Institute of Education, School Capacity for Problem Solving, 1977.

Parker, A. "Some Challenges for Disseminators Building Networks." Speech delivered at the National Seminar, Networking: An Essential Dissemination Process, Washington, D.C., Oct. 3, 1979.

Peterson, P. "Schools, Groups and Networks: A Political Perspective." Unpublished manuscript. Washington, D.C.: National Institute of Education, Network Development Staff, School Capacity for Problem Solving Group, 1977.

Rosenbaum, A. "Social Networks as a Political Resource: Some Insights Drawn from the Community Organizational and Community Action Experiences." Unpublished manuscript. Washington, D.C.: National Institute of Education, Network Development Staff, School Capacity for Problem Solving Group, 1977.

Sarason, S. B., and Lorentz, E. *The Challenge of the Resource Exchange Network.* San Francisco: Jossey-Bass, 1979.

Schön, D. A. "Network Related Intervention." Unpublished manuscript. Washington, D.C.: National Institute of Education, Center for Policy Research, 1977.

Sirotnik, K., and Goodlad, J. (eds.). *School-University Partnerships in Action: Concepts, Cases and Concerns.* New York: Teachers College Press, 1988.

PART FOUR

RETHINKING POLICY
FOR TEACHER LEARNING

CHAPTER ELEVEN

Organizing the Other Half of Teaching

Julia E. Koppich and Charles Taylor Kerchner

In big cities and small towns, rural communities and suburbs, in the thirty-four states that have collective bargaining laws and in those that do not, public school teachers continue to join the American Federation of Teachers (AFT) and the National Education Association (NEA). Teaching is, in fact, the most unionized occupation in the United States. The AFT and NEA are large, powerful, politically influential, and vocal. Yet thoughtful consideration of the productive role these organizations might play in reshaping American education has largely been absent from the debate about school reform.

The unions' sharpest critics paint the AFT and NEA as principal barriers to education improvement. They advocate eliminating collective bargaining (or at least greatly reducing its scope) as at least a powerful palliative, if not the cure for what ails American education. The unions' staunchest defenders portray the organizations as the last best line of defense against the infidels who would destroy public schools. The research community largely ignores them (Bradley, 1996).

We believe teacher unions have vast and largely untapped potential to catalyze a revitalized system of public schooling in this nation. But before unions can be catalysts for fundamental change in the institution of education, they must first transform themselves. These unions have been successful at organizing the

---

This chapter, prepared for the National Commission on Teaching and America's Future, was adapted from Kerchner, C. T., Koppich, J. E., and Weeres, J. W. *United Mind Workers: Unions and Teaching in the Knowledge Society.* San Francisco: Jossey-Bass, 1997.

first half of the occupation—salaries and working conditions. Now we argue that they must organize the second half—the actual work of teaching. Unions must shift their emphasis from organizing around work rule standardization, job control, and member protection to organizing around quality, schools, and a flexible labor market for teachers.

THE IMPETUS FOR REFORM

We place ourselves firmly in the camp of those who believe large-scale change must come to American education. We arrive at this position not simply because American students' scores on national or international exams (the National Assessment of Educational Progress, the Third International Mathematics Study, for example) are disappointing, though indeed they are. Rather, we are convinced that the institutional structure of schooling in this nation is ill suited to the new American imperatives.

Fundamental changes are taking place in the organization of society and the economy. One need not look very far to see the wrenching of a society in transition. The rapid shift from an industrial economy, to a service-based economy, to an economy increasingly dependent on "smart workers" with high-level technological skills has both redefined America's industrial base and produced a widening gap between the economic haves and have-nots. We are entering what has been dubbed the knowledge era in which the strategic use and manipulation of information increasingly will be a source of wealth and power. Concurrently the devolution of governmental authority and responsibility to state and local entities, part of the "reinventing government" trend, is tearing at the fabric of decades-old social policy, reshaping the arena of public versus private responsibility.

These changes will cause fundamental reorganization of education. Preparing students to meet the workplace challenges of the new century requires a much different education system from the one created for and adequate to an economy based on farms and factories. Policy taste for devolving authority will continue to create pressure on the traditional education hierarchy to move decisions to local schools and communities.

At the core, many of the necessary changes in education are about reorganizing learning. What is learning, who is capable of learning, and what is the responsibility of teachers in creating learning? We call these relationships the instructional core of education. The instructional core contains the transactions between teachers and students, books and blackboards, corridors and curriculum, through which learning takes place.

Changes in the instructional core will, we believe, cause major dislocations in the way schools are organized and governed. The schools we have now rest on behavioral psychology. The behaviorists conceived of the mind as a kind of black box. Learning could be broken down into a series of small steps, the process was basically sequential, and all students would learn in the same way, at the same rate, and with the same results.

Since World War II, however, behavioral approaches to learning have been increasingly challenged by the rise of cognitive science, which has provided new and dramatic insights into how the brain functions and how children learn. We know now that the mind is not a black box. The brain creates its own mental images, interpreting and reinterpreting reality. Learning, we have come to understand, is enormously complex and often quite nonlinear. The same teaching methods or the same teaching materials do not necessarily produce the same results in all students.

This volatile combination—rapid changes in workplace requirements and emerging knowledge about how learning happens—portends a new role for teachers. Teachers must become knowledge workers, able to synthesize and create knowledge in their classrooms, able to diagnose students' instructional needs, and adapt strategies and materials to students' particular learning styles, able to provide students with the requisite skills that will serve them well in their years after schooling ends. Teachers must have autonomy, but that freedom to teach must be framed by a well-developed, and continuously improving, knowledge of practice.

SCHOOLS, UNIONS, AND THE INDUSTRIAL TRADITION

It has often been said that American schools are based on the factory model. Although schools do not operate as factories, industrial assumptions came to rule education decisions. The idea that bigger was better drove the consolidation of school districts in rural areas and the unification of districts in cities. The number of school districts in the United States fell from 300,000 in the early 1900s to fewer than 15,000 today. The idea that specialization was efficient gave rise to high school departmentalization and separate career paths for teachers and administrators. The tenets of scientific management offered school administrators the mantle of technical expertise and clearly established their organizational superiority over teachers.

As teachers began to organize in increasing numbers, they too sought guidance in industrial examples. With the widespread advent of collective bargaining in the 1960s, the unions increasingly came to resemble their industrial forbears. Thus, both the AFT and NEA modeled their operation on the unions that had served American factory workers so well in the post–World War II period.

Teachers' contracts—districtwide agreements between teachers as represented by their union and local school boards—developed largely in response to centralized education decision making. As power and authority accrued to school district headquarters (and, not incidentally, was lodged firmly in the hands of administrators), so too did unions consolidate their efforts in master contracts to influence the terms and conditions of employment of those whom they represented. Viewed in this light, the centralized collective bargaining agreement appears as a rather rational development.

The contract is the vehicle through which the union establishes the rights of individual teachers and protects its members from arbitrary actions by the employer. Contracts establish teachers' rates of pay and benefit packages. They delineate procedures by which teachers who desire to transfer to a different school or a different assignment may do so. They outline agreements for setting the level of class sizes, define the length of teachers' salaried workday and work year, establish procedures for evaluating professional performance, and provide a mechanism for adjudicating procedural and substantive disputes that arise between teachers and the school or district administration.

Contracts are meant to create fairness in a bureaucracy. The union is deputized by its members to represent their economic interests, through salary and benefit arrangements, and to protect their employment security, through standardized work rules and districtwide personnel procedures. Negotiated agreements apply a districtwide template to teachers' conditions of employment. The same professional rules of engagement attach equally to all teachers in a given school district.

Collective bargaining also assumes a division of interests between labor and management. The union, through the contract, represents the economic and day-to-day work concerns of the employees. Management establishes policy and makes operational decisions. In other words, collective bargaining assumes that bread-and-butter issues of compensation, benefits, job security, and general conditions of employment are properly part of the employee's concern. The mission of the institution and the conduct of the work are not.

This presumed bifurcation of union-management interests is reinforced by the statutorily restricted scope of bargaining. State laws define those issues about which union and management can bargain and those that are excluded from negotiations. Thus, salaries, benefits, and transfer policies are bargainable; curriculum and education goals typically are not. The statutorily defined separation of interests contributes to adversarial union-management relations as both parties to the agreement spar over how to maximize the gains each seeks.

DRIFTING TOWARD CHANGE

Over the past decade and a half of education reform efforts, as the country began to shed industrialism and try to define its successor, unions too have attempted to confront their past and look toward the future. The late Albert Shanker, the AFT president whose tenure spanned twenty-two years, fought as loud and hard for rigor and high expectations from teachers as he did for general bread-and-butter issues. He became the catalyst for—and often the lightning rod in—the national debate on curriculum standards, certification examinations for teachers, and salary scales that reflect performance and professional responsibility.

In a February 1997 speech to the National Press Club, "A New Approach to Unionism—It's Not Your Mother's NEA" (Chase, 1997), that organization's president, Robert Chase, called for a "reinvention" of the union: "Industrial-style adversarial tactics are not suited to the next stage or reform," Chase declared as he pledged the union to build partnerships with administrators, work to improve school quality, and help incompetent teachers improve or remove them from the classroom.

TURN, the Teacher Union Reform Network, is an alliance of twenty-one presidents of large AFT and NEA locals that aims to "restructure the nation's teachers' unions to promote reforms that will ultimately lead to better learning and higher achievement for America's children" (Teacher Union Reform Network, 1996).

Local Efforts

Some local school districts have undertaken bold and visible efforts to change union practice in the name of new education imperatives. Most of these have centered on the union contract.

Labor scholars describe two modes of bargaining: distributive and integrative (Walton and McKersie, 1965). In *distributive negotiations,* the parties see the bargaining table as laden with items each side wants to claim, or preserve, for itself. Bargaining is about dividing up the spoils—money, rights, power—and carrying them away. *Integrative bargaining* focuses on union and management's seeking common roads for mutual benefit. The parties treat each other as professionals and consciously consider the issues that are important to both and the trade-offs each side can accept. It is this conception of negotiations that has given rise to locally based union reforms.

Dampening union-management conflict generally has been patterned on the principles of win-win bargaining. Popularized in *Getting to Yes* (1981) by Roger Fisher and William Ury of the Harvard Negotiation Project, the win-win approach promotes collaborative negotiations. "Hard on the problem, not hard on each other" is win-win's functional slogan, embraced by union and management adherents who work through the process of identifying common goals and "inventing options for mutual gain" that allow both sides to claim victory.

For some districts, *collaborative bargaining,* the generic name for win-win and its multiple spin-offs, has come to be viewed as an end in itself. Achieving union-management cordiality is the goal as negotiations then proceed, with rather predictable results, along the usual path of topics.

Other districts have understood that the reason to change the form of the relationship is not simply to alter the tenor of the discourse. In fact, union-management relations, although they do not need to be steeped in animosity permanently, are likely to be periodically conflictual as teachers assert rights and responsibilities lodged firmly in traditional management domains. These districts have endeavored to confront the more vexing—and ultimately more important—issues of what kinds of educational decisions are being made, the operating level at which they are struck, and the cumulative impact of these decisions on student achievement. Reforms generally have proceeded along three paths: joint union-management committees, educational policy trust agreements, and contract waivers.

Joint committees extend union-management decision making into relatively uncharted cooperative waters. Pittsburgh, Pennsylvania, established a joint committee to oversee the district's school-based management undertaking. In Cincinnati the union and the district removed the thorny issue of resolving class size disputes from the contract grievance procedure and placed it in the hands of a joint committee. The peer review system of Poway, California, is overseen by a committee composed of union and management representatives. Under the unique labor-management constitution of Glenview, Illinois, much of the district's decision making on instruction, personnel, and finance takes place in joint committees. Joint committees, then, are meant to expand the portfolio of the negotiated agreement and move substantive discussions of education policy and practice beyond the legally restricted scope of bargaining.

Trust agreements, legally binding bilateral accords that sit outside the collectively bargained contract, are designed to deal with issues that arguably fall outside the scope of bargaining (particularly important when discussions of legally allowable scope are likely to eclipse discussions of substance) or that are better handled in an arena less formal than negotiations with an outcome less rigid than a contract. A four-year-long California experiment involving twelve school districts resulted in union-management trust agreements covering issues such as peer review, professional development, and school site collaborative management and decision making. Another means of expanding union-management cooperative decision making, trust agreements also serve as vehicles for expanding the envelope of union involvement in education policy formation and implementation.

A few contracts have established procedures that enable individual schools to request *waivers* from specific portions of the agreement for school-determined educational reasons. For example, a school wants to experiment with some very large classes and some quite small ones, but that would violate the class size provision of the contract. A waiver provision allows the school to request relief from that portion of the agreement.

Tinkering at the Margins

Joint committees, trust agreements, and waivers are designed to loosen the constraints of the contract without losing the purpose of collective bargaining. They are meant to provide schools and teachers with new opportunities for flexibility and innovative instructional practice while preserving the routines and protections so key to industrial unionism. However, these reforms (some of which we have participated in and even led), no matter how faithfully conducted and thoughtfully executed, have failed to move unions and districts much beyond the education reform starting gate.

Trust agreements and joint committees expand the range of union-management discussion, but they are themselves centralized accords that tend to focus on preserving equity and extending teacher rights. Waivers, the clearest effort to decentralize decision-making authority, are enmeshed in their own web of rules.

Moreover, waivers, trust agreements, and joint operating committees sit outside the regular bureaucratic structure and have about them a perpetual air of impermanence. Generally accorded about equal status as other "pilot projects" in a school district, these efforts at reforming the labor-management relationship tend to be seen by teachers and administrators as temporary educational aberrations. The bureaucracy continues to operate as if little had changed. In the inevitable test of wills between change and the status quo, change invariably blinks first.

Finally, the problems these bargaining reforms endeavor to solve in practice are not the fundamental issues of educational quality and student achievement. It is these issues that unions must confront.

We return now to our point of departure. Teacher unions have organized teachers' economic lives and brought stability to working conditions. Now they have an opportunity to lead the transformation of education by embracing a new set of first principles of unionism: organizing around quality, organizing around schools, and organizing a flexible teacher labor market.

ORGANIZING AROUND QUALITY

Teachers care deeply about teaching and learning, and they know a great deal about how children learn and think and what it takes for students to achieve. But teaching is not organized to take advantage of this knowledge. The idea of the knowledge worker who creates, synthesizes, and interprets information dominates the literature on the modern workplace. Schools, however, still think that real expertise lies somewhere outside the classroom. Organizing around quality, then, is an expression of professional expertise, captured by two issues:

(1) advocating for and participating in the debate on standards for student achievement, and (2) establishing and maintaining standards of professional practice.

Standards for Students

The United States is engaged in a furious debate about what student learning standards should be, how we should measure them, and what kinds of rewards and consequences should attach to meeting or failing to meet them. By and large, teachers have been absent from this debate. Unions need to advocate for and enforce standards. They need to make it possible for teachers to lend their voices and their expertise to the debate.

The task for unions will not be an easy one. Teachers are chary of testing programs they have seen or experienced. They are aware, often painfully so, of the political tensions created by the standards debate. But teachers must be involved, for it is teachers who will be called on to implement any standards that are developed by doing the hard day-to-day work in classrooms over a sustained period of time.

Standards for Teaching

Unions can also link themselves to educational quality by developing and ensuring quality of teaching practice. Peer review is probably the most powerful demonstration of teacher creation and demonstration of a knowledge of practice. In the twenty or so districts that have tried it—Cincinnati; Rochester, New York; and Columbus, Ohio, for example—peer review brings higher standards to teaching. It significantly changes the conception of teaching work by recognizing the importance of engagement and commitment as well as skill and technique. It recognizes a legitimate role for teachers in establishing and enforcing standards in their own occupation. Peer review also fundamentally changes the role of the union. As Al Fondy, president of the Pittsburgh Federation of Teachers, notes, "It is not the primary purpose of the union to defend the least competent of its members."

Peer review began in 1981 when the Toledo, Ohio, schools and the Toledo Federation of Teachers added to their collective bargaining agreement a one-sentence clause by which teachers agreed to police the ranks of their veterans in return for the right to review the professional performance of new teachers. In the last decade and a half, peer review has spread among a number of progressive school districts.

Peer review brings higher standards to teaching in two ways. First, peer review systems generally have more resources, and thus put forward a more thorough system of evaluation, than do conventional administratively driven evaluation schemes. In districts with peer review plans, unions and districts negotiate substantial financial set-asides (approximately $2,000 for each teacher to be reviewed) for purposes of implementing the evaluation system.

Second, peer review systems link good teaching and professional development. The traditional evaluation system captures only a sliver of a teacher's work, principally that which can be observed in a brief administrative visit to a teacher's classroom. It is designed as a kind of checklist accountability system. Peer review, on the other hand, taps a broader segment of a teacher's professional portfolio through prolonged and extensive engagement with and observation by teaching colleagues and an emphasis on enhancing professional practice.

Most peer review systems are patterned after the Toledo plan. Novices are supervised, assisted, and evaluated by experienced teachers, who are selected in a competitive process by others who have done the same job. The evaluators, called consulting teachers, spend full time for up to three years in their positions as peer reviewers.

Another component of the peer review system involves the effort to assist experienced teachers "in trouble." Cooperating teachers work with these individuals, recommend a program of remediation, and at the end of a designated period of time assess the success of the improvements efforts.

In the case of both novices undergoing their early-years assessments and experienced teachers participating in the remediation (often called "intervention"), consulting teachers report to a joint union-management board of review, which makes recommendations to the district school board regarding the status of continuing employment for the teachers who have been evaluated.

Anecdotal evidence suggests that peer review is tougher than conventional administrator-driven evaluation. In the years that the Toledo program has been operating, approximately 6.4 percent of the new teachers resigned, were not renewed, or were terminated for inadequate performance. In the five years before the program began, when evaluation was conducted by administrators, only one new teacher was terminated (Dal Lawrence, personal communication, 1985).

There is no evidence that teachers will soft-pedal evaluation in order to save the jobs of colleagues. More than administrators, teachers bear the burden of incompetent colleagues. Evidence suggests clearly that unionized teachers will vote to fire other union members who are not living up to teacher-established standards of professional practice.

Peer review changes the stakes in evaluation. As Miles Myers, executive director of the National Council of Teachers of English and former president of the California Federation of Teachers, has observed, "Peer review forces teachers to define good teaching. Teachers have to be able to express good teaching in language that other teachers understand and accept" (Miles Myers, personal communication, 1996).

Peer review also represents a radical departure for teacher unions from established industrial norms in which evaluation is the province of school administrators. The union's role in this scenario is to watchdog the process and protect members from violations of their due process rights. Under peer review, the union's role becomes one of balancing protection of individual teachers with the protection of teaching.

We believe teachers have little to lose and much to gain from organizing around the quality dimensions of teaching. Peer review is capacity building for teachers and unions. It creates an important building block for using unionism to improve schools.

ORGANIZING AROUND SCHOOLS

Flexibility, creativity, the ability to adapt to changing circumstances, and an ethic of continuous improvement are hallmarks of successful modern organizations. These organizations develop a passion for quality and improvement. As they seek or create opportunities for growth, they are also highly responsive to their customers and clients. Individuals, work teams, and small operating units gain substantial autonomy about how work is to be done and how resources are to be used.

Public education has barely begin to adopt this organizational spirit. The evolution of school districts as centralized bureaucracies has created a structure, and an organizational demeanor, that stymies rather than supports change and innovation. Indeed it is hard to fathom a school district that could match the efficiency of a Federal Express, the innovativeness of a Saturn plant, the entrepreneurial corporate culture of a Hewlett-Packard. The structure of collective bargaining agreements tends to reify the centralized nature of decision making.

We believe that public schools need to adapt to educational purposes some of these fundamental characteristics of successful business firms. They need to be entrepreneurial and flexible, and adopt an ethic of continuous improvement. Rethinking collective bargaining agreements is a place to begin.

We propose that the comprehensive districtwide contract be replaced by two new forms of written union-management agreement: a slender district-level contract and a much more encompassing school site educational compact. These agreements would have the effect of recognizing the union as an equal participant in educational improvement, refocusing negotiated agreements on institutional rather than individual welfare, and placing significant educational authority and responsibility in the hands of schools.

The new central agreement, which would provide a kind of bare-bones philosophical and operational architecture, would be structured around consensually arrived at educational goals toward which union and management would agree all schools would strive. The document would also contain a few basic wage and working condition provisions, many of which would be subject to school site modification. More comprehensive agreements would be forged at local schools in school site educational compacts.

We borrow the notion of the modern-day workplace compact from the work of Irving Bluestone and Barry Bluestone. In their book, *Negotiating the Future* (1992), Bluestone and Bluestone write:

> A contract is essentially adversarial in nature, representing a compromise be-
> tween the separate interests of each party to the agreement. In contrast, a com-
> pact is fundamentally a cooperative document, providing for a mutual vision
> and a joint system for achieving common goals that foster the general well-being
> of all stakeholders in a given endeavor. [With a compact], labor takes on greater
> responsibility for productivity and quality; management assumes a greater oblig-
> ation to provide employment security. Together, management and the . . . union
> work jointly to make decisions at every level of the [enterprise] [p. 27].

The term *compact* has both substantive and symbolic meaning here. The agreement would be developed at individual schools by the administrators, teachers, and support staff who work there. Rather than serving as an enumer-ation of accrued employment rights, the educational compact would represent a kind of social contract between the school and its community.

The parties to each agreement—union and management in the case of the districtwide contract, the school community in the instance of the site-based compact—would reach decisions based on their assessment of a common vision of education and common goals for the district or school. Both kinds of agree-ments would adopt improving the quality of the educational enterprise as their organizational and operating framework. In order to focus on continuous im-provement, all issues of educational purpose and policy would be expected top-ics of discussion.

The New Central Agreement

Six basic provisions would compose the districtwide contract:

- Union-district joint responsibility for improving education
- A new kind of pay schedule and a basic benefits package
- Professional development and assessment of professional performance
- A standard minimum school year calendar
- Union and employment security guarantees
- A mechanism for resolving disputes

Joint Responsibility. This would be a clear statement of the union's and district's intention to assume mutual obligation for improving and maintaining the health of the educational enterprise. Both parties—the union as the recognized representative of employees and the district as the employer—would commit to joint action that furthers the district's educational mission. The agreement would be grounded in the assumption that union and management share a common purpose in improving schooling. Thus, the union would be recognized to represent members' interests in all areas of educational improvement.

As a means of framing joint action and establishing a clear course and direction, the union and the district together would set broad-based, measurable educational goals toward which the district, and all schools in it, would strive. Goals would be focused on student achievement as defined in multiple ways: levels of academic performance, school attendance and completion rates, rates of student participation in extracurricular activities, levels of parent and community participation in schools and school-related activities, and the like. They would be specific enough to be measurable, but not so specific as to limit schools' ability to adapt the goals to the needs of their particular student populations. Measurable educational goals would serve as a public statement to the community of the union's and district's commitment to educational improvement and their willingness to be held accountable for the results of their efforts. As an additional component of assuming joint responsibility for educational quality, the union and district would develop a quality review procedure for nonperforming schools. The contract would spell out procedures for certifying schools as nonperforming as well as processes by which the district would assume responsibility for such schools.

Salaries and Benefits. A new kind of salary structure, based on teachers' demonstrated knowledge and skills, is key to the new contract. In essence teacher pay would focus on a "value-added" orientation: what the individual professional adds to the needed repertoire of his or her own classroom or to the school. The plan would structure financial compensation around the acquisition of three types of knowledge and skills (Kelley and Odden, 1995):

- Demonstrated depth in the areas of content, curriculum, and instructional expertise
- Breadth skills, such as curriculum development and professional development
- Management skills critical to schools involved in school-based management efforts

Union and district jointly would agree on both the set of skills that would translate into higher compensation for teachers as well as the method for assessing these skills. Skill-based pay increments might, for example, be based on passing a content test in an area of licensure, becoming licensed in a second area, achieving demonstrated proficiency in an additional language, or being certified an "accomplished teacher" by the National Board for Professional Teaching Standards. The decision as to which skills would produce pay increments would be based on the union's and district's assessment regarding district needs.

The districtwide schedule would represent teachers' minimum or basic rates of pay. These could be enhanced by individual school sites. Pensions and benefits would be portable, enabling teachers to move from district to district or state to state without jeopardizing either retirement or health care.

Professional Development and Professional Performance. Means for assisting teachers to improve their professional skills, and procedures for assessing the results of their professional efforts, would constitute two of the fundamental components of the centralized union-management agreement.

We know the dimensions of quality professional development. It is largely teacher driven, teacher directed, and continuous. Perhaps most significant, good professional development is school based and directed at what teachers actually do in schools and classrooms (Little, 1993; Corcoran, 1994).

In the new bargaining model we propose, the majority of professional development would be school based. However, the union and the district, as part of their central agreement, might choose to join forces on some development dimensions. For example, the National Board for Professional Teaching Standards might be the focus of some districtwide professional development efforts, particularly if certification by the national board carried with it added financial compensation for teachers. Together the union and district could offer courses to assist teachers to prepare for national board certification. Or they might set aside funds to reimburse teachers who achieve board certification for the fees required to undergo the process.

In addition, the district and union might take the long view, extrapolate the district's future needs, and determine areas of anticipated teacher shortage. Joint professional development programs might then be organized for the purpose of "retraining" teachers willing to develop new professional skills and competencies designed to meet the district's future educational needs.

The principal purpose of districtwide statements about and programs for professional development would be to reinforce joint expectations for and commitment to ongoing professional growth. This would be an additional tacit signal that the teaching career is not static; rather, learning is a continuous undertaking both for those who teach and for those whom they teach.

Peer review, the process by which teachers assess the professional competence of their colleagues, is an essential component of the union's assuming responsibility for the quality of the teaching profession. Thus, a procedure for implementing peer review would be contained in the new districtwide contract.

School Year Calendar. The majority of a conventional district-based collective bargaining agreement centers on work rules and content—days and hours of employment, class size parameters, and delineation of nonteaching duties. The new districtwide agreement would contain just one work rule provision: the contract would establish a standard school year calendar that would specify the days during which schools typically would be expected to be in session. Individual sites, through their educational compacts, would be free to modify this calendar by increasing the minimum number of school days. All other workload matters that typically would be part of a district wide negotiated agreement would be included in school-based educational compacts.

Union and Employment Security. The district's obligation in this new mutual arrangement would be to guarantee to teachers employment security and to guarantee to the union organizational security. The purpose would be to provide a stable work environment and a ready supply of qualified labor without imposing undue restrictions on either school site flexibility or professionals' ability to market their services and accept the most attractive job offer.

We differentiate here between employment security and job security. Employment security—the right to a teaching position in the school district, assuming satisfactory performance—would be ensured by a no-layoffs provision in the agreement. Job security—the right to remain at a particular school—would not be a contractual guarantee. Decisions about which teachers were assigned to which schools would rest with school staffs and be based on schools' particular needs.

The district and union would also agree to a union security contract provision in the form of the hiring hall. This portion of the agreement would have the effect of preserving the institutional integrity of the union as the source of the supply of competent professional labor for the district.

Dispute Resolution. Disagreements regarding the application or interpretation of contract provisions are bound to arise. Thus, the union-district pact would include means by which to resolve these kinds of disputes.

The emphasis in adjudicating disputes would focus largely on preserving the integrity of the educational institution and the goals it is attempting to achieve. Thus, this new sort of grievance procedure would need to balance institutional welfare with individual rights, ensuring at the same time that school-based educational programs remain intact and that the system does not treat individual teachers in an arbitrary or capricious manner.

For purposes of adjudicating disputes regarding the districtwide agreement, the union and the district jointly would select an individual to serve as a kind of permanent umpire. Disagreements that are not resolved through informal district and union discussions would be submitted to the umpire, who would be empowered to render a binding decision that would take into account the obvious language of the disputed contract provision as well as the intent of the parties in developing it. In other words, the permanent umpire would enter the dispute resolution process with a clear sense of the district's and schools' goals, missions, and rules of engagement. That understanding would contribute substantially to the umpire's resolution of the dispute.

The Educational Compact

The new districtwide contract serves to frame the basics. Much of the heart of the educational enterprise would be shaped by and incorporated into a new educational compact whose authority is lodged at the school site. By means of the compact, employees would gain the right to make essential workplace decisions. In exchange for this new authority, the parties to the compact would assume responsibility for the educational performance of the school. In order to ensure that the compact was structured in a manner designed to assist the school in reaching established educational goals, the school district would retain authority to approve these agreements.

The enterprise compact would have the following basic components:

- A statement of educational philosophy and student performance targets
- Resource allocation mechanisms
- Hiring procedures
- Means for achieving salary decisions
- Class and course organization procedures
- Programs for professional development and assessment of professional performance
- A statement about quality assurance and community support
- A dispute resolution plan

Educational Philosophy and Student Performance Targets. An initial feature of the compact would be a statement of the school's operating mission and principles. In effect, this provision would provide an opportunity for the school staff and community mutually to determine the fundamental philosophy and educational underpinnings of the institution. The purpose of this section would be to reach consensus on the answer to the question, "What is it our school stands for?"

The compact would contain a set of measurable student performance targets. Keyed to the student achievement goals enunciated in the central union-district pact, the compact targets would be tailored to the school's clients and mission. Targets would be more specific than goals but would, like the goals, focus on measures of student achievement.

Compact-enshrined targets would serve as a set of quality indicators for the school. Annually the school would assess and make public the degree to which it was making progress toward reaching the targets and achieving the districtwide goals. The school would also be obliged to study, attempt to understand, and explain to the wider school community conditions or impediments that might prevent the school from reaching its anticipated targets in any given year.

Resource Allocation. The majority of resources—as much as 90 percent—would be controlled at the school site. Resources would be allocated to the school by the district on a per pupil basis. In other words each school would be able to anticipate its complement of fiscal resources based on its student enrollment. The principal purpose of the per pupil allocation arrangement is to prevent the central district office from skimming resources that ought to be the province of the school. Insofar as schools are able to predict their student populations, they ought to be able to predict their revenue streams. Parties to the school-based educational compact would establish procedures by which to determine resource allocation priorities. All resource decisions would be stated in terms that clearly link resource distribution to efforts to further the educational program of the school. Here is where the staffing rubber meets the conventional union road.

Should a school collectively decide that an individual teacher's skills, while perhaps valuable in past years, no longer meet the needs of that school, the staff would have the authority, based on the school's mission and educational targets, to replace that teacher with another staff member (another teacher with different skills, an administrator, a classified employee). The displaced teacher's seniority would not provide him or her with an extra advantage in terms of remaining at the school. Instead that teacher would contact the union and, through the hiring hall, seek a position more clearly suited to his or her particular professional skills.

Hiring. Hiring would be a school site function. Prospective teachers would be sent for interviews from the union hiring hall to schools with advertised positions. Schools would develop procedures by which to make decisions regarding the numerical and job-specific composition of their staffs, as well as mechanisms for adding and deleting staff positions. Hiring decisions would be grounded in judgments about the welfare of the educational program and school-determined priorities regarding resource allocation.

Salary Decisions. Teachers' pay would be structured on the basis of demonstrated knowledge and skill. The districtwide salary schedule would serve as the baseline. Schools would be free, within the limits of their available resources, to offer teachers additional financial compensation.

Added compensation might be paid as a kind of "signing bonus" to induce a particularly well-thought-of or well-suited teacher to come to a school. Or a school might decide to award added dollars to a teacher or a group of teachers who have made an especially significant contribution to the school in reaching its performance targets.

Teachers who receive financial compensation above that to which they would ordinarily have been entitled by virtue of their placement on the salary schedule would not have those dollars permanently attached to their pay scheme. Instead these would become one-time bonuses, renewable at a school's discretion. Determination of the distribution, if any, of added salary to teachers or groups of teachers would be made at the school using the procedure established in the compact.

Allowing schools to supplement teachers' basic compensation serves two essential purposes. It enables schools to compete for teachers' services and to reward tangibly those professionals whose contributions measurably advance the school toward fulfilling its mission and achieving its performance targets.

We are aware that the option to award teachers added financial compensation selectively might appear to offer the prospect of encouraging a kind of unhealthy interpersonal competition that could constrain teachers from cooperating with one another. We believe in practice, however, that this system would have a different result. It would contribute to the ability of individual teachers or groups of teachers to be entrepreneurs. Moreover, in most instances of furthering school programs, we believe the advantage would accrue to collective rather than individual efforts.

Class and Course Organization. Schools would be free to determine the length of the school day, the number of days school would operate (though they would not be permitted to fall below the minimum specified in the districtwide contract), and the organization of time. Fifty-minute periods might give way to two-hour class blocks in high schools. Elementary schools might structure their day so as to allow teachers to team-teach. Class sizes would float depending on the school-determined needs of the educational program.

The educational compact would acknowledge time as a flexible and precious resource. The agreement would contain a set of school-determined procedures detailing the ways in which decisions about the allocation and use of time would be made.

Professional Development and Professional Performance. Each school would determine a regular, ongoing program of professional growth and development. This program would be tied specifically to increasing teachers' capacity to improve student educational performance in order to meet school-developed targets and district-promulgated goals. The compact might, for example, include a set of school-specific incentives, supports, and rewards for teachers who become certified through the National Board for Professional Teaching Standards. Or it might designate particular areas of needed staff knowledge and skill and establish a program designed to assist teachers to achieve these.

Performance assessment would be accomplished by means of the peer review system. Schools would adhere to the districtwide peer review scheme, although they might contribute additional components of professional accomplishment that individually they elect to assess.

Quality Assurance and Community Support. The educational compact is not simply a bargain among school staff members. It is also an agreement with the school's public—a statement of mutual obligation and commitment, and professional as well as public accountability.

Teachers would agree to guarantee the quality of the educational program. They would agree to act in the service of improved student achievement, make every reasonable effort to meet measurable educational goals, and to continually upgrade and assess their own professional practice so as to contribute to the welfare of the school.

In exchange, parents and the community would commit to support teachers and the school. Support might be achieved in various ways. Parents, for example, would agree to encourage students at home, assist students to the degree possible with homework, attend parent conferences and back-to-school events, and, to the extent their schedules permit, volunteer at their children's schools. In addition, parents and the broader community would commit to preserving the fiscal viability of schools.

We believe that by including this kind of provision directly in the educational compact, parents and the broader community are included as partners in the educational program. Partnership does not simply imply some form of modest participation in school or schooling activities. Rather, this arrangement requires a mutual and symbiotic commitment of educators, parents, and the full school community in insuring student success.

Dispute Resolution. The agreement would include a set of procedures to resolve compact issues that fall into contention. As in districtwide disputes, the school-based resolution process would, in developing a proposed solution to the problem, take into account the welfare of the school and the furtherance of its educational mission, as well as the rights of the individual or individuals who are asserting that they have been wronged.

CREATING A LABOR MARKET FOR TEACHERS

The structure we outline anticipates a highly decentralized system. We assume, in other words, that the individual school becomes the primary employer. We assume, moreover, that unions must become part of the market solution to obtaining an adequate supply of qualified workers.

The literature on modern, productive organizations, those that have come to be called knowledge era organizations, suggests that they put a premium on flexibility and organic change, the very qualities that cause problems for existing bureaucratic and union structures. We suggest rearranging the teacher labor market to make it simultaneously self-advancing and socially productive. We attempt here to strike a balance between the two legs of unionism: workers' rights of self-determination and society's need for institutions that are simultaneously productive and just. This goal requires several major changes in the teacher labor market.

Emphasizing Career Security Rather Than Job Security

Classically organizations have been defined by their boundaries. One was either part of an organization or was not, and employee status set the boundary. If one had a job, one belonged to the organization. No job, no membership.

In teaching, belonging has been achieved through the hiring process. It has been secured with the passage of time, the accumulation of seniority, and the granting of tenure. Seniority and tenure have provided teachers with a comfortable kind of security of employment and position. To be sure, job protection is not now, and never has been, absolute. Teachers are not shielded from layoff in times of fiscal crisis, and, conventional wisdom notwithstanding, bad teachers can be fired. Nonetheless, a teacher has been relatively safe in assuming that absent some sort of crisis, a job with the district, and even a position in a particular school, was secure. Union contract provisions in large measure created this kind of stability for teaching employees.

But the historical relationship of the teacher to the education institution is beginning to break down. The organization we know as school increasingly operates with part-time employees who are part of the organization but not entirely, contractual services where people perform vital functions but are not on the payroll, consultants who perform highly strategic activities but for only a short period of time, and volunteers or community resources from other organizations and agencies in which the participant may never have an economic relationship to the school.

One gains a picture of a highly organic organization that changes rapidly with conditions and combines and recombines itself with fluidity. In this setting the union's historical weapon of building a set of rights around a particular job is challenged. The union has two possible avenues of action. One is to fight each of the boundaries: redefinition of teacher work, contracting out, the use of interns, substitution of volunteers or employees of other organizations or agencies. Or the union can begin to organize around career security rather than job security. By career security we mean that union members would be buffered from the winds of organizational change through a series of mechanisms that would allow members to move relatively easily from school to school, job to job, and one type of economic relationship to another. A new version of an old union classic, the hiring hall, would make this possible.

Creating the Modern Hiring Hall

The hiring hall grew from the craft tradition of project-based employment, relatively frequent job changes, and peripatetic workers. In an era when the nature of work is rapidly changing, it is an idea whose time has come again.

The union ought to become the exclusive provider of teachers to the schools in a district for which it is the recognized exclusive representative. As in the case with the old craft unions, a teacher would gain access to work through the union. Unlike the historic craft union hiring hall, where individuals lined up daily for their work assignments, this hiring hall would function as a sophisticated human resources organization offering placement and counseling services and access to training and development.

Historically teacher supply has been a primary problem for school districts. Teacher shortages cause districts to compromise greatly the standards they use in hiring teachers. The union, through the hiring hall, could bring the supply and demand of labor into balance and assure schools that there will be a supply of qualified people to work.

In our conception, the hiring hall would have multiple functions:

Registration. Just as a personnel office now does, the hiring hall would receive and qualify applications. It would determine whether the person had the basic legal requirements for a job and whether the person met the requirements of an individual posting.

Preparation and recommendation. The hall would assist applicants in preparing employment portfolios, more compact versions of the kinds of presentations now being required for certification by the National Board for Professional Teaching Standards. Of course, the certification of board-certified teachers would become part of their registration information. The hall might also provide screening, career counseling, and assistance in interview training.

An electronic database. Registration information, including selections from a teacher's portfolio, would be made available to all schools in a hiring hall's service area and, given compatible data formats, could be transferred among geographic locations as well. A school could thus screen applicants according to criteria they chose, with the knowledge that if they followed the proper screening techniques, their search would meet all the antidiscriminatory and civil rights requirements. All the information, including registrant preferences and work experience, would be available to a school.

Employment broker. Particularly for employees with highly specialized skills or a desire to work an unusual schedule, the hiring hall would serve an additional brokerage function. The hall, for example, would be able to create full-time employment for teachers of art or music, who might not be affordable at a single elementary school but might find a shared arrangement among several schools. Or it would be able to assist teachers who choose a practice centered on creating curriculum or developing educational software, skills that a single school might have need of for an intense period of development lasting only a few months but that several schools might require over the course of an academic year. The hiring hall, in other words, would enable teachers to develop the kinds of professional practice options suited to their talents and needs while maintaining steady employment.

Under the hiring hall plan as well, persons who were not employed at a school would become part of a pool of workers in transition between jobs. Members of the pool would be supported by a fund financed by all employees as part of districtwide bargaining agreements. The length of time an employee would be economically supported while in the pool would depend on the employee's seniority in the union.

We recognize the possibility of poorly run hiring halls that discourage or discriminate against applicants. Thus, the hiring hall would be the personnel office of first resort. Schools would be obliged to seek teachers through the hiring hall mechanism before turning to other sources. A persistent failure of a school or schools to use the hiring hall or of the hiring hall to have qualified workers available would be grounds for an unfair labor practice complaint, just as failure to bargain in good faith is now.

Developing a Career Ladder with Teaching at the Top

Decades after the publication of *Schoolteacher* (Lortie, 1975), teaching remains an "unstaged career." To be sure, informal leadership and positions of respect and influence accrue with experience. And over the past twenty years we have witnessed substantial differentiation in teaching work in the form of job specialization and job enlargement. But these arrangements, whether they are mentor teacher programs or career ladders, fall far short of constituting the kind of career progression that other occupations of highly trained individuals enjoy.

We focus here on the career ladder. Most existing career ladder plans take entry-level teaching as their bottom rung. Classroom teachers, the individuals who work with children every day, are at the bottom of the ladder. The message that is sent is clear: those who work with children have the lowest status, and those who work with adults have the highest.

We suggest a different ladder, one that places teaching at the top and creates an orderly career progression into teaching. The duties and responsibilities now ascribed to lead teachers would become part of the normal responsibility of senior teachers, part of the world into which they become socialized.

Putting teaching at the top of a career ladder allows those who are classroom teachers to have a teaching relationship with other adults. It makes possible real apprenticeships in the schools. It creates a natural situation in which teachers can train and socialize new entrants and ensure their quality.

These arrangements would enable paraprofessionals, or teachers' aides, for example, to work their way toward college degrees, teaching certification, and employment as full-fledged teachers. Paraprofessionals bring important qualities to schools. They generally live in the community in which the school is located and often, particularly in immigrant communities, speak the home language of the students. These individuals have worked in classrooms. If they indicate a desire to earn the title of teacher, one can have reasonable confidence that the commitment is a serious one.

Portable Pensions and Benefits

Localized pensions and benefits create pronounced rigidity in the teacher labor market. Just as teacher job protection is tied to a particular employer, so too are benefits. Pensions are largely part of state plans in which employee contributions are matched by the state only at retirement. Moving employment out of state carries heavy penalties. Other fringe benefits, particularly health benefits, are usually specific to the school district. Career security for teachers means that they have the ability to move from place to place. Their leverage in the market is the capacity to move, whether or not they exercise it.

In health care and other benefits, where services must be locally delivered, the unions themselves should serve as the plan holder, contracting with health maintenance organizations and other care providers. The key is to move access to health care from the employer to the occupation so that benefits continue when employment status changes.

In terms of pensions, we advocate the establishment of a nationwide pension system for teachers, perhaps patterned on the model of TIAA-CREF. A nationwide system would be portable, with teachers free to move to different states without jeopardizing accrued retirement benefits. Because interstate pension plan differences would disappear, the system would also be equitable. Portable pensions and benefits, then, would contribute to a flexible teacher labor market.

Teacher Ownership of Professional Practice

Teachers need ownership of their craft or work, and they need ownership of the intellectual property involved. Unions can help in two ways. First, unions can allow, even encourage, teachers to create schools themselves—cooperative enterprises, professional service corporations, teacher-run schools. To the extent to which schooling operates like a market, unions will need to assist their members in the full participation in those markets. Otherwise the outside market forces will be pitted against the core of unionized teachers.

Second, unions ought to provide avenues for teachers to develop the materials with which they work—books, software, manipulatives—and should help to ensure that those products belong to their creators. Unions can assist teachers or groups of teachers to negotiate royalty payments. Or they might provide venture capital—a little seed money to allow a good idea to take root and flourish.

Contracting Out

Contracting out seriously threatens existing union structures. Historically in education most contracting out has been done in ancillary service areas—food service, maintenance, and janitorial services. But increasingly the use of contract workers has come closer to the core functions of teaching and learning. As schools decentralize and budgetary decisions are made at school sites, teachers themselves, as members of school site decision bodies, are likely to be involved in decisions about how labor is to be divided. Some services are likely to be contracted out.

Unions ought not simply to adopt the conventional anticontracting-out stance. At a minimum this position will diminish the support of those of their members who believe some educational services at their particular schools can be better provided through contract workers from outside the district. Instead we believe unions ought to insist on and help to establish a set of baseline enforceable rules about contracting out. We suggest two rules in particular. First, no one should be forced to accept bad services. No local site council should be required to accept the services of either bad employees or bad contractors. Since the people most affected by bad services are those in the schools, decisions about contracting out should be lodged in schools. Second, all contracts should require basic worker protections. Ensuring basic rights in contracts tends to level the field and allow groups of workers internal to an organization to compete with outsiders for contract relationships.

The goal of this set of proposals is to link union security with an institutionally useful labor market, one that provides high-quality workers, allows the market to adjust for supply and demand, and provides career continuity for educators without hobbling school reform and change in the process.

A NEW LAW OF WORK

The principles underlying current labor policy are found in the National Labor Relations Act (1935) and two laws that amended it: the Taft-Hartley Act (1947) and the Landrum-Griffin Act (1959). These laws apply to the private sector, but many of their tenets have been employed in the development of state labor relations laws governing teachers and other public employees.

The National Labor Relations Act (NLRA), an outgrowth of increased pro–organized labor public sentiment in the wake of the New Deal, defined the rights of employees to select an exclusive representative, established the right of unions to bargain collectively, required that employers negotiate in good faith, and created the National Labor Relations Board to administer the act. The Taft-Hartley and Landrum-Griffin acts refined the responsibilities of unions and the rights of employees and employers. Taft-Hartley restricted some union activities, such as the secondary boycott, and created the Federal Mediation and Conciliation Service for the purpose of resolving union-management disputes short of resorting to legal action. Landrum-Griffin, also called the Labor-Management Reporting and Disclosure Act, was designed to regulate the relationship between the union and its members. Labeled by some as the "bill of rights for union members," Landrum-Griffin allows members to sue unions for inappropriate or unfair representation.

U.S. labor law is built on an industrial model. Collective bargaining statutes, whether federal laws for private employees or state statutes covering teachers and other public employees, create separate functions of labor and management, assume that employers and employees have different interests in the workplace relationship, and shelter adversarial union-management interactions.[1]

The protections of labor law were intended to apply to those whose work content and condition were controlled by others, explaining the emphasis on separation of labor and management responsibilities. The 1980 U.S. Supreme Court *Yeshiva* decision (*NLRB v. Yeshiva University,* U.S. 672, 1980) reinforced this separation in higher education. Faculty members at Yeshiva University were denied collective bargaining rights because their faculty senate and its committees made substantive decisions at their university.[2] Although this federal legal doctrine has never been applied in any state case governing public school teachers, it has a potentially chilling effect on reshaping the boundaries between labor work and management work.

Fearing the continuance of company-dominated unions, the NLRA created a clear prohibition against management acts that would help unions. Subsequent case law made the barrier explicit and reinforced the ideal that labor relations properly understood and practiced require an arms-length, adversarial relationship.

What we believe is required is not simply amended labor law but a new law of work—a statute that countenances the enormous changes taking place in the nature of work. The law would need not only to grapple with conventional organizational power inequities that unions are designed to overcome, but must also deal with the special problems of knowledge workers on matters such as ownership of professional practice and protection of intellectual property.

The substantive areas with which the new law of work will need to deal include these:

- Coverage. Which workers are eligible for protection under labor statutes?
- Bargaining unit. Which employees should be grouped together to be represented by unions?
- Cooperation. Under what legal aegis can unions and employers develop joint working arrangements?
- Scope of bargaining. What issues are unions and employers supposed to discuss?

- Peer review. How can employees assume professional responsibility for judging the quality of work performed by their colleagues?
- Hiring hall. How can educational workers' jobs be organized around schools rather than school districts?
- Dispute resolution. How can workers and managers learn to solve workplace problems peacefully, and what recourse will the system provide for when they fail?
- Statute administration. What role do state labor boards for other jurisdictional bodies play in making the statute run smoothly?

BRINGING THE NEW SYSTEM INTO BEING

We are convinced of the need for a fundamental transformation of the purposes and operational procedures of teacher unions. Unions can, and should, play a central role in bringing into being a new institutional structure for education. Building the new institution will cause unions to let go of tradition and concurrently open new opportunities for organizing. We believe a new teacher unionism can embrace the quality and productivity that educated workers want and institutions need with the dignity of work dimensions to which unions have traditionally been dedicated.

We do not underestimate the challenge set before unions. The system we have outlined here represents a radical departure from established norms. We also do not underestimate the power of unions to persuade. Should unions embrace fundamental institutional reform, we believe they can succeed not only in preserving their own organizational integrity but, more important, can be instrumental in bringing into being a revitalized system of public schooling in America.

Notes

1. All public sector labor-management statutes are state laws. There is no federal law covering public employees in their right to organize and bargain collectively with their employees.
2. Yeshiva is a private university. Thus, its employees are covered by the provisions of the National Labor Relations Act.

References

Bluestone, B., and Bluestone, I. *Negotiating the Future: A Labor Perspective on American Business.* New York: Basic Books, 1992.

Bradley, A. "Education's 'Dark Continent': If Teacher's Unions Are So Influential Why Do Researchers Ignore Them?" *Education Week*, Dec. 4, 1996, pp. 25–27.

Chase, R. "A New Approach to Unionism—It's Not Your Mother's NEA." Speech to the National Press Club, Washington, D.C., 1997.

Corcoran, T. B. "Transforming Professional Development for Teachers: A Guide for State Policymakers." Paper prepared for the National Governors' Association, Oct. 1994.

Fisher, R., and Ury, W. *Getting to Yes: Negotiating Agreement Without Giving In.* Boston: Houghton Mifflin, 1981.

Kelley, C., and Odden, A. "Reinventing Teacher Compensation Systems." CPRE Finance Brief. New Brunswick, N.J.: Rutgers University, Consortium for Policy Research in Education, 1995.

Lawrence, D. "The Toledo Plan for Peer Evaluation and Assistance." *Education and Urban Society*, 1985, *17*(3), 347–354.

Little, J. W. "Teachers' Professional Development in a Climate of Educational Reform." *Educational Evaluation and Policy Analysis*, 1993, *15*(2), 129–151.

Lortie, D. C. *Schoolteacher: A Sociological Study.* Chicago: University of Chicago Press, 1975.

Ponessa, J. "Seeking 'Reinvention' of NEA, Chase Calls for Shift in Priorities." *Education Week*, Feb. 12, 1997.

Teacher Union Reform Network. Proposal to the John D. and Catherine T. MacArthur Foundation, 1996.

Walton, R. E., and McKersie, R. B. *A Behavioral Theory of Labor Negotiations.* New York: McGraw-Hill, 1965.

CHAPTER TWELVE

The Frame and the Tapestry

Standards-Based Reform and Professional Development

Charles L. Thompson and John S. Zeuli

I t is now widely accepted that in order to realize recently proposed reforms in what is taught and how it is taught in mathematics and science (NCTM, 1989, 1991; Rutherford and Ahlgren, 1989; NRC, 1996), teachers will have to unlearn much of what they believe, know, and know how to do (Ball, 1988) while also forming new beliefs, developing new knowledge, and mastering new skills. The proposed reforms constitute a new curriculum for teacher learning. If they do not specify precisely what teachers should know and be able to do, they do outline it rather clearly and exemplify aspects of it with a nearly literary vividness.

Systemic reform, which in its canonical form (Smith and O'Day, 1991; O'Day and Smith, 1993) consists of states' adopting some variant on the principal reform manifestos as standards for curriculum and teaching, then aligning the major instruments of state policy to support widespread attainment of the standards, may be viewed as a large-scale effort to teach teachers what they need to know in order to carry out the reforms. Indeed Cohen and Barnes (1993) have argued that all policy might profitably be viewed as an effort to teach those who

Preparation of this chapter was supported in part by a National Science Foundation Statewide Systemic Initiative Grant (Grant No. OSR-9250061) to the Michigan Department of Education, with a subgrant to Michigan State University. The interpretations and opinions offered here do not necessarily reflect the views of the National Science Foundation or the Michigan Department of Education. We thank Andy Anderson, David Cohen, Michael Huberman, Deborah Smith, Jim Spillane, and Gary Sykes for reviewing and commenting on early drafts of this chapter. Any flaws in it are, however, solely our responsibility.

must carry it out rather than solely as an effort to induce or constrain them to behave differently. Any serious policy—that is, any policy that does not simply endorse existing practice and call for more of it—requires some learning on the part of those who must implement it. To carry out policies based on the proposed reforms will require a great deal of learning—not merely additive learning (the addition of new skills to an existing repertoire) but transformative learning (thoroughgoing changes in deeply held beliefs, knowledge, and habits of practice).

From this point of view, all of systemic reform—not just one component of it—is a vast project in professional development. It is, of course, too soon to judge whether the project will succeed. (One is reminded of Chou En-lai's response when asked for his assessment of the French Revolution: "It's too early to tell.") But the current signs are not good, and neither are the portents for the future. Not only is it proving predictably difficult to effect the coherence in state policy characterized as "supremely rational" by one advocate for systemic reform (Fuhrman, 1991). The difficulty is predictable because, as Cohen (1982; also Cohen and Spillane, 1993) has pointed out, fragmentation was deliberately designed into our system of government by founders deeply distrustful of all concentration of power, a system stratified into levels, divided into branches within levels, and open to influence by a host of ever-shifting and conflicting interests. But even in some of the states where significant components of systemic reform have been put in place, they do not appear to be producing the intended changes in curricular and instructional practice. Our own research (Spillane and Zeuli, 1997; Thompson, Zeuli, and Borman, 1997), employing qualitative methods with a sample of teachers strategically chosen on the basis of questionnaires administered to larger quantitative samples, confirms and elaborates earlier case studies that showed how difficult and partial are the reforms in many classrooms (Ball, 1990; Cohen, 1990; Grant, Peterson, and Shojgreen-Downer, 1996; Peterson, 1990; Wiemers, 1990; Wilson, 1990).

Yet we come not to bury systemic reform. It is, as Chou En-lai would doubtless agree, too early for that. But we do not quite come to praise it either. Instead we argue that implementation of Smith and O'Day-style systemic reform is quite unlikely, perhaps not fully necessary, probably helpful, potentially harmful, and almost certainly not sufficient to effect the changes in teaching practice major reform documents advocate. The standards-based policy coherence that systemic reformers envision, though unlikely for reasons already alluded to, would probably be helpful in defining desirable goals for local educators, stimulating movement toward the goals, and reducing conflicts among the policies that local educators labor under. But the role assigned to professional development in systemic reform—construed more broadly than the traditional workshop but more narrowly than systemic reform as a whole—is far too small and the proposed changes in professional development insufficient. As others have argued in this book, professional development is a key, if not the key, to the realization of the proposed reforms in subject matter teaching and learning.

Just increasing the amount of professional development will not necessarily help. But neither will just aligning professional development with new standards for curriculum and instruction to make it more coherent and sustained. Nor will replacing traditional formats with new forms, contexts, and social arrangements for professional development through collegial exchange within schools and in cross-school networks, or through an expansion of teacher participation in the learning opportunities embedded in such tasks as the development of new local standards, selection of curricular materials, design and use of new assessment approaches, and the like. The emergence of these promising new forms of collegial and task-embedded professional development—or perhaps the reconstrual of these activities as professional development in order to legitimize and expand them—will prove little more helpful than their unlamented forebears unless they get the core content and pedagogy right.

What it would mean to "get the core content and pedagogy of professional development right" is one of the principal subjects of this chapter. Another is what it would take to get the content and pedagogy of professional development right on a very large scale. After all, the whole point of systemic reform is that it is not enough to offer a curriculum of understanding for a few students in a few places. Scientific literacy and mathematical power for virtually all students is the putative aim of systemic reform.

If the problem of realizing the reforms is centrally (though not exclusively) a problem of teacher learning on a very large scale, and if most traditional approaches to professional development do not work very effectively, and if standards-aligned and even promisingly innovative professional development forms and formats may not prove much more effective, then we are at a very dangerous point in the evolution of the reforms. At the federal level, what passes these days for a great deal of money has been spent to promote systemic reform in science and mathematics education, not to mention other subjects. As the implied promissory notes come due in the Congress, one can almost see the anxiety and blood pressure rise at the National Science Foundation, and one can also see the pressure passed along to statewide systemic initiatives in the form of demands to "scale up" quickly and to provide evidence that student outcomes are already improving. For reasons largely independent of federal policy, impatience for results is also growing at the state level. Within Michigan, for example, a process of summary accreditation based on results of a state assessment aligned with national standards is being used to turn up the heat on low-performing schools.

It may be argued that at both levels, the pressure is necessary and is accompanied by support: special funding and a strategy from the federal level and technical assistance for unaccredited schools from the state. The combination of pressure and support is not difficult to justify. After all, a good deal of research suggests that just such a combination is necessary to promote change (McLaughlin, 1987; Huberman and Miles, 1984). But what if the support is ineffective or at least not sufficiently effective to produce authentic change in curriculum, instruction, and student learning, rather than more frenetic activity at the state level and narrowly test-focused activity at the school level (exhortations and rewards for doing well on the tests, instruction in test-taking skills, practice on items similar to those on the assessment)? What if there is little to scale up except policy activity and rhetoric because so few teachers understand the ideas at the heart of the reforms and because so few policymakers, administrators, and professional development providers know how to help them learn—or even understand the kind of transformative learning that is required, or even that transformative learning is required? What if, further, the prevailing mode of scaling up is ill suited to the realities of teacher learning, a central unsolved problem?

When someone thinks that A causes B, and yet can offer no plausible mechanism through which A does cause B, offering instead diffuse notions of influence at a distance, Piagetians call this "magical thinking." One hesitates to suggest that federal and state policymakers may be engaged in such magical thinking. If anything, what they propose and insist that others do seems so hard-headed, so full of practical steps, action plans, and coordination of hard-nosed policy instruments—in a word, so pragmatic. But what if all of this activity is based on a misapprehension or, at best, a partial apprehension of the problem and the process of realizing the reforms? What if the central problem at this point is not insufficient pressure or uncoordinated policy messages but teacher learning and, indeed, teacher learning of a particular sort? Then what we are observing might be called "magical pragmatism," a set of apparently pragmatic policies that are unlikely to produce the desired consequences because they grow diffuse and fail to address the core content and pedagogy of professional development.

As the evidence accumulates that systemic reform is not (yet) working, policymakers pursuing the strategy confront three broad choices: redouble the pressure, abandon the strategy, or try to understand and address the learning problem. If the principal problem at the moment is, as we have argued, centrally one of capacity (teachers' beliefs, knowledge, and skill) rather than of will (teachers' motivation), then redoubling the pressure is unlikely to work. It is likely instead to suppress genuine reflection on why reform is not yet working in favor of feverish efforts to produce data showing that it is working, along with determined efforts to scale up on an engineering model.

Although redoubling the pressure is unlikely to work, it is likely to be tried, at least for a time. During this period, many of the professional organizations and academics that originated the standards may need to provide a buffer against unproductive governmental pressures on teachers, administrators, and others who are seriously engaged in reform. For the past decade or so, the apparent consensus on standards among educators, scientists and mathematicians, business leaders, and policymakers has blurred the lines among these groups and may have obscured their sometimes divergent interests. Yet standards-based reform is not identical to governmentally driven systemic reform. While the new standards have been first praised, then appropriated, and most recently used as a hammer by federal and state policymakers, they were initiated and developed almost exclusively by professional scientists, mathematicians, and educators working through professional associations. (Indeed there are those who say that this is part of the problem, but that is an issue for a different chapter.) If the same professional groups that originated the standards were to explicate the problem and the process of transformative teacher learning clearly and persistently, the notion that promoting such learning is the central challenge for the next few decades might well achieve the status of a pervasive "idea in good currency" (Schön, 1971) and begin to influence policy at all levels.

The second choice, abandoning the systemic reform strategy, seems likely to leave the field even more wide open than it is now to the strategy of enlarging market competition in education. It might be possible, even within a thoroughly competitive environment, for professionals who believe in standards-based reform to sustain the process and push forward on the problem of teacher learning at the heart of it. It is even conceivable that standards-based reform, steadily and cleverly pursued, might prosper in such an environment. With at least some publics in many places, the fact that a school is working to realize standards set through a consensus of leading scientists, mathematicians, and educators might well prove a selling point. And schools choosing to embrace the standards would not be so whipsawed by publics that reject them. Parents and students who reject the standards could go elsewhere. To our knowledge, no one has thought very carefully about, much less investigated empirically, the implications of the market movement for standards-based reform.

The third choice open to systemic reformers is to try to understand what the core content and pedagogy of professional development should be like and to figure out how to propagate such professional development. Our purpose in this chapter is to aid the pursuit of the third choice, while also suggesting what reform-minded professionals might do regardless of which way policymakers choose to turn.

THINKING TO LEARN: THE HEART OF THE REFORMS

If the reform manifestos in science and mathematics education outline a curriculum for teacher learning, and if one thinks of reformers and policymakers as teachers of teachers, then it would be useful for them to understand what aspects of the curriculum teachers seem to be having trouble with. Perhaps most striking about teachers' efforts to learn and put into practice the current reform ideas in science and mathematics education is that it is possible—indeed, fairly common—to get a great deal right and still miss the point of what Sykes (1990) has called the "inner intent" of the reforms. For example, in Cohen's (1990) famous study of a California teacher, Mrs. Oublier had adopted some features of the new practice advocated by California's mathematics framework, including the use of concrete manipulatives, the use of small groups, and the incorporation of estimation and problem solving as important mathematical topics. But Mrs. O. combined traditional and new approaches into "an extraordinary melange" of practices that took no account of the conflicts between elements traceable to her earlier training in direct instruction models and the new features she had recently adopted. Cohen's colleagues in the California Study of Elementary Mathematics (Peterson, 1990) found, at most, similar interminglings of new and older practices without much recognition of the contradictions among the conceptions of content, teaching, and learning that undergird the disparate elements (Ball, 1990; Peterson, 1990; Wiemers, 1990). In fact, the one teacher who rejected the reform ideas outright seemed more aware of the differences than did the teachers who adopted them (Wilson, 1990). In our own research on science and mathematics education reform in Michigan (Spillane and Zeuli, 1997; Thompson, Zeuli, and Borman, 1997), we have found a few teachers who did seem to understand and work at realizing the inner intent of the reforms but a predominance of practice was remarkably similar to the patterns revealed in the California study several years earlier.

The essential point—the inner intent—that seems so seldom grasped even by teachers eager to embrace the current reforms is that in order to learn the sorts of things envisioned by reformers, students must think. In fact, such learning is almost exclusively a product or by-product of thinking. By "think," we mean that students must actively try to solve problems, resolve dissonances between the way they initially understand a phenomenon and new evidence that challenges that understanding, put collections of facts or observations together into patterns, make and test conjectures, and build lines of reasoning about why claims are or are not true. Such thinking is generative. It literally creates understanding in the mind of the thinker. Thinking is to a student's knowledge as photosynthesis is to a plant's food. Plants do not get food from the soil. They make it through photosynthesis, using nutrients and water from the soil and energy from sunlight. No photosynthesis, no food. Students do not get knowledge from teachers, or books, or experience with hands-on materials. They make it by thinking, using information and experience. No thinking, no learning—at least, no conceptual learning of the kind reformers envision.

These assertions about thinking and learning are rhetorical simplifications of or metaphors for familiar constructivist notions. Although there are many constructivisms, differing significantly if sometimes subtly along several dimensions (Phillips, 1995), for our purposes it will suffice to characterize two major streams: psychological constructivism and sociocultural constructivism. In psychological constructivism, we "schematize" the profuse flow of everyday experience—James's "blooming, buzzing confusion"—in order to make it manageable, and we use the resulting schematic versions of earlier experience to process subsequent experience. Learning is the product of encounters between schematic representations of objects and processes derived from prior experience and new experiences that cannot be readily processed in terms of or assimilated into those schemas. When new information does not quite fit the existing pattern or model, one may sometimes gloss over the discrepancy, but if the conflict becomes too pronounced to assimilate into mental business as usual, one is driven to resolve the discrepancy by revising or extending existing schemas. Situations of mismatch between the mental equipment one has in hand and the experience or information one has in view are, to a greater or lesser extent, "problems" (Hiebert and others, 1996). "Problem solving" may involve tinkering with the equipment to make it work in the new situation, devising an extension here or an extra connection there, reconstructing whole components, or even abandoning the existing model in favor of one that handles the situation more adequately.

Sociocultural constructivists emphasize the role of social interaction: employing culturally defined symbol systems, categories, and conventions including but not limited to linguistic ones—in the construction of beliefs or "knowledge" shared by communities of knowers. What is accepted as knowledge at a given time by a set of people is created through processes of discussion and negotiation carried out in accord with the norms of the group, not to mention a set of assumptions that its members hold. Both the norms and the assumptions may be tacit or carefully examined and embraced, or a combination of the two. Individual members' beliefs and knowledge are in considerable measure a function of social processes.

Key reform documents envision the classroom as a scientific or mathematical community governed by roughly the same norms of argument and evidence as govern discourse within communities of scholars in the disciplines themselves. Classrooms are scientific or mathematical communities writ small. Although this image of exchange among teacher and students is formed originally on the model of scientists' and mathematicians own collective work (or, more accurately, an idealization of it) rather than on a model of the learning process, it is nonetheless consistent with a sociocultural form of constructivism. Science and mathematics education reformers portray effective classrooms as small communities that adopt scientific or mathematical modes of communication and other conventions to help them struggle with challenging problems, thus developing systems of shared knowledge that gradually evolve in the direction of the knowledge held by communities of scholars in the disciplines. Discussion is an externalized, social way of thinking things through—interactive thinking out loud. At key points in the discussion, the teacher may present current scientific accounts of the phenomenon under study, but such presentations should come as answers to questions or solutions to problems that students are actively puzzling over—thinking about—not as answers to questions they never asked, about phenomena they never wondered about.

It is in the context of such a community that the individual student is held to construct his or her own knowledge, or "knowing," to adopt Smith's (1995) distinction between the individual's construction and the "knowledge" constructed and held by a community. In the reformers' vision of learning we have, in essence, a moderate form of psychological constructivism nested within a moderate form of social constructivism (Phillips, 1995). In other words, individual students create their own understandings by struggling to solve problems or resolve dissonances, but both the situations of dissonance themselves (problems) and the process of resolution (scientific or mathematical discourse) are to a considerable extent socially defined. The functions of thought—the generative, critical, and executive control functions that Brown, Collins, and Duguid (1989; see also Collins, Brown and Newman, 1989) discussed in their work on cognitive apprenticeship and situated cognition—are "externalized," or played out overtly by the teacher and students through social interaction, sometimes employing manipulatives, diagrams, experimental apparatus, tables, graphs, and the like as media of representation. The assumption is that over time students will not only construct their own understandings of scientific and mathematical ideas, but will also "internalize" the processes—learn how to carry out for themselves some version of the thinking processes that are carried out by the class as a community under the guidance of the teacher. That is, they will eventually learn to think like scientists and mathematicians, though as Hiebert and others (1996) point out, in the short run they will do well to think like children struggling with mathematical or scientific problems.

As this implies, reformers recognize that left to their own devices, students will not necessarily recapitulate the history of scientific and mathematical development for themselves (romantic constructivists notwithstanding). They need teachers to pose problems that lie along the path between their existing knowledge and current disciplinary knowledge in various domains—though posing such problems is a useful first step and difficult enough in its own right, since it requires both disciplinary knowledge and knowledge of the state of students' understandings at a given point in time. They also need teachers to establish appropriate norms and social arrangements for interaction; to orchestrate the interaction through questions, clarifications, and the like; to provide tools and materials; to track the evolution of their thinking in order to continue to guide it effectively; and at appropriate points (not prematurely), to introduce current scientific or mathematical ideas.

What may be lost in all of this tinkering and reconstruction and problem solving and norm-governed discourse is that they are metaphors for or modes of thinking. Learning—meaning conceptual advance, the development of new and usable understandings—is largely a product of such thinking, not of efforts to remember. "Knowledge is," according to Dewey (1929, in Hiebert and others, 1996), "the fruit of the undertakings that transform a problematic situation into a resolved one." Thus, what is important about the types of tasks teachers assign, the materials and equipment they use, their grouping practices, the nature of classroom discourse, and teachers' assessment practices is whether they are designed and employed to provoke, provide opportunities for, and support thinking by students.

WHAT TEACHERS NEED TO KNOW AND WHY IT IS ELUSIVE

If the important thing about nearly all dimensions of teaching is whether and how they encourage students to think, then for the reforms to be realized in classrooms across the country, teachers need to understand that fact. They need to understand it because only teachers can ensure that students have abundant opportunities and support to think their way through puzzling, dissonance-inducing phenomena and problems. Virtually all of the effect that any combination of policy instruments exerts on students' learning—if any—will be filtered through teachers, mediated by what teachers believe and know and are able to do. The key questions for reform, then, are whether teachers understand that students must think in order to learn and whether they know how to provoke, stimulate, and support students' thinking.

That students must think in order to learn may seem blatantly obvious. But if it is so obvious, why do so many teachers—in fact, nearly all teachers—fail to see it? They fail to see it in part because, as Cohen (1988) has pointed out, the notion that students must think in order to learn contradicts some of our most deep-seated ideas about teaching and learning. The idea that students must create their own understandings by thinking their way through to satisfactory resolutions of puzzles and contradictions runs counter to conceptions of knowledge as facts, teaching as telling, and learning as memorizing. Telling is the dominant mode of teaching most of us experienced in our families, churches, sports teams, and other childhood settings, not to mention school, where we underwent a twelve- to twenty-year "apprenticeship of observation" (Lortie, 1975) in teaching as telling and learning as remembering. We may think that we have shucked off such outmoded ideas, but such deeply ingrained schemas do not go easily. Changing such habits of mind and habits of practice is more like unlearning the patellar reflex than like changing one's normal route to work by introducing a two-block detour.

Another reason is that teachers change their practice through what Huberman has called "bricolage," or tinkering (Huberman, 1993, 1995). According to Huberman (1993), teachers are like independent artisans, always picking up a new technique here, a new activity there, and a new piece of curricular material somewhere else. They choose techniques, activities, and materials that seem to fit their own styles, settings, and students (Doyle and Ponder, 1977), then adjust them on the basis of their goals and experience. This kind of craftsmanly tinkering is quite practical and eminently sensible, but it is also quite conservative. It enables a teacher to preserve a style and set of fundamental ideas about subject matter, teaching, and learning while elaborating a repertoire that "works" with a widening array of students. By "works" we mean that the repertoire enables teachers to maintain order by keeping most students engaged in activities that seem related to the subjects being taught.

A third reason is that many teachers believe they know it already, when what they know is a little different from what we mean. A fairly common response to our assertion that students must think in order to learn is, "Well, of course. We all know that thinking skills are important." Such a response converts "thinking to learn" into "learning to think," where learning to think is construed to involve learning certain skills in the usual way—by practicing them. It is true that we are using the word *think* in a rather special sense. It is also true that students do need to learn how to think, whether by participating in classroom communities whose norms and patterns of communication help them do so, or through more explicit approaches. But thinking to learn is different from learning to think, and it is thinking to learn we see as central to reformed practice in science and mathematics.

In sum, the reforms call for very deep changes—even a transformation—in teachers' ideas about and understandings of subject matter, teaching, and learning. But most teachers' ideas about these matters are very deep-seated and resistant to intervention. Moreover, their conventional way of making changes, their preferred way of learning, is evolutionary and fundamentally conservative, not revolutionary and transformative.

WHY SYSTEMIC REFORM IS INSUFFICIENT TO TEACH TEACHERS WHAT THEY NEED TO KNOW

If it is indeed transformative learning that would be required to realize science and mathematics education reformers' visions of curriculum and teaching, it should not be too surprising that most of the policy instruments that systemic reform seeks to align and employ fail to bring about the necessary conceptual transformation. Let us consider some of them:

Frameworks or Standard-Setting Documents

From one point of view, frameworks and other standard-setting documents are designed simply to point out the goals toward which all other policy instruments are to be aligned. But if they do so well, one might expect the frameworks to be effective instruments of reform in their own right. Yet a good deal of research suggests that even very high-quality frameworks are open to wide variations in interpretation and do not get the core message of reform across very effectively (Cohen and Ball, 1990; Darling-Hammond, 1990). Further, much of what we know about learning for conceptual change shows that written documents ("texts") alone are inadequate to bring about a revolution in most learners' beliefs and knowledge. Why should teachers be different from other learners on this count?

Curricular Materials

Good curricular materials that are clearly aligned not merely with the topics specified in the frameworks but also with the core ideas about subject matter, teaching, and learning expressed in them can undoubtedly help teachers who already understand the core ideas to carry them out effectively in their classrooms. But most teachers do not now understand these ideas, and a great deal of prior research shows how teachers can bend or distort new materials to fit their existing conceptions. There are undoubtedly some examples of teachers' grasping reform ideas from close examination and use of materials that are carefully designed to support the reforms, but they do not turn up prominently in our research, and in prior waves of reform, such as those of the post-*Sputnik* era, new materials by themselves have proved a relatively weak instrument for changing pedagogy.

Assessment and Accountability Systems

Our research on science and mathematics education reform in Michigan shows clearly that the combination of the Michigan Educational Assessment Program (MEAP) and the summary accreditation process has captured the attention of local district administrators, and most local districts seem to have aligned their curriculum guides with the topics specified in the Michigan Essential Goals and Objectives for Science and Mathematics Education (Spillane and Thompson, 1997). Some have even gone on to rework their curriculum guides at a deeper level, so that they reflect the new ideas about what should be taught and how it can be taught effectively. But considering how deep-seated most teachers' ideas are about subject matter, teaching, and learning as well as teachers' typical tinkering mode of professional learning, one would not expect these topically or even substantively aligned documents to produce conceptually transformative teacher learning on a broad scale. Our classroom-level research confirms that they have not (Spillane and Zeuli, 1997; Thompson, Zeuli, and Borman, 1997).

It is also clear that more and more teachers have begun to examine the MEAP and their students' responses to it. In principle, close examination of students' responses could be very educative, especially responses to the more open-ended questions or problems. Coming face to face with the fact that what students have learned is not necessarily what one has taught can be the kind of dissonance-inducing, puzzling, even shocking experience that prompts some teachers to begin an extensive reconsideration of their own fundamental ideas about teaching and learning (Darling-Hammond, Ancess, and Falk, 1995).

But lest we grow too optimistic about the power of examining assessment responses to bring about the necessary revolution in teachers' understandings, we would note that confrontation with students' misconceptions can be assimilated into business as usual, just as novel materials can. In our research, we have encountered teachers who talk knowledgeably about students' misconceptions and even report carrying out "clinical interviews" (their term) in order to uncover students' ideas. But many of these teachers seem to assume that the erroneous ideas, once uncovered, can be corrected in much the same way that errors have always been corrected: by telling the student that his or her idea is wrong, perhaps explaining why it is wrong, and presenting the correct answer. In other words, one can understand a great deal about students' thoughts—the conceptions and misconceptions they hold concerning matters mathematical and scientific—without understanding the centrality of thinking as the process through which conceptual learning takes place and without appreciating the implications for one's teaching.

Professional Development

Perhaps it is not all that surprising that curriculum frameworks, curricular materials, and assessment and accountability systems do not seem adequate to promote the necessary revolution in teachers' beliefs and knowledge. But what about professional development? In theory professional development is specifically designed to promote learning. Yet there is little evidence for and a strong argument against the proposition that professional development as traditionally organized and conducted is effective in helping teachers understand the core of the reforms.

Advocates of systemic reform (Smith and O'Day, 1991; O'Day and Smith, 1993) have criticized most district-sponsored professional development as fragmented or scattered, brief rather than sustained, and not aligned with well-specified curricular and instructional standards. They also find the professional development that universities offer remote from practice and consisting of a loose collection of courses that are neither coherent nor aligned with curricular and instructional standards.

If professional development were well aligned, coherent, and sustained but unchanged in any other way, would it then be effective in promoting the kind of transformative learning necessary to equip teachers to carry out the reform? There is little evidence bearing directly on this question, perhaps in part because sites where such programs of professional development exist are relatively rare. But there is little reason to believe that aligned, coherent, sustained professional development conducted in the standard training mode or in the generally pre-sentational mode characteristic of most university courses would challenge teachers' existing ideas and support rethinking and revision sufficiently to bring about major changes. In prevailing conception and practice, the content of pro-fessional development is largely techniques, its pedagogy is training, and the learning it promotes consists of remembering new things to try in the classroom. In other words, most current professional development reflects the same deep-seated schemas of knowledge as facts and skills, teaching as telling, and learn-ing as remembering that govern traditional K–12 teaching practice.

WHY NEW FORMS AND FORMATS FOR PROFESSIONAL DEVELOPMENT ARE NOT NECESSARILY THE ANSWER, AND WHAT MIGHT BE

If the alignment of standard policy instruments called for in systemic reform seems unlikely to promote the kind of transformative rethinking required for re-alization of the reforms, what might? The past few years have seen enthusiasm for a variety of new formats and arrangements for teachers' professional devel-opment and learning, including teacher inquiry groups, action research net-works, mutual classroom observation and feedback by teachers, journal writing and exchange, and a variety of job-embedded or task-embedded opportunities to learn through curriculum development or revision, design and use of new as-sessment instruments and approaches, and the like (Little, 1993).

But as Ball (1995) has suggested, it is as much of a mistake to focus principally on the structural or surface features of professional development for teachers as it is to focus on surface features of instruction for K–12 students (such as the use of manipulatives and the use of small groups). The really critical questions about these new forms of professional development concern their substantive content and pedagogy. Huberman (1995) has noted how easily collegially oriented efforts can create a "discussion culture" unhinged from actual changes in classroom prac-tice. "Inquiry groups" in name can turn out to be emotional support groups in practice, valuable to the morale and mental health of participants but unlikely to effect real changes in their beliefs or knowledge. Similarly, without some signifi-cant conceptual reframing, teacher participation in the development of curricula or assessment tools may do no more than extend intraparadigm tinkering into new forums beyond the classroom.

If the organizational arrangements and social forms through which professional development is conducted may not matter, what does matter about learning opportunities for teachers? Their content and pedagogy, yes. But what is it about their content and pedagogy that matters?

As for content, professional development needs to focus on some combination of (1) the ideas and the connections among the ideas that students are to learn, (2) students' thinking and learning—what they bring to encounters with these ideas, some typical paths along which the encounter frequently proceeds, and how teachers can assess or track students' thinking within the normal flow of classroom activity, and (3) teaching, construed largely as a process of provoking students to think, supporting them as they do, and guiding them along productive paths. To realize this conception of teaching, teachers need to know how to choose or design problems whose resolution will advance their students' understanding at different points along the developmental pathway toward current disciplinary knowledge, how to help students represent and express their ideas in a variety of ways, how to establish and maintain norms appropriate to a scientific or mathematical classroom community, and how to orchestrate student discourse. The last certainly includes knowing how to hold one's tongue, but the role of the teacher in classrooms where students are genuinely engaged in thinking and talking things through for themselves is not simply to refrain from telling. It requires posing questions framed with one eye on students' existing ideas and the other on the ideas to be learned; listening with one ear trained in each of these directions; asking students to explain their thinking; asking other students whether they agree or disagree and, in any event, why; deciding which unexpected turns of thought to pursue and which to ignore for the moment; and a great deal more (Ball, 1993; Lampert, 1992; Schifter, 1996a, 1996b).

The difficult remaining question is what features must characterize the pedagogy of professional development if it is to help teachers learn these things. In addressing this question, it seems most productive to begin with an image of the teacher as a learner. Over the past decade or more, the by-now-classic image of the teacher as an isolate within the egg-crate structure of the school (Lortie, 1975) has been challenged increasingly (see, for example, McLaughlin and Yee, 1988). A few years ago Huberman (1993) sounded a contrarian note by counterposing the image of the teacher as an independent artisan to the increasingly popular image of the teacher as a professional colleague among colleagues. More recently he has relented to a degree, allowing that under certain conditions, collegial networks can indeed improve teaching (Huberman, 1995). But Huberman still argues, persuasively in our view, that networks and other forms of collegial professional development are challenged by the "tinkerer," "instructional handyman," or "bricoleur" habits and dispositions of most teachers:

Adapted from Levi-Strauss, this image of the "bricoleur" entails a continuous dialogue with the instructional situation as it evolves; it is inherently personal and pragmatic, and makes both technical communication and changes in instructional procedures, a difficult exercise. . . . [In the "artisan" model, there] . . . is a general plan, as in the Commedia dell'arte or in jazz groups, but within it are nested a series of not-yet defined "moves," should the course of events prove unworkable or less interesting than the challenges one fashions for oneself [Huberman, 1995, p. 196].

It is through examination of experience, adjustments, and the incorporation of new materials and activities that seem to fit the teacher's "virtually idiosyncratic practice" (which is only "loosely harmonized with others") that the teacher learns and changes—"solitary problem-solving through iterative chains of reasoning and direct action" (Huberman, 1995). Any professional development experience intended to promote serious change in teaching is up against this pattern of "productive tinkering," a pattern of both practice and change in practice that is not only deeply ingrained and normally adaptive, but also resiliently conservative. Even interventions intended to transform practice in fundamental ways seem frequently to be assimilated into the established pattern, their contents reduced to techniques and tools that expand the teacher's repertoire incrementally but leave her basic mode of practice undisturbed. Since teachers, like other artisans, are more interested in learning from more advanced peers than from formal training, networks and other collegial arrangements do seem appealing and appropriate, but unless there is some intervention to perturb the established pattern, these collegial formats may do nothing more than provide contexts for the exchange of craftsmanly techniques within the existing paradigm of teaching—a useful function, no doubt, but probably not a transformative one.

This image of the teacher-bricoleur, counterposed against the image of practice proposed by science and mathematics education reformers and considered in the light of research in the constructivist traditions discussed earlier, suggests a set of five requirements for transformative professional development:

• A first requirement is to create a sufficiently high level of cognitive dissonance to disturb in some fundamental way the equilibrium between teachers' existing beliefs and practices on the one hand and their experience with subject matter, students' learning, and teaching on the other (Nelson and Hammerman, 1994; Ball and Cohen, this volume). Dissonance significant enough to provoke a transformation in teachers about knowledge, learning, and teaching rather than mere tinkering seems to arise infrequently in the normal flow of teaching, other task performance (such as curriculum revision), and collegial exchange. Some deliberate intervention is probably required to convert normal practice from an inert fact or a basis for tinkering into the "abundant resource for learning" whose potential Ball and Cohen (this volume) see.

• A second requirement is to provide time, contexts, and support for teachers to think—to work at resolving the dissonance through discussion, reading, writing, and other activities that essentially amount to the crystallization, externalization, criticism, and revision of their thinking. A good deal has been written about the need to provide time and contexts for teachers to talk with each other and learn, but unless the time and contexts are used to promote and support dissonance-resolving thinking, they probably will not help much. Here we are not merely beating once more the oft-beaten drum of time for collegial learning, but arguing for more opportunities for teachers to think, where "think" has the special dissonance-resolving sense we have employed throughout this chapter.

• A third requirement is to ensure that the dissonance-creating and dissonance-resolving activities are connected to the teacher's own students and context, or something like them (Huberman, 1995; Brown, Collins, and Duguid, 1989; Ball and Cohen, this volume). The literature on situated cognition suggests that knowledge is most readily mobilized for use in situations resembling those in which it was acquired. Although recent work by Anderson, Reder, and Simon (1996) seeks to correct some of the excesses of that literature, the general premise seems to remain useful. Ball and Cohen (this volume) provide a nice metaphor for the idea of situated cognition: learning about teaching in isolation from the contexts of practice is "like trying to learn to swim on a sidewalk." Teaching, as they point out, is a performance. By this they do not mean that useful learning can occur only during actual or simulated teaching performance. A certain amount of distance from practice, in a situation less rushed than the actual contexts of classroom practice, may be essential to serious learning. Teachers may be connected to practice in the way that matters and yet not be in the midst of practice—for example, by examining and discussing samples of students' written work, videotapes of teachers and students at work, and other artifacts that embody some aspect of practice. But there is a tricky issue embedded here: such reflective activity would presumably produce conceptual knowledge (understanding) rather than, say, the new habits of practice that may be acquired through trial performances successively approximating a new ideal. We would argue, however, that such conceptual knowledge is crucial because of the very nature of reformed practice as conceptually guided improvisation. A new performance repertoire will be needed, but so will the knowledge and insight to recognize when and decide how to draw on it effectively. Learning solely at the level of behavior (say, through operant conditioning) would not be very helpful.

• A fourth is to provide a way for teachers to develop a repertoire for practice that is consistent with the new understanding that teachers are building

(Huberman, 1995). This point is the obverse of the one we have just made. That is, although conceptual knowledge or understanding is essential, it is not sufficient. Teaching is, in fact, a performance, and the process of moving from an in-principle understanding to action in the blizzard of stimuli blowing in most classrooms is not trivial. Knowledge derived from reflection on practice and close to practice may be more readily mobilized in practice than knowledge acquired in situations more remote from practice, but there is still another step. We do not wish to dichotomize knowledge ("theory") and practice, but neither do we wish to pretend that invoking terms such as *praxis* or decrying the distinction between theory and practice is the same as integrating theory and practice in practice. It is still possible to understand and yet not be able to do. Professional development has to come to grips with this challenge too.

• The fifth requirement is to provide continuing help in the cycle of (1) surfacing the new issues and problems that will inevitably arise from actual classroom performance, (2) deriving new understandings from them, (3) translating these new understandings into performance, and (4) recycling (Huberman, 1995). In a sense this phase of teacher learning represents a return to within-paradigm tinkering, perhaps carried out collegially, and thus might not appear to require continued support. Indeed it should be possible for professional developers to withdraw support gradually, particularly if support from peers remains accessible. But tinkering within the new paradigm—the paradigm of practice enunciated in major reform documents—seems a more deliberate, explicit, conceptually driven process than is typical in current modes of practice and adjustment. In the early going, at least, it would seem to involve a great deal of what Perkins and Salomon (1988) call "high road transfer." Perkins and Salomon distinguish between "low road transfer," or the transfer of learning through practice of a given skill in many slightly varying contexts, so that its application is slowly generalized laterally, and "high road transfer," in which a procedure or technique is quite explicitly conceptualized and deliberately applied, perhaps overleaping many small variations in context to contexts quite different from the one in which it was originally learned. Something like low road transfer is probably necessary to achieve the degree of automaticity required for real-classroom application on a steady basis, but in making such a major change as reformers envision, substantial high road transfer will be required initially, and that is very hard work and likely to need extra support.

These requirements can be met—indeed, are being met, in whole or in part, through theoretically driven design or intuitive improvisation—in a variety of different ways. For example, Schifter and her colleagues (Schifter and Fosnot, 1993; Schifter, 1996a, 1996b; Ball and Mosenthal, 1990) have created a whole program of experiences designed to challenge teachers' beliefs and knowledge of mathematics, the learning of mathematics, and their identities as mathematical thinkers and teachers. SummerMath for Teachers is designed to initiate what Schifter and her colleagues call "a complex process of active reflection" on mathematical knowing and student learning, enabling teachers, as one staff member put it, "to construct constructivism."

The first phase of the program is a two-week summer institute. During the initial stages, teachers respond to a series of nonroutine mathematical problems drawn from elementary and secondary curricula. The problems chosen resist any rule-based computational answer with which teachers may already be familiar. In groups of three or four, teachers engage in a process of active, verbalized problem solving in which they explore mathematical ideas, devise different representations, and determine their validity in the light of the problem. In both small group and whole group sessions, staff provoke cognitive conflict by asking questions that invite teachers to reason out loud and take issue with each other. They refrain from giving answers to participating teachers. The experience often induces anxiety about teachers' knowledge of mathematics and prompts them to rethink their assumptions about learning. Some teachers are initially disconcerted by the subject matter: "I don't have any idea what 8 divided by 12 means in the real world [though] I know the answer is 2/3." Others are troubled by being asked to find two methods of solving a problem. "Finding the correct answer was important to me. . . . Once I felt I had a correct answer, it was difficult for me to think of another way." Teachers also surface pedagogical questions, such as, "How are the students going to know what's right if the teacher doesn't tell them? Isn't the teacher being irresponsible by letting a student leave class believing that something is wrong?" "Is it okay to argue about different solutions?"

This process of reflection on mathematical knowing and learning continues throughout the two weeks. Following teachers' explorations of mathematical problems, the participants interview students and view videotapes of students' attempts to solve problems, often the same ones with which teachers themselves had struggled. As teachers probe and assess students' thinking, another set of questions emerges that go to teachers' underlying assumptions about learning. Teachers begin to doubt whether students' correct answers signify that students "really understand what they are doing." Teachers also begin to question the degree to which their own pedagogical practices give them access to their students' thinking: "Watching the videos I begin to ask myself, what is learning?" During the latter stages of the institute, teachers are asked to design a lesson and teach it based on what they learned in an interview about how a student thinks about a particular mathematical idea. Throughout the two-week period, teachers keep reflective journals.

Taken together, these experiences often cause distinct discomfort among teachers whose sense of competence as teachers of mathematics is uncertain. But the program softens and offsets the anxiety by maintaining a consistently supportive atmosphere. The activities provide teachers with extended opportunities to think about mathematics without any formal evaluation. And there is no expectation that teachers already know what it means to "construct mathematical knowledge." While teachers confront feelings of anxiety about themselves as learners and teachers of mathematics, they also experience success as they learn to think through and solve problems. They come to expect that some measure of confusion and frustration often precedes and attends the emergence of new mathematical understandings.

Teachers' work at the two-week institute, though intense, represents only a beginning. Throughout the following academic year, a SummerMath staff member visits each teacher's classroom once a week to observe, interview, and in general provide support as the teacher enacts changes at the core of his or her practice. Teachers may also enroll in a course designed to deepen their understanding of mathematical content and in an advanced institute in which they continue to evaluate their mathematics teaching in a safe environment. Schifter and Fosnot (1993) suggest that significant change in instructional approach can take anywhere from six months to a year and that most of what teachers need to learn in order to change their teaching significantly is actually learned as they teach their own students. "But whether the transformation takes six months or three years or more," they note, "the process is developmental and comprises a series of discernible stages, each building on the achievements of its precursors while overcoming their limitations in a more embracing and coherent unity" (p. 85).

When teachers return to their classrooms, they start to experiment with the instructional strategies that reflect the new principles of learning they encountered during the summer institute. Once their use of these strategies becomes routine, teachers are then prepared to turn their attention to students' thinking and plan and adapt lessons in the light of what advances this thinking. At that point, teachers are prepared to reconsider content and focus on identifying the big ideas in the curriculum. As Schifter and Fosnot make clear, teachers' movement through this process of change is neither straightforward nor invariant. And teachers often seem to have greatest difficulty gaining the deeper understanding of the nature of mathematics that, these authors argue, is key to having insight into students' learning process.

Another approach to meeting the requirements for transformative professional development is exemplified in the teacher inquiry group organized by Featherstone under the auspices of the National Center for Research on Teacher Learning (Featherstone, Pfeiffer, and Smith, 1993; Featherstone and others, 1995). The inquiry group was initiated to support teachers' explorations of innovative approaches to teaching mathematics that parallel those recommended by the National Council of Teachers of Mathematics (NCTM) *Standards* documents. Teachers met weekly with researchers and collectively studied materials related to mathematics teaching and learning, such as videotapes of mathematics lessons, teacher and student journal entries, observers' field notes, and articles. Featherstone emphasizes that these sorts of materials can raise provocative questions about participants' practice by "making the familiar strange" (Featherstone, personal communication, 1996). Like Schifter, she stresses that to provoke thought and learning rather than defensiveness, an environment of trust and mutual support must surround the process of posing challenging questions and observations.

During the initial meetings, teachers observed videotapes of a prominent mathematics educator, Deborah Ball, as she investigated with third graders the addition and subtraction of positive and negative numbers. In one session, for example, third graders were discussing "number sentences equal to 10" that they had invented. In another session, students discussed number sentences that they had written to describe the movements of an elevator that had twelve floors above and twelve floors below ground. Before viewing the videotapes, teachers in the inquiry group responded to the same tasks Ball gave to her own students. After the viewing, teachers discussed the merits and limitations of the representations Ball had used to help students navigate the mathematical terrain. Teachers also examined students' math journals as well as Ball's own journal that recorded her reflections on the progress of students' thinking.

Even before entering the inquiry group, most participating teachers had some familiarity with the NCTM *Standards* and were committed to teaching mathematics differently. But the content in Ball's classroom and the conversations she facilitated among students were considerably different from teachers' experiences. Some teachers, for instance, claimed that they had been "worried and upset" when Ball, after twenty minutes of discussion, did not resolve by the end of class whether 200–190 equaled 10, or 190, as one student had argued. Another teacher commented that she "was shocked" that a teacher would spend three days on only one problem. Other teachers remarked, after examining Ball's journal entries, that they had not considered identifying the different ways students thought about solving the number sentences. The inquiry group continued to meet over the course of a year to support members' attempts to resolve the divergence between new ways of teaching mathematics and teachers' own practice. Discussions increasingly focused on individual teachers' classrooms, and teachers explored different ways to teach their own students.

As Featherstone and her colleagues report, however, translations of initial understanding into performance required struggle. Part of the struggle involved a shift in teachers' professional identity. Teachers in the inquiry group had been taught mathematics in traditional ways and had had little opportunity to gain conceptual knowledge of mathematics. Their participation in group activities and discussions, although useful for creating dissonance and encouraging some changes in practice, did not alter the way teachers felt about mathematics and did not help them gain a greater understanding of specific subject matter, such as operations with integers. Major changes occurred only as teachers attempted to teach their students more conceptually, sometimes in concert with another teacher or researcher. Featherstone and her colleagues argue that teachers probably learn subject matter best while teaching it. She finds that teachers feel a greater sense of pride and curiosity about ideas generated by students in their own classrooms than in ideas generated elsewhere. Further, they expect to understand what is said about mathematics by students in their classrooms and do not expect to be confused, as they often are in university settings. This expectation that they can understand supports their efforts to make sense of the mathematical ideas and of what students say about these ideas. Featherstone and her colleagues believe that teachers need opportunities to engage in mathematical discussions and play with alternative representations. They note that teachers can get such opportunities in their own classrooms, where they can also participate in a community of mathematical thinkers and learners—their own students. And finally, say Featherstone and her colleagues, there are powerful psychic rewards for learning the mathematics that teachers expect students to understand.

A third example of ways the requirements for transformative professional development can be met is found in Riverville, a small semirural district in Michigan (Spillane and Thompson, 1997). Over the past eight years, Riverville has transformed its mathematics program quite radically. District administrators initially encouraged and supported a small number of teacher leaders who were interested in revising their practice, releasing them from classroom duties to attend workshops and conferences and helping them to initiate connections with mathematics experts outside the district. The teacher leaders learned about the mathematics reforms through course work at a neighboring university and later participated in piloting innovative mathematics curricula in their own and their colleagues' classrooms.

We have not yet examined in detail the teacher leaders' own learning and growth, but the teachers with whom they worked report a process of change in their thinking about mathematics instruction that, with some notable exceptions, parallels the experiences of teachers in SummerMath and Featherstone's teacher inquiry group (see Spillane and Zeuli, 1997). With encouragement and support from district administrators, teacher leaders were expected in their day-to-day interactions with colleagues to challenge the content and pedagogy of their peers' mathematics instruction. But unlike the situations in SummerMath and in the teacher inquiry group, teacher leaders in Riverville had already established a high level of trust and camaraderie with their peers. Teacher leaders had taught beside their peers for years and were perceived to be experimenting with new practices of potential value; also, administrators at the district and building levels had established support for teachers' voluntary efforts to change. Perhaps because of these combined factors, the teachers we interviewed did not report high levels of inner dissonance in their initial observations of reformed mathematics instruction. But they did recognize the sharp contrast between the way they taught mathematics and the teacher leaders' practice. Typically the process began when a teacher leader asked a colleague to observe her teaching:

> The whole thing started just because [the teacher leader] and I were friends and I trusted what she was talking about. She asked, "Can I try some things with your kids?" That started five years ago, and I said, "sure, because anything's better than the textbook right now." So we did that, and then we piloted the entire fractions unit with five teachers in this building.

Teachers highlighted the value of observing more advanced colleagues even though, or perhaps because, it gave rise to observations at odds with a teacher's beliefs about content and how students learned. As one teacher commented, "I realized that I didn't know enough about powerful problems in mathematics." Another teacher said, "The things kids came up with, and the misconceptions they had. I saw how giving kids more time to talk helped students' understanding." After observing teacher leaders on several occasions, teachers began to change their curriculum content and experimented with reform-oriented pedagogies. Teacher leaders served to support these initial attempts, observing their peers' teaching and discussing with them what happened in class, and why. Through district-supported summer workshops and interchanges with university-based mathematics educators, many teachers gained learning opportunities paralleling those through which teacher leaders had rethought their own practice.

Many Riverville teachers report that their mathematics classroom is now quite different from the way it was a few years ago. Students now grapple with substantive mathematical problems, teachers recognize the importance of students' arguing about ideas, some form of visual representation of student thinking is common, and students' writing about their mathematical ideas is part of the curriculum. Observation corroborates their reports (Spillane and Zeuli, 1997). Interestingly the process of change these teachers report overlaps with aspects of the change process that Featherstone and her colleagues, as well as Schifter and Fosnot, portrayed. Riverville teachers generally report that close attention to student thinking came after they had established manageable routines associated with the new pedagogy. They also report that guiding student thinking represented a significant shift in how they think about their practice. Said one teacher, "I let students try ideas and fail. Now I realize by struggling it helps them to make sense of the idea." Riverville teachers also seemed to recognize, after they had taken strides toward reformed practice, that they needed to gain a deeper understanding of the mathematics they were expected to teach. A willingness to grapple with understanding the mathematical content seemed to emerge later in the process of change.

In somewhat different ways, each of these professional development efforts creates sufficient dissonance to disturb teachers' existing ideas about content, pedagogy, and learning; provides time, contexts, and support for teachers to think through the conflicts to new ideas; enables them to connect the new ideas to their own students and contexts; helps them develop a repertoire of strategies and techniques to draw on in the ongoing flow of practice; and supports the continuing reconstruction of practice over an extended period.

Underlying each of them are two models of learning: reflective problem solving and cognitive apprenticeship. By *reflective problem solving* we refer to individual or collaborative efforts to resolve some puzzle or conflict between a teacher's (or teachers') existing ideas and new information arising from observed or actual practice, interaction with students, or encounters with subject matter. (Hiebert and others, 1996, refer to such a process as "reflective inquiry and problematizing.") By *cognitive apprenticeship* we refer to learning that results from "apprenticeship" of a novice (in some area) to an expert, who models desired performance, provides scaffolding or support for the novice to try out the performance in part or whole, and coaches, or provides feedback on, the novice's performance and tips on how to improve it, then gradually withdraws or "fades" (Collins, Brown, and Newman, 1989).

As Hiebert and others (1996) pointed out in the context of K–12 students' mathematics learning, the two models may be viewed as complementary rather than competing. In combination the two are adequate to meet the five requirements for professional development enumerated above, as well as to help us understand what is going on in the several examples of good professional development. Their relationship is indeed complementary, but more specifically, in the case of learning to teach in new ways, they seem frequently to form parts of a cycle or to be embedded in each other in complex ways.

Although it seems logical to begin by inducing dissonance, the order of events does not seem to be inevitable. As in the case of Riverville teachers, one could learn the general shape of reformed practice—that is, develop an initial performance repertoire—through the modeling phase of cognitive apprenticeship and could begin to extend the repertoire to a variety of specific "moves" through the scaffolding and coaching phases. But the initial modeling phase also induced a certain amount of cognitive dissonance in the teachers (not, apparently, a highly threatening level). Further, reformed practice will always require a certain amount of improvisation because students' thinking is at its core, and students' thinking (indeed, all thinking) is inherently mercurial in its particulars. If improvisation is to be more efficient than simple trial and error, a cognitive infrastructure is required to support and guide it. The infrastructure would have to include subject matter knowledge, knowledge of students' thinking, misthinking, and learning, and cognitive models of how teaching may help students develop more adequate understanding of the subject matter.

To be really deep and flexible, such an infrastructure would have to be developed through the kind of dissonance-resolving reflective problem solving sketched earlier. In SummerMath the basic foundation of the infrastructure is constructed through fairly troubling encounters with new problems and ideas in the initial summer institute. But Schifter also attributes much of the cognitive reconstruction to teachers' work within their own classrooms. Featherstone gives even more prominence to classroom-based reconstruction. And, as we have seen, in Riverville the process of cognitive restructuring appears to be less traumatic, undertaken, perhaps, in many more small steps rather than through an initial revolution followed by a period of consolidation. It may be that cognitive apprenticeship is the primary mode of practice change in Riverville, while the supporting conceptual infrastructure is developed through such a long chain of reflective problem solving that teachers become aware only in retrospect of the major revolution they have undergone. We thus have two basic models of learning, interrelated in complicated ways and playing out in varied forms and formats.

SCALING UP AS A PROBLEM OF LEARNING, NOT ENGINEERING

Now suppose the argument we presented is roughly right:

- In order to learn, students must think.
- If this is to happen on any significant scale and with any regularity, teachers must understand that students must think in order to learn as well as how to promote and support students' thinking.
- Understanding these things will require a major transformation in teachers' beliefs and knowledge.
- In order to learn them, teachers must think. (Obviously teachers think all the time, but they generally lack the provocations, support, and time to think in the special sense developed in this chapter.)
- Even properly aligned with curricular and instructional standards, the policy instruments embraced by systemic reform are inadequate to promote such learning.
- Popular new forms and formats for teachers' professional development may be promising, but they too will prove ineffective unless the content and pedagogies at their core exhibit certain characteristics.
- Some examples of such learning opportunities may be found, and their critical characteristics can be identified, but they are few in number and still developing.

If this argument is correct, then what might be done to broaden effective opportunities for teacher learning in order to realize the reforms on a much larger scale?

Darling-Hammond and McLaughlin have suggested a series of policies that support professional development in an era of reform (1995). They argue for going beyond skills-oriented training to "providing occasions for teachers to reflect critically on their practice and to fashion new knowledge about content, pedagogy, and learners." So far, so good. Their policy recommendations largely concern new structures and institutional arrangements such as school-university collaboration on curriculum development, change efforts, and research; cross-school networks that provide shared experiences and "critical friends" to join in reflecting on them; partnerships with neighborhood-based youth organizations that offer windows on students' interests and accomplishments, homes, and neighborhoods; and district, regional, or national groups engaged in standard setting, revision of curriculum frameworks, and assessment of teaching practice and school practices.

They also call for reassessment of a whole range of existing policy instruments and practices "for their compatibility with two cornerstones of the reform agenda: a learner-centered view of teaching and a career-long conception of teachers' learning" (Darling-Hammond and McLaughlin, 1995, p. 601). They invite reconsideration and adjustment of curriculum frameworks; student assessment systems; administrative licensing; accountability systems; teacher education institutions; testing, licensing, and evaluation of teachers; allocation of resources between teaching and administrative functions; and other system components in order to ensure that they support and do not impede teachers learning. Taken together these amount to a thoughtful revision and extension of systemic reform specifically to support professionals' development.

Yet although their recommendations would probably reduce impediments to reformed practice and open up new opportunities for teachers to learn, they seem to adjust the frame for reform without sufficient attention to what must go on inside the frame. That is, they deal largely with organizational arrangements, institutional structures, resource allocation, systems of incentives, and formats and general types of activities that teachers might engage in, not with the core content and pedagogy of the learning opportunities, whether specifically designed for professional development or task-embedded occasions for teacher learning.

It may be objected that these are simply the sorts of things that policy deals with—structures, arrangements, incentives, resources, constraints, and entry standards. This may be so, and yet be the source of the limitations of policy to effect the changes in teachers' beliefs and knowledge that are necessary to the realization of the reforms. The workings of the formal policy system depend critically on cultural variables (beliefs, deeply embedded ways of looking at things, knowledge) within the profession and in the society at large, variables that are not readily manipulable by the formal policy system. (Cohen and Spillane, 1993, made this point in a somewhat different context.)

Not only are there limitations on the capacity of formal policy to bring about reform, but actual dangers presented by policy as well. One of the great dangers of any proposal involving policy or governmental intervention is that adoption of the recommended approach by federal or state agencies almost inevitably brings in its wake terrific pressures for large-scale implementation and immediate results expressed in measurable (indeed, measured) student outcomes. In the race to respond to these pressures, careful attention to core matters of content and pedagogy is commonly lost, as is any serious attention to whether and how the intervention actually promotes transformative learning by teachers. In place of serious attention to learning, a great tide of rhetoric and activity is released, followed by the collection of a great deal of data that cover over the fact that the activity, though feverish and well intentioned, is not producing the projected results. Thus, governmental interventions to engineer large-scale implementation of the new forms of professional development that are undertaken before understanding of their core content and pedagogy has developed and spread broadly within the professional sector are likely to prove not merely ineffective, but actually counterproductive.

In somewhat less inflammatory terms, Ball and Cohen (this volume) have pointed out government's weak record in promoting reform, especially reform that requires sustained attention to ideas. While conceding that the record and capacity of the professional sector for such work is not much stronger than that of government, they also argue that building and broadening understanding of the new teaching is properly professional rather than governmental work.

With its strategy of standard setting and alignment, systemic reform can offer a framework for realization of the reforms, but the implementation of systemic reform policy is not the same as reform of actual practice. The alignment of curricular materials, assessment, accountability systems, teacher education requirements, initial and continuing teacher licensure requirements, and other system components may reduce impediments to reform, send a coherent message supporting reform, create incentives for reform, and make available some useful tools for reformed practice, but even if it could be achieved and sustained, such alignment by itself cannot change teachers' fundamental ideas about subject matter, teaching, and learning and cannot teach them how to promote learning through thinking.

In another context, our colleague Andy Anderson once remarked, "To make a tapestry, you need a frame, but the frame is not the tapestry." We would argue that the next few years—indeed, the next few decades at least—are a time for weaving the tapestry, not for creating new frames—that is, not for entirely new structural interventions from the governmental sector. Of course, to call for a moratorium on new policy interventions while we weave this tapestry of understanding within the professional sector is futile. The political system will inevitably cast new waves of initiatives up onto the shore. Certainly there will be new initiatives outside the framework of systemic reform. Market-based reforms such as choice, charters, and vouchers are virtually certain to expand. Yet whether these market-based reforms take hold or not, schools will still need teachers, and achievement of new kinds of learning by students will still depend on the steady expansion of transformative learning by teachers. There are also mounting public and political pressures opposing the ideas in the reform frameworks themselves. Consider, for example, the debates regarding creationism, back-to-basic mathematics instruction, and such whole language practices as invented spelling that have recently raged within the Michigan State Board of Education.

But consider also the possibility that the professional sector, as a major component of civil society, can serve as a buffer against disruptive intervention from the policy sector, as well as the context within which "professional development"—meaning learning by widening circles of teachers, so that it is not only these teachers' knowledge but the whole profession that develops—can proceed. The basic premise of the civil society argument is that nongovernmental organizations or voluntary associations such as churches, guilds, unions, social clubs, civic associations, and the like serve two important functions: (1) they form the habits of spontaneous association and the disposition to trust on which both effective government and robust economic activity depend, and (2) they serve as bulwarks against governmental dominance and social atomization (Fukuyama, 1995; Putnam, 1993, 1995; Hall, 1995). Although they have been embraced by government, the new standards that define the directions for reform are products of professional rather than governmental organizations. These associations and their state affiliates have strongly influenced states' curricular, instructional, and assessment standards—so much so that the line between the professional and governmental sectors has become even more blurred than usual. But reform of practice based on professional standards could proceed somewhat independent of federal, state, and even local district policy. In fact, it could proceed, to a certain extent at least, in the teeth of governmental policy. To do so would require greater self-consciousness about the distinction between the two sectors and perhaps greater self-confidence within the professional sector as well. It would be greatly preferable to have governmental policy that supports professionally conducted reform financially, in regulatory terms, and even pedagogically, but governmental policy may be a shakier frame for reform than are professional standards.

The development of the professional culture—widely shared new beliefs and understanding—on which realization of the reforms depends is really a two-level problem: the level of the climate of opinion and the level of broadening capacity. The first is a matter of popularizing the ideas that transformative teacher learning is crucial to the realization of the reforms and that the required kind of teacher learning involves dissonance-inducing and dissonance-resolving thinking by teachers. As we suggested earlier, if scientists, mathematicians, science and mathematics educators, and prominent policy researchers were to embrace these ideas and articulate them persistently, they could become the kinds of "ideas in good currency" that tend to dominate professional and policy activity during a given period (Schön, 1971).

The second level of the problem—that of broadening capacity—would be aided by such a changed climate but would nevertheless remain a major challenge for some time to come. The confluence of the already burgeoning popularity of increased collegial exchange within schools and through cross-school networks, with popularization of the idea that transformative teacher learning is crucial to the realization of the reforms in science and mathematics education, could create a rich matrix of potential for teacher learning. But even this combination of trends will fall short of what is necessary without a deliberate effort to build broadening capacity for professional development. The full set of requirements for professional development is unlikely to emerge naturally in most collegial groups. For example, even if the diversity of views among teachers within a given group were great enough to create a high level of cognitive dissonance for its members, the norms of discourse that enable a group to resolve such dissonance by constructing thoroughly new understandings will probably not arise spontaneously. The prevailing culture of exchange in the teaching profession does not seem to support the necessary sustained mutual challenging within an atmosphere of trust.

It is for these reasons that the development of widespread capacity for deliberately designed and conducted professional development of the sorts we have described is essential. Such programs help participants gain a certain conceptual elevation, helping them rise above the plane of tinkering within existing modes of practice to see that a thoroughly different way to construe knowledge, learning, and teaching is possible. Fortunately it is probably not necessary for every teacher to experience such specially designed, expertly conducted, and therefore expensive programs of professional development directly. As the Riverville example suggests, if a few members of a school's faculty or a network's members had the benefit of such experiences, and if they have moral and material support from district leadership, these direct beneficiaries might be able to help their colleagues by making conceptual trouble and modeling appropriate ways of resolving it. In this scenario deliberately designed and conducted programs of professional development prime the pump for transformative learning in the task-embedded and collegial formats now growing in popularity. As the scenario plays out, strategic investments in building broadened capacity for programs of transformative professional development could add value to the whole array of more loosely organized, emergent, dispersed contexts for teacher learning. (If federal or state agencies could make such investments without demanding to see results the next day, such investments might help. One way to help ensure such restraint would be to identify the activity supported quite clearly as research. Research there certainly would be. There is no direct empirical evidence to support many of the arguments we have made here.)

"Building" such capacity, with its dangerous resonance with the engineering metaphor of "scaling up," is really the wrong term. A more productive, if also more awkward, way to put the question is, How could broadened capacity be learned? As Ball and Cohen (this volume) point out, the capacity to promote powerful teacher learning is heavily person dependent. Persons acquire it by learning. We have argued elsewhere (Spillane and Thompson, 1997) that local districts' capacity to support reform rests in key administrators' and teacher leaders' capacity to grasp the central reform ideas for themselves and to help others within their district learn them. Here we wish to extend the array of institutions and actors whose capacity to support reform consists largely of their capacity to promote learning. Our current conception extends beyond local administrators and teacher leaders to include such current or potential providers of professional development and technical assistance as district mathematics and science curriculum coordinators, mathematics and science centers, and university-based mathematics and science educators. So the question is, How might more among this array learn how to conduct transformative professional development?

The answer is through variants on the same processes employed in the exemplars of transformative professional development described previously. For example, those programs and groups (and others like them) could offer apprenticeships enabling other professional developers to emulate them. The point here is not to replicate specific programs but to widen the circles of people who understand how to design and conduct programs appropriate to their own settings. In part, these cognitive apprenticeships would involve professional developers' participating in the same fashion that a teacher would participate. Professional developers in training would first be participant-observers, both learning much of what their fellow participants are learning and observing how those who run the programs or groups do what they do. In fact, reflection on the pedagogy of the professional development program in order to articulate conceptual guidance for classroom teaching is a feature of the SummerMath program. Such reflection, articulation, and application would be even more direct for professional developers in training than for teachers. Professional developers in training would use what they learn in contexts more like the contexts in which they had learned it, which should lead to readier application (Collins, Brown, and Newman, 1989) or transfer (Perkins and Salomon, 1988).

Apprenticeships might also include cotraining or coteaching experiences during which expert professional developers could provide scaffolding and coaching for relative novices, as well as follow-up observation and consultation in the learner's own setting, paralleling the kinds of follow-up provided to teachers in their classrooms. As is probably obvious, this process would be intended to produce the same sort of revolution in professional developers' ideas about the content and pedagogy of professional development as teacher participants seem to undergo in their ideas about knowledge, learning, and teaching. Ball and Cohen (this volume) have suggested a series of other ways to help increasing numbers of professional developers—in their phrase, "bricolage guides"—learn how to promote transformative learning.

CONCLUSION

Even if we manage over the next decade or two to make some real headway on the problem of teacher learning, the current reform movement faces other potentially fatal challenges. As Cuban (1993) has shown, earlier waves of reform failed, through a combination of exhaustion from within and political opposition from without, to realize similarly ambitious changes in teaching on a broad scale. Making the change to the kind of teaching that reformers envision makes extraordinary demands on time, energy, and aroused intelligence, and if a teacher succeeds in making the change, she or he has won through to a steady state in which teaching continues to make almost equally extraordinary demands of the same sort. Reformed teaching is hard work, even harder than traditional teaching. Teachers who are learning to teach and are teaching in progressive ways are also virtually certain to meet skepticism and outright opposition from peers, parents, and politicians. The backlash against progressive ideas is no less fierce now than in earlier waves of reform.

So why might the current wave of reform succeed when previous ones have failed? What resources do we have now that they did not have then? As a profession, we know a great deal about students' thinking and learning in several subject areas that was unknown or only dimly understood in Dewey's day. We also know a certain amount more about teaching. We know more about processes of change in education. These are important resources, but they will not be adequate to the challenge unless we avail ourselves of some additional resources that the past few decades of attempts at reform should have created for us: perspective, persistence, and a greatly lengthened time horizon. As Cohen (1988) has pointed out, we are in the midst of "a long, slow collision" between traditional and progressive ideas about knowledge, learning, and teaching. If we keep thinking hard about our problems, we may learn enough to make some advances even among the certain setbacks, losses, and outright failures of the next few decades.

It may be argued that what we are proposing is no more than what is happening already. To a significant degree, this is true—but not completely. For one thing we are proposing a deliberate, sustained shift in focus from the governmental policy sector to the professional sector. We do not argue that states should dismantle or abandon the implementation of systemic reform or that the federal government should reduce its support for systemic reform. We do argue that the shift of focus from policy to the professional sector should be made deliberately, knowing what we are about, refusing to be drawn into new governmental initiatives or to be distracted by escalating pressures for immediate, large-scale improvements in measured student achievement through engineered efforts to scale up. Not that more rapid improvements in student achievement are not desirable. They are. But if our reading of what lies at the heart of the reforms is correct—transformative learning by teachers, leading to students' learning by thinking—then increased pressures for quick results will prove ineffective at best, counterproductive at worst, and enormously wasteful of time and attention for a certainty.

A second difference between what is already happening and what we are proposing is that we explicitly recognize the person-dependent nature of reconceiving scaling up as a process of learning rather than a process of design and engineering. That is, "scaling up" as it is commonly conceived seems to result in designs, jargon, and activities that bear only the most indirect relationship to the fact that this is all about students' and teachers' learning by thinking. Ball (1995) called for "conceptual" scaling up rather than a scaling up of models. This moves the discussion in the right direction, but perhaps a still better way to conceive scaling up is as a process of propagating transformative professional development, construed to include a wide variety of learning processes that combine expert guidance and peer interaction, carried out within a conceptual framework provided by professional standards for curriculum, instruction, and assessment. Reconceiving what it means to scale up by recognizing that it really means supporting the development of wider and wider circles of learning around people who already know how to design and conduct transformative professional development will not bring about rapid change in teaching practice or in student achievement, but it should help to produce more authentic change than we are now seeing.

References

Anderson, J., Reder, L., and Simon, H. "Situated Learning and Education." *Educational Researcher*, 1996, *25*(4), 5–11.

Ball, D. L. "Unlearning to Teach Mathematics." *For the Learning of Mathematics*, 1988, *8*(1), 40–48.

Ball, D. L. "Reflections and Deflections of Policy: The Case of Carol Turner." *Educational Evaluation and Policy Analysis*, 1990, *12*(3), 263–275.

Ball, D. L. "With an Eye on the Mathematical Horizon: Dilemmas of Teaching Elementary School Mathematics." *Elementary School Journal*, 1993, *93*(4), 373–397.

Ball, D. L. *Developing Mathematics Reform: What Don't We Know About Teacher Learning—But Would Make Good Working Hypotheses?* Craft Paper No. 95–4. East Lansing: Michigan State University, National Center for Research on Teacher Learning, Oct. 1995.

Ball, D. L., and Mosenthal, J. H. *The Construction of New Forms of Teaching: Subject Matter Knowledge in Inservice Teacher Education*. Research Report No. 90–8. East Lansing: Michigan State University, National Center for Research on Teacher Learning, 1990.

Brown, J. S., Collins, A., and Duguid, P. "Situated Cognition and the Culture of Learning." *Educational Researcher*, 1989, *18*, 32–42.

Cobb, P. "Where Is the Mind? Constructivist and Sociocultural Perspectives on Mathematical Development." *Educational Researcher*, 1994, *23*(7), 13–20.

Cohen, D. K. "Policy and Organization: The Impact of State and Federal Educational Policy on School Governance." *Harvard Educational Review*, 1982, *52*(4), 474–499.

Cohen, D. K. "Teaching Practice: Plus Que Ça Change…" In P. W. Jackson (ed.), *Contributing to Educational Change: Perspectives on Research and Practice* (pp. 27–84). Berkeley, Calif.: McCutchan, 1988.

Cohen, D. K. "A Revolution in One Classroom: The Case of Mrs. Oublier." *Education Evaluation and Policy Analysis*, 1990, *12*(3), 327–345.

Cohen, D. K., and Ball, D. "Policy and Practice: An Overview." *Educational Evaluation and Policy Analysis*, 1990, *12*(3), 347–353.

Cohen, D. K., and Barnes, C. A. "Pedagogy and Policy, and Conclusion: A New Pedagogy for Policy?" In D. K. Cohen, M. W. McLaughlin, and J. E. Talbert (eds.), *Teaching for Understanding: Challenges for Policy and Practice*. San Francisco: Jossey-Bass, 1993.

Cohen, D. K., and Spillane, J. P. "Policy and Practice: The Relations Between Governance and Instruction." In S. H. Fuhrman (ed.), *Designing Coherent Education Policy* (pp. 35–95). San Francisco: Jossey-Bass, 1993.

Collins, A., Brown, J. S., and Newman, S. E. "Cognitive Apprenticeship: Teaching the Crafts of Reading, Writing and Mathematics." In L. B. Resnick (ed.), *Knowing, Learning and Instruction: Essays in Honor of Robert Glaser*. Hillsdale, N.J.: Erlbaum, 1989.

Cuban, L. *How Teachers Taught: Constancy and Change in American Classrooms, 1890–1990* (2nd ed.). New York: Teachers College Press, 1993.

Darling-Hammond, L. "Instructional Policy into Practice: 'The Power of the Bottom over the Top.'" *Educational Evaluation and Policy Analysis*, 1990, *12*(3), 233–241.

Darling-Hammond, L., Ancess, J., and Falk, B. *Authentic Assessment in Action: Studies of Schools and Students at Work*. New York: Teachers College Press, 1995.

Darling-Hammond, L., and McLaughlin, M. W. "Policies That Support Professional Development in an Era of Reform." *Phi Delta Kappan,* Apr. 1995, pp. 597–604.

Doyle, W., and Ponder, G. A. "The Practicality Ethic in Teacher Decision Making." *Interchange,* 1977, *8*(3), 1–12.

Featherstone, H., Pfeiffer, L., and Smith, S. P. *Learning in Good Company: Report on a Pilot Study.* Research Report No. 93–2. East Lansing: Michigan State University, National Center for Research on Teacher Learning, 1993.

Featherstone, H., and others. *Expanding the Equation: Learning Mathematics Through Teaching in New Ways.* Research Report No. 95–1. East Lansing: Michigan State University, National Center for Research on Teacher Learning, 1995.

Fuhrman, S. H. *Putting the Pieces Together: Systemic School Reform.* CPRE Policy Briefs: Reporting on Issues and Research in Education Policy No. RB-06-4-91. New Brunswick, N.J.: Rutgers University, Consortium for Policy Research in Education, 1991.

Fukuyama, F. *Trust: The Social Virtues and the Creation of Prosperity.* New York: Free Press, 1995.

Grant, S. G., Peterson, P., and Shojgreen-Downer, A. "Learning to Teach Mathematics in the Context of Systemic Reform." *American Educational Research Journal,* 1996, *33*(2), 509–541.

Hall, J. A. "In Search of Civil Society." In J. A. Hall (ed.), *Civil Society: Theory, History, Comparison.* Cambridge, England: Polity, 1995.

Hiebert, J., and others. "Problem Solving as a Basis for Reform in Curriculum and Instruction: The Case of Mathematics." *Educational Researcher,* 1996, *25*(4), 12–21.

Huberman, M. "The Model of an Independent Artisan in Teachers' Professional Relations." In J. Little and M. McLaughlin (eds.), *Teachers' Work.* New York: Teachers College Press, 1993.

Huberman, M. "Networks That Alter Teaching: Conceptualizations, Exchanges and Experiments." *Teachers and Teaching: Theory and Practice,* 1995, *1*(2), 193–211.

Huberman, A. M., and Miles, M. B. *Innovation Up Close: How School Improvement Works.* New York: Plenum Press, 1984.

Lampert, M. "Practices and Problems in Teaching Authentic Mathematics." In F. Oser, A. Dick, and J. L. Patry (eds.), *Effective and Responsible Teaching: The New Synthesis.* San Francisco: Jossey-Bass, 1992.

Little, J. W. "Teachers' Professional Development in a Climate of Educational Reform." *Educational Evaluation and Policy Analysis,* 1993, *15*(2), 129–151.

Lortie, D. C. *Schoolteacher: A Sociological Study.* Chicago: University of Chicago Press, 1975.

McLaughlin, M. "Learning from Experience: Lessons from Policy Implementation." *Educational Evaluation and Policy Analysis,* 1987, *9*(2), 171–178.

McLaughlin, M., and Yee, S. "School as a Place to Have a Career." In A. Lieberman (ed.), *Building a Professional Culture in Schools* (pp. 23–44). New York: Teachers College Press, 1988.

National Council of Teachers of Mathematics (NCTM). *Curriculum and Evaluation Standards for School Mathematics.* Reston, Va.: Author, 1989.

National Council of Teachers of Mathematics (NCTM). *Professional Standards for Teaching Mathematics.* Reston, Va.: Author, 1991.

National Research Council. *National Science Education Standards.* Washington, D.C.: National Academy Press, 1996.

Nelson, B. S., and Hammerman, J. K. *Reconceptualizing Teaching: Moving Toward the Creation of Intellectual Communities of Students, Teachers and Teacher Educators.* Newton, Mass.: Center for the Development of Teaching, Education Development Center, 1994.

O'Day, J., and Smith, M. S. "Systemic Educational Reform and Educational Opportunity." In S. H. Fuhrman (ed.), *Designing Coherent Educational Policy* (pp. 250–312). San Francisco: Jossey-Bass, 1993.

Perkins, D. N., and Salomon, G. "Teaching for Transfer." *Educational Leadership,* 1988, *46*(1), 22–32.

Peterson, P. "The California Study of Elementary Mathematics." *Educational Evaluation and Policy Analysis,* 1990, *12*(3), 257–262.

Phillips, D. C. "The Good, the Bad, and the Ugly: The Many Faces of Constructivism." *Educational Researcher,* 1995, *24*(7), 5–12.

Putnam, R. D. *Making Democracy Work: Civic Traditions in Modern Italy.* Princeton, N.J.: Princeton University Press, 1993.

Putnam, R. D. "Bowling Alone: America's Declining Social Capital." *Journal of Democracy,* 1995, *6*(1), 65–78.

Rutherford, F. J., and Ahlgren, A. *Science for All Americans.* Project No. 2061. New York: Oxford University Press, 1989.

Schifter, D. (ed.). *What's Happening in Math Class? Envisioning New Practices Through Teacher Narratives* (Vol. 1). New York: Teachers College Press, 1996a.

Schifter, D. (ed.). *What's Happening in Math Class? Reconstructing Professional Identities* (Vol. 2). New York: Teachers College Press, 1996b.

Schifter, D., and Fosnot, C. T. *Reconstructing Mathematics Education: Stories of Teachers Meeting the Challenge of Reform.* New York: Teachers College Press, 1993.

Schön, D. A. *Beyond the Stable State.* New York: Random House, 1971.

Schön, D. A. *The Reflective Practitioner: How Professionals Think in Action.* New York: Basic Books, 1983.

Smith, E. "Where Is the Mind? Knowing and Knowledge in Cobb's Constructivist and Sociocultural Perspectives." *Educational Researcher,* 1995, *24*(6), 23–24.

Smith, M. S., and O'Day, J. "Systemic School Reform." In S. H. Fuhrman and B. Malen (eds.), *The Politics of Curriculum and Testing.* Bristol, Pa.: Falmer Press, 1991.

Spillane, J., and Thompson, C. "Restructuring Notion of Local Capacity—The Local Education Agencies' Capacity for Ambitious Instructional Reform." *Education Evaluation and Policy Analysis,* 1997, *19*, 185–203.

Spillane, J. P., and Zeuli, J. S. "The Mathematics Reforms: Mapping the Progress of Reform and Multiple Contexts of Influence." Paper presented at the Annual Meeting of the American Educational Research Association, Chicago, Mar. 1997.

Sykes, G. "Organizing Policy into Practice: Reactions to the Cases." *Educational Evaluation and Policy Analysis,* 1990, *12*(3), 243–247.

Thompson, C., Zeuli, J., and Borman, J. "The Science Reforms: Mapping the Progress of Reform and Multiple Contexts of Influence." Paper presented at the annual meeting of the American Educational Research Association, Chicago, Mar. 1997.

Wiemers, N. J. "Transformation and Accommodation: A Case Study of Joe Scott." *Educational Evaluation and Policy Analysis,* 1990, *12*(3), 297–308.

Wilson, S. M. "A Conflict of Interests: The Case of Mark Black." *Educational Evaluation and Policy Analysis,* 1990, *12*(3), 309–326.

CHAPTER THIRTEEN

Investing in Teaching as a Learning Profession

Policy Problems and Prospects

Linda Darling-Hammond and Milbrey Wallin McLaughlin

The chapters in this book suggest that strategic investments aimed at dramatic improvements in education should focus on the preparation and ongoing professional development of teachers and other educators. This final chapter evaluates the lessons these authors have offered for the development of policy that supports teacher learning needed for high-quality teaching. Before we discuss the kinds of policies that might guide such investments, however, we confront directly the question of whether and how teacher knowledge matters. From a theoretical perspective it might seem obvious that the goal of educating a much more diverse student body to much higher standards than ever before would require enormous skill on the part of teachers. If schools are to educate virtually all students for "knowledge work" and for complex roles as citizens in a technological world, teachers will need to know how to design curriculum and adapt their teaching so that it responds to student understandings, experiences, and needs, as well as to family and community contexts. This task cannot be prepackaged or "teacherproofed." It stands to reason that teaching challenging content to learners who bring very different experiences and conceptions would depend on the capacity of practitioners to create powerful and diverse learning experiences that connect to what students know and how they most effectively learn.

WHY INVEST IN TEACHERS' LEARNING?

These desiderata are not just a matter of theory, however. Growing evidence demonstrates that what teachers know has substantial influence on what students learn. In an analysis of nine hundred Texas school districts, Ronald Ferguson (1991) found that teachers' expertise, as measured by scores on a licensing examination, master's degree, and experience, accounted for about 40 percent of the explained variance in students' reading and mathematics achievement at grades 1 through 11 more than any other single factor. He also found that every additional dollar spent on more highly qualified teachers netted greater increases in student achievement than did less instructionally focused uses of school resources. The effects were so strong and the variations in teacher expertise so great that, after controlling for socioeconomic status, the large disparities in achievement between black and white students were almost entirely accounted for by differences in the qualifications of their teachers.

Similar findings about both the influence of teacher expertise on student achievement and the unequal distribution of skilled teachers to white and minority students have resulted from studies in Alabama (Ferguson and Ladd, 1996), Tennessee (Sanders and Rivers, 1996), Dallas, Texas (Jordan, Mendro, and Weerasinghe, 1997), and New York City (Armour-Thomas et al., 1989). National studies and local research in Georgia, North Carolina, Michigan, and Virginia have found that students achieve at higher levels and are less likely to drop out when they are taught by teachers with certification in their teaching field, by those with master's degrees, and by teachers enrolled in graduate studies (Druva and Anderson, 1983; Hawk, Coble, and Swanson, 1985; NAEP, 1994; Council for School Performance, 1997; Knoblock, 1986; Sanders, Skonie-Hardin, and Phelps, 1994).

These findings are reinforced by those of a recent review of sixty production function studies that found that teacher education, ability, and experience, along with small schools and lower teacher-pupil ratios, are associated with significant increases in student achievement (Greenwald, Hedges, and Laine, 1996). This study's estimates of achievement gains associated with expenditure increments found that spending on teacher education swamped other variables as the most productive investment for schools.

What Kind of Teacher Education Matters?

Other research confirms that teacher knowledge of subject matter, student learning and development, and teaching methods, along with skills developed through expert guidance in clinical settings, are all important elements of teaching effectiveness. More than two hundred studies have found that teachers who have more background in their content areas and have greater knowledge of teaching and learning are more highly rated and more successful with students in fields ranging from early childhood and elementary education to mathematics, science, and vocational education (for reviews, see Ashton and Crocker, 1986; Begle, 1979; Darling-Hammond, Wise, and Klein, 1995; Evertson, Hawley, and Zlotnick, 1985; Guyton and Farokhi, 1987; NCTAF, 1996).

Not only does teacher education matter, but more teacher education appears to be better than less—particularly when it includes carefully planned, extended clinical experiences that are interwoven with course work on learning and teaching. Recent studies of redesigned teacher education programs offering a five-year course of study that includes a year-long internship find that their graduates are more successful and more likely to enter and remain in teaching than graduates of traditional undergraduate teacher education programs (Andrew and Schwab, 1995; Denton and Peters, 1988; Shin, 1994; NCTAF, 1996).

What may be a critically important feature of such programs is that they allow teachers to learn about practice *in* practice (Ball and Cohen, this volume), in settings that deliberately construct integrated study of content, learning, and teaching and create strong connections between theory and practice. Learning to teach diverse learners for deep understanding requires approaches to professional development that help teachers negotiate the divide between general propositions about learning, development, and teaching and the situated realities of subject matter, students, and classrooms.

Situated learning about teaching in curriculum contexts also appears to be an important attribute of inservice education. David Cohen and Heather Hill's study (1997) of California mathematics teachers found that those who participated in sustained professional development grounded in the curriculum they were learning to teach were much more likely than those who engaged in other kinds of professional development to report reform-oriented teaching practices, and their students had higher mathematics achievement. Other studies have found similar results for intensive curriculum-based professional development in which teachers have the opportunity to study curriculum and teaching strategies while engaged in implementing and reflecting on new approaches (Wiley and Yoon, 1995; Brown, Smith, and Stein, 1995).

If it is increasingly clear that teacher learning is a linchpin of school reform, it is equally apparent that if teachers are to negotiate the demands of new standards and new students, they must have access to a deeper base of knowledge and expertise than most teacher preparation programs and inservice staff development programs now provide (see, for example, Kennedy, this volume; Ladson-Billings, this volume). While individual projects already demonstrate that new models of teacher development can be successfully launched and that they make a difference for what teachers can do in schools, these occasional exemplars are not yet part of more far-reaching efforts to create systemic change. In the long run, teachers' and other educators' capacities for much more powerful practice and for leadership in school renewal can be widely acquired throughout the teaching force only by major reforms of teacher (and administrator) preparation and major restructuring of the systems by which states and school districts license, hire, induct, support, and provide for the continual learning of practitioners. This argues for a focus on developing new policy as well as new practices in professional development.

Lessons for Investing in Teaching and Teacher Learning

How can policymakers construct policies consistent with the teacher learning goals addressed in this book? Although there are many dilemmas for which we do not have answers, a good deal has been learned from research and from past reforms about the influences of policy on teaching, and the influences of teaching on policy. We highlight two broad sets of lessons here.

Lessons about Teaching and Teacher Learning. One set of lessons has to do with what we know about teachers' thinking and practice, their work, and the process of change. First, teachers' participation in solving the problems of teaching practice is essential. Policymakers cannot mandate what matters most, which is the combination of knowledge, skills, and commitments that practitioners bring to their work and to their engagement with any innovation (McLaughlin, 1987). From the earliest work on the "remote control" of teaching (Shulman, 1983) to more recent work on teacher learning and the processes of school change (Lieberman, 1995; Darling-Hammond and McLaughlin, 1995), much research suggests that the locus of most relevant problem solving regarding the issues of teaching practice lies among teachers themselves. Not surprisingly research on successful school-based reforms makes repeated reference to the collective problem-solving capacity of school staff (Fullan, 1993; Newmann and Wehlage, 1995). Efforts to build school capacity rest on the premise that teachers can forge a stronger, collective dialogue regarding practice, informed by access to greater knowledge about learning and teaching (Little, this volume).

Professional norms and knowledge are the proximate causes of teachers' actions, and they are crucial in any approach to improvement. However teachers interact around the issues that concern their practice, they bring various degrees and forms of knowledge about teaching, children, learning, and subject matter to the table. In addition, they bring norms and expectations about students, each other, schooling, and good practice itself. What teachers know, know how to do, and believe to be right are critical, and they clearly constrain or enable efforts aimed at teaching improvement. Attempts to reshape governance or school structure will come to naught if means are not available to develop new professional norms and knowledge (Elmore, Peterson, and McCarthy, 1996; Cohen, 1996; McLaughlin, 1993; Bryk, Lee, and Holland, 1993).

If teachers' norms and knowledge are crucial, we also know that changing teachers' knowledge, beliefs, and norms of practice requires long-term learning opportunities based in practice as well as research. The deep-seated learning—and unlearning—that teachers must do to realize ambitious reform goals has been the focus of much recent research in various areas of the curriculum (Ball and Cohen, this volume; Kennedy, this volume; Hawley and Valli, this volume; Lampert and Ball, this volume). Given the wide array of learning needs demanded by teaching and by current reforms, it is important to figure out how policy can stimulate and support a rich mix of learning opportunities connected to practice and to a growing knowledge base about effective teaching.

Teaching—and teacher learning—are situated in subject matter contexts. Recognition of the subject-specific nature of "pedagogical content knowledge" (Shulman, 1987), has led to research that illustrates how teachers' actions and their learning are heavily conditioned by the subject matter context (Stodolsky, 1988; Grossman and Stodolsky, 1994; Siskin and Little, 1997). Put another way, teachers' norms of practice, knowledge of content, and images of good teaching do not exist in the abstract or in the wholly generic form featured by much staff development of decades past (regarding, for example, classroom management techniques or lesson planning techniques). Instead much pedagogical knowledge is encoded in the content of reading, mathematics, science, social studies, the arts, and so on. Because subject matter contexts are profoundly different, efforts to change norms and knowledge must be substantially situated in school subjects (Lampert, 1987; Ball, 1994).

Teaching—and teacher learning—are also situated in student contexts. As recent studies have found, the students' context is what is most immediately important to teachers (Darling-Hammond, 1997b; McLaughlin, 1993; McLaughlin and Talbert, 1993). Making subject matter understandable to students requires an understanding of the cultural and community contexts that shape their experiences, so that representations of content can connect to those experiences and can take into account the ways these contexts shape students' ways of knowing and modes of learning (Ladson-Billings, this volume; Moll, 1996). Effective teachers develop "pedagogical learner knowledge" (Grimmett and MacKinnon, 1992) based on what they know about learning and development, and based on what they learn from strategies that help them come to know how their students think, what they know and believe, and what they care about.

Furthermore, today's teachers teach different students and teach them in different settings than did yesterday's. Significant and often swift changes in student demographics and language backgrounds, particularly in states with high rates of immigration, present significant challenges to school teachers. The diversity of language, culture, academic preparation, and interests added by changes in who comes to school is increased by shifts in who stays in school. Students who in years past would have left the classroom for jobs in fast food businesses, service industries, or other low-skill occupations stay in school in greater numbers. Regardless of their social backgrounds or national origins, today's students come from home and community circumstances much more stressful and challenging than they did even ten years ago (Children's Defense Fund, 1997; Crowson and Boyd, 1993). As schools become more socioeconomically and ethnically diverse and more diverse in learning needs as a result of inclusion policies, policies must be sensitive to fact that standardized practices will not allow teachers to address differences among students, and that strategies for doing so are a major area of needed learning.

Lessons Concerning Change Processes and Agents. A second set of lessons concerns what we know about how teachers change their ideas about and approaches to their practice. A phenomenon little appreciated in earlier eras of school reform is that professional communities are key agents in shaping teachers' norms and knowledge and in sustaining change. As research has increasingly noted the collective nature of professional learning (indeed, all learning), attention has become focused on the professional communities of which teachers are a part and the cultures these communities represent (Hargreaves, 1992, 1993; McLaughlin and Talbert, 1993, in press; Talbert and McLaughlin, 1994). Such cultures and communities are an inescapable feature of life in schools, and arise organically as well as by administrative contrivance. As recent research has argued, the possibilities for individual teacher learning increase greatly as professional communities move from individualistic or "balkanized" cultures to "collaborative" cultures, and towards what can be described as "learning communities."

There are many manifestations of professional community, some conforming to school boundaries and some transcending these boundaries through networks or other associations (Firestone and Pennell, 1995). But clearly, the development of viable professional communities within and across schools holds much promise for supporting teachers' growth and development (Little, this volume; Lieberman and Grolnick, this volume). Recent work has begun to demonstrate that the kinds of professional community vary greatly among schools, and that the type of community may be critical to the effects of restructuring on student learning (Louis, Marks, and Kruse, 1995). The formation, sustenance, and life cycle of such communities, as well as their import for student learning, bear careful consideration as a focus of teacher policy.

Initial teacher preparation and mentoring in the formative years matters as well. Only in the past decade has careful, convincing research begun to illuminate the links between initial teacher preparation experiences and teachers' approaches to teaching. The early socialization that occurs in preservice programs and initial experiences on the job is clearly powerful. In addition evidence is beginning to accumulate that well-conceived teacher education and induction programs can provide much more extensive and useful knowledge about learning, teaching, students, and subjects than was once the norm, establishing important groundwork for the development of significantly more sophisticated kinds of classroom practice and ongoing learning in collaboration with peers (National Commission on Teaching and America's Future, 1996). The task for teacher policy is to shape more useful government, professional, and institutional policies to encourage the spread of such teacher education programs.

Finally it is clear that external agents can play important catalytic roles in introducing new ideas to teachers, helping form professional communities, and mentoring teachers through periods of learning. Change agents come in various forms: professional associations and networks, professional development organizations, unions that take improvement-oriented activity to be central to their role (Koppich and Kerchner, this volume), and "linkers," who broker ideas and techniques among schools and teachers (Lieberman, 1996). These sources can play an important catalytic role in bringing ideas to teachers' attention and in supporting them through an extended process of change (Fullan, 1993). Policies have not yet begun to take full advantage of these various agents.

WHAT KINDS OF POLICIES MATTER?

The chapters in this book suggest that changes in policy and practice are likely to be most productive if they focus on the relationship between student learning and teaching as it unfolds in different community and organizational contexts; the development of strong professional communities that foster practitioner learning connected to curriculum and organization reform; and strategies for restructuring schools and schools of education as learning organizations that build knowledge through collegial inquiry. An overarching concern is how to develop knowledgeable teachers and learning-centered schools in all communities, especially in low-income communities where children have least access to competent and caring teaching and schooling. The deep-seated inequities in students' access to high-quality teaching and teachers' access to professional learning are a driving force for more systemic policy strategies.

While policymakers and practitioners may tend to think of professional development as the specific set of activities that provide teachers with in-service training once they have entered the profession, this limited view does not account for many factors that critically influence teachers' expertise and the quality of teaching. Efforts to improve teaching in ways that are both widespread and lasting must address several key areas at once: (1) attracting, recruiting, and retaining people in teaching who have the ability and disposition to teach well; (2) helping teachers—and the profession as a whole—develop strong professional norms, knowledge, and skills; and (3) creating incentives and organizational conditions that support teachers' and students' learning in schools. In addition, policy strategies should be evaluated in terms of their possibilities for bringing changes to scale and enhancing equity—in short, their ability to address the persistent inequalities, enormous fragmentation, and growing diversity that are inherent in American public schooling.

Attracting, recruiting, and retaining capable people in the classroom require attention to incentives and conditions for entry (training subsidies, salaries, working conditions, and entry requirements); the availability of high-quality preparation programs for both current college students and individuals who want to enter teaching from other careers; district hiring and induction practices, which may either alienate good teachers or recruit and retain them; and compensation systems that either reward teachers for leaving the classroom or are redesigned to support the development of accomplished teaching (Darling-Hammond, Berry, Haselkorn, and Fideler, this volume).

The distribution of all of these factors is equally critical. If traditional resource allocations are not mediated by equalizing policies, teacher salaries, working conditions, and development opportunities will continue to be allocated extremely unevenly, leaving some communities and students with much less access to expert teachers and much less professional knowledge on which to build. Barriers to teacher mobility rooted in fragmented state licensing and pension systems can also prevent well-qualified teachers in areas with surpluses from moving to areas of high need (NCTAF, 1996). All of these factors are subject to the control of government and professional bodies that can, in principle, exert useful leverage to change the character of the teaching force.

Efforts to develop professional norms and expertise implicate many policy actors. State policymakers, university leaders, teacher educators, and those who set standards for preparation programs (standards boards, accrediting bodies, and state agency officials) must puzzle over what it is teachers need to know for today's and tomorrow's schools. Many different policies—some of them governmental and others professional—influence the definition and transmission of knowledge in professions: standards that govern professional education, licensing, and certification; tools like accreditation and state approval that shape preparation programs; mechanisms like induction programs that shape early socialization into the field; assessments of teacher knowledge, skills, and abilities that cast a long shadow on training, evaluation, and practice; and school organizational factors that determine whether and how teachers work together, toward what ends, and with what guidance or support.

The creation of workplace incentives and conditions that support high-quality teaching touches areas of policy often considered under the rubric of school management and organization. These organizational concerns are frequently ignored when questions of pedagogy and teaching policy are under consideration. For example, the allocation of time for teaching and the ways in which students' and teachers' work is organized determine how deeply material can be studied; the allocation and organization of time for planning determine how much discourse about practice among teachers is likely to occur; the size of schools or school units within which teachers attend to shared students determines the extent to which a group can easily function as a learning community that shares norms, knowledge, expertise, and decisions; the structures that exist or do not exist for reflecting and deliberating on shared work determine the extent to which teachers can learn from one another and effect changes in their collective practice that add up to more than the sum of their separate parts (Little, this volume).

The problem of realizing change on a large scale and in an equitable manner involves a triple challenge to policymakers: how to get from central plans (such as state-level standards-based reforms) to broad enactment in large numbers of districts, schools, and classrooms; how to get from a few promising small-scale efforts to many, as in instances where large numbers of teacher or schools learn from demonstration programs; and how to do so equitably, within a system that is funded unequally and managed in a decentralized fashion.

In addressing these problems, the ultimate challenge to policymakers lies in realizing the results of investment in teachers and teacher development in student learning (Sykes, this volume). It is one thing for teachers to participate in and appreciate professional development experiences; it is quite another for their learning to be translated into classroom practice that makes a difference. For many reasons, the professional development scene is littered with examples of learning experiences that do not connect particularly well with teachers' practice in classrooms. Among them are faulty assumptions about how teachers learn, a lack of match between the pedagogy of professional development and the desired pedagogy in the classroom, a focus on generic skills that do not map onto the subject-specific world in which teachers actually work, and failure to address issues and concerns about students that are most on teachers' minds (McLaughlin and Oberman, 1996).

A first challenge to professional development, then, is to engage teachers in ideas, materials, techniques, and learning that have direct relevance and application to their teaching and in settings (including the context of practice itself) in which those applications are most powerfully experienced. Achieving the link between exposure to new ideas in teacher development and the realization of these ideas in student learning is a complex undertaking. Although some evidence establishes that these links are there under certain conditions, the linkage is often not realized or even examined.

As we have implied, the problems of teacher recruitment, preparation, and support are intertwined. Solving any one of them requires solutions to the others. Even if one attracts more qualified people to teaching, many will leave or end up teaching in suboptimal ways if workplaces do not support high-quality teaching and teacher learning. Enhancing some teachers' access to useful knowledge will not help traditionally underserved students' access to high-quality teaching if these efforts do not reach the teaching force that serves the lowest-wealth schools. Changing teachers' early preparation is likely to be of limited value unless there are companion efforts to change the norms that govern the school workplace as well. Hence encouraging excellence in teaching requires coordinated action on a range of fronts, involving a range of actors in legislative, bureaucratic, and professional positions.

POLICY TOOLS TO SUPPORT TEACHERS' LEARNING

Policymakers have a number of strategic choices available. In current reform efforts, at least three broad classes of policies have been promoted as means for improving practice: standards-based strategies, school-based strategies, and development-based strategies that focus on teachers' professional learning (see Figure 13.1). These are overlapping rather than discrete policy tools; however, each pursues a somewhat different logic as a support, incentive or occasion for teachers' learning.

Standards-Based Strategies

Standards-based strategies establish goals for teachers' professional performance; they have evolved primarily in two domains. Strategies that feature changes in student learning goals, curriculum, and assessment as levers for the improvement of teaching practice comprise one well-known set of initiatives. Recent efforts to create standards for students have focused on content and performance

Figure 13.1. Promising Strategies for Promoting Teacher Excellence.

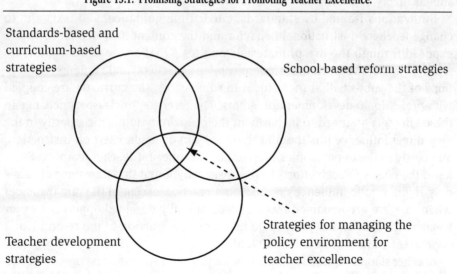

Standards-based and curriculum-based strategies

School-based reform strategies

Teacher development strategies

Strategies for managing the policy environment for teacher excellence

standards that outline what students should know and how they should demonstrate their understanding. The logic of standards-based reform is that once clear goals are specified, the other mechanisms of schooling—curriculum, teaching, teacher training, organizational features, and other resources—will be marshaled to attain them (O'Day and Smith, 1993).

Some governmental bodies and professional associations have focused on outlining learning standards and curriculum guidance. The work of the National Council of Teachers of Mathematics in developing standards for curriculum and teaching constituted one of the first efforts by the profession (Lampert and Ball, this volume). Maine, Vermont, New York, Kentucky, and other states, have developed standards followed by the adoption of new tests with high or low stakes attached. Others have focused on defining the curriculum to be taught. The state curricular framework reform movements in various subject areas in the late 1980s are an example of this strategy in action; California and Maryland provide two well-known cases. In the former case, new tests were also developed but never widely implemented. In the latter case, ambitious performance tests resulting in school-level scores are still in use.

In previous eras, reformers focused on innovative instructional packages or materials as the key lever of action, as in the well-known science and mathematics curriculum innovations supported by the National Science Foundation in the 1960s and 1970s (Welch, 1979), and more recently in some mathematics series, such as Cognitively Guided Instruction. These voluntary classroom-directed efforts, however, were not embedded in instructional systems influencing large-scale testing programs or expectations for the learning of most students. Thus, they stopped short of systemic ambitions, although they held a similar theory of change.

Innovations framed by standards, curriculum guidance, and tests aim to change teachers' instructional behavior and the content to which students are exposed through the use of materials and tests that shape the assignments teachers make, the work that students do, and teachers' and students' conceptions of the subjects that they study. In some cases, the curricula are coupled with professional development programs. The leverage for classroom change in these efforts is assumed to lie partly in their proximity to practice, partly in the very direct influence it is thought that they can or might exert on instruction, and partly in the opportunities they sometimes offer for teacher learning. Studies of the effects of such efforts have consistently found that they typically have only slight, erratic influence on classroom practice, except in the rare instances when they are accompanied by extended, carefully designed opportunities for teachers to learn and to participate in the co-construction of the reform (for a review, see Darling-Hammond, 1997b).

Another standards-based approach, sometimes linked to the first one, is the setting of standards for what teachers should know and be able to do. Two leading examples are the efforts of the National Board for Professional Teaching Standards (NBPTS), a professional body that has set standards of accomplished practice and offers voluntary assessments to certify veteran teachers who meet them, and the Interstate New Teacher Assessment and Support Consortium (INTASC), a consortium of more than thirty states that has developed standards and assessments for licensing beginning teachers. The INTASC approach sought to incorporate standards for students developed by national professional associations as well as to be compatible with the more advanced teaching standards developed by the NBPTS.

Although the two efforts are institutionally different (a private national professional body versus a state government-based effort), both create ambitious standards for teachers' work and invite individuals or jurisdictions to meet the standards. The INTASC standards have also been incorporated into standards for teacher education programs applied by the National Council for the Accreditation of Teacher Education (NCATE), creating the possibility of a coherent continuum for teacher development, from initial preparation, through licensing and induction, to the development of accomplished practice. Together these initiatives assume that the key element in educational change is teachers' knowledge, skills, and norms of practice and that a cadre of teachers who meet such standards will be a powerful lever for change. They further assume that a critical agent for change is the profession itself, in concert with the agencies that license, educate, hire, and reward the work of teachers.

Although too new to have widely demonstrated effects on teachers' practice or student outcomes, a number of studies have found that teachers report that their experience with the National Board and INTASC standards and assessments has caused them to change their teaching in ways they feel are important, and that a growing number of teacher education programs are changing their curricula in response to the standards (Darling-Hammond, in press). Thus, these efforts may hold promise for translating the aspirations of student standards into a set of supports and incentives that better prepare teachers to meet them.

School-Based Reform Strategies

Another class of reforms centers attention on the school and the community of practice that operates there. Specific programs and policies vary, but all focus on creating a schoolwide approach to change, through either governance changes (for example, site-based management), structural changes (for example, new schedules and grouping policies), and/or curriculum changes (for example, schoolwide goal-setting leading to the creation or adoption of new approaches to teaching). Following on the heels of the "effective schools" movement of the early 1980s, efforts like those of the Coalition of Essential Schools, the School Development Program, Accelerated Schools, and others have sought to foster a community of shared practice within the school. Generally the effort to create greater participation and a collective perspective among school staff is viewed as a resource for reform and an opportunity for teacher learning and change. The leverage for change is thought to lie initially in the transformation of professionals' sense of purpose and mission and, consequently, in renewed instructional work they undertake together (Darling-Hammond, 1997b).

Some of these reforms emphasize the transformation of school structures (the creation of decision-making teams or teaching teams focused on shared students, the establishment of longer classes and multiyear relationships between teachers and students, the creation of collaborative planning time and tasks for teachers). These seek to change what is possible by changing the conditions for students' learning and, in some cases, teachers' learning as well. Some school-based reforms emphasize teacher-to-teacher collaboration, coaching, and staff development. Others highlight inquiry or "action research" as a way for teachers to examine critical questions of teaching and learning in their school (Cochran-Smith and Lytle, 1996) and to make changes that emerge from their own findings.

Teacher inquiry is presumed to offer occasions for teachers to engage in learning activities that rely on the primary material of their classrooms. Schools playing a leadership role in the Hewlett-Annenberg–sponsored Bay Area School Reform Collaborative, for example, are expected to feature teacher learning as part of a "cycle of inquiry" in which faculty collect and analyze data about their students' performance and structure their own professional development activities to support the work they have identified as crucial for their school's progress (Center for Research on the Context of Teaching, 1998). Teacher inquiry, when it functions as reformers expect, not only provides evidence teachers can use to make changes in their practice; it also functions as a "disequilibrating" element, unsettling prior ideas and paving the way for constructing new, more effective ones (see Thompson and Zeuli, this volume).

A related contribution of a dynamic learning community at the school level is its "integrative capacity," or ability to help teachers come to a shared understanding of their goals for teaching and student learning (Bryk, 1995, regarding Catholic high schools; Meier, 1995, for an example of public elementary and middle schools). This seems to be particularly likely when teachers' work has been structured around shared students or subject matter, including the examination of student work and teaching activities. The resulting shared theory of practice is assumed to help teachers know how to make their individual and collective efforts more coherently related to one another and to establish indicators that teachers can use to assess their work (Darling-Hammond, Ancess, and Falk, 1995; Hill, 1995; McLaughlin, 1993; McLaughlin and Talbert, 1993).

Efforts to build a school-based learning community assume that the teachers' community affords a rich context for learning where teachers can build on the faculty's collective expertise in the course of critical reflection and change (Little, this volume). However, the contemporary array of school-based strategies reflects distinctly different starting points, from efforts to "reculture" a school environment around more constructive professional habits of practice, to initiatives aimed at rehabilitating schools identified as "failing." Each point of departure carries different incentives and signals for teachers, and different resources for their efforts.

From the point of view of promoting teachers' learning, the promise of the various school-based strategies lies in their capacity to mobilize and focus teachers' energies on a collective and improved vision of students' education and, along with it, a situated vision of and support for their own learning. Experience with these initiatives over the past decade suggests that local school capacity in the form of staff expertise, material resources, and community supports makes an important difference for the outcomes of school-based reforms, as do school district and state contexts which may be supportive of or hostile to the changes undertaken, and the availability of external sources of legitimation, help, and knowledge when they are called for by those working to transform practice inside the school. In addition, schools that have made important changes frequently flounder if they are not able to hire incoming staff who share their knowledge and beliefs when vacancies need to be filled (Darling-Hammond, 1997b; Elmore, Peterson, and McCarthy, 1996; Lieberman, 1995).

Development-Based Strategies

A large array of professional development policies comprises the third class of efforts to support teachers' learning. These focus on the development of individual teachers' capacities, from preservice teacher education programs to the diverse occasions for development that teachers encounter throughout their careers. This class of policy variously locates opportunity for learning in such diverse institutional settings as universities, districts, special projects, networks, and professional organizations, and it takes different shapes and forms along teachers' professional paths. The assortment of national, state, and local public and private programs that provides resources for teachers' learning throughout the various phases of teachers' careers can be made intensive and coherent, as in New York City's District 2 (Elmore and Burney, this volume), or may remain scattershot and contradictory in the implicit views of important knowledge and skills and how those might be acquired.

Both preservice teacher education programs and in-service development consistent with the premises of teacher learning outlined in this book provide explicit opportunities for teachers to learn how to be learners themselves and to learn about practice in practice that is both theoretically and practically grounded. Professional development available to practicing teachers outside their school workplace takes many forms, from district in-service activities, to subject matter networks, to school-university partnerships, to the activities associated with special reform projects (Lieberman and Grolnick, this volume).

Professional development consistent with the ideals of a learning profession—whether pre- or in-service—understands teachers' learning as an intellectual problem as well as a problem of enactment (Kennedy, this volume), and situates leverage for change in teachers' active engagement in wrestling with new experiences and ideas, in unlearning as well as learning new professional habits and expertise (Lampert and Ball, this volume; Lieberman, 1996).

Whereas the usual "in-service" activities available to (or required of) teachers supply information for teachers to assimilate into an existing system of ideas and practices, professional development activities that promote more fundamental learning challenge "taken-for-granteds" and enable teachers to examine the normative structures underlying their work. Professional development of this stripe offers opportunities for teachers not only to master new technical skills but also to reconceptualize their practice in fundamental ways. Some of the work of subject matter networks, for example, engages teachers in rethinking relationships between students and content, and the associated classroom roles and expectations (Lieberman, 1996). Professional learning activities such as these derive power as change strategies from their ability to provide teachers with experiences of alternative practices and an accessible path from the old to the new.

The effectiveness of professional development strategies depends not only on the extent to which they individually create more powerful contexts for and approaches to teacher learning, but also the extent to which teachers encounter comprehensive, cumulative, and reinforcing learning opportunities over the course of their careers, rather than spotty, erratic, and conflicting experiences that leave them with gaps in their knowledge, uncertainty, and confusion. In addition the outcomes of professional development depend on the extent to which teachers work in settings that allow them to incorporate what they have learned into their classroom practice. If school norms and structures do not support the enactment of new practices, or if evaluation and supervision practices enforce a different set of expectations for teaching, what teachers have learned in networks, courses, study groups, or seminars will not take deep root.

Implications of Different Starting Points for Policy

Each of these classes of policy stems from a different logic about what stimulates and supports student learning and teacher competence. Standards-based policies reflect a belief that setting expectations for student learning and teacher performance will produce more focused effort on the part of institutions and hence more productive practices. In standards-based efforts that attach rewards and sanctions to student or teacher performance, there is an additional belief that such incentives function as motivators and can produce change. Alone, these policies do not treat questions of how students or teachers will learn to meet the standards, or how schools will be organized to support them.

School-based strategies assume that student learning will be enhanced by a more coherent approach to practice within the school. The unit of change is thought to be the school, not the individual teacher. In some versions of this approach, incentives include the rewards of heightened professional exchange and empowerment brought about by broader faculty participation and inquiry. In others, for example, policies that designate penalties for "failing" schools, negative consequences are thought to motivate improvement. Alone, such policies do not look beyond the school for sources of expertise for solving teaching problems, nor do they concern themselves with the ways in which the resources, regulations, and conceptions of education emanating from other agencies—school districts, federal or state governments—affect the school.

Professional development approaches target individual teachers' professional growth and provide access to knowledge of different kinds. This may include comprehensive programs of preparation or specific areas of learning focused on particular reform initiatives, subject domains, or student characteristics (language, culture, or achievement, for example). The incentives associated with such approaches are both intrinsic—the satisfaction of becoming more effective and feeling more efficacious—and extrinsic—salary credits or mandates that stimulate or require participation. Alone, such approaches do not solve problems of what students or teachers should learn, how schools will be organized to ensure that such learning opportunities are available, and whether the strategies learned will support or conflict with other policies, practices, or structures that affect teachers' work.

It is easy to see how even in the best of circumstances, none of these strategies by itself can produce high-quality teaching. Without some systemwide agreements about what constitutes useful teaching and teaching knowledge and some systematic supports for acquiring it, as well as school contexts for enacting it, the knowledge that teachers may gain from particular independent development experiences may be at best partial and at worst unusable, leaving them feeling "all dressed up with no place to go." Thus, the three policy strategies ultimately rely on one another and serve as complements rather than as single solutions to the problems of improving teaching and schooling.

MAKING POLICY CHOICES

Different starting points for policy can be productive so long as other elements of the system are considered as well. Among the issues that should be important to policymakers are considerations of coherence, context, and fit, that is, the match between a policy's logic and the situation to which it is applied.

Coherence and Comprehensiveness

A seminal learning from policy analysis is that, like other policies, teacher policies that push on only one feature of the system are unlikely to work. The past several decades abound with examples of single-focus policies aimed at instructional improvement, among them the National Science Foundation (NSF)–supported curriculum improvement investments of the 1950s and 1960s (Welch, 1979); discrete professional development activities such as the NSF-supported summer institutes for mathematics and science teachers in the 1960s and 1970s (Fox, 1978; Stake and Easly, 1978); tests, like those instigated as the basis for measurement-driven instructional improvement strategies (Cohen and Barnes, 1993; Popham, 1987); and graduation requirements, as in the wave of state actions in the early 1980s to increase the number of mathematics and science courses students needed for a high school diploma (Clune, 1989).

All of these failed for inattention to other parts of the system. Curriculum changes could not be implemented without massive changes in teacher preparation; preparation initiatives could not overcome the conditions of teaching that precluded the use of new practices; tests alone did not change instruction; course-taking requirements could not ensure high-quality teaching or school supports for struggling students; and so on. Similarly, many standards-based reforms have fallen short for lack of support for teachers' learning (Darling-Hammond, 1997a, 1997b).

Because single-issue policies are unlikely to be fruitful and policies do not land in a vacuum but on top of other, often contradictory policies (Darling-Hammond, 1990), attention to the cumulative effect of policies, and their coherence where they intersect, is crucial. Figure 13.1 depicts the policy intersection at which standards-based policies, school-based strategies, and professional development initiatives meet. The power of policies at the intersection lies in their potential to leverage multiple, reinforcing incentives and supports for students' and teachers' learning and improved practices. The premise of cumulative effects underlies a spate of policy strategies, many of them stemming from the state level, which have sought to orchestrate the different strands of influence promulgated by government education agencies, including state curriculum frameworks, assessments, accountability requirements, and professional development resources (O'Day and Smith, 1993).

There is evidence that some carefully crafted state systemic reforms in place for several years have reached large numbers of teachers and helped them engage in the use of new materials and practices (e.g., Shields, Corcoran, and Zucker, 1994). However, not all policies are mutually supportive. For example, new incentives for teachers to achieve National Board Certification conflict with behaviorist models of teacher evaluation and supervision mandated in some states in the 1980s. New curriculum frameworks ask teachers to teach for goals that are inconsistent with existing student tests. Thus, policy coherence is as often undermined as enhanced by the avalanche of new and often contradictory state and local policies that address curriculum and testing as well as the ways teachers are prepared, credentialed, supported, evaluated, assigned, and compensated. These can impede education when they confuse educators, dilute resources, or pile incompatible demands on schools (Darling-Hammond, Ancess, and Falk, 1995).

Similarly, the "Christmas tree" strategy of pursuing multiple grants and projects in many schools or districts often neglects the core functioning of the school and the careful use of staff time and efforts, while creating conflicts among the normative structures of different strategies. For example, although both inquiry-oriented strategies and direct instruction policies aim to improve student achievement, they are differentially appropriate for different learning goals and offer fundamentally different perspectives on teaching. Teachers who encounter both sets of requirements operating simultaneously in their district or school are bound to be confused about the sort of teaching they are expected to undertake and the kinds of expertise they are expected to develop. Since such policies are usually adopted as mandates for curriculum, staff development, supervision, or teacher evaluation, teachers are expected merely to comply with different conceptions of teaching rather than to learn about the different appropriate uses of various teaching strategies for different learning goals and students in specific contexts. The necessary standardization of policy conflicts with the demands of effective teaching. As Lee Shulman (1983, p. 488) observes:

> Why is the juxtaposition of "teaching" and "policy" the statement of a problem? We are wont to think of teaching as a highly clinical, artful, individual act. Since instruction is interactive, with teachers' actions predicated on pupil responses or difficulties, it appears ludicrous in principle to issue directives regarding how teachers are to perform.

In fact, studies find that when prescriptive policies violate professional standards, teachers experience internal conflict resulting in dysfunctional practices (Darling-Hammond, 1997b; Lipsky, 1980; Sykes, 1983).

The Implications of Context for Professional Policy

The widespread strategy of using mandates to legislate teaching practice assumes that there is one best answer to teaching problems rather than presuming that there are a variety of approaches to teaching that are differentially effective in different circumstances. Recognition that contexts matter for teaching—that teachers must shape their actions to fit the needs of their students, the nature of their communities, and the demands of their subject matter—leads to a fundamentally different starting point for policy: one that seeks to build the knowledge of practitioners to make sound judgments in nonroutine situations rather than to prejudge and prescribe the actions they should take. The fact that teaching is complex, knowledge-based work that is contingent on many factors that cannot be controlled from afar suggests large arenas of instructional improvement that are not amenable to traditional policy tools aimed directly at constructing or constraining what teachers do (Sykes, 1983). Instead one might argue that efforts to engage the profession in strengthening practitioners' abilities to respond intelligently to the diverse circumstances they must confront would be more fruitful in accomplishing these goals (see Thompson and Zeuli, this volume).

Engaging the profession in this way requires policy of another sort. While the acknowledgment of professionalism might sometimes suggest an absence of policy (that is, that policymakers not act in arenas where regulation is a counterproductive substitute for professional judgment), the creation of a widely shared professional knowledge base that would justify less governmental intrusion in classroom matters actually depends on a host of policy actions. It requires policies that draw on professional knowledge and legitimize the authority of the profession in standard setting, by, for example, establishing professional standards boards to take responsibility for licensing and certification and providing incentives for teachers to meet those standards (as when states relicense teachers who have met the standards of the National Board for Professional Teaching Standards or pay them higher salaries). It requires policies that use the results of professional standard setting to inform professional education through vehicles like accreditation of preservice programs or the involvement of professional associations in the construction of professional development and teacher evaluation, rather than relying on bureaucratic mechanisms that do not represent the expertise of skillful professionals. And it requires policies that provide incentives for teachers to build their professional knowledge and to use it, through, for example, rewards for knowledge and skill that operate in hiring processes, compensation systems, and the construction of teachers' roles in relation to their expertise.

These kinds of policy, which we call professional policy, emphasize the development of expertise to be used for problem solving rather than the imposition of standardized prescriptions for practice that impede teachers' ability to handle diversity. The preparation of teachers to work effectively in distinctive contexts with diverse learners is a hallmark of the new standards created by expert teachers through the National Board for Professional Teaching Standards, INTASC, and state standards boards in states like Minnesota and Iowa (Darling-Hammond, Wise, and Klein, 1995). These standards share a view of teaching as reciprocal and contingent, with teachers' actions and responses dependent on students' prior knowledge and learning. The development activities they foster emphasize teachers' abilities to understand their students from multiple perspectives—in terms of their stages of development; approaches to learning;

cultural, language, and family backgrounds; and community contexts—and to develop learning opportunities that build on this understanding.

In the past these considerations were not viewed as important, since teaching was understood as the straightforward implementation of set procedures. Consequently teachers had few occasions to learn about the families, communities, and cultural backgrounds of their students, and they lacked access to the "funds of knowledge" that could equip them to teach more effectively (Au and Kawakami, 1994; Moll, 1996). Policies that could assist teachers in working more effectively with contemporary students include those that incorporate new professional standards that would shape more intensive preparation in this regard and those that facilitate new ways of connecting teachers to children's families. The Harvard Family Research Project's recommendation that education schools incorporate a family focus in their teacher training programs through community-based field work (Bradley, 1997) follows the lead of these new standards and a number of teacher education initiatives that have already begun to reconfigure preparation in this way (Ladson-Billings, this volume; see also Dalton and Moir, 1996, for a description of the innovative University of California, Santa Cruz, teacher education effort, and Tellez and Cohen, 1996, for a discussion of how the University of Houston has engaged preservice teachers in the communities from which their students will be drawn).

Some innovative principals incorporate this kind of learning into in-service development, using professional days to enable teachers' involvement in their students' communities. Teachers visit homes, volunteer in churches and youth organizations, and participate in other activities that connect them with families and communities. By teachers' reports, the knowledge they have acquired has translated into more effective teaching and learning (McLaughlin and Talbert, 1993; NCTAF, 1996). Tellez and Cohen (1996) name this important form of teacher learning "grinding cultural lenses." At root it is the development of an appreciation for the many and various contexts of learning and a growing ability to use these in the service of higher achievement for students.

Policy that can take account of and foster the complex subject- and student-specific knowledge that undergirds effective teaching must somehow enlist the resources of professional entities that influence teachers' learning opportunities: professional associations, teacher unions, subject matter groups, licensing and certification boards, informal professional development groups, private foundations, and others. Coherence among governmental and professional initiatives is crucial (Elmore, Peterson, and McCarthy, 1996; Cohen and Hill, 1997; McLaughlin, 1998). Reforms that ignore teachers' professional organizations waive critical opportunities to engage them as active agents of change. Overlooking unions as partners in reform also misses occasions to affect the culture of unions (Koppich and Kerchner, this volume) and mend the adversarial relations that have often crippled reform efforts (see, for example, Useem, 1996, who describes how contentious relations between union and district in Philadelphia undermined the efforts of local professional development teams).

Teachers' organizations can contribute critical expertise and resources to government-sponsored efforts to invest in teachers' learning. We have already described the roles of professional standards boards, subject matter associations, and accrediting bodies as one set of examples. In addition organizations like IMPACT II have forged learning communities among teachers through a confederation of sites implementing a grants-and-networking model of support for teachers' professionalism and growth. As teachers' organizations strive to move increasingly from industrial-style unionism to professional unionism (Koppich and Kerchner, this volume), the Teachers' Union Reform Network (TURN), a union-led effort to restructure teachers' unions to support high-quality teaching, has provided substantive leadership in identifying effective practices for urban school settings. And the National Education Association (NEA) has established the National Foundation for the Improvement of Education, which awards grants that enable "teachers to take charge of their own learning." A central precept of this NEA initiative is that "this work can and should be initiated by the teaching profession itself" (National Foundation for the Improvement of Education, 1996).

In a number of settings, policymakers are beginning to use both the norms of practice held by the profession and the important resources that professional associations afford as partners in promoting teaching as a learning profession. Recent research illustrates how governmental and professional initiatives can be integrated to achieve greater power and coherence through thoughtfully managed standards-based reforms (see Ball and Cohen, this volume); through district-level initiatives, where leaders mediate higher-level policy influences while aligning their own district-initiated professional development activities (see Elmore and Burney, this volume); through governmental supports for professional bodies, like the National Board for Profession Teaching Standards (NBPTS) or comparable state standards boards; and through public-professional partnerships, as in the case of the Interstate New Teacher Assessment and Support Consortium (INTASC) working with state agencies, standards boards, and schools of education (Darling-Hammond, in press). These findings suggest that policy bundles that thoughtfully combine government action with private professional activity across levels of the system hold greater potential than the unplanned accumulation of policies and practices based on inconsistent and uninformed visions of teaching by a variety of bodies working in isolation.

Achieving a Fit Between Policy and the Realities of Practice

Ultimately the coherence that matters most is that which pertains at the level of schools and classrooms. Policy coherence requires that policymakers at all levels examine both the various elements of the system, such as standards, school environments, and learning opportunities, and the demands associated with policies that compete for the same time, attention, and resources. They must be prepared to "unmandate" those vestigial remnants of earlier reforms that now collide with productive schooling and teaching. They must also learn to evaluate the compatibility of the assumptions and values of policies operating in the same practical environment and the ways in which they can be expected to promote teachers' learning, students' learning, and effective practice (Little, this volume; Sykes, this volume).

We have learned that effective policy not only motivates; policy also teaches, and policymakers learn (Cohen and Barnes, 1993). Policymaking involves substantial, ongoing teaching and learning on the part of those who formulate and carry out policy, as well as by classroom teachers. The act of promulgating policy is an educative act, whether or not the promulgators conceive of it that way. Policy communicates messages to teachers about what they should teach and how, and the manner in which the policy is communicated has something to do with how it is received, absorbed, and learned by those who will implement it in classrooms (Cohen and Barnes, 1993). Of particular concern, then, is the fit between the policymakers' "teaching" strategy and the "material" they are trying to teach, which in many cases involves ambitious conceptions of curriculum and pedagogy. Research has begun to uncover the general mismatch that often exists in such cases, and the kinds of learning that all must do, at all levels of the system, for the messages of policy to be heard and internalized by those for whom they are intended (Wilson, Peterson, Ball, and Cohen, 1996; Peterson, Prawat, and Grant, 1994).

To realize investment in teachers' learning, policies need not only cohere with one another and make sense in teachers' contexts, but they must also correspond with the needs and circumstances of the teachers who are expected to benefit from them. A "one size fits all" approach cannot work as a program design or as a resource allocation strategy. The professional development opportunities valued by veteran teachers often differ from those new teachers find helpful. Teachers working in different school settings often have different needs for particular knowledge and expertise. And the challenges confronting schools and teachers are not evenly distributed throughout the public education system.

Because political, social, and professional conditions differ substantially, teaching practices and teacher policies have different meanings and effects in different contexts (Talbert and McLaughlin, 1994; Cohen, 1996; Spillane, 1994). Teacher and administrator beliefs, abilities, and commitments strongly influence how policies are realized in particular schools and classrooms, as do the state and local policy contexts through which a policy moves (Weatherley and Lipsky, 1977; Spillane, 1994; Elmore, Peterson, and McCarthy, 1996). Policymakers must either accept differential responses or tailor policies to anticipate different adaptations and needs for resources.

As we noted earlier, policymakers who want to encourage educational reform have a number of choices available, including standards-based, school-based, and professional development-based strategies. Each set of tools has a different logic and different assumptions about the conditions under which it will be most effective as a support for learning and change. An important question for policymakers to consider is the extent to which each of these strategies is likely to be useful for particular purposes in specific contexts; that is, whether the logic of the policy instrument fits the situation and goals to which it is applied. Policymakers have at hand a repertoire they can employ in response to different labor force conditions as well as teachers' needs and school contexts.

One element of policy fit is the extent to which learning incentives and supports are appropriate to teachers' existing knowledge, their needs for knowledge and skill development, and their stages in their careers. In some states, longstanding attention to teacher education and licensing may mean that teachers share a strong body of knowledge about teaching, learning, and subject matter; in others, low standards and large-scale emergency hiring have meant that many teachers lack even the most rudimentary knowledge about teaching and content (Darling-Hammond, 1997a).

Teachers of different skill levels are likely to be differentially distributed across schools and districts, due to unequal local resources and uneven concerns for teaching quality. Thus policies that would rely on school-based reforms might be successful in high-capacity schools and utter failures in schools where teachers lack the core knowledge needed to implement the reforms. In such a case, an overhaul of state and local standards for preparation, licensing, and hiring, coupled with equalization of core funding and massive infusions of professional development in low-capacity schools, would be needed for school-level reforms to succeed.

Ironically, policies that aim to support teachers' learning generally are not structured to reflect teachers' development. New teachers typically enter the classrooms with the same teaching demands placed on them as on their veteran colleagues, yet they have little opportunity to learn how to use their new skills and get their feet wet as professionals. They need practical supports. On the other hand, well-prepared new teachers may have encountered areas of knowledge that were not part of the training of teachers in earlier eras. Hence, some experienced teachers may profit from access to new insights about, for example, how children learn and how to teach students with special needs while they also look for opportunities to pursue particular topics in depth and to rethink their practice. An effective professional development investment strategy recognizes that teachers' knowledge needs reflect their career paths and prior learning opportunities.

However, effective investments in professional development must also be balanced between meeting the needs of individual teachers and furthering the organizational goals of their schools and districts. This means that policies must simultaneously consider means for addressing individual and organizational needs and balancing ideas about professional development investments that might push in different or incompatible directions.

Perhaps the most difficult challenges to the fit between policy and practice lie in the need to distribute resources and incentives in ways that support equity for teachers and their students. Reformers and policymakers who are aiming to increase teaching excellence in the nation's schools must wrestle with the great diversity that exists among schoolteachers' local school contexts, work experiences, and teaching challenges (Darling-Hammond, 1997b; Metz, 1990). Neither challenges nor resources for teaching are evenly distributed throughout state or local education systems. High-wealth districts in most states spend at least twice as much as low-wealth districts, and they offer higher salaries, better teaching and learning conditions, and greater professional development supports for teachers. Recruitment and retention of teachers and administrators are difficult in many inner-city schools, where professional supports and personal security often are not guaranteed. Rural communities also suffer from the inability to attract and retain talented young teachers.

Both teacher resources and resources for teachers are unevenly distributed among the nation's schools and communities. The suburbanization of American society attracted middle-class families of all race and ethnic backgrounds from the central cities, leaving the inner city with disproportionate concentrations of families with the greatest needs (Kantor and Brenzel, 1992). Teachers in both poor urban and rural communities also profit from fewer of the community supports such as health care, child care, libraries, museums, transportation systems, and recreational facilities that complement teachers' work in more advantaged settings.

The educational system is not currently organized to ensure that every student has a competent, caring teacher—and to ensure that all teachers have access to the knowledge resources necessary for them to provide high-quality teaching for all students. Policymakers who want to ensure that all students have access to high-quality teaching must develop strategies for equalizing the currently unlevel playing field and for ensuring that professional development resources reach the teaching force that serves the most needy schools.

RESPONDING TO THE CHALLENGE:
EXAMPLES FROM THE FIELD

The factors that affect policy outcomes and should inform policy choices are intertwined. Responding to any one of them implicates the others. For example, if policymakers are serious about setting standards that all students and teachers are expected to meet, they must also reallocate resources in ways that attend to the different learning situations in which teachers and students find themselves. Efforts to involve the profession in the provision of professional development may complicate efforts to integrate policy at the intersection, even as it enhances the possibilities of reaching teachers across multiple contexts. Bringing all of these considerations together to achieve coherent investments in teachers' learning requires the hard work of rethinking policy relationships, bringing new perspectives to the table, and discarding policies and practices that may have been operating for some time.

Promising instances of the kind of rethinking and re-forming needed can be found in a number of districts around the country. In Toledo, Columbus, and Cincinnati, Ohio, as well as Rochester, New York, and Seattle, Washington, for example, teachers' organizations and school boards have initiated programs of peer review and mentoring designed to provide a comprehensive, career-long approach to professional development. These efforts to mentor beginning teachers and provide supports to other teachers, including special interventions for those who are having difficulty, are "about teachers taking charge of the profession" (Chase, 1997). The mentoring programs have been so successful in all of these cities that 85 to 90 percent of new teachers are still teaching in these districts after three to five years, in contrast to only 50 or 60 percent of new teachers in many other urban school districts. In addition, the new teachers and their colleagues report that they achieve higher levels of competence sooner than other beginning teachers do (NCTAF, 1996). The teachers' union also was the engine behind promoting professional development for all district teachers in Minneapolis. Through its contract, the union acted to integrate and expand the piecemeal professional development formerly available in the district and to place the profession in the lead both as support and review for high-quality teaching.

New actors have entered the district professional development scene to stimulate and support innovative approaches to teachers' learning and change. In Denver, for example, the Public Education and Business Coalition sponsors what is considered a successful example of a new professional development model where a cadre of coalition-sponsored trainers—all experienced classroom teachers—works in teachers' classrooms. Schools start by participating in the coalition's three-year Literacy League project and then can move on to three years of a reading or mathematics project. In Cincinnati the business community endowed a professional development academy that draws on the expertise of local teachers, university faculty, and professional developers to create highly successful programs of ongoing learning that use innovative technology to give teachers' constant access to one another's practice and expertise (NCTAF, 1996). Cincinnati, like New York City's School District 2 (Elmore and Burney, this volume), and New Haven, California, is among those districts that have worked to create a coherent approach to teacher development across the entire career.

Cross-Sector Collaboration in Support of District-Level Reform

The Jefferson County Public Schools, which serves the Louisville, Kentucky, area, is another school district that illustrates how local professional organizations can join with local school districts and state agencies in creating systemic supports for the improvement of teaching and learning. At the heart of teachers' professional development in Louisville is the Center for the Collaborative Advancement of the Teaching Profession, located in the University of Louisville's School of Education, which has played a key integrating role for professional development in the area, especially in the wake of the Kentucky Education Reform Act (KERA) of 1990. The center was established in 1987 by the Kentucky Council on Higher Education and grew out of a longstanding collaborative relationship between the Jefferson Country Public Schools and the University of Louisville. The work of the center is shaped by an advisory committee that includes representatives from the University of Louisville Education and Arts and Sciences departments, Gheens Academy (the primary professional development agency in Louisville), various county school systems, the Ohio Valley Education Cooperative, and local principals and teachers. This advisory board comprises the occasion for representatives of the broad education community to identify common goals and wrestle with developing a comprehensive, coherent strategy for the area.

The state context for these efforts is a comprehensive reform act that has sought to equalize school funding, overhaul curriculum and assessment to make them more performance-based and intellectually ambitious, create a new accountability system for schools, enact new standards for teacher licensing and preparation, fund widespread professional development for practicing teachers and other staff, dramatically increase access to early childhood education programs and transform primary grades education into multiage classrooms focused on developmentally appropriate teaching, enhance the use of technology, and create full-service schools connecting community resources to education. Shortly after KERA was passed, the legislature created an autonomous Education Professional Standards Board to assume responsibility for credentialing teachers, and it transferred the state education department from the domain of an elected superintendent to one who is appointed.

All of these changes were intended to professionalize the management and conduct of education in the state and to improve dramatically the caliber of practice across a system that had been severely undernourished in terms of tangible resources and access to professional knowledge. The state's investment in professional education and development has continued to increase throughout the 1990s, with noteworthy results. In a large-scale national survey, Kentucky's teachers reported that they had access to more extensive professional development in their content areas and on issues of teaching and assessment than teachers in any other state (Darling-Hammond, 1997a). Furthermore, more than 90 percent of Kentucky's newly prepared teachers in 1996 reported that they had been very well prepared by their teacher education programs (Wilkerson and Associates, 1997), a startling finding given traditional complaints about teacher education.

The new three-tiered credential system encourages teachers to complete a fifth year of teacher education and requires them to complete a one-year internship in their initial year on the job, with both initial licensure and continuation based on the passage of performance-based assessments tied to the INTASC standards. Colleges of education are now approved based on the NCATE standards (which also incorporate INTASC standards). And teachers may secure a Rank I credential by achieving National Board certification or by pursuing additional graduate work beyond the master's degree. State-funded regional service centers, universities, district consortia, a state-supported cadre of Distinguished Educators, and five hundred teaching coaches supported by the Kentucky Education Association provide professional development supports in technology, curriculum and assessment, school-based decision making, teaching strategies, and exceptional child education.

Louisville has done a remarkable job of taking advantage of all of these reforms and marshaling resources for educator support. The Center for the Collaborative Advancement of the Teaching Profession has focused its work in the past few years on restructuring the university's teacher preparation programs in line with the state reforms and establishing a network of twenty-five professional development schools (PDS). Professional development offered through the center deals expressly with the social contexts of teaching. For example, the PDS sites were selected with explicit attention to their community contexts and student characteristics and so provide opportunities for both experienced teachers and preservice teachers (as well as University of Louisville faculty) to work within diverse school contexts all seeking to develop state-of-the-art practice. The fifth-year master of arts in teaching program places top priority on preparing students to work effectively with diverse student populations and communities. Students must not only complete successful work in their home PDS, they also must rotate to partner PDS schools for a six-week period. A student assigned to a PDS school in an isolated small town outside Louisville, for example, may go to an inner-city PDS for six weeks. Students are also required to complete thirty hours of service to a local social service organization that supports the healthy development of children and their families. The placement must be "outside the students' cultural comfort zone."

Collaboration between the center's preservice programs and the local districts supports a tightly integrated normative conception of high-quality teaching and learning outcomes that builds on state reforms in curriculum and assessment. The center is one of several university-based programs that supports the Kentucky Collaborative for Elementary Learning, which has enabled three thousand teachers to be trained in a program called Different Ways of Knowing, developed by the Galef Institute. The Different Ways of Knowing project, along with the normatively compatible Child Development Project, is deeply embedded in districts' schools and in the professional development available through the Gheens Academy. Both inform the elementary teacher preparation programs at the University of Louisville.

Similarly the secondary teacher preparation programs and professional development schools are informed by the work of the Coalition of Essential Schools, which, like Kentucky's reforms, emphasizes ambitious performance-based curriculum for all students. Because of these collaborations, Louisville teachers, novice and veteran, hear consistent messages about valued practice and student outcomes, and they have many opportunities to develop their ability to enact such practice. The center plays a major role in making Louisville a system of schools, using teachers' professional development as the cornerstone of a coherent pedagogical and professional framework.

State Initiatives That Integrate Standards and Development-Based Reforms

States such as Vermont and California have taken an active role in making knowledge resources available to many teachers in the state (see NCTAF, 1996, and EDWEEK Quality Counts for elaboration). For example, through the California Subject Matter projects, extensive statewide networks were set up to provide teachers access to professional development related to state curricular frameworks. These and other professional development resources appear to have been instrumental in advancing California teachers' learning in many instances (Firestone and Pennell, 1995). Vermont also established teacher networks tied to the state's portfolio system of assessment in writing and mathematics in fourth and eighth grades (Murnane and Levy, 1996). In both cases a number of teachers were able to get access to sustained professional development directly tied to their work with students, which they found extremely valuable. However, in cases like these, where professional development has been voluntary, accessible to relatively small proportions of the teaching force, and unconnected to reforms of preservice preparation or teacher credentialing, the salutory effects have been uneven.

Connecticut provides an especially instructive example of how state-level policymakers have used a standards-based starting point to integrate policies to support and motivate teachers' learning throughout the state in a more systemic way. As part of its 1986 Education Enhancement Act, Connecticut coupled major increases in teacher salaries with greater equalization in funding across districts, higher standards for teacher education and licensing, and substantial investments in beginning teacher mentoring and professional development. In 1987 student learning standards were adopted in an early effort to link teaching standards with student learning. Since 1986, the state's efforts have included

> legislative changes in licensure and teacher preparation program approval requirements, the development of curriculum guides, redesigned student assessments that clearly communicate desired student outcomes coupled with dissemination of teaching practices to produce those outcomes, and state-funded school improvement efforts to encourage the reorganization of schools [Connecticut State Department of Education, 1991].

Since these reforms were undertaken, the state's students have posted significant gains on the National Assessment of Educational Progress, becoming one of the top-scoring states in the nation in mathematics and reading, despite an increase in the proportion of students with special needs during the 1990s.

An initial investment of $300 million was used to boost minimum beginning teacher salaries in an equalizing fashion that made it possible for low-wealth districts to compete in the market for qualified teachers. An analysis of the outcomes of this initiative found that it eliminated teacher shortages, even in the cities, and created surpluses of teachers within three years of its passage (Connecticut State Department of Education, 1991). At the same time, the state raised licensing standards by requiring a major in the discipline to be taught plus extensive knowledge of teaching and learning as part of preparation; instituted performance-based examinations in subject matter and knowledge of teaching as a basis for receiving a license; created a state-funded beginning teacher mentoring program that supported trained mentors for beginning teachers in their first year on the job; and created a sophisticated assessment program using state-trained assessors for determining who could continue in teaching after the initial year.

Connecticut also required teachers to earn a master's degree in education for a continuing license and supported new professional development strategies in universities and school districts. Recently the state has extended its performance-based licensing system to incorporate the new INTASC standards and to develop portfolio assessments modeled on those of the National Board for Professional Teaching Standards. As part of ongoing teacher education reforms, the state agency has supported the creation of seventeen professional development schools linked to local universities and more than one hundred school-university partnerships. In addition Connecticut has developed ten advanced credit-earning courses on teacher and student standards, which can be applied toward the required master's degree. The state also funds and operates a set of Institutes for Teaching and Learning.

Connecticut's process of implementing INTASC-based portfolios for beginning teacher licensing is as much a professional development system as a measurement activity, and educators are involved in every aspect of its development and implementation so that these opportunities are widespread. Each assessment is developed with the assistance of a teacher in residence in the department of education; advisory committees of teachers, teacher educators, and administrators guide the development of standards and assessments; hundreds of educators are convened to provide feedback on drafts of the standards; and many more are involved in the assessments themselves, as cooperating teachers and school-based mentors who work with beginning teachers on developing their practice, as assessors who are trained to score the portfolios, and as expert teachers who convene regional support seminars to help candidates learn about the standards and the portfolio development process. Individuals involved in each of these roles are engaged in preparation that is organized around the examination of cases and the development of evidence connected to the standards.

Together these activities can have far-reaching effects. By one estimate more than 40 percent of Connecticut's teachers have been prepared and have served as assessors, mentors, or cooperating teachers under either the earlier beginning teacher performance assessment or the new portfolios. By the year 2010, 80 percent of elementary teachers, and nearly as many secondary teachers, will have participated in the new assessment system as candidates, support providers, or assessors. Because the assessments focus on the development of teacher competence, not just its measurement, and are tightly tied to student standards and lead to sustained, sophisticated discourse about practice, the assessment system serves as a focal point for improving teaching and learning.

CONCLUSION

We have suggested that the task of learning to teach diverse learners for much more challenging learning goals is a complex problem that requires the unlearning of old practices as well as the learning of new, highly sophisticated strategies for drawing connections between students' experiences and ambitious curriculum ideas. We have argued that the task of making policy in support of these ends is a nontrivial problem as well—one that requires the unmandating of previously enacted, conflicting policies as well as the creation of new approaches based on a coherent vision of teaching and learning, the skillful deployment of professional and governmental resources across different levels of the system, and an appreciation for the diverse contexts in which teachers and students learn.

Although both of these tasks might appear daunting, there is growing evidence that it is possible to create a policy infrastructure for good teaching that systematically supports the development of professional knowledge, norms, and practices within and across schools. Where this is being done, policymakers and educators are creating webs of learning opportunities in professional communities that develop capacity for teacher decision making rather than seeking to mandate the procedures of teaching. In this way, the juxtaposition of "teaching" and "policy"—rather than being only the statement of a problem—may begin to describe new possibilities for enriching and equalizing students' opportunities to learn to high levels, because their teachers are continuously supported in learning to teach.

References

Andrew, M. D., and Schwab, R. L. "Has Reform in Teacher Education Influenced Teacher Performance? An Outcome Assessment of Graduates of Eleven Teacher Education Programs." *Action in Teacher Education,* 1995, *17*(3), 43–53.

Armour-Thomas, E., Clay, C., Domanico, R., Bruno, K., and Allen, B. *An Outlier Study of Elementary and Middle Schools in New York City: Final Report.* New York: New York City Board of Education, 1989.

Ashton, P., and Crocker, L. "Does Teacher Certification Make a Difference?" *Florida Journal of Teacher Education,* 1986, *38*(3), 73–83.

Au, K. H., and Kawakami, A. J. "Cultural Congruence in Instruction." In E. R. Hillins, J. E. King, and W. C. Hayman (eds.), *Teaching Diverse Populations: Formulating a Knowledge Base.* Albany: State University of New York Press, 1994.

Ball, D. L. "Developing Mathematics Reform: What We Don't Know About Teacher Learning But Would Make Good Working Hypotheses." Paper presented at the Conference on Teacher Enhancement in Mathematics, K–6, Arlington, Va., 1994.

Begle, E. G. *Critical Variables in Mathematics Education.* Washington, D.C.: Mathematical Association of American and National Council of Teachers of Mathematics, 1979.

Begle, E. G., and Geeslin, W. *Teacher Effectiveness in Mathematics Instruction.* National Longitudinal Study of Mathematical Abilities Reports No. 28. Washington, D.C.: Mathematical Association of America and National Council of Teachers of Mathematics, 1972.

Bradley, A. "Teacher Training Ignores Students' Families, Study Finds." *Education Week.* Nov. 12, 1997.

Brown, C. A., Smith, M. S., and Stein, M. K. "Linking Teacher Support to Enhanced Classroom Instruction." Paper presented at the annual meeting of the American Educational Research Association, New York, 1995.

Bryk, A. S. "Lessons from Catholic High Schools on Renewing Our Education Institutions." In M. T. Hallinon (ed.), *Restructuring Schools: Promising Practices and Policies* (pp. 81–98). New York: Plenum Press, 1995.

Bryk, A. S., Lee, V., and Holland, P. *Catholic Schools and the Common Good.* Cambridge, Mass.: Harvard University Press, 1993.

Center for Research on the Context of Teaching. *Assessing Results: The Bay Area School Reform Collaborative at Year Two.* Stanford, Calif.: Stanford University School of Education, 1998.

Chase, B. "Teacher vs. Teacher? Nonsense." *Education Week,* October 22, 1997.

Children's Defense Fund. *The State of America's Children.* Washington, D.C.: Author, 1997.

Clune, W. *The Implementation and Effects of High School Graduation Requirements.* New Brunswick, N.J.: Rutgers University, Consortium for Research on Policy Education, 1989.

Cochran-Smith, M., and Lytle, S. L. "Communities for Teacher Research: Fringe or Forefront." In M. W. McLaughlin and I. Oberman, *Teacher Learning.* New York: Teachers College Press, 1996.

Cohen, D. K. "Systemic Reform: Policy, Practice and Performance." In H. Ladd (ed.), *Holding Schools Accountable: Performance-Based Reform in Education.* Washington, D.C.: Brookings Institution, 1996.

Cohen, D. K., and Barnes, C. A. "Conclusion: A New Pedagogy for Policy." In D. K. Cohen, M. W. McLaughlin, and J. E. Talbert (eds)., *Teaching for Understanding: Challenges for Policy and Practice* (pp. 240–275). San Francisco: Jossey-Bass, 1993.

Cohen, D. K., and Hill, H. "Teaching and Learning Mathematics in California." Paper presented at the annual meeting of the American Educational Research Association, San Francisco, April 1997.

Connecticut State Department of Education. *Research Bulletin, School Year 1990–91, No. 1.* Hartford, Conn.: Bureau of Research and Teacher Assessment, 1991.

Council for School Performance. *Teachers with Advanced Degrees Advance Student Learning.* Atlanta: Council for School Performance, Georgia State University, 1997.

Crowson, R. L., and Boyd, W. L. "Coordinated Services for Children: Designing Arks for Storms and Seas Unknown." *American Journal of Education,* 1993, *101,* 140–179.

Dalton, S., and Moir, E. "Text and Context for Professional Development of New Bilingual Teachers." In M. W. McLaughlin and I. Oberman (eds.), *Teacher Learning* (pp. 126–133). New York: Teachers College Press, 1996.

Darling-Hammond, L. "Instructional Policy into Practice: The Power of the Bottom Over the Top." *Educational Evaluation and Policy Analysis,* 1990, *12*(3), 233–242.

Darling-Hammond, L. *Doing What Matters Most: Investing in Quality Teaching.* New York: National Commission on Teaching and America's Future, 1997a.

Darling-Hammond, L. *The Right to Learn: A Blueprint for Creating Schools That Work.* San Francisco: Jossey-Bass, 1997b.

Darling-Hammond, L. *Reshaping Teaching Policy, Preparation, and Practice: Influences of the National Board for Professional Teaching Standards.* Washington, D.C.: National Partnership for Excellence and Accountability in Teaching, in press.

Darling-Hammond, L., Ancess, J., and Falk, B. *Authentic Assessment in Action: Studies of Schools and Students at Work.* New York: Teachers College Press, 1995.

Darling-Hammond, L., and McLaughlin, M. W. "Policies That Support Professional Development in an Era of Reform." *Phi Delta Kappan*, 1995, *76*(8), 597–604.

Darling-Hammond, L., Wise, A. E., and Klein, S. *A License to Teach: Building a Profession for 21st Century Schools.* Boulder, Colo.: Westview Press, 1995.

Denton, J. J., and Peters, W. H. "Program Assessment Report Curriculum Evaluation of a Non-Traditional Program for Certifying Teachers." Unpublished report. College Station: Texas A&M University, 1988.

Druva, C. A., and Anderson, R. D. "Science Teacher Characteristics by Teacher Behavior and by Student Outcome: A Meta-Analysis of Research." *Journal of Research in Science Teaching*, 1983, *20*(5), 467–479.

Elmore, R. F., Peterson, P., and McCarthy, S. J. *Teaching, Learning and School Organization: Restructuring and Classroom Practice in Three Elementary Schools.* San Francisco: Jossey-Bass, 1996.

Evertson, C., Hawley, W., and Zlotnick, M. "Making a Difference in Educational Quality Through Teacher Education." *Journal of Teacher Education*, 1985, *36*(3), 2–12.

Ferguson, R. F. "Paying for Public Education: New Evidence on How and Why Money Matters." *Harvard Journal on Legislation*, 1991, *28*(2), 465–498.

Ferguson, R. F., and Ladd, H. F. "How and Why Money Matters: An Analysis of Alabama Schools." In H. Ladd (ed.), *Holding Schools Accountable* (pp. 265–298). Washington, D.C.: Brookings Institution, 1996.

Firestone, W. A., and Pennell, J. R. *State-Run Teacher Networks: Capacity Building and Policy Supporting Approaches*. New Brunswick, N.J.: Rutgers University, Eagleton Institute of Politics, Consortium for Policy Research in Education, 1995.

Fox, G. T. "Limitation of a Standard Perspective on Program Evaluation: The Example of Ten Years of Teacher Corps Evaluations." In J. P. Steffensen, G. T. Fox, and B. Joyce (eds.), *Teacher Corps Evaluation*. Omaha: University of Nebraska, Center for Urban Education, 1978.

Fullan, M. *Change Forces: Probing the Depths of Educational Reform.* Bristol, Pa.: Falmer Press, 1993.

Greenwald, R., Hedges, L. V., and Laine, R. D. "The Effect of School Resources on Student Achievement." *Review of Educational Research*, 1996, *66*, 361–396.

Grimmett, P., and MacKinnon, A. "Craft Knowledge and the Education of Teachers." In G. Grant (ed.), *Review of Research in Education* (Vol. 18, pp. 385–456). Washington, D.C.: American Educational Research Association, 1992.

Grossman, P., and Stodolsky, S. "Considerations of Content and the Circumstances of Secondary School Teaching." In L. Darling-Hammond (ed.), *Review of Research in Education* (Vol. 20, pp. 179–221). Washington, D. C.: American Educational Research Association, 1994.

Guyton, E., and Farokhi, E. "Relationships Among Academic Performance, Basic Skills, Subject Matter Knowledge and Teaching Skills of Teacher Education Graduates." *Journal of Teacher Education,* Sept.–Oct. 1987, pp. 37–42.

Hargreaves, A. "Cultures of Teaching: A Focus for Change." In A. Hargreaves and M. Fullan (eds.), *Understanding Teacher Development.* New York: Teachers College Press, 1992.

Hargreaves, A. "Individualism and Individuality: Reinterpreting the Teacher Culture." In J. W. Little and M. W. McLaughlin (eds.), *Teachers' Work: Individuals, Colleagues, and Contexts.* New York: Teachers College Press, 1993.

Hawk, P., Coble, C. R., and Swanson, M. "Certification: It Does Matter." *Journal of Teacher Education,* 1985, *36*(3), 13–15.

Hill, P. *Reinventing Public Education.* Santa Monica, Calif.: Institute on Education and Training, RAND Corporation, 1995.

Jordan, H. R., Mendro, R. L., and Weerasinghe, D. *Teacher Effects on Longitudinal Student Achievement.* Dallas, Tex.: Dallas Public Schools, 1997.

Kantor, H., and Brenzel, B. "Urban Education and the 'Truly Disadvantaged': The Historical Roots of the Contemporary Crisis." *Teachers College Record,* 1992, *42*, 521–562.

Knoblock, G. A. "Continuing Professional Education for Teachers and Its Relationship to Teacher Effectiveness." Unpublished dissertation, Michigan State University, 1986. *Dissertation Abstracts International, 46*(02), 3325A, University microfilms no. AAC8529729.

Lampert, M. *Teachers' Thinking About Students' Thinking About Geometry: The Effects of New Teaching Goals.* Issue Paper TR-88-1. Cambridge, Mass.: Harvard Graduate School of Education, Education Technology Center, 1987.

Lieberman, A. *The Work of Restructuring Schools: Building from the Ground Up.* New York: Teachers College Press, 1995.

Lieberman, A. "Practices That Support Teacher Development." In M. W. McLaughlin and I. Oberman (eds.), *Teacher Learning* (pp. 185–201). New York: Teachers College Press, 1996.

Lipsky, M. *Street-Level Bureaucracy: Dilemmas of the Individual in Public Service.* New York: Russell Sage, 1980.

Louis, K. S., Marks, H. M. and Kruse, S. "Teacher's Professional Community in Restructuring Schools." Paper prepared for the Center on Organization and Restructuring Schools, Wisconsin Center for Education Research, Madison, 1995.

McLaughlin, M. W. "Learning from Experience: Lessons from Policy Implementation." *Educational Evaluation and Policy Analysis,* 1987, *2*, 171–178.

McLaughlin, M. W. "What Matters Most in Teachers' Workplace Context." In J. W. Little and M. W. McLaughlin (eds.), *Teachers' Work: Individuals, Colleagues, and Contexts.* New York: Teachers College Press, 1993.

McLaughlin, M. W. "Listening and Learning from the Field: Tales of Policy Implementation and Situated Practice." In A. Lieberman (ed.), *The Roots of Educational Change.* Netherlands: Kluwer, 1998.

McLaughlin, M. W., and Oberman, I. *Teacher Learning: New Policies, New Practices.* New York: Teachers College Press, 1996.

McLaughlin, M. W., and Talbert, J. E. *Contexts That Matter for Teaching and Learning.* Center for Research on the Contexts of Teaching, Stanford University, 1993.

McLaughlin, M. W. and Talbert, J. E. *Secondary Schoolteaching in Context.* Chicago: University of Chicago Press, in press.

Meier, D. *The Power of Their Ideas.* Boston: Beacon Press, 1995.

Metz, M. H. "How Social Class Differences Shape Teachers' Work." In M. W. McLaughlin, J. E. Talbert, and N. Bascia (eds.), *The Context of Secondary Schools: Teachers' Realities* (pp. 40–107). New York: Teachers College Press, 1990.

Moll, L. "Funds of Knowledge: Using a Qualitative Approach to Connect Homes and Classrooms." *Theory into Practice,* 1992, *31*(1), 132–141.

Murnane, R. and Levy, F. *Teaching the New Basic Skills.* New York: Free Press, 1996.

National Assessment of Educational Progress. *1992 NAEP Trial State Assessment.* Washington, D.C.: U.S. Department of Education, 1994.

National Commission on Teaching and America's Future (NCTAF). *What Matters Most: Teaching for America's Future.* New York: Author, 1996.

National Foundation for the Improvement of Education (NFIE). *Teachers Take Charge of Their Learning.* Washington, D.C.: Author, 1996.

Newmann, F., and Wehlage, G. (eds.). *Successful School Restructuring: A Report to the Public and Educators by the Center on Organization and Restructuring of Schools.* Madison: University of Wisconsin, 1995.

O'Day, J. A., and Smith, M. S. "Systemic School Reform and Educational Opportunity." In S. Fuhrman (ed.), *Designing Coherent Education Policy: Improving the System.* San Francisco: Jossey-Bass, 1993.

Peterson, P., Prawat, R., and Grant, S. "Rising Expectations and Declining Resources: Learning to Make Reform in the Best and Worst of Times." Paper presented at the annual meeting of the American Educational Research Association, New Orleans, 1994.

Popham, J. "The Merits of Measurement-Driven Instruction." *Phi Delta Kappan,* 1987, *9*(2), 679–686.

Sanders, S. L., Skonie-Hardin, S. D., and Phelps, W. H. "The Effects of Teacher Educational Attainment on Student Educational Attainment in Four Regions of Virginia: Implications for Administrators" Paper presented at the annual meeting of the Mid-South Educational Research Association, Nov. 1994.

Sanders, W. L., and Rivers, J. C. *Cumulative and Residual Effects of Teachers on Future Student Academic Achievement.* Knoxville: University of Tennessee Value-Added Research and Assessment Center, 1996.

Shields, P. M., Corcoran, T., and Zucker, A. *Evaluation of the National Science Foundation's Statewide Systemic Initiatives (SSI) Program: First Year Report, Vol. 1: Technical Report.* Washington, D.C.: National Science Foundation, Directorate for Education and Human Services, 1994.

Shin, H. "Estimating Future Teacher Supply: An Application of Survival Analysis." Paper presented at the annual meeting of the American Educational Research Association, New Orleans, 1994.

Shulman L. "Autonomy and Obligation." In L. Shulman and G. Sykes (eds.), *Handbook of Teaching and Policy* (pp. 484–504). White Plains, N.Y.: Longman, 1983.

Shulman, L. "Knowledge and Teaching: Foundations of the New Reform." *Harvard Educational Review*, 1987, *57*(1), 1–22.

Siskin, L., and Little, J. W. *The Subjects in Question*. New York: Teachers College Press, 1997.

Spillane, J. "How Districts Mediate Between State Policy and Teachers' Practice." In R. F. Elmore and S. H. Fuhrman (eds.), *The Governance of Curriculum* (pp. 167–185). Washington, D.C.: Association for Supervision and Curriculum Development, 1994.

Stake, R., and Easly, J. A. *Case Studies in Science Education* (Vol. 2). Washington, D.C.: U.S. Government Printing Office, 1978.

Stodolsky, S. *The Subject Matters: Classroom Activity in Mathematics and Social Studies*. Chicago: University of Chicago Press, 1988.

Sykes, G. "Public Policy and the Problem of Teacher Quality." In L. S. Shulman and G. Sykes (eds.), *Handbook of Teaching and Policy* (pp. 97–125). White Plains, NY: Longman, 1983.

Talbert, J. E., and McLaughlin, M. W. "Teacher Professionalism in Local School Contexts." *American Journal of Education*, 1994, *102*, 123–153.

Tellez, K., and Cohen, M. "Preparing Teachers for Multicultural, Inner-city Classrooms: Grinding New Lenses." In M. W. McLaughlin and I. Oberman (eds.), *Teachers Learning* (pp. 134–160). New York: Teachers College Press, 1996.

Useem, E. "Reforming Alone: Barriers to Organizational Learning in Urban School Change Initiatives." Paper presented at the annual meeting of the American Educational Research Association, New York, Apr. 8–12, 1996.

Weatherley, R., and Lipsky, M. "Street-Level Bureaucrats and Institutional Innovation: Implementing Special Education Reform." *Harvard Education Review*, 1977, *47*, 171–197.

Welch, W. W. "Twenty Years of Science Curriculum Development: A Look Back." *Review of Research in Education*, 1979, *7*, 282–306.

Wiley, D., and Yoon, B. "Teacher Reports of Opportunity to Learn: Analyses of the 1993 California Learning Assessment System." *Educational Evaluation and Policy Analysis*, 1995, *17*(3), 355–370.

Wilkerson and Associates. *The Preparation of Teachers for Kentucky Schools: A Survey of New Teachers*. Frankfort: Kentucky Institute for Education Research, 1997.

Wilson, S. M., Peterson, P. L., Ball, D. L., and Cohen, D. K. "Learning by All." *Phi Delta Kappan*, 1996, *77*, 468–474.

NAME INDEX

SUBJECT INDEX

419